On Pain of Speech

FLASHPOINTS

The series solicits books that consider literature beyond strictly national and disciplinary frameworks, distinguished both by their historical grounding and by their theoretical and conceptual strength. We seek studies that engage theory without losing touch with history, and work historically without falling into uncritical positivism. FlashPoints will aim for a broad audience within the humanities and the social sciences concerned with moments of cultural emergence and transformation. In a Benjaminian mode, FlashPoints is interested in how literature contributes to forming new constellations of culture and history, and in how such formations function critically and politically in the present. Available online at http://repositories.cdlib.org/ucpress.

Series Editors

Judith Butler, Edward Dimendberg, Catherine Gallagher, Susan Gillman
Richard Terdiman, Chair

1. *On Pain of Speech: Fantasies of the First Order and the Literary Rant,* by Dina Al-Kassim
2. *Moses and Multiculturalism,* by Barbara Johnson

On Pain of Speech

*Fantasies of the First Order
and the Literary Rant*

Dina Al-Kassim

UNIVERSITY OF CALIFORNIA PRESS
Berkeley · Los Angeles · London

University of California Press, one of the most
distinguished university presses in the United States,
enriches lives around the world by advancing
scholarship in the humanities, social sciences,
and natural sciences. Its activities are supported
by the UC Press Foundation and by philanthropic
contributions from individuals and institutions.
For more information, visit www.ucpress.edu.

University of California Press
Berkeley and Los Angeles, California

University of California Press, Ltd.
London, England

© 2010 by The Regents of the University of California

Library of Congress Cataloging-in-Publication Data

Al-Kassim, Dina, 1966–.
    On pain of speech : fantasies of the first order
and the literary rant / Dina Al-Kassim.
        p.   cm.—(FlashPoints, 1)
    Includes bibliographical references and index.
    ISBN 978-0-520-25925-6 (pbk. : alk. paper)
    1. Modernism (Literature).   2. Speech acts
(Linguistics) in literature.   3. Psychoanalysis in
literature.   4. Postcolonialism in literature.
5. Subjectivity in literature.   6. Protest literature.
I. Title.
PN56.M54A47 2010
809'.9112—dc22   2009020575

Manufactured in the United States of America

19 18 17 16 15 14 13 12 11 10
10 9 8 7 6 5 4 3 2 1

This book is printed on Cascades Enviro 100, a
100% post consumer waste, recycled, de-inked fiber.
FSC recycled certified and processed chlorine free.
It is acid free, Ecologo certified, and manufactured
by BioGas energy.

In memoriam,
Gary Fisher and Lindon Barrett

Contents

List of Illustrations — ix

Acknowledgments — xi

Introduction: The Politics of Address — 1

1. On Being Stubborn — 61
   Oscar Wilde and the Modern Type

2. "The Bar Was Not Very Gay" — 119
   New Kinship and the Serious Writer's Block

3. "A Long Tirade for a Direct Interjection" — 178
   Talismano Rebukes the Oriental Tale in
   Jacques Lacan's *Séminaires*

Notes — 233

Bibliography — 271

Index — 281

Illustrations

1. Meddeb's Talisman — 213
2. A spiral letter, 1917 — 220
3. Brinkley Messick's schematic of the spiral letter — 221
4. Map of Tunis showing old city spiral and new city grid — 222

Acknowledgments

My thanks go out to all the friends, colleagues, and anonymous readers whose insight and care have supported and encouraged my writing. For intellectual sustenance I thank Samirah Alkassim, John Culbert, Ali Dadgar, Lara Deeb, Jonathan Mark Harrington Hall, Donna Jones, Dan Katz, Eric Peterson, Kavita Philip, Jon Platania, Targol Mesbah, Ute Hugo Rupp, Ward Smith, Rei Terada, and Christine Wertheim. Ali Dadgar graciously permitted me to use as cover art his painting, an image that has accompanied my imagination of the central argument of this book. The Albanians who gave me my first opportunity—Brett Benjamin, Don Bird, Tom Cohen, Pierre Joris, Paul Kottman, Nicole Peyrafitte, Charles Shepardson, and David Wills—are gratefully remembered here. For the invitation to publish in *Public Culture* and for enlightening conversations about the work, I thank Emily Apter, Elisabeth Povinelli, and the editorial board at *Public Culture*. Purushottama Bilimoria generously invited me to speak on Lacan's Muslim patient at the International Association for Philosophy and Literature Conference, which led to a meeting with Gayatri Chakravorty Spivak, whom I also thank for her generosity and for her reading of Kant's wild man. Jody Greene invited me often to review for *GLQ*, which helped sharpen my sense of the field of sexuality studies as something more than the local. Afsaneh Najmabadi and Kathryn Babayan invited me into an ongoing conversation about

Foucault and history that has influenced these pages in every chapter. I thank Samuel Weber for prompting me to think through the *réseaux* in Meddeb's work, a key intervention at a key moment. My editors at University of California Press deserve more thanks than I can give; Dick Terdiman and Catherine Gallagher as well as the two anonymous readers at UC Press made these pages possible. Caroline Knapp, Hannah Love, and Sharron Wood patiently shepherded the text through the production process with enthusiasm and understanding. Busy colleagues in the field who took the time to read and evaluated the work in draft form and whose insightful comments and criticisms have vastly improved the final result include Carla Freccero, Daniel Katz, David Lloyd, Jean-Michel Rabaté, and Daniel Tiffany. My mentors John Bishop, Judith Butler, Celeste Langan, Michael Lucey, Afsaneh Najmabadi, and Stefania Pandolfo taught by example and set high standards but always with a utopian possibility. I have been privileged to work with brilliant students whose insights and promise have inspired my own work: Olivia Gunn, Dorothy Stringer, Lisa Nolan, Margaux Cowden, Anna Cavness, Emma Heaney, Kyle Wanberg, Duy Lap Nguyen, Robert Wood, Tamara Beauchamp, Burcu Polat, Mariana Razo-Wardwell y Botey, and Travis Tanner. Thanks are due to the Irvinians who generously read my work—Susan Jarratt, Adriana Johnson, R. Radhakrishnan, Annette Schlichter—and to my colleagues at the Critical Theory Institute for their warm and critical interrogation of chapter 3 during a CTI works-in-progress session: Ackbar Abbas, Lindon Barrett, Alex Gelley, Akira Lippit, Bliss Lim, Steve Mailloux, George Marcus, Bill Maurer, Mark Poster, Gaby Schwab, and John Smith. Vicki Ruiz, Dean of the School of the Humanities at the University of California at Irvine, generously supported the production of this work. Many thanks to my family for everything: A. S. Alkassim, Sharon Alkassim, Helen Heath, Faris Alkassim, Samirah Alkassim, Rakan Salameh, and Fawwaz Salama. For constant political and intellectual friendship and late-night emailia, Judith Butler. And for unstinting criticism pushing me to believe that one can write a book about ranting, John Culbert.

INTRODUCTION

The Politics of Address

Je veux bien qu'on n'entende plus rien, mais on parle, on crie: pourquoi ai-je peur d'entendre aussi ma propre voix? Et je ne parle pas de peur, mais de terreur, d'horreur. Qu'on me fasse taire (si l'on ose)! Qu'on couse mes lèvres comme celles d'une plaie!
Georges Bataille, L'Expérience intérieure

We are dealing . . . with a discourse that turns the traditional values of intelligibility upside down. An explanation from below, which is not the simplest, the most elementary, the clearest explanation but, rather, the most confused, the murkiest, the most disorderly, the most haphazard.
Michel Foucault, Society Must Be Defended

The very "I" is called into question by its relation to the one to whom I address myself. This relation to the Other does not precisely ruin my story or reduce me to speechlessness, but it does, invariably, clutter my speech with signs of its undoing.
Judith Butler, Undoing Gender

In the fall of 1983, only months before his death the next summer, Michel Foucault delivered the lectures that would later appear as *Fearless Speech* and which propose "to construct a genealogy of the critical attitude in Western philosophy."[1] Appropriately, this discourse took place on the campus of the University of California at Berkeley, where two decades earlier the student-led Free Speech Movement successfully militated to lift the ban on political speech and to protect academic freedom. One might think that the lectures, which traced attitudes toward frank talk and free speech, *parrhesia,* in classical Greece, were motivated by the progressive freedoms gained through the resistance of militant groups from the 1960s onward. And yet, Foucault's lectures, like his publications of the late 1970s, were to turn this assumption on its head by challenging his audience to consider that the courageous practice of "speaking truth to power" might have become already, and in the very moment of its exercise, a form of instituted power and political authority not accessible to all. In an audacious suggestion that picked up a thread from his lectures of the 1970s, Foucault argued that indeed practices of freedom may not proceed from clear and sovereign intelligibilities.[2] This suggestion that the critical attitude owes its existence not to rational clarity but to the murky depths and a speech not bound by reason's law and order resonates with another theme of the late work.[3] Shortly before his death and against a common misreading that held that the central object of his work was the analysis of power and its epistemological rather than mystical foundations, Foucault distinguished the goal of his research from the 1960s onward in these terms: "my objective . . . has been to create a history of the different modes by which in our culture, human beings are made subjects."[4] Resistance, key to the manufacture of the subject under modern regimes of biopolitical power, proliferates in intimacy with power as its constant companion and domestic familiar. On the importance of resistance, Foucault quite precisely identifies the struggle against subjection, subjectivity, and submission.[5] But by underscoring the significance of popular and individual resistance to domination, Foucault did not relinquish the critique of conventions of resistant expression, which, he argued again and again, are allied to power and in fact represent it.

Against the humanist assumptions of sovereign speech that enable speaking truth to power, our concern in *On Pain of Speech* will be this notion of struggle that Foucault argues is immanent to power but takes the form of haphazard and murky speech at the margins of accepted intelligibility. Judith Butler reformulates the Foucauldian *problématique* in terms of address and specifies the intersubjective event of a speech act "cluttered with signs of its own undoing." This clamor of a speech addressed to another but undermined in its singular enunciation complicates the notion of autonomy that burdens our thinking of rebellion and revolt. Further, the notion that the speaking subject, the "I" of my speech, is itself a quasi-fictional creature whose speech is dependent upon the other of address flies in the face of that other fictional character, the sovereign speaker who defines my intelligibility. The late Foucault, so devoted to a study of the technology of the self and the ways that subjection might afford us the means of its own undoing, was drawn to precisely this question of the complex interdependence of speaker and addressee insofar as his understanding of modern subjection passed through a prior notion of discourse, which he inherited from Georges Bataille, the philosopher of subjectivity and sovereignty who stooped to pornographic novels and ranting texts.[6] Foucault's notion that resistance is immanent to power and that excess or unintelligibility exposes the presence of a norm, its contours and its authority, these ideas are drawn directly from the work of this dissident philosopher who pushed himself to the very edge of his own capacity for self-understanding. I propose the term "rant" to describe this complex of address, entreaty, and attack that characterizes the haphazard and murky speech that only sometimes gathers itself into a counterdiscourse and which has become a symptom of modernist writing, avowed to truth telling but unable to secure its own speech from the clutter of its own undoing.

I have chosen to call this modernist symptom of abject appeal the "rant" because of its echo of the seventeenth-century rakish libertinage and popular antinomianism, ranterism, a form of religious dissent credited, along with other groups, with inspiring resistance to England's Blasphemy Act of 1650. Characterized by their enemies as cursing noisemakers who preached their doctrines of spiritual and moral autonomy and sexual and bodily license in alehouses, brothels, and the streets, ranterism roused the interest of Marxist scholars curious to track the origins of public dissent, notions of free speech, and powers of mayhem in the modern period. Individual ranters left few inflammatory rants; they are best known through the slander they inspired. As harbingers of modernist decadence and avant-garde antics, the ranters are an emblem of manic dissent and provocative speech addressed against God, king, and country that cannot resolve itself into a unified and universal social program. Historical ranterism dissipated its energies and suffered the king's justice but left a trace in popular memory of a public speech that took sovereign, state, and church law as its enemy. Other early modern associations with the word "rant" include wild frolicking and raving youths. As an emblem of the discrete cases treated here, in Oscar Wilde, Jane Bowles, and Abdelwahab Meddeb, the rant connects to elements of each: the suggestion of savagery in the epithet "wild Irish," the rude and unruly feminine in Bowles, and the coffeehouses where gather dissident antinomians, postcolonial critics, calligraphers, and Muslim heresies in Meddeb's fictional landscape. The complex of social contestation, public disorderliness, and bodily disarray resonates with modernism's exploration of normative subjectivity and the social limits enjoined upon the subject but brought to crisis by the abject appeal of the rant's address. England's series of civil wars opened a mythic space for the imagination of a total scandal, the ranter, whose strutting sovereignty and sexual freedoms belied the quick collapse of individual ranters under torture and state censure; this legendary figure, whom we cannot seem to decide if a hero or a horror, is a harbinger of the self-invention that haunts modernity. And although academic references to the Levellers, the Ranters and the Diggers are not rare—Janet Lyon's recent book on manifestos, for example, recalls these early dissidents—ranters left so little in the way of incontestable testament that even their existence has been disputed by some seventeenth-century historians. Worse than marginal, ranters get no hearing and have fathered no legitimate legacy.

Such a failure to come into historical focus has been appropriated to a *tradition* of oppositional speech anchored in easily transmissible forms like the manifesto which then authorizes genre study of the voice from below; however, the "style" of ranting admits of no such legacy and leaves no heirs in form. Rather ranting repeats symptomatically without the regular identity of form that legitimates genre. Foucault's notion of a counterdiscourse differs from the inspiration for Christopher Hill's Marxist historical sketch of ranterism, for counterdiscourse does not commit us to the Benjaminian dialectic of victor and vanquished, nor does it oblige us to a literal imagination of class consciousness. The murky speech from below cannot organize a program or manifest itself as a consciousness; its disorderly and haphazard speech does not even aim at a broader social intelligibility that exists ready-made for the claiming, and these features of counterdiscourse set it at odds with a Marxist approach that would seek to redeem the experience of the vanquished. Taking Theodor Adorno as a guide, we might turn to entry ninety-eight of *Minima Moralia* to situate the role of critical thinking in a world characterized not only by the dialectic of victor and vanquished, but also by an inassimilable element. Writing, he tells us, "should also address itself to those things which were not embraced by this dynamic, which fell by the wayside—what might be called the waste products and blind spots that have escaped the dialectic." For, "it is in the nature of the defeated to appear, in their impotence, irrelevant, eccentric, derisory. . . . Theory must needs deal with cross-grained, opaque, unassimilated material, which as such admittedly has from the start an anachronistic quality, but is not wholly obsolete since it has outwitted the historical dynamic."[7] Waste products—here, significantly, children's stories, which, Adorno says, "contain incomparably more eloquent ciphers even of history" than do high drama—are dissonant with the dominant order not only because hierarchies of value disdain their graces. The eccentric and derisory are the ciphers of history, portending new values or speaking an as yet unintelligible tongue. Neither victor nor yet vanquished, they address us through discordant tones and dissonant notes. In line with this concern for history's inassimilable element, Foucault will shift the dialectical picture of power and its representations of law by attending to the shadows and waste as domains available for the cultivation of new practices of life.

PANGS OF SPEECH, CÉSAIRE TO GENET

As an example of what appears eccentric and derisory and which always speaks in discordant tones, Aimé Césaire's *Discourse on Colonialism* of 1950 is an irresistible reference. Written by a major surrealist innovator and poet, founder of the influential *l'Etudiant noir* and *Tropiques*, originator of Négritude, and literary parliamentarian in his native Martinique, Césaire conceived the pamphlet as a clear articulation of the direct connection between colonialism, slavery, European fascism, and American postwar imperialism. He delivered up a theoretical broadside that launches volleys in all directions yet still opens the possibility or potential for self-transformation and thus political revolution in and by the reader. This complex of affect, aim, and modes of address comprises a field of truth telling that cannot be contained by our weak slogan "speaking truth to power," nor by a long historical tradition of *parrhesia,* or "fearless speech." Rather, here rebellious speech takes revolt as its means and along with it, the inevitable abjection revolt confers upon the speaking subject. Césaire's discourse addresses itself to the very law that subjects its speaker and its listener, here the law of history and racist imperialism, but turns that address to another purpose and another audience, one that can give a hearing to the phantasmagoria of his discourse.

> Therefore, comrade, you will hold as enemies—loftily, lucidly, consistently—not only sadistic governors and greedy bankers, not only prefects who torture and colonists who flog, not only corrupt, check-licking politicians and subservient judges, but likewise and for the same reason, venomous journalists, goitrous academics, wreathed in dollars and stupidity, ethnographers who go in for metaphysics, presumptuous Belgian theologians, chattering intellectuals born stinking out of the thigh of Nietzsche, the paternalists, the embracers, the corrupters, the back-slappers, the lovers of exoticism, the dividers, the agrarian sociologists, the hoodwinkers, the hoaxers, the hot-air artists, the humbugs, and in general, all those who, performing their functions in the sordid division of labor for the defense of Western bourgeois society, try in diverse ways and by infamous diversions to split up the forces of Progress—even if it means denying the very possibility of Progress—all of them tools of capitalism, all of them, openly or secretly, supporters of plundering colonialism, all of them responsible, all hateful, all slave-traders, all henceforth answerable for the violence of revolutionary action.[8]

Such fiery rhetoric is not, of course, without precursors, and indeed belongs to a certain political tradition. As literary parliamentarian Césaire inherits the progressive voice of protest of Hugo, the righteous antiracism of Zola, and the anticolonial manifestos of surrealism found, for instance, in the final sections of Artaud's *The Theatre and its Double*. Nor should we forget the revolutionary legacy of Toussaint L'Ouverture. This moment of ranting in Césaire encapsulates the denunciation of primitivism that is discussed below at great length in chapter 1's treatment of Oscar Wilde and which establishes the nineteenth-century decadent engagement with "race" as a conceptual shorthand for culture itself. Bursting with glittering formulations, this seemingly wandering monologue stoops to sarcasm, invective, ventriloquy, copious citation, falsetto, personification, and theatrical asides. In that spirit, *Discourse on Colonialism* shakes off whatever lingering commitments it has to the surrealist genre of manifesto and lays claim to a new mode of address, the rant.

> Oh! The racism of these gentlemen does not bother me. I do not become indignant over it. I merely examine it. I note it, and that is all. I am almost grateful to it for expressing itself openly and appearing in broad daylight, as a sign. A sign that the intrepid class that once stormed the Bastille is now hamstrung. A sign that it feels itself to be mortal. A sign that it feels itself to be a corpse. And when the corpse starts to babble you get this sort of thing. (DC, 49)

A subtle turn away from the politics of revolt, such restraint sidesteps the invitation to become the master's voice and instead proffers its partial, provisional, and watchful attention to the coming of the new age. This unsovereign voice of contestation denounces the law of European moral and political decadence without "dissipating its energies in revolt," as Wilde once observed of the rebel. This almost-gratitude has become a trait of postcolonial writing, as has the careful repetition of voices and the permeation of discourse by the nondiscursive moans and gestures of postcolonial legacies.[9] Intimate with censorships of all kinds, and directly—even impulsively—addressing the laws of order in the very speech acts to which they commit themselves, these moments of ranting appeal can only manifest themselves through abjection.

More difficult to contain, however, is the veering politics of address in the righteous invective above, which solicits a "comrade" where Césaire found such brothers-in-arms lacking.[10] Further, Césaire's nearly exhaustive inventory of colonialists, a list both righteous and ridiculous, and culminating in the summary judgment of "all of them," takes that motley group not only as object of defiance but as implicit addressee as well. As a result, something quite strange happens to our convention of direct address when comrades and enemies are both invoked and dispatched in the same space. Butler's observation that the other of address troubles speech with signs of undoing is apt here. One might ask which other, the abstract comrade or the materialized enemy, is responsible for the undoing we witness. An irresolvable negotiation between direct address and the fracturing of a broad public address to many causes rhetorical turbulence. This unraveling address cannot be simplified or contained, and the *Discourse on Colonialism* is exemplary in its refusal to jettison the irrelevant waste product that produces ranting excess. Instead, Césaire carefully preserves the text's tendency toward parabasis, or swerving address, and in so doing establishes a tolerance for its own rant as an ethical choice. This productive undoing is also the opening for a different iteration of known styles and familiar words; the moment the text is infected with the babbling that it rejects becomes by that same capitulation the moment when a new intelligibility may be registered. A promising failure, splintering address to launch a faltering and compromised speech, this felicitous speech act articulates a form of subjectivity and orientation in the world that derives its terms from the given word. A symptom of modernist knowledge and literary practice, the rant overlaps with manifesto as form without conceding the latter's fundamental belief in communication: even provocative nonsense believes in its gesture of approach to the other. The rant can harbor no such belief but moves toward its readers in a veering kaleidoscopic field of multiplied address. This voice of enmity and embrace, which makes of its own misfiring the claiming of a new subjectivity, as is the ultimate goal of Césaire's rant, can also be heard echoing through Fanon, whose debt to Césaire can best be gauged in the fracturing and splintering address of his own political rants.[11]

The multiple address of the rant complicates one tradition by which we apprehend contestation, namely speech act theory, which since J. L. Austin first approached the question of the performative speech act and the possibility of misfire has been refined and extended by the work of feminists, philosophers, and psychoanalysts. In his famous exchanges with J. D. Searle, Jacques Derrida spelled out the ambivalent force of the performative, which depends upon iteration of convention in new contexts; with this observation, Derrida shifted the discussion away from rule-governed codes and conventions and toward the ever-changing context of performative repetition to show that the promise of the performative is itself dependent upon a temporality neither past nor future but best characterized as a future anterior. Thus the performative repetition of convention is radically dependent upon the event of repetition, and so open to the surprise of a failed performance or an unexpected happening; for this reason the performative is never identical to itself. The salient example is the signature, which we know to be an indispensable attestation of identity while knowing just as well that the graphematic mark is never self-identical, for every mark admits of perverse performance. Shoshana Felman brought to the discussion of the performative speech act and the slipperiness of its iteration a consideration of the intersubjective space of performative utterance, and in a psychoanalytic reading of the act of promising she noted that every repetition of a promise depends on not only the context of its utterance but also the "context" of its ever-changing effect on speaker and listener. Thus iteration not only changes the performative; it changes the subjects of speech as well. Wilde crystallized this paradox in the title *The Importance of Being Earnest*. This psychoanalytic twist on the performative and iteration comes through her spare and careful reading of promising in Molière's *Don Juan* and Mozart's *Don Giovanni* and builds up a convincing argument for the constantly shifting and, indeed, undecidable energies surrounding Don Juan's sincerity and belief in his own promises. Making profitable use of Lacan's maxim that "speech is the body arising as such," Felman argues that no theory of the performative speech act can do without an account of persuasion, and, equally, that persuasion is not a temporally transparent or causal category. Finally, Felman's invocation of the speaking body reminds us of a psychoanalytic principle; namely, that the speaking subject is an embodied subject and thus responsible and responsive to the other of address in the ways signaled by Judith Butler's account of undoing. "A speech act is reducible neither to the body nor to a conscious intention, but becomes the site where the two diverge and intertwine. In this sense, the speaking body scandalizes metaphysics, in particular, its penchant for clear dichotomies."[12]

Neither solely embodied nor purely conscious, speech acts do more than convey information, execute a command, or phatically gesture toward traditions of belonging. The central idea of this book is that the kind of speech act exhibited by Bataille's demand, "Shut me up (if you dare)!" betrays a fantasy of addressing the social order that denies the rights of speech to the speaking subject but simultaneously demands incessant communication. Here the figure of the mouth that would continue to cry after we have sewn up its lips captures the paradox of an embodiment that is neither fully conscious nor only the literal body, but rather the "place" where the clean distinction between speaker and addressee is both knotted and undone in the same gesture. In this sense, the moment of ranting attests to a voice foreclosed in the public spaces of its circulation yet still resounding. At the limit of what is legitimate and legible, the rant materializes a speaking subject whose resistant speech emerges or, more aptly, irrupts to contest the public space that abjects it. This practice of contestation through ranting address also constructs its "addressee" by multiplying the field of address. Through the conceit of a direct address to the law that subjugates, the rant shows publicly the symbolic law that orders it while simultaneously the literary rant draws the witness into complicity or violently denounces the reader. For example, in *Journal du voleur* Jean Genet evokes this dynamic bondage and resistance when he writes, "Je crois que j'avais besoin de creuser, de forer une masse de langage où ma pensée fût à son aise. *Peut-être voulais-je m'accuser dans ma langue*" (I think I needed to dig, to drill through a mass of language so that my thoughts could be at ease. *Perhaps I wanted to accuse/insist myself in my language*).[13] Here Genet plays upon the meanings of "m'accuser," which vacillates between the moral sense of "accuse" and the more abstract sense of "emphasize" or "underscore." This hesitation between insisting on one's rights to expression and to be heard in public and the irresistible attraction to self-confession and self-indictment is not resolved by

Genet's text, which frequently breaks into direct denunciation of "you," the reader; if Genet's writing voice must conjure a "you" to repudiate, it is because "you" come to represent the law of ordinary values and transparent because sanctioned utterances. Thus to denounce the law that abjects him, the ranter must in fact constitute or construct that law, but this can only be affirmed in a fictional direction.[14] The fantasy of speaking in one's own name goads expression, but because sovereign speech can exist only in fantasy, it cannot anchor the rant to ensure a hearing, nor can it secure the rant against the risk of further unintelligibility and breakdown.

Ranting persists in the political space constituted by a social foreclosure of the speaking position. The difficulty of this figure of address is heightened by the fact that in being dispossessed of the right to speech, the rant is not, however, unable to speak. In line with this folded border that appears as an absolute limit, my framing of the rant depends upon a psychoanalytic concept, foreclosure, which names a founding negation that establishes a kind of generalized law for the subject; while a contingent form, the result of an individual, historical, infinitely local encounter with the other, the negation at issue, *Verwerfung,* as it has developed in what now constitutes a psychoanalytic tradition from Freud through Lacan, Mannoni, and Laplanche, supplies the terms by and through which we appear in public as intelligible beings. As resistant speech, the rant must invent its own terms from a censored encyclopedia of experience and social naming, which is to say that the rant materializes a speaking subject at the limit of intelligibility where none is authorized. In Jean Genet's *Journal du voleur* the thief's liminality is literally expressed through spittle, snot, sperm, and other quasi-fluid, semisolid emissions. These are not metaphors for his social status; they are the abject terms by which Genet generates a field of images and meanings far in excess of the social foreclosure he lives. Ranting attests to negation by supplementing it in a generative negativity that proliferates the terms of subjection but with the promise, not always realized, of setting subjection to work to expose, invent, and manifest new terms for the particular subject. Radically dependent upon a particular history of injury, the rant's abject appeal flows from and indeed fosters the singularity of a speech that is imbricated and embedded in subjection.

The resonance between the freedom to take oneself to task and the necessity to underscore or insist oneself into a language that only belongs improperly to one repeats throughout the examples of ranting assembled here. Genet's concise formulation presents us with a paradox of belonging and address that cannot be described as a simple relation of norm to its excluded other. Here, the speaker not only desires to perform a speech act; he desires to perform it in and as his own tongue; this emphasis on the tongue brings the category of language and its border into crisis, for the one who speaks has a ready access to the language and can easily respect its laws. What constitutes the transgression effected by this lawful exercise of grammar that at once undermines the transparency of understanding and the simple declaration of a desire? According to Marie Redonnet, Genet wanted nothing more than to "glorify France in poetry that attacks it and strips it bare, such is the paradoxical and scandalous task of Genet as poet. The betrayal of a poet is an act of love. The betrayal is the invention of a new love, condition of a new ethics." While Redonnet emphasizes the transgression of Genet's writing against the state at the very moment it was under German occupation, Genet's explanation of his need to simultaneously insist and accuse himself concerns theft during his wanderings across Europe, for he comes to realize that he was never more a representative of the state of France as when he tried to practice his thievery abroad. In order to seize upon his own uniqueness, he could not remain in literal exile because his thoughts and sense of self had been cultivated in French. Thus, to become who he is, the true betrayer, the writer Genet must return to the language that binds him. To transcend the social designation that inhabits him, he must find at home the becoming-foreigner that countersigns his uniqueness.

The rant is a speech act embedded in its own attachments, bound by the word and by the social terms of its own subjection; from out of the negation of social foreclosure and the subjection of determination the rant crafts its "mots-défis"[15] and reaches within a social network of division and exclusion to participate in the power of the word. Significantly, Genet notes that he could not simply speak in argot but was compelled to write in the language of the enemy, the dominant classes. As he puts it, only Céline could make that choice and still be recognized a genius of modern French literature because "it took a doctor." No juvenile convict and war deserter could hope to transgress the language with his social class; this comment has nothing in it of an identification with the working classes, nor particularly anything against luxury, for his point lies elsewhere than the dialectic of victor and vanquished. For Genet, there are the absolutely abject, for instance, the children reared in juvenile prisoners to become adult outcasts.[16] The notions of center/periphery with which we are even now redrawing the map of modernism to become more inclusive are themselves insufficient to describe the examples of modernist speech treated here, for these writers do not add an interesting marginal variant, nor do they represent the views of the periphery to the ears of the metropole.[17] Modernist ranters, like Césaire and Genet, expose the social deformation of the system of subjection, and as such they speak from within and not from a distant frontier. Not condemned to silence but sidelined in a symbolic economy that determines reception before the speech act is heard, the rant grows and even thrives in the internal fold prepared for it. And it is this liminality to which the rant bears witness in a form of speech that does not shatter the delimitations and exclusions of the norm but rather expands the borderline by widening the path of its own audition.

MODERNISM: FROM PARRHESIA TO REVOLT

This figure of a defiant speech in excess of the norm is salient in modernism, and on this point it is worth recalling that Charles Baudelaire, that combative wellspring of modernist sensibility, had at least three distinct faces. Famously the lyric poet of modernity, he was the translator-critic who proclaimed Edgar Allan Poe the first modern poet. Yet Baudelaire was also the ranter who, exiled to Brussels in search of an editor willing to publish poetry deemed blasphemous and licentious in France, compiled the interminable and never-completed stream of curses and invective "Pauvre Belgique!" Brussels, the "Capital des singes," could only ape the imaginary refinements of a bankrupt Paris, making it nothing more than an "asterisk of history." Baudelaire's denunciations echo down through the works of high modernism even as his more presentable face, that of the lyric poet harshly censored by state morality, continues to dominate his reception. This unbridled and frankly unhinged practice of critique, which comprises only one aspect of "spleen" in his ethos but which can be heard throughout the poems that make up *Spleen de Paris,* resonates in the high modernism of Pound and Lewis and in the singular blend of refinement and abjection practiced by Céline. Flaubert, like Baudelaire, had no shortage of ire, which he used to great effect in his *Dictionnaire des idées reçues* to satirize the dominant tics of the bourgeoisie but which equally bound him to the object he loved to hate by trapping him in a discursive loop.[18] To rail against the bourgeois love of denouncing all difference, Flaubert was obliged to "thunder against" *(tonner contre)* the same. As Richard Terdiman's study of nineteenth-century aesthetics and opposition shows, writers like Flaubert and Baudelaire were forced to find more subtle means to resist the mortifying norms that limited desire and expression to commodifiable forms, and thus they engaged in counterdiscursive negotiations with the norm. Fundamentally, modernism demanded that its aesthetic labors contest the symbolic laws of ordered social rationality, but not all social resistance can be neatly contained in the dialectic. Even the nimble modernist mediation with which Benjamin credits Baudelaire, as the voice of nineteenth-century modernity itself, comes to crisis under pressure of dissident exile and mindless mimicry of the metropole. Meeting refusal and negation with the same, modernism cultivated the voice of revolt and rebellion into practices that have yielded a lineage of contestation, but that tradition of righteous and militant speech and the more subtle mediations that Terdiman explores issue from a subjective experience that is at once self-aware and self-contained and easily transmissible as a style of writing, a social attitude or pose, and a form of subjectivity. Critical denunciation of middle-class morality, cultural degeneration, and commonplace idées fixes are by the end of the nineteenth century the stock in trade of aestheticism, although decadence, which practices its own form of ranting, as my discussion of Oscar Wilde will demonstrate, continued to trouble critique with excessive spleen.[19] A tradition of revolt paradoxically enforces a subjective style as a social norm in this writing, while that same style remains uncannily animated by a rage or exigency that strains the pose of masterful renunciation, militant critique, sovereign self, and secular antinomian.[20] The rant irrupts precisely at the point when negotiation of this difference between an autonomy claimed and servility collapses.

We approach the topic of ranting at this crisis of autonomy and servility through two aspects articulated in the subtitle: the literary rant, the first aspect, summons the question of fantasy in the constitution of the subject; the second aspect represents its relation to power and symbolic law. This double optic entails a consideration of the figure and function of the "primitive" or fantasies of the first order in modernity and especially in literary modernism and psychoanalysis. It also proposes that modernist ranting exposes a boundary or limit that is lived as a law, beyond which lies unintelligibility and social death; this double function structures the three chapters of the book as each moves through a critical elaboration of the different constitutions of normative subjectivity and the scripted transgressions the norm enjoins while also describing the rant's challenge to that normativity through its unsovereign speech. Thus each chapter pursues both the figure of the primitive as a constitutive feature of normative subjectivity and simultaneously, the irruption of literary ranting in my three examples. The modernist soundings of the three chapters have in common the binding character of the recursive figuration of primitivism, the politics of ranting address, and the psychoanalytic optic that, while highlighting different analytic terms in each discussion—sublimation, fetishism, and foreclosure, respectively—keeps in view the notion of a founding negation that constitutes a social limit. Chapter 1 sets out the role of sublimation and fantasy in Oscar Wilde's political aesthetic, and examines his attempt to put racializing discourses to antiracist purpose in "De Profundis," a ranting letter written while he was imprisoned for consensual sex with another man. Chapter 2 looks at Jane Bowles's shift of modernist lesbian expatriatism from the Parisian metropole to colonial Morocco to argue that Bowles's writing block and ranting practice were sustained by a racial form of fetishism. Psychoanalytic concepts of the primitive and fetishism are key to understanding her detours. Though ranting is self-consciously depicted in her fiction as dramatic crisis, for Bowles ranting has much to do with silence and blocked expression, which breaks out in a furious epistolary career in her personal life. Chapter 3 builds upon this modernist culture of primitivism and expression, alternately blocked and excessive, through a close reading of the novel *Talismano*, by the Tunisian Abdelwahab Meddeb, and turns to a particular kind of primitivism that also carries the stigma of infantilism, medievalism, and arrested development: orientalism. In this chapter the rant becomes part of a self-conscious and knowing poetics of ranting, and thus lifts *On Pain of Speech*'s discussion from a reading of symptoms to a reading of the postcolonial avant-garde uptake and reuse of a pathological form. Meddeb's appropriation also extends to psychoanalytic categories and the styles and history of decadent literary forms and high modernism. The whole culminates in the way that *Talismano* is able to turn the staging of outburst and breakdown or raving and reveries into a repeatable style that can usefully reflect on the history of orientalism and the forms of normative subjectivity enforced in the postcolonial state while simultaneously refusing the implicit racialization of psychoanalytic theory.

The psychoanalytic argument that proceeds from chapter to chapter follows the intuition of a symbolic law, without which no voice of modernist revolt need or could be raised, beginning with Wilde's literary and critical reflections before Freud's major publications; this is followed by a midcentury example of an abject feminine writing that acts out feminine refusal and compensates with fetishistic fantasy. My discussion of a gay Irish decadent and a queer lesbian who voluntarily exiled herself to Morocco explores two unconventional ways of embodying the norms of sexuality, which include the norms of dissident sexuality underway since the middle of the nineteenth century. The arguments of the first two chapters, each a consideration of a single writer whose complex relation to colonialism and to empire inflects questions of sexual and gendered identity, converge in the final chapter's postcolonial critique of symbolic relations. *Talismano* is unusually able to find the utopian potentiality hidden in a history of foreclosures and refusals perpetuated in the present. Key to this capacity to imagine utopian figures is *Talismano*'s foregrounding of the body in all the registers of its modernity; thus, the mechanism of modern subjection—the racially marked and sexed body—is apparent in *Talismano*'s emphasis on representing the "disorder of the body more than the law." This is one reason why the novel so clearly signals its debt to French decadent writing. This progression of chapters builds toward a major criticism of Jacques Lacan's theory of foreclosure, which has become a key term in feminist and postcolonial critique in recent years. Like the literary texts pursued in these chapters, psychoanalysis is treated as a form of modernism, which, as Foucault argued consistently after 1966, developed to diagnose and resist the biopolitical power that represents subjectivity as determined by degeneracy and hereditary taint.[21] In this sense, psychoanalysis participates in the modernist critical project to undo the consolidation of social fantasy that privileges normative identity as the only attainable form of social life.

Postscripts, letters, afterwords: marginal genres at the edges of masterful texts are often the site of the rant's emergence, but what I am calling the rant is not in itself a genre. The literary rant may be turned into a full-blown poetics, as in the case of Meddeb, or may remain a telling and poignant symptom of a failed strategy of self-invention, as in the case of Wilde's prison letter. Felman proposes a novel way to think of failure that helps us grasp this recursive genrelessness. Failure, she tells us, is not the problem of something that fails to happen; rather, something else happens instead, and this something else that happens is a parataxis that surprises and scandalizes, throwing the whole story into uncanny association. In Bowles I have found an example between the catastrophe of *De Profundis* and the formal triumph of *Talismano*;

what makes Bowles perhaps unique as a ranter is the way that she turned protest, plaints, and anxious agonizing into the textual relays of a writerly life held in suspense—death driven, manic, blocked, and blaming, but life nonetheless. This would be a parataxis of writing itself where the failure to write creates other effects of writing.

Clearly, such a paradoxical set of conditions and rhetorical operations does not constitute a genre, though the politics of address that is powerfully exposed by this linking of life and writing becomes familiar when viewed as a constant production of the predicament of modernist self-elaboration conducted in opposition to an unspoken norm. Symbolic resistance in its guise as counterdiscourse both denaturalizes congealed ideological forms and discloses or materializes the seemingly impossible position of an excluded and marginal otherness.[22] By this account counterdiscourses are forceful but ultimately not revolutionary, for they cannot subvert the dominant power that frames them. Ranting must materialize the law of its abjection as a precondition of rebuke and a putatively vindicating speech, and thus differs from the notion of counterdiscourse in at least two ways: the rant cannot build upon itself because as an event of the materialization of the law, it cannot rally a movement or gather the troops. Rather, it appeals without mastery. Further, margin and center are not the best figures for approaching the rant, for this is not speech projected from an exotic outside but a speech from within the entanglement of law with itself. As Butler puts it in her discussion of Antigone, the crisis of representation engendered by a perverse performative is a crisis from within the very terms of representation; it is the social deformation within the system that brings the system to crisis rather than the violent intruder who triumphs over law.[23] If there is a dominant figure in my discussion of the rant, it is this asymmetrical chiasmus that cannot reverse a system nor bring it to its knees but engenders catachrestic effects that promise new freedoms from within the bondage of existing limitations.

Foucault's history of *parrhesia* and counterdiscourse sheds light on the genealogy of modernity; by the late nineteenth century, the confessional discourses of the subject extended to medicine, law, sociology, education, and literature; by multiplying the resonance and meaning of things sexual the frank talk of the classical world was subsumed in the scientific data and personal identity of the modern norm. This historical perspective caused Foucault to reason that speaking the sexual truth of the subject had come to a position of power, that it is, in fact, the modern institution of an authority of speech and subjective support for a normative version of truth and self. In a utopian move, Foucault urged his readers to proliferate the modes of subjectivation beyond the reach of power's norm. This project is not one that eschews power or seeks to purify resistance of its intimacy with the power to speak, but rather it attempts to shift the center of the norm away from itself; *parrhesia* is not banished in the biopolitical deployment of sexuality and race. It is, however, substantially complicated by the diffusion of sovereign power in the networks of biopolitical relation, and, as Foucault writes, "When a philosopher criticizes a tyrant, when a citizen criticizes the majority, when a pupil criticizes his teacher, then such speakers may be using *parrhesia*."[24] Yet the use of *parrhesia* does not confer upon the pupil, citizen, or philosopher the status of *parrhesiastes*, nor does it extricate the speaker from the web of power relations that entangle him.

Fearless speech that speaks the truth is still possible, but it is now performed from a position of subjection and subjectivation that does not always offer the clarity of a single addressee or prime target. An ideal act of *parrhesia* haunts the modern subject with the promise of being done, once and for all, with subjection or denouncing finally the power that subjects. By Foucault's own analysis, the ethical act of *parrhesia* corresponds to one element of critique but cannot account for the diffusion of disciplinary power in the forms of truth that we, moderns, both accept and resist. For this reason, the act of *parrhesia* is more often a fantasy we keep alive than a reality that we live. But the ethical drive that inspired *parrhesia* and the ethical hearing that allowed for truth to be determined in the relation of listening, these are not arts violently lost in history and unattainable in the present dispensation of power.

More than a literary influence, this lineage from Baudelaire to decadence and surrealism and the postcolonial avant-garde attests to an attitude of resistance—or what Bataille called a "rage of revolt"—and, more specifically, to an obligation or vocation of self-invention; as Foucault learns from Baudelaire, "to be modern is not to accept oneself as one is in the flux of the passing moments; it is to take oneself as object of a complex and difficult elaboration," which paradoxically must take place in writing and thus in a context of address that destines self-invention to the vagaries of public audience. The burden of self-invention brings with it both a realist acceptance of ruin and a utopian wager that hopes for transformation. In *Fearless Speech*, and at greater length in the seminar *The Hermeneutics of the Subject*, Foucault dwells on the transformation of *parrhesia*, protest speech or speaking truth to power, into a technology of the self. *Parrhesia* represents "a sort of 'figure' among rhetorical figures, but with this characteristic: that it is without any figure since it is completely natural. *Parrhesia* is the zero degree of those rhetorical figures which intensify the emotions of the audience."[25] *Parrhesia* is an experience of speech that establishes truth through conviction and risk, but the "figure of no figure," which claims a natural and unembellished character, bears new burdens in the modern period. C. L. R. James, as we shall see below, is a good example of this insofar as the *parrhesia* he risks is caught up in the apologia he compulsively performs. Ranting, a speech under duress, loses the subject in the stream of words that overwhelm his speaking. But the appeal, abject though it is, is directed both at the law that condemns, the self who defends, and the audience who may receive it. No longer a zero-sum speech shorn of artifice and thus authorized as truth telling, the rant is a modern speech destined to that complex and difficult elaboration that establishes the self through the address to the other of speech. This address cannot be entirely direct nor wholly allegorical, for the scene of face-to-face communication has been mediated not only by the alienation of speech in the public space of modernity, but also by the division of the self through the interiorization of that "complex and difficult elaboration" by which one must "take oneself as object."

To speak of the politics of address is to invoke the knowledge that no speech can master its effects or know fully what hearing awaits it, and thus the aim of address, its approach to the other, will always bear the trace of that knowledge. This knowing incapacity or capable nonknowledge lurks in the address of writing as a precondition of what wants and needs to be said, even at moments of urgency when, we are told, engagement and political commitment demand sovereign mastery of our speech and the self-control to put aside childish things. This latter will be important as we consider ranting, because although marginal texts and movements do belatedly reap the benefit of canonization, the rant—as an event—is not a stable genre and cannot be defined by a formal poetics. Although imitation may have its way, no two rants will exhibit the same formal structure, despite the fact that ranting can yield a poetics by determining an individual writer's obsessions and interventions.

If modernity conserves *parrhesia* but only as a foreclosed inscription, which binds it within subjection, how does this politics of address characteristic of modernity account for the postcolonial difference?

Chiefly through the strategy of a biopolitical limit rewritten as the difference between modernity's rational man and its primitive other. In a unique discussion of contemporary postcolonial subjectivity and systems of rationality, Stefania Pandolfo explores a contradiction confronting Moroccan modernity and subjectivity. Moroccan psychoanalysts, committed by their technical training to cutting-edge therapies informed by Lacanian psychoanalysis, are challenged in this faith by the fact that their modern postcolonial patients have quite a different practical understanding of healing through the talking cure. For the physicians the cure is understood in Lacanian terms as requiring a symbolic assumption of one's subject position effected through the arrival or irruption of "true speech" in analysis.[26] For the cure to take place, the subject must accede to this full speech act in a narrative of self that abandons the detritus of everyday chatter or, in Lacanian terms, empty speech. This heroic narrative of the newly sovereign subject produced through the intersubjective analytic encounter runs up against an obstacle, and not only in theory, for increasingly Moroccans seeking remedy in analysis also seek out folk, religious, and magical healing, and quite without any sense of contradiction or immiscibility of practices. For the medical practice this simultaneous appeal to the laws of science and the "hallucinations" of folklore requires an explanation. How, indeed, is a modern form of rationality to contend with a persistent social fact that shows that the authentic speech of healing can and does take place in the context of magical thinking? One physician's reluctant admission that for many patients the truest attestation and articulation of their pain may not arrive in the zone of medical technical superiority but rather within the mystical reassertion of unregulated practices suggests that some in the medical establishment can hear the message of Moroccan modernity as one fractured by other experience, which is pathologized in the postcolonial context as "tradition." As Pandolfo's critical work and ethnographic investigations show, contemporary Moroccans struggle in the limitations of this medical theory when subjective experience and local practices attest to another truth, namely, that the phantasmagoria of alienation and modern loss—where time is out of joint and culture is both lagging and never equal to itself—must be spoken to produce the means of new subjectivity, new life and new truths. This productivity of the imaginary when addressed by the subject to and through the "law" is a truth attested to by literary movements as early as Baudelaire's invocations of a satanic vocation. Aestheticism, decadence, surrealism, and postcolonial and modernist literature can all be understood as forms of attestation to social losses, gaps, foreclosures, and contradictions that realist and self-reflective forms of knowledge cannot always access.

Not all contemporaries accept this complicated and crosshatched modernity. Pandolfo cites Abdallah Laroui's bracing conclusion that only through the repudiation of primitive attachments and the total renovation of the self can the postcolonial Arab subject overcome the impasse of the present and move toward emancipation.

> Laroui sees it as an emancipation from the image of the west within, from the melancholic attachment to a vanished Arab past, from culture, always already lost, from phantasmatic desire, from a lingering sense of loss. Only those who have accomplished the path of emancipation are entitled to speak, have a voice in the present. All others dwell in an incommensurable past. The patient's speech, if one were to extrapolate from Laroui, can never be encountered in the present. It is already, and by definition, "folklore"; it belongs to a remote past, the archeological past of cemeteries. (TLM, 142)

Against this staunchly rationalist Marxist argument for an uncompromised modernity—itself indebted to a Freudian model of melancholia and working through—Pandolfo contrasts the work of Driss Chraibi, whose surreal novel of 1954, *Le Passé Simple,* dramatizes the consequences of Laroui's categorical and inflexible attitude in the face of the archaeological return of the "remote past." There a young Moroccan passes through an infernal and hallucinatory night-town epic replete with references to the surrealist canon and Céline and Joyce, among others; he is accompanied by an enigmatic figure of cultural severance, a "thin line" that speaks his greatest shames and castigates him for abandoning his African roots. Enraged rants, profane acts, futile rebellion, and the gender problem are absolutely central to the problem of modernity in the novel and continue to appear in the next generation of Maghrebian novelists for whom Chraibi was a serious influence. Pandolfo argues through her reading of Chraibi that "the loss, which is modernity itself, cannot be overcome and returns as a phantasm." And the subject, "wrenched" and "torn in every direction discovers in this non-resolution the possibility of speech and perhaps the path of another emancipation" (TLM, 143). In literary terms, the rant proceeds from this possibility inherent in the situation of impasse, discord, and severance that modernity enjoins upon its subjects as a defining negativity. Thus the discourse on East/West relations and modernity is conveyed by a figure that can only be rendered as figure; it cannot be decanted to a single premise or rationalist narrative. The "inauthenticity" of hallucination and complaint, of excess and inaudible meaning, these are all hallmarks of a modern experience explored at great length in chapter 3 through an analysis of *Talismano,* a novel that stages intervention and transformation but only via the imaginary and figural relay of a ranting text for which Chraibi's heretical novel is a precursor.

It is in the encounter with what Pandolfo calls the "other scene" and which we might understand as the imaginary that the Moroccan subjects who so worry the medical establishment are able to produce an address and find the hearing they seek. The psychiatrist she cites says clearly that the symptom of Moroccan modernity is increasingly addressed to the doctor but never spoken in that encounter; rather, the sociohistorical symptom finds its voice and speaks its truth only in the hallucinatory space of ritual, dream, or literary reverie. This is a modernity that can be described as a particular situation of speech foreclosed seeking its proper outlet. In "Aggressivity in Psychoanalysis," Lacan writes that in seeking analysis the patient presents himself as someone capable of being understood. Presenting oneself as intelligible to an other is a complex symbolic act that need not happen only in the space cleared by enlightenment reason. The hallucinatory spaces of incantation and ritual or the culturally sanctioned space of avant-garde literature are equally apt to render this presentation. As the psychiatrist admits, the "true speech" of symbolic self-understanding is more often heard in the phantasmagoric theater of ritual and incantation than in the clinical setting; thus the analyst's concern for the finality of cure runs aground in the uneven and striated spaces of social practice where cure may not arrive once and for all, but may in fact require a lifetime of repetition. Pandolfo argues that literature is a social practice that can register lacerations of the modernity's severance by voicing this imaginary discourse. And in *Le Passé Simple* she finds an example of the imaginary yielding a knowledge about one's symbolic inscription in a historical problem and a cultural moment. This "successful" speech of an excessive, surreal, and ranting text performs what it knows about the foreclosure of the symbol by indulging in the imaginary and empty speech of fiction.

Scholars of Anglo-American modernism may be surprised to find the term modernism applied to late nineteenth-century decadence and writings of the postwar era, as well as to postcolonial authors who write in Arabic, which has a much older literary lineage than English, and French. One of the broader aims of this book is to decenter modernist definitions of period and style by arguing that modernism is a practice that always had a global reach and which continues well into the 1980s in the texts of the Francophone and Arabic literature of the Mashreq and the Maghreb, as well as the few Anglophone texts of the Middle East at the very least.[27] This is not to say that avant-garde experimentation, stream-of-consciousness psychological narrative, themes of memory, fragmentation, and subjectivity, and moods of political despair and resistant rage do not color other literary styles or schools, but rather that the political and aesthetic intervention of the Caribbean, queer modernism, and the Arabic and Francophone literature of the Middle East have been practicing literary modernism in forms and styles that have been politically daring , formally innovative, and critical since at least the late nineteenth century. The Arabic and Francophone literature of the Maghreb and the Mashreq has found inspiration in the gesture of the Euro-American modernist avant-garde. The influence of American poetics, T. S. Eliot and Whitman especially, was felt early on,[28] while it is difficult to find a major author untouched by Baudelaire, which is to say that the fundamental response of decadent avant-gardism to modernity and the subjection it enjoins became a resource for anticolonial critique and a critical reception of modernity coeval with the major texts of high modernism. Maghrebian Francophone literature has been marked by a passionate reading of Faulkner, while Maghrebian authors such as Rachid Boudjedra and Abdelwahab Meddeb, both novelists and poets who write in Arabic and French, attest in their works and in interviews to a capacious absorption of American, Arabic, Irish, and French literature.[29] Contra our habits of periodization in Anglo-American modernist studies, modernism did not end with the Second World War; in the Middle East the 1950s were a time of modernist innovation,[30] while the 1970s and 1980s witnessed the arrival of the first Arabic language avant-garde novels. When I speak of what will be for most modernist scholars "alternative modernism," I do not have in mind a dialectic of metropole and its periphery, as do others working comparatively through world literature or attempting to expand the reach of modernism, for there are alternative modernisms at home, for instance in the pages of Bowles's letters and published fiction. The fundamental presumption of such a dialectical model avers a belated and inherently imitative export of American expatriate or Parisian metropolitan culture to the outskirts of empire. As a caution against this developmental model, we might recall that Césaire is a major surrealist whose staggering poetics insists the legacy of Lautréamont into the twentieth century in ways unparalleled in French poetics. The queer modernism of decadence and the postcolonial avant-garde have in common their avant-garde investment in the project of self-invention and an unstinting critical posture toward normativity of all kinds; this double commitment sets apart a lineage of decadent modernism from the literary realism that dominates much national literature, postcolonial writing, and gay and lesbian literature avowed to a confessional style. With this in mind, marginality should be understood not on the model of excluded identity, ready-made but ignored, nor on the model of alternative modernisms, if that means simply expanding the map of modernism geographically; rather, here we are concerned with subjects in process, determined by the laws they rebuke but constructing them nonetheless: a gay Irishman in Reading Goal, a Jewish sexual tourist in Morocco, a Caribbean socialist on Ellis Island, a juvenile vagrant moving between national borders and allying himself with the enemies of the state, a Muslim patient called up to secure a system, Lewis the enemy who enters the center only to throw himself out, and an avant-garde Tunisian writer who resists postcolonial nationalism and its determination of marginals. Marginality—not as a group identity but as the resistant effect of having become a subject—engenders writing in the mode of a critical examination of the social world.

Foucault's account of biopolitical modernity finds ample support from the field of modernist literary production; in fact, modernism, as a global field of writing that addresses the phantasmagoria of modern severance and loss, registers the subjective torsions that Foucault's speculative history indexes, but until recently literary explorations of subjection and efforts to bring about new subjectivation were not viewed as ciphers of this imbrication of state, sex, and race but rather as avant-garde or humanist resistance to power manifest as the alienation of the human subject in a social world lamenting the loss of its idols in the disenchantment of modernity. That this theme constitutes a tradition of modernist revolt and rebellion is incontestable. As our discussion of Foucault suggests, however, resistance is an insufficient lens through which to view the wide array of modernist negotiations with power, its prohibitions, and the creativity it has called forth. The resistance narrative is, of course, a valuable and certainly a valid one to apply to modernist texts. I am interested in another narrative that attends to the strategies of survival in the modernist text. This implies a certain seizing upon power, participating in its reach and rerouting its potential through untrafficked or unprecedented terrain. In each of the three chapters that follow, I pursue individual authors who adopt discrete strategies of writing to usurp sovereign power and redirect it through their own exigency. Personal sovereignty of the writing subject is one result of this rerouting, but no such sovereignty can be displaced outside the frame of writing or exercised in its absence. As Bataille would have it, this is a sovereignty that disappears in the moment of its exercise. What inheres, then, in its wake is a practice of writing that proceeds from its mode of address and its active ability to foreground or expose the forms of power's reach, the symbolic law and order that subtends it.

Working toward chapter 3's broader understanding of the ways that foreclosure operates in the historical spaces of modernity, whether metropolitan or postcolonial, the first and second chapters explore psychoanalytic concepts and literary engagements that disclose exclusions of an increasingly deepening kind. From the open secrecy of Wilde's social status as aesthete dandy exhibiting a "new ideal for life" on the stage and in the elegant hotels and male brothels of London to the clarity of his prison letter, which brooks no secrecy nor harbors any liberal illusions about the English prison, the fin de siècle example presents us with layers of permission and outright avowal of sexual dissidence and juridical prohibition of homosexuality. In this regard, queer historiography has corroborated the main thesis of Foucault's *Discipline and Punish,* which argues that violent spectacles of punishment were replaced in the modern dispensation of power by invisible or hidden incitements to docility. As early as Crompton's *Byron and Greek Love: Homophobia in 19th Century England* critics have argued that the abolition of the death penalty for sodomy and modern requirements of admissible evidence did not result in a decriminalization of homosexuality in England comparable to that of the "Declaration of the Rights of Man" on the continent. What Wilde's example discloses is the development of expressive display in homosexual culture simultaneous with new mechanisms of social control, including the mediatic sexual scandal and panic; this collision of extreme publicity with the veils of discretion and expression that characterized late nineteenth-century sexual culture and the active practice of a social taboo on homosexuality exposes the ways that seemingly forbidden behavior thrived in public and as an object of public consumption. Far from describing a shadowy and marginal exclusion, the place of homosexuality in public life is rather one of an intimate fold within. Here the psychoanalytic concept of sublimation as a means to queer kinship and a transcendence of racial determinism illuminates the tight relation between prohibition and creative expression; as Foucault explains, "homosexuality is an historic occasion to reopen affective and relational virtualities, not so much through the intrinsic qualities of the homosexual but because of the 'slantwise' position of the latter . . . the diagonal lines he can lay out in the social fabric allow these virtualities to come to light."[31]

With a similarly uncanny ability to expose the slantwise force of a limit, Jane Bowles, whose writings appear to be apolitical, produces subtle reflections on the marginalization of gender, the difficulty of forming alternative family structures, and the impossible negotiation of desire across cultural differences, and does so fully within a language of domesticity and feminine complaint framed by helplessness and frustration; this language, while it bears some resemblance to the tropes of feminine domestic discourse established as a nineteenth-century American norm, in its new context serves a very different function, one that is evident only if we attend to the dynamic disavowals found throughout her ranting letters. Here we seem to be very far from a consideration of state regulation of bodies; however, the fact that Tangier was seen as sufficiently remote from American home life to enable a lesbian household anchored by servitude suggests that the expatriate life was not so much a refusal of state regulation and a flight from the norm as it was the site of the reaffirmation of the rule of kinship centered on that modern conception of sexual regulation in the family. Further, far from allowing a revolutionary thwarting of all convention, being American in Tangier enabled a form of domesticity that closely mimicked not the gender roles of butch-femme performance but the domestic economy of flows and stoppage of money, where intimacy is engendered in the sharing of scarcity and wealth. My reading of Bowles's desire to turn prostitution and servitude into home life argues that her erotic attachments and frustrations bound her within a domesticity that provided her a respite from the struggle with writing that consumed her days and the paralyzing gender enforcement that made her cringe before her lesbian elders in the Parisian American expatriate scene. This domestic alternative to the "isolation" of her writing block grounds her epistolary ranting by securing for her a space from which to rebuke a normative law of kinship and comportment, adult development, and gendered behavior, all of which she suffered as failure. In this chapter I develop the core argument that the rant is a form of address that has as its twinned purpose the exposure of symbolic laws that prohibit and the simultaneous disavowal of the law. Such a disavowal of what one is in the process of expressing or highlighting can only founder on its own speech, but when a writer turns that failure into the material reworked by ranting and by fiction she performs a further alteration of the law. In Bowles the themes of failure and inadequacy embrace the terms of derogation and put true criticism in the mouth of those least authorized to speak.

In the course of these chapters, our gaze remains fixed on the link between a mobilization of the trope of the primitive, variously expressed as degenerate, decadent, or regressed, and a literary symptom, the rant, that emerges as a riposte to the modern technologies of discursive sexuality that run through the speaking subject and determine his position of enunciation; sexualization and racialization are twin processes that collude to produce in the speaking body the conditions of intelligibility and recognition by means of which power ensures its own survival. Figurations of infantile regression, femininity, homosexuality, race, and "actual" primitive or tribal societies are tied in the literary avant-garde to the difficult intuition that social groups appear to be governed by invisible, unstated symbolic laws of kinship and repression, and for this reason sensitivity to the phantasm of the law produces a ranting excess characteristic of literary decadence and which later modernisms try to contain. In the manner of Foucault's notion of *problématiques,* we will pursue the question of why and how did the modernist construction of race and sexuality, of margin and center, of public and private produce this symptom of ranting excess, but rather than offer a sweeping or comprehensive history or genealogy of what I am arguing is an unmasterable terrain, we approach the topic through selected soundings of this set of preoccupations. I say unmasterable, for the rant's address exposes a set of relations that dramatize a problem of power's inscription. The rant does not offer us a genre's list of formal attributes or the accidental, but conventional features of a received identity. Yet there is a family resemblance between moments of ranting, one we might describe as a staging or materialization of an encounter with the "law" that can only happen in fantasy and through the performance of ranting address.

An important link between these authors exists in their shared presumption that writing can be a recourse against the disciplinary power that menaces and subjects them. In this sense, the outbreak of ranting evident in the texts considered here is distinct from what may be a broader cultural phenomenon of complaint and vigorous protest widely observed by modernist mass cultural critics like Wyndham Lewis and

Theodor Adorno, two theorists who diagnosed the cultural production of infantilism. The literary rant believes in writing and puts its faith in the peculiarly dislocated and disorienting address of ranting appeal. More potently invested than a ranting crank letter to the editor or a late-night blog, the literary rant disarms its author through a commitment to writing as a form of power uncontained by but still beholden to hierarchies of institutional authority or the armies of convention. Marxist critic C. L. R. James, whom I discuss at length in the next section, responded to his incarceration at Ellis Island by producing a literary critical assessment of *Moby Dick* in which he argued that the novel presciently foretold the arrival of modern totalitarianism through the development of middle management in the administered society. That he turned to writing about writing while facing indefinite detention attests to modernism's acute sensitivity to the power of the word while it underlines James's equal attunement to writing as both a technology of subjection and the modern form of subjectivation by which we are "incited to recognize our moral obligations."[32]

REPROBATE WORDS

Incarcerated indefinitely at Ellis Island in 1951 for "passport violations," C. L. R. James, Trinidadian socialist and postcolonial theorist avant la lettre, set himself the task of explaining that a work of fiction written in 1850 was the single most exhaustive examination of the social world of the 1950s. Doubtless few are the writers who, arrested on grounds of engaging "in activities 'prejudicial to the public interest' or 'subversive to the national security,'"[33] could find in literary criticism the resources of a resounding apologia and public address. James, however, begins his polemical postscript to *Mariners, Renegades and Castaways: The Story of Herman Melville and the World We Live In*, titled "A Natural But Necessary Conclusion," with the assertion of the "inseparability of great literature and social life" revealed to him by the writing of the book.[34] This fusion of literature and life shone with uncanny clarity as James found himself "just about to write, suddenly projected onto an island isolated from the rest of society, where American administrators and officials, and American security officers controlled the destinies of perhaps a thousand men, sailors, 'isolatoes,' renegades and cast-aways from all parts of the world."[35] It was from this "space of absolute malediction"[36] that James sought to refashion the terms of his indefinite detention into the language of protest and critique and to show that the labor of analytic reading was and could still be transformative.

> I came to the conclusion that I would never be able to recover from the shame and disgrace if I let all this pass without saying a word, or waited until my case was decided before speaking. Some time or other someone had to speak and not some philanthropist, but someone who was involved. I publish the protest with the book on Melville because as I have shown, the book as written is a part of my experience. It is also a claim before the American people, the best claim I can put forward, that my desire to be a citizen is not a selfish nor a frivolous one.[37]

However outraged he may be, James is not speaking truth to power when he recounts the details of his incarceration. Indeed, the form of his address and its political force pose a challenge to conventional theories of protest, contestation, freedom of expression, and the public sphere. He addresses an audience that cannot be limited to the state nor to the petty officials and fellow prisoners who tormented him. If he does address power, it is the power diffused throughout a readership as diverse as the crew of the *Pequod* and as unable to attend to him as they. A claim set before the American people but cast adrift in the uncertain fate of publication, James's protest aims in several directions at once as it defends against an accusation, proclaims a desire, sets the record straight, criticizes an abuse of power, and appeals to the reader to uphold a discrete set of values that he then labels American.[38] If the address is kaleidoscopic in its aim, it gathers into that fractured space the postscript's many purposes and multiple destinations such that the claim set forth is also a claiming of the rights of address. Insofar as the book of criticism entails a protest, for having been "part of my experience," *Mariners* takes this particularity and makes of it the ground of a universal project of freedom performed uniquely by and through critique, but the universality regained in the practice of writing is one tied to a politics of address and a labor of interpretation rather than a revolutionary exhortation to simple action.

Donald Pease's analysis of the contortions of address to which the state condemned James exposes with economy the complexity of the speaking position at the core of *Mariners* and its postscript. A naked act of power, the sentence of indefinite detention depended first upon the reassignment of subjects to new classification beyond the laws to which citizens might appeal. Reassignment was a tool of silencing as effective against new immigrants denied entry on grounds that they posed a threat to national security as it was against persons like James, who had begun the naturalization process in 1938; as Pease recounts, the state's "reclassification of James as an illegal alien and the transporting of him to Ellis Island had removed from James the power to speak in his own name. The state's pronouncement that he was a foreign subversive had disallowed the possibility that James would ever be brought to give testimony before a congressional committee" (*MRC*, xxv). Radically foreclosed from a citizen's rights of expression and due process and accused of subverting American democracy in his books, James is "forced to this public protest" (*MRC*, 155) where he must actively assume the label of alien if he is to expose the "grave injustices that are being perpetrated in the name of the law" (*MRC*, 165) when the "Department of Justice now assumes the right to say what a citizen or would-be citizen should study" (*MRC*, 157). But reassignment beyond the bounds of testimony to a silence without legal appeal was only the first turn of the screw, as Pease notes.

> After the state pronounced James a security threat, James's legal subjectivity underwent demotion to the status of "you." As its secondary addressee, James was subject to the law's powers of enforcement but he was no longer recognized as the subject of its norms. James's loss of the power to speak as "I" also deauthorized the testifying phrases through which he could convey his claims before a court and invalidated his interlocutory privileges within the civil society. The state's restriction of his pronominal identifications to the "you" who must obey the law had also disallowed James membership in the "we" of "we the people" whose sovereign will the state was understood to represent. "You" could never become "we" because "you" named the subversive with whom the state had refused the rights of dialogue as an "I." (*MRC*, xxvii)

The "you" of reassignment commands silence as both the condition of its power to designate the alien and as its corresponding effect; unlike an interpellative speech act, the separation of "you" from "we" requires no recognition from the alien to authorize the act. Nor is the category "We, the people" stabilized through the active foreclosure of "you." Rather, the legal subjectivity established by the act of reassignment from "we" to "you" disarticulates the citizen-voice potential within the space of "we, the people" to substitute that of an absolute sovereignty defined not by the contents of its borders but by its power of address. Not only can "you" never become "we," as Pease observes; "we" are spoken for and live under threat of direct address and through it, reassignment by the state, for testimony itself, as was witnessed in the McCarthy hearings, becomes a test of the speaker's worthiness to be recognized by the state's social norms rather than a right guaranteed in advance by those norms. According to James the McCarran Act enabled a lawlessness of the law itself, which violated the juridical norms and cultural principles of American democracy and effectively rendered alien freedom of thought and expression.

Despite James's claim that the protest was an essential part of the larger argument launched by *Mariners,* the postscript was subsequently suppressed partially or entire in the 1978 and 1985 reprints of the 1953 original, itself printed in only two thousand copies. Dismissed as "special pleading" by literary critics and historians alike, the postscript, in its abject appeal to the American citizen, disqualified the work from serious consideration, at least in the eyes of his detractors.[39] Yet it is precisely this quality of special pleading that turns a pathetic appeal for sympathy into an active appeal of the accusation of subversion. The strategies of address in James's postscript constitute a political intervention that nearly all his readers have failed to hear. It is, after all, only by assuming the position of alien, judged an enemy of the state, that James is able to take up the first person and challenge the terms of the juridical foreclosure enacted through a politics of address and expressed in the spatialization of time that is indefinite detention. Meeting his accusers on the very same ground, James reverses the operation of alienation and, rather than make of the law a lawlessness as do his jailers on authority of the sovereign state, he transfigures the alien outside into the credible testimony of American values. The margin becomes a fold within, and the border that would hold the barbarians at bay becomes instead the intimate and native interiority, the very expression of the truth of law rescued from a perverse inversion by an excessive, because empty, sovereignty.

Yet the subversion of the law by the law only lifts James to greater rhetorical heights as he calls on the American people to acknowledge his sincere desire to become a citizen. The rhetorical excess of special pleading, even where such pleading operates a reversal of alienation, strains the conventional form of the apologia or true testimony that serves as authorial alibi for the postscript. Shrill and composed by turns, James's rant against the state and his fellow inmates at Ellis Island castigates the prison system and calls out individual representatives of state legality, judges, congressmen, and wardens alike; by calling attention to his special circumstances and those of particular guards or inmates as well, this ranting text, rather than undercutting its universal theme, underscores the necessary defense of particularity and the singular subject. Addressing the law, but on its own terms, this turbulent postscript engages a fantasy of speaking in its own name where no right to speak is granted and where only the exceptional claim of special pleading authorizes its unlicensed speech.

What James's editors and critics dismiss as excessively particular and self-regarding in the suppressed postscript scandalizes the conceit of analytic neutrality, the conventions of rational debate and dispassionate description upheld by the preceding seven chapters. And yet, despite its rebarbative and unruly nature, ample continuity of ideas binds the last chapter to the whole. James's insistence on foregrounding his own experience as further corroboration of the book's argument; his attention to the withholding of medical care as a form of torture and the bodily details disclosed; his relentless narration of his judicial nightmare, told in the rising tones of near hysteria: it is this "scandal of the speaking body"[40] that perturbs and inspires both censorship and disdain. By transgressing writerly decorum and inserting his bodily subject into the account, James contaminates the imaginary divide between public and private, personal tragedy and world historical event, subjective trauma and objective social theory. In *Mariners,* special pleading names the operation by which kaleidoscopic address is set to work to magnify difference and to break open the condensation of social fantasy that imagines community along the lines of docility and subversion, or, as James clearly saw, of "national races, national stocks and national bloods" (*MRC,* 13). Against the grain of a Marxism that would subordinate race to class, James challenges critical pieties by resorting to a kind of literalism or an excess of self-evidence, saying, "Who doubts this has only to read the McCarran Immigration Bill of 1952, which is permeated with the doctrine of racial superiority" (*MRC,* 13).[41]

Explicitly targeting the law of this racial fantasy, James invokes the body as both testamentary evidence and juridical target of the state. It is this explicit binding of accountability to particularity, so disquieting to his fellow travelers, that grants the postscript its passional center. The body, in its sickness, vulnerability, bondage, and alienation, is also the basis for the claims to health, safety, freedom of thought, and naturalization that transform his appeal from a simple legal challenge likely to fail into a principled claiming of alien rights based upon sincere desire, in this case the desire to become a citizen and thus to destroy the racial basis for such becoming. Careening in and out of defensive self-justification and an almost wandering argument, the protest falls outside a convention of free speech where speech musters the self in sovereign self-representation. In this sense, *Mariners'* rant, by continuing to dispute, well beyond the legal proceedings, the terms of his incarceration as subversive alien, makes a virtue of the fall into embodied subjection; by conjuring the law's true lawlessness, the convicted writer regains a speaking position to rebuke that very law. *Mariners* insists that James's subjection at the hands of the state only fed his subjective powers, giving him more cause to cultivate the self besieged by sovereign power. This interlacing of subjection and subjectivity with the creativity of his subjectivation echoes the theme of James's reading of Melville, whose prescient understanding that capital forges emotion and desire as well as economic and class relations authorizes James to claim that Melville foresaw the subjectivities that would produce and be produced by totalitarianism.

When Benjamin, in the opening lines of his essay "On Some Motifs in Baudelaire,"[42] tells us that the poet wrote for an audience unable to read him, an audience whose powers of attention had been shattered by the very conditions from which Baudelaire wrote and which were for him the richest resource of his poetry, Benjamin offers a clue for an imagination of a new mode of address, always speaking from an intimate margin, a space of irrelevance and desuetude that Genet signals in his eloquent testimony to prison narrative that introduces George Jackson's *Soledad Brother*.

> A book written in prison—or in any place of confinement—is addressed perhaps above all to readers who are not outcasts, who have never been and will never go to prison, and that is why in some sense such a book proceeds obliquely. Otherwise, I know that the one writing it would only have to take words and fling them onto paper, the forbidden and accursed words, the bloody words, the words spit out in a lather, discharged with sperm, the slandered, reprobate words, the unwritten words—like the ultimate name of God—the dangerous, padlocked words, the words that don't belong in the dictionary, because if they were written there, complete and not maimed by ellipses, they would say too quickly the suffocating misery of a solitude that is not accepted and that is whipped and prodded only by what it is deprived of: sex and freedom.
>
> It is therefore prudent that any writing that reaches us from this infernal place should reach us as though mutilated, pruned of its overly tumultuous adornments.
>
> It is thus behind bars, accepted only by them, that its readers, if they dare, will guess at the infamy of a situation that a forthright vocabulary could never reconstruct: but behind the permitted words, learn to hear others![43]

Both James and Genet know the dangers of an appeal from prison to a reader who will never spend a night as outcast, marked by judgment and confined apart from the common stream of "forthright vocabulary." Oblique address demands a pruning of language's wilder and more violent truths; the ear of the "normal" reader will need to listen for the unwritten, reprobate words behind prudent writing from prison; such listening requires an apprenticeship in reading the disaggregated absences and censorships that mutilate efforts to enter the public sphere and practice free speech from prison. Defensively, James justifies his need to publish the protest; indeed, for James, "someone had to speak" of a sincere desire to become another or, in the language of his detention and the law that justified it, to become a citizen. The expressions of an imprisoned author, compelled to speak but not authorized to address his public, are born already under a ban such that no act of censorship need be made; the space of writing is already that of foreclosed inscription, and the words that emerge in the public space of free expression have endured a prior violence more profound than prohibition. They are destined for the "you" of a difference now absolute, for the book of the outcast aims at the insider's ear in hopes that the attentive listener will intuit the reprobate word whose ghostly absence clings to the printed page. James's postscript addresses a reader who, having read *Mariners,* is equipped for but not yet ready to assume the subjectivity elaborated in James's act of interpretation. Desiring to become, but not yet ready to assume, the orientation of writer and reader defies a commonplace dialectical framing of address and destines address to a political space of engendering, engaging, seducing, and affirming, or what I will call the political space of ranting that, in James's case, ranges lawful freedoms against lawless sovereignty. For this reason, James's intimate marginality, both temporal and spatial, structures the mode of address as a message sent out to a people who cannot hear him and a law that continues to bind him.

Neither the autonomous speech of the manifesto nor the cursing, reprobate word, this rant is rather the unsovereign speech to which the writer is both constrained and compelled. James strikingly captures the dilemma of Genet's oblique address, which must mediate rage through the precision and restraint of its genre. In so shaping his postscript, James conjures a complex figure of modernity, that of the simultaneous absence and dissemination of sovereignty in the disciplinary mechanisms of the modern state, which depend for their operation on an intricate nexus of speech and writing, interpellation and reassignment, subjection and subjectivation. Responding to state discipline, James's rant far exceeds the "Caliban" model of protest and rebuke, that classical topos of postcolonial theory, because rather than giving in to the unwritten word, spat out in a lather, he binds rage to a formal structure of multiple and fracturing address.[44] In a sense a failed manifesto, James's text foregrounds his difference—as black, colonized, immigrant, writer, invalid, and socialist—rather than his fundamental identity with his reader. This strategy presumes abjection in order to mount its appeal and thus refutes an imaginary construction of heroic and sovereign speech, making abject appeal the ground of another hearing. For these reasons I take James's protest to be exemplary of that modernist literary symptom, the rant. Neither a genre nor a reliable indicator of a psychological state, the rant is an event of address that irrupts in the modernist text of contestation. Dependent upon a fantasy, that one could speak in one's own voice and denounce the law, the rant unwittingly constructs the law it seeks to rebuke. This paradoxical address, engaging as it does a fantasy of sovereign speech, establishes the very symbolic order it resists, for the rant must testify to its own abjection if it is to accuse the law that orders it. The ranter is always at war, but the rant itself is a moment unhinged, a point of breathless furor that flashes and subsides, so precarious is its purchase on the sovereign subject it so desires to be. Monstrous *tyros,* abject enemies, and pathetic complainers project their voices, as the ranter tangles with the phantom sovereignty it avows but cannot retain.

The image of the writer at war may call up our modern romance with the defiant avant-garde issuing manifestos for reform and cutting judgments right and left. James and Genet offer a different imagination of this being-at-war in the care with which they craft the very position of appeal and in their acute awareness that their singular contestations leave them out on a limb, righteous and gesturing but solitary. We might continue to call the predicament of their address, and thus their self-stylization, "oblique address," but the spatial metaphor fails to capture entirely what is at stake; for though mediation is the rule, well-crafted rage is the substance. "The story that exposes life's possibilities may not necessarily appeal, still, it calls up a moment of rage without which its author would have been blind to its excessive possibilities."[45] So writes Bataille in the preface to his autobiographical account of the utterly futile contributions of Parisian surrealists and other avant-gardists to the Spanish Revolution. Fury born of excessive ordeal drives any writer fit to be read. Without this authorizing experience, "how can we linger over books to which the author had not been, palpably, constrained?" Bataille identifies a capacity for writing in the ordeal of unsovereign insight that finds expression only through the detours of discursive language. He eventually comes to rail against the veils of mediation dividing him from himself and his readers, but the essential declaration of a contestation that transgresses the dialectic of address by suspending it and transforms writing into a fundamental *relation* of address remains a constant preoccupation for him.[46] The social antagonism underlying the rant appears in its approach to the other of writing and thus materializes not in an orderly dialectics of opposition but in the rant's tactical ability to set unintelligibility to work in an attack on the given terms of subjection—for Bataille, the rage of experience is not rendered up to and in the lucidity of prose; rather, the experience drives one to communicate. Such tactics of address are denied a hearing within the framework of even the most progressive theories of free speech and contestation. Thus theories, from Bakhtin on the carnivalesque to the Habermasian public sphere,[47] of the "explanation from below" that order textual contestation into dialogic exchange and limpid communication can only repeat the marginalization of these singular texts, incapable as they are of occupying the knowing position of sovereign speech. Such theories offer no purchase on this consistent symptom of modernism, impossible to capture in a counterdiscourse or counterhistory.

Inheritor of C. L. R. James's generation of anticolonial militancy and cultural critique, postcolonial studies has of necessity foregrounded resistant speech both as a feature of colonial histories and as an essential technique of anticolonial revolutionary movements. A particularly acute meditation on political subjectivation emerges in postcolonial writing as a debate around the question of address and the right to be heard, and takes many methodological forms framed by the complex histories emergent in the area studies where popular and state sovereignty are still at stake. In a foundational text of Latin American literary criticism, Roberto Retamar examines tactics of resistant speech expressed in the history of appeals to the theatrical figure of Shakespeare's Caliban. New world rebel, monstrous yet poetic, grotesquely inhuman but given the most seductive lines, Caliban, as Retamar notes, served up for the European imagination a controllable image of the monstrous and despised racial other; reduced to impotent cursing where vital anticolonial action is both most warranted and most feared by his masters, *The Tempest*'s Caliban provided a compensatory phantasm, expressing but encasing social anxieties aroused in the European imagination by the first consolidation of English imperialism in the Caribbean. For Retamar, in contemporary terms the historical construction of a despised and cannibal race merges with the conflicted identity of Latin American elites and intellectuals to produce a simultaneous acknowledgment and defensive denial of the figure. The history of the Caliban myth folds resistance into the grotesque imagery and racial polemics of a burgeoning modern discourse on the primitive, which can easily be turned to antidemocratic and protofascist ends in the metropole, as is best illustrated by Ernst Renan's study *Caliban: Suite de la Tempête,* or to native efforts to transcend the Caliban, with his mestizo heritage, in oneself through a form of colonial mimicry self-imposed as literary, subjective, and civilizational ideal. According to Fredric Jameson, who introduces the English translation, the essay "Caliban" is interested to map the paradoxes and dilemmas of the dialectic of otherness and employs polemics to this end.

Key to Retamar's explanation is the reclamation of the term *mambí,* a colonial insult leveled at Cuban nationalists but extensible to all Latin Americans. "This is the dialectic of Caliban. To offend us they call us *mambí,* they call us *black;* but we reclaim as a mark of glory the honor of considering ourselves descendants of the *mambí,* descendants of the rebel, runaway."[48] By reclaiming the insult as a form of resistant speech, the new Calibans, in a kind of symbolic cannibalism, rely upon resignification to desublimate the socially unspeakable and thus to appropriate its destructive power. While Retamar's approach advocates a similar act of reclamation through full identification with Europe's derogation of the Caribbean in the figure of Caliban, and thus proposes an assumption of the history of racial abjection, his striking manifesto falls prey to its own dialectical machinery as he situates literary politics as a war between the militant Martí on the one side, and the accommodationist, Sarmiento, and outright counterrevolutionary Fuentes on the other. The "attitude that is at the root of our historical being" of absolute and monstrous defiance admits of no difference and only perpetuates antagonisms as a means of self-definition.

His own essay, heavily invested with a bitter castigation of counterrevolutionary writers—the list of betrayals is long, though not unconvincing—speaks the curse of Caliban quite readily and without a clear sense of how the Latin American writer is to avoid falling into the same traps. Tropes of resistant speech recur throughout Retamar's manifesto to draw for us in negative terms the portrait of the hero of sovereign speech rousing his people against the powerful forces of imperialism, yet this avowed polemics offers little to readers hungry to learn how to bring about such a response; indeed, it offers nothing beyond the broad claim that literature should serve its people by reflecting and expressing their real, material circumstances; all else is counterrevolutionary dross, decadent pandering to bourgeois sensibilities or a failed social realism. And while we may agree with the rolling waves of judgment and bile, defiant back talk of this kind forecloses difference in the public sphere even as it violently exposes the workings of a symbolic law of abjection, which the polemic is only too happy to aim at the other.

We can see the limitations of Caliban's back talk, as an approach to resistance, repeated in Sartre's "Black Orpheus," the introduction to Leopold Senghor's pathbreaking 1948 compilation of Francophone poetry.[49] Sartre cannot restrain his compulsion to describe the voices of African, Malagasy, and Caribbean poets in the language of Caliban's curse, saying, "What then did you expect when you unbound the gag that had muted those black mouths? That they would sing your praises?"[50] One limitation of Retamar's and Sartre's characterizations of radical literary speech acts lies in their shared assumption that the address of the literary follows only along the paths of identification and expression. A literary harangue that does not assume identification nor seeks to express only "real, material" relations but also symbolic relations would, according to Retamar's "Caliban," fail to be properly literary and open the work to charges of vulgar formalism or decadence. For Sartre, the purpose of *la poésie nègre* is to express African rhythm, historical trauma, and essential humanity while offering the "you" of colonial power a window into other experience,[51] with the strange result that he appears to be introducing a volume of black poetry addressed explicitly to a solely white audience. In contrast, Fanon's reply to these lines reported in *Black Skin, White Masks* argues the revolutionary perspective with more nuance, saying, "If I cry out, it will not be a black cry."[52] Fanon refuses the place allotted him in the dialectical machine of progressive history to which Sartre would confine him. Ironically, both Retamar and Sartre had read Fanon, yet none of the complexity of Fanon's politics of address informs their speculation about the nature of resistant speech, neither its orientation, its limits, nor its fundamental imbrication with the power it seeks out.[53]

James signed the introduction to *Mariners* in November 1952, the same year that saw the publication of *Black Skin, White Masks*. Together these texts provide a powerful reading of a social reality that neither Retamar nor Sartre envisions; whereas for Sartre black writing signals the emergence of a new voice on the scene of revolutionary literature, the predicament shared by James and Fanon consigns their speech to a space of foreclosed inscription from which they must materialize a speaking subject by risking innovation of form and, thus, illegibility. To mount his own position and speak in his own name, Fanon must first navigate a host of racial phantasms projected into him by the public discourse he endeavors to breach. *Black Skin, White Masks* begins with the claim that "to speak is to exist absolutely for the other" set against the fact that "the Negro of the Antilles, whoever he is, has always to face the problem of language" (*BSWM*, 17–18); Fanon struggles in his rant with a status of foreclosed other because he must refuse the role assigned to him in and by the public sphere. His quest for disalienation from racist subjectivity and his refusal to "forever absorb himself in uncovering resistance, opposition, challenge" expose him as an outsider to the conventions of free speech that have prepared for him an "alterity of rupture, of conflict, of battle." Fanon rejects the role of antithesis ready to be dialectically sublated into history and repudiates both the limitation of his subject to race consciousness and the abstraction of his being from his own singularity and attachment to his body, his culture, his people, and his language.[54] *Black Skin, White Masks* is not an avant-garde manifesto of humanist universality as is sometimes claimed, even by his most sensitive critics. It is rather what Abdelkebir Khatibi has called a "labour of decolonization" that necessarily takes the form of the rant because it must speak in the symptom of modernity rather than from the piety of the public sphere, but this labour of decolonization, with all the associations of birth and toil, enables a working-through the symptom.

The rant labors to wrest from particularity the very condition or instance of contestation. This work of unworking, what we might call analysis or unraveling, sets the rant apart from the manifesto as form. The salient feature of the manifesto as genre is its assumption that in speaking, it speaks for "you." Such a vanguardism is amply illustrated by Retamar's scathing indictment of his fellow writers and reflects the tactical relation to truth meted out by the manifesto's address. Truths self-evident are its stock-in-trade, and should its complaint not rouse approval in its hearers, they seal their own fates and fall behind the line of demarcation that separates the manifesto's polemic from all comers. The texts of James and Fanon, however, speak more aptly to the contradiction of a voice foreclosed whose speech contests the very framing of contestation in the public sphere. This oblique address cannot contain its speech for the simple reason that its form is not given in advance; it must re-create its genre, and thus its limits, within the content of its own writing. As a consequence, the precision of the rant's formulations is, paradoxically, shot through with the abject affects of an orphan writing. The rant is not a genre; it is, rather, an event of ranting that irrupts like the *furor-inanitas,* speaking a desire at times unintelligible from within the confines of social norms, including norms of radical contestation. Written under the sign of this contradiction *Black Skin, White Masks* defies generic ascription though its disordered and intermittently incoherent avowal of self becomes a seductive proof of its argument and a performative instantiation of its purpose.[55]

Nonetheless, the manifesto remains the genre closest to the rant, and perhaps is the one most likely to produce the ranticle. In what is surely the most considered and detailed attempt to account for the manifesto as a modernist genre, Janet Lyon's *Manifestoes: Provocations of the Modern* argues that "the manifesto is a constitutive discourse of modernity," which voices popular polemic and acute frustration at the uneven and unequal distribution of universal freedoms. For Lyon the manifesto becomes central to modernity because it embodies in a transmissible form the speaking position of counterdiscourse and conveys in a common and widely legible style the narrative of radical resistance. "The manifesto's revolutionary speaking position constructs political certainty . . . not just by reinforcing polemical fields, but also by assuming control of the language of history, the conditions of plot" (*MPM,* 60). Through its ringing phrases announcing permanent revolution, the manifesto turns the political unconscious into a narrative and so represents the steady state of revolutionary storytelling. This is political speech straightened by generic ascription and presented as archon of the revolutionary spirit because it offers a "reliable discursive form" for the expansion of revolution beyond local and national culture and onto the world stage (*MPM,* 24). The global and expanding reach of manifest protest is an essential attribute of the genre, for the fundamental conceit insists on the universality of the claims of justice and truth, what Lyon carefully identifies as "certainty,"[56] beyond the local scene of contest. In the face of clear and present wrongs, the manifesto claims manifest rights to be inserted into the universal narrative of the just and the true. Relying upon a Habermasian understanding of the public sphere and free speech, this account of the speech of protest situates resistant speech generically and locates its impetus to speak in the realization that the claims for universality of the liberal state are both overstated and unevenly applied.

If "one takes 'public sphere' to mean, as Habermas elaborates it, a common, public, discursive space within which citizens bracket their socioeconomic differences in order to deliberate about their common concerns" (*MPM*, 54), then the perspective brought by postcolonial, sexuality, and race studies very soon exposes the limits of the communicative model of public discourse; the Habermasian conception of the public takes as its ideal image a bourgeois society that guarantees free speech, open to all, only through the prior establishment of several interlocking prerequisites, "merely private interests were to be inadmissible; inequalities of status were to be bracketed; and discussants were to deliberate as peers. The result of such discussion would be 'public opinion' in the strong sense of a consensus about the common good."[57] Like the manifesto, the rant contests the given, but, as the speech of foreclosed subjectivity, it cannot aim for the abstract common good because it injects the "merely" private into public space. As *Mariners* illustrates, particularity and special pleading are the necessary attributes of a bid to speak where no populist front awaits the speaker to urge him on and thereby sanction polemic. The ranter speaks as subject; he shares with the many others of his address a profound subjection to the other of speech, to the definitions of the state, to his affective attachments, and thus he can only conjure the enabling fantasy of such sovereign speech by countersigning his own abjection.

Although critical of Habermas's failure to consider women and minorities as excluded participants in public discourse, Lyon appears to take the Habermasian conception of the public sphere, counterdiscourse, and the universal subject of reason as givens, arguing that public exchange "produces universality as an immanent criterion and regulative norm"; in this way public exchange, even framed by exclusion, lays the foundation for the perfectibility of the public sphere and the extension of universality to marginalized others. For Habermas, exchange establishes as a feature of the norm an immanent possibility of critique, which then comes to constitute "a counterdiscourse inherent in modernity itself."[58] Modernity's counterdiscourse, which "set out from Kantian philosophy as an unconscious expression of the modern age and pursued the goal of enlightening the Enlightenment about its own narrowmindedness" (*MPM*, 33), meets the dominant in the space cleared for the exercise of freedom; counterdiscourse follows from enlightenment to augment it such that discourse and the one that rises up to meet it become one flesh.

When dissent is imagined as dialectical opposition in the teleology of perfectibility, the manifesto, in offering a ready-made model of "back talk," appears as the privileged site and form of political contestation in the public arena. As a result, dissent is always oriented toward a norm or center and seeks through a political challenge to be folded back into the capacious reach of true universality. Lyon reads the fate of the political avant-garde forward into the construction of an aesthetic avant-garde. And, following Peter Bürger's understanding of the avant-garde, in which aesthetic rebellion targets bourgeois institutions of a depoliticized and autonomous art, Lyon argues that the manifestos of the avant-garde were alternately dependent upon "the discourse of the plebian public sphere"[59] and damning of mass culture. As critic of modernity, the avant-garde represents the values of the public sphere, reversed but intact. The universal form of the manifesto allows for a continuity of dissent insofar as the exercise of dissent is evident, within the framework of Lyon's study and of the theorization of the public sphere it establishes for literary history, in the features of the ready-made form. Thus, the argument locates a sociopolitical formalism in the structure of address constitutive of the manifesto; despite Lyon's stated desire not to limit the manifesto by offering formal descriptions of convention, the manifesto form and the structure of address it carries with it constitute the historically unchanging convention of dissent in her study and, we might argue, beyond it, in the political unconscious for which a rousing and defiant speech so often substitutes for political understanding and action. Which is to say that Lyon taps into a tautology of democratic expression, one whose circularity and symbolic sedimentation produce monsters of the mind to be broadcast as the spectacular because commodifiable individualism of the airwaves, or so thought Wyndham Lewis. However, in naturalizing the mode of address in resistant speech Lyon shows one of the limitations of the revised (by feminism and an awareness of racial difference) Habermasian approach to counterdiscourse.[60]

This tendency to bypass the conundrum of address inherent in the manifesto becomes especially evident when Lyon attempts to account for its passional features. Although shrewdly viewing the affective appeal of the manifesto as its most elemental and inescapable quality—anger, frustration, fury, and suffering are noted in Lyon's argument but chiefly as rhetorical instruments—rarely is affective force subjected to analysis. For instance, "the manifesto also asserts its rhetorical certainty, inevitability, and 'irresistibility' (to recall Arendt's term) through the use of the discourse of passionate, righteous anger" (*MPM*, 61). Lyon's brief invocation of a Greimasian taxonomy of emotional states serves to register, while containing, the common passional feature of manifesto, anger, in an explanatory formalism that captures the feeling only to sideline it to the advantage of a rhetorical description where speaking positions and moods are stable; in short, anger is a stable instrument of address and ensures through its allure and the clear legibility of its form the consensus of its audience. This is nowhere more evident than, when claiming that the manifesto's audience is called into being through the genre's sensible and affective appeal, she writes, "the manifesto . . . is a text of radicalism which forges an audience through its efforts at affective and experiential intelligibility. That is, an audience crystallizes as the manifesto formulates and performs a future audience's experience of and response to oppression" (*MPM*, 28). The theme of intelligibility is also harnessed to the notion of affect,

> if the manifesto seeks to provide a rationale for its figuratively violent repudiation of hegemony, it must make itself intelligible to dominant ideology. . . . The paradoxes of the manifesto form—its conflicts between participation and political marginalization, anger and restraint, threat and argument, mythic time and urgent agendas—can easily be projected onto the subjects who use the manifesto form. Magnified by the fish-eye lens of universalist normativity, such tensions may be read as symptoms of an inherent irrationality that threatens the stability of democratic ideals. (*MPM*, 61)

Unintelligibility or nonsense, the very affect of the manifesto's appeal is also a danger to be warded off lest the subject of protest be contaminated by what it must handle. This may very well be an accurate account of the manifesto and its political situation, but the logic of contamination and, therefore, the limit of legibility inscribes the speech of protest within the very norms it comes to dispute. It is here that both the irruption of ranting and the dynamics of foreclosure come into play for, as Lyon argues, the speech of protest opens the subject to the threat of disappearance and sudden dismissal from the sphere of public exchange. Living in this risk, the rant breaks into discourse, bringing it to crisis by speaking in its language but to alien purpose.

Illegibility demands both an account of subjective and affective states and how they are braided into or fray out of the social pact; if the manifesto tarries with the positivities that are social givens and rigorously stays on the side of sense, ranting falls into illegibility and nonsense at the very moment it broaches the "unspeakable, [because] language carries a violence that brings it to the limits of speakability."[61] For this reason there is no ready-made genre that captures the problematic of what I am calling foreclosed inscription; no history of the availability of a "reliable discursive form" unfolds in the archive of contestation, failed manifesto, or ranting complaint. Rather the critical posture, which in Habermas's articulation of counterdiscourse is a sensible and straight-talking augmentation of enlightenment, of the rant's address repeats itself as an aftereffect or residue of a foundational foreclosure. In the opening passages of *Critique of Postcolonial Reason,* Gayatri Spivak presents us with one such foundational foreclosure when she reads the figure of the natural man in Kant and draws our attention to the disturbing way that the primitive, specified by Kant as a native of Tierra del Fuego, is brought onto the stage of philosophy only to be summarily dismissed as the antithesis of human progress, civilization, and enlightenment. This founding foreclosure evacuates the primitive but establishes the act of evacuation as the indelible characteristic of post-Kantian philosophy, that is, of enlightenment. And through this establishment of an inclusion made in order to immediately exclude the other of Western rationality, the act of foreclosure becomes a sanctioned and hallowed institution repeated through the decades. Progressively, it becomes impossible to name the symptom of this relation because it is the founding gesture of relation between north and south, east and west. The primitive man becomes the native informant and then the postcolonial critic: "As the historical narrative moves from colony to postcolony to globality, the native informant is thrown out—to use the Freudian concept-metaphor of *Verwerfung*—into the discursive world as a cryptonym, inhabiting us so that we cannot claim the credit of our proper name."[62] Crypts do not give up secrets in the open exchange of the public sphere. But postcolonial speech can produce a crisis for a public sphere by pointing to the reproduction of the founding foreclosure in the framing of reason, enlightenment, and inclusion. By doing so, such speech gives the lie to dialectical models of history, which would assign to the postcolonial voice its role as antithesis to be transcended and absorbed into the totality.[63]

Earlier I argued that the rant materializes a complex figure of modernity representing the simultaneous absence and dissemination of sovereignty in the disciplinary mechanisms of the modern state and its culture; this absence (the sovereign is not sovereign) and dissemination (the McCarran Act can be repealed by sovereign citizens) redoubles the paradox of subjection and subjectivation whereby the chance of the latter is bought at the price of the former; but more acutely than any quid pro quo, the freedom of a new subjectivation is itself conjured from within the knot of subjection. To illustrate the point that the form of power preceding modernity inheres in modern discipline and regulation, Foucault begins his lectures entitled *Psychiatric Power* with two scenes highlighting the commingling of sovereign and disciplinary power. Referring to the "founding scene of psychiatry," the lecture of November 14, 1973, opens with the tableau of Pinel freeing the "mad" inmates of the infamous prison Bicêtre, who, once unfettered, were put on the path to eventual cure. In contrast to this inaugural and liberatory moment of psychiatric power, Foucault presents a case reported by Pinel in his 1800 *Traité medico-philosophique* (Year IX) concerning the madness of King George III. Basing his account on the narrative supplied by the king's physician, Pinel describes the sovereign at a moment of utter abjection. Bereft of reason, confined to a padded chamber where his servants, on doctor's orders, informed him with calm insistence that he was no longer the sovereign and that he must obey their dictates, the monarch was forced to submit to greater physical force as part of a medical cure. Predictably, one day the patient welcomed his doctor with a rain of excrement and other filth. As a consequence restrained, stripped, cleaned, and confined, the unsovereign king, having stooped to a peasant's protest, endured more months of similar treatment before he was finally declared cured after having become docile and compliant. Whereas the almost mythic tableaux of madmen freed from their chains by sovereign reason and the rights of man as represented by Pinel still operates both semiotically and institutionally through the metaphor of sovereign power, the account of George III's cure disperses the power and force of sovereignty within the scene of confinement and abjection and between the agents of cure, the body servants and physician who tend the subject king. From this contrast Foucault is able to argue that unlike King Lear, George III is brought under a "completely different type of power which differs term by term, I think, from the power of sovereignty. It is an anonymous, nameless and faceless power that is distributed between different persons."[64]

Viewed from the encroachment of disciplinary power, the absence and dissemination of sovereignty in the social order alters the address of writing as well. "In a word, we can say that disciplinary power, and this is no doubt its fundamental property, fabricates subjected bodies; it pins the subject function exactly to the body . . . Disciplinary power is individualizing because it fastens the subject-function to the somatic singularity by means of a system of supervision—writing."[65] Bound to the growth of psychiatric power in the asylum, writing also became a site for resistance to that power. As scientific writing recorded the fits of a marginal subject it unwittingly wrote the subject-function into the very heart of disciplinary power, and by writing the subject into the body, discipline, paradoxically, inscribed that bodily subject in a system of representation dependent for its power upon that very bodily subject. The figure drawn by Foucault's history of modern subjection is not a vicious circle endlessly revolving around or through the abject subject body; rather, as he explains in "Preface to Transgression," limit and transgression describe a relation of spiraling influence rather than dialectical stalemate or historical progress. Modern power and resistance occupy the same discursive space and engender their effects through the same medium, writing, without which modern subjection could never have dethroned sovereign force. In the example of the asylum, psychiatric power draws its authority from its intensive catalogue of hysterical symptoms; thus, the very science of psychiatric "truth" grew from the mysterious resistance and enigmatic behavior of mad women, which in turn demanded architectural and civic innovations of time, space, and finance.

While the law imposes norms of legibility through which one is recognized as a subject, this recognition in turn means that the subject has taken in the law, made it his own and thus recognized the law as a form of truth. "The law is what established the criterion of subjecthood according to which the subject can be recognized at all."[66] Fastened to his somatic singularity, the subject can use the truth of subjection against the law of legibility. Thus, modern subjectivation, inventing "new ideals for life," as Oscar Wilde said was the purpose of art, jeopardizes the subject—and his body for modernity marks the arrival of a subject-body disciplined through writing—precisely in his relation to truth when it brings the subject to the limit of the law and thus the very border of legibility. Unlike the sovereign subject of the manifesto, the ranter risks himself when he takes the unintelligibility to which he has been consigned and folds it into discourse; translating the limitation of a social abjection into the terms of a new subjectivity, the modern subject, like the *parrhesiastes* of the classical scene of frank talk and free speech,[67] risks losing himself in the moment of resistance; "to question the norm, to call for new norms, is to detach oneself from oneself.... The moment of resistance, of opposition, emerges precisely when we find ourselves attached to our constraint."[68] Whereas Lacan situates the subject after the law as the effect of the prior symbolic inscription of law and order,[69] ranters address the law, performing before the law to materialize the web of entanglements and intimacies that subject them. Ranting is not a practice or genre in dialectical opposition to state sovereignty or a capitalist ruling class, although these may be targets of the rant; it is a symptom of modern subjection, and as such it opens the individual subject to the marginality of his own speaking position. The fantasy of addressing the law allows a tropic recentering of that shattering exteriority, which can serve the purpose of a denial or an engagement with power. Unlike the claims of the manifesto, the rant opens the subject to an unprecedented speech that promises a wrenching transformation and manifests itself only as abject appeal.

Any speaker can be thrust suddenly into an experience or perception of this exposure, for no subject can defend against the upsurge of "truth" when truth is no longer the fearless speech of a philosopher denouncing a tyrant.[70] As Foucault in his last seminar continues to ask the question how did the subject become the medium of truth's production, he sketches a genealogy from frank talk to contemporary biopolitical production of subjectivities; the increasing subjection of speakers to technological rationalities and social intelligibilities confirms the picture of a landscape saturated by limits rather than bordered by them, for the speaker who brings a complaint or attempts to engage in *parrhesia* is beset by a constant risk that he may become unintelligible himself. This knowledge of a norm bounded and sealed by the risk of the fall, into deviancy, criminality, abjection, or sheer meaninglessness, is pervasive in modernist cultural production. Levi-Strauss's structuralist anthropology, building upon Freud's architectonic of unconscious psychic mechanisms and folded temporalities, inspired Lacan's speculations regarding the symbolic order and its articulation with a phantasmatic sphere of imaginary images and unconscious ciphers. In this Lacan showed himself an uncanny reader of modernity, for modern subjection demands and invents the "primitive" to figure the symbolic law. This primitive constitutes an indelible aspect of modern subjection and takes on a new specificity in the deployment of sexuality where the intensification of the body through technologies of child rearing, hygiene, medical scrutiny, management of populations, and the development of racial categories of regulation, demands a new primitivism as well; this is the primitivism of the body, which is to say that the older image of the state of nature and primitive man as the twin antitheses to civilization is usurped by a savage, raced body within the borders of European rationality. In gothic tales—Stoker's *Dracula,* Stevenson's *Dr. Jekyll and Mr. Hyde,* and Wells's *The Island of Dr. Moreau,* for example—this body materializes as a menacing primitivism within, figuring unconscious sexual urges, criminality, and hereditary taint. Later anti-psychoanalytic texts like D. H. Lawrence's charged vituperations in *Fantasia of the Unconscious* or Wyndham Lewis's *Time and Western Man* attempt to map systematically the ontological hierarchies of an imagined symbolic order that assumes the primitive as origin and potentially as a source of cultural purification and renewal.

The following chapters approach a series of related tropes and preoccupations that circulate within literary modernism under the sign of the primitive and which have led me to theorize a relationship between writing and subjection in the modern period. Foucault defines modernity, within the framework of the deployment of sexuality, as a new regime of power operating to arouse a deafening and endless discourse about the body. This noisy sexuality is foundational for the modern subject but appears in the modern imagination as a fettered silence enjoined by a repressive master. The implications of such a paradoxical modernity for thinking about the role of literature, only one among many forms of an "intensification of the body," are manifold, but guiding my interests throughout the following discussion is the fundamental claim of the *History of Sexuality* that the deployment of modern power takes as axiomatic the distinction of normal from abnormal.[71] The literature of this modernity necessarily participates in the larger cultural work of derogating and defending the deviant modes of the subject while it simultaneously repeats, perpetuates, and invents new norms. The modernism here pursued is a marginal modernism where normativity and abjection intermingle in ways that illuminate the costs as well as the functioning of modern subjection.

AN EAR FOR AN EYE

We are beginning to develop a sense that Foucault's notion of subjection retains elements that are central to psychoanalysis; sublimation, fantasy, and traumatic transfiguration are not identical to but are clearly related to the elements in Foucault's own thought, for instance, the sublimation of exhibitions of state violence described as the prologue to *Discipline and Punish,* or the bodies and pleasures he exhorts us to cultivate at the end of *History of Sexuality,* or the notion of epistemic break developed in his archaeologies of science. As I have argued elsewhere,[72] Foucault actually names sublimation in his discussion of the *scientia sexualis* and, certainly, his notion that prior technologies of power do not disappear but are folded into new configurations of power depends upon tropes of diversion, translation, and conservation that also underlie the different accounts of sublimation given in Freud, Lacan, and Laplanche. Without reducing Foucault's insights into the mechanisms of social transformation and transmission to mere repetitions of fundamental Freudian views, it is worth noting that Foucault often drew upon his familiarity with clinical terms—he was a certified psychologist and had served the requisite apprenticeship in a psychiatric hospital—to articulate relationships of temporal complexity involving figures of deferral, retroaction, and utopian transfiguration. Not only is it a fundamental error to claim, as so many do, that Foucault repudiated psychoanalysis; his most often quoted phrases—for instance, the exhortation to find new "bodies and pleasures"—owe much to the psychic figures sketched above.[73] In fact, he makes the case that until the 1940s psychoanalysis led the battle against the racialist theories of cultural "mind" that dominated psychiatry throughout the nineteenth century and still persist today. Consistently, from the publication of *The Order of Things* through the lectures on psychiatric power and abnormality and beyond, Foucault held psychoanalysis apart from the racist discourse of perversion, degeneration, and heredity that dominated the public and scientific discourses of man. This particular discourse is a fundamentally modernist one, and insofar as psychoanalysis sought to wrench the subject and his knowledge away from bondage to the primitive nationalism fundamental to this discourse, psychoanalysis was itself participating in the critical modernist stance against a particular form of racism; by so engaging itself with the social world, psychoanalysis entered the public sphere not only as a species of clinical language but as a participant in a characteristic modernist public discourse, that of the decline of the public sphere itself.

In contrast to a common misapprehension that pictures Freudian psychoanalysis through the lens of biological determinism and civilizational stages, my use of Freud as a modernist theorist sensitive to the constant intimacy between race and sexuality in the configurations of modern power situates psychoanalysis in the context of the racial industry of modernity that Foucault describes at length in *History of Sexuality, Volume I*. Reading Freud through Foucault's genealogy of modern state power and the deployment of sexuality as a tool of governmentality yields an understanding of the discipline of oedipal guilt and bondage as also a regulatory mechanism for the cultural production of subjective norms well beyond the familial scene. This regulatory function is affected through the cultivation of what we could call actuarial types that standardize risk and inscribe guilt or innocence. We may take up this theme of decline, as a conditioning element in the loss of the public, in two ways: first, through the cultural enfeeblement so widely diagnosed in European modernist cultural critique (in this our guides will be Wyndham Lewis and Adorno),[74] and, second, as the object of a psychoanalytic reflection on the cultural intelligibility of social norms.

Today contemporary discussions of media, public mind, and propaganda repeat a major modernist habit in their agreement that a crisis of legitimacy afflicts our public sphere, infantilizing our citizenry, laying waste the fine architecture of democratic inclusion.[75] Echo of an older lament, this discourse of decline repeats in significant ways modernist critiques of public culture and mass identifications. As one critic has noted, "the list of writers that announce the decline, degradation, crisis or extinction of the public is long and steadily expanding. Publicness, we are told again and again and again, is a quality that we once had but have now lost, perhaps irretrievably so."[76] Always already done for, lost before its collapse, the public, if there is one, would seem to be bounded by its lack.[77] Ambivalently, the theoretical elaborations of the antimodern modernists toward the inescapably libidinal nature of political life and the familial construction of social norms suggest that a genealogy of this lament of the loss of the public as a loss of innocence constitutes a tradition of critical intuitions registering the trace of kinship or what in chapter 3 will emerge as the inscription of the faded bond of kinship, a spectral kinship no longer legible in the institutions charged to reveal its form. As a public discourse on the loss of the public and the erosion of community, this language of decline offers in the negative a set of terms with which to approach the loss of a common sense conceived as a clear social intelligibility while our focus on ranting allows us to consider the seemingly unintelligible as a source not only of survival but of living on and beyond the social inscription of foreclosed life.[78]

In the chapters that follow we will pursue the figure of the primitive as he reappears in our ranting texts as an Irishman, a queer, a child, a woman, an African, an Arab, and an oriental; this recursive figure, whose return betokens the rant's intent to materialize normative abjections, is also linked indelibly with a Euro-American project of racialization that takes specific forms by enjoining the specificity of bodily identity as the major social intelligibility for apprehending the particular. Indeed, in *Eurocentrism* Amin argues that race emerges to resolve the antinomy between universality and particularity or, more precisely, between the universality dictated by the necessity of a global reach for capital and the particularity of European exceptionalism or a self-understanding as a civilizing force. Etienne Balibar adjusts this narrative a degree when he adds that European humanist universality depends upon its racial logic "to constitute the human race and improve it or preserve it from decline."[79] If race resolves this fundamental antinomy by supplying an inexhaustible store of phantasms, then the fear of decline can been viewed as a motor for increased expansion. "Eurocentrism implies a theory of world history and, departing from it, a global political project."[80] Discourses on the decline of the public bear the trace of this racial history symptomatically, as the object to be protected and conserved.

An example of such a discourse of racial decline lies behind the phrase "global village," a coinage usually attributed to Marshall McLuhan, but who in fact got it from Wyndham Lewis.[81] Typical of Lewis's caustic assessment of the publics, "global village" identified a worldwide degeneration of civic *virtus* as the "small-man" loses his bearings and vertical dignity in a maelstrom of rumor, gossip, consumption, and unending trivialities. For Lewis, both painter and writer, the global village trades in the self-possessed eye of the eighteenth-century ideologues and European perspectival line for the uncloseably receptive ear of a mediatic world not to be dominated by man's senses. The global village is nothing less than an insult, another resolution of universality in exceptionalism; where McLuhan could celebrate what he viewed as the retribalization of western logocentric man gone native in the new waters of orality, Lewis could only excoriate or, at best, as he did in 1944 in his *America and Cosmic Man,* go west and unconvincingly advocate a utopia of racial fusion in the form of Cosmic Man, cosmopolitan of the coming atomic age. The global villager, seed of the *effeminatus* of political theory, which is to say, luxuriating, self-interested, and parasitic, takes many forms for Lewis; the most enduring of these are the invert, the youth, and the child. And the public sphere, saturated with low journalism and advertisement, breeds only subjection and degeneration. The peculiarity, and truly the vitriolic genius, of Lewis lies in his linking of this political decline with the racial industry of the family; from his masterwork of social critique, 1926's *The Art of Being Ruled,* through his pamphlets of the 1930s Lewis constantly makes this connection between family, politics, and race.

> All politics today are, in one degree or another, "Youth-politics." . . .
> In the great democracies of the West we live more or less under Press-government by *suggestion* and *education* of course, by absorption daily of column after column of gossip, breezy social articles, selected "news", "controversial" special features, . . . plus Talkies. . . . Really novel forms and modes of expression are not taken on with an equal zeal and promptitude: the true innovator is as badly off as ever he was. . . . The term "Youth-politics" signifies the management of this system of education and propaganda-politics, in which Ma and Pa Everyman are two childlike persons, of course. But the *Everymans,* as a family, are very decadent—they in fact do become more infantile every day.[82]

A perilous social project of ignorance attached to infantile desires collapses the personal and private realms. Lewis, denouncing the "infantilizing" trend in public discourse, argued that the intellectual must take up the task of speaking the foreign to analyze power, but he could never shake his indignation that no one particularly wanted to hear him with the result that he doggedly repeated his fundamental tenet of infantilization in the critical works *Time and Western Man, Men Without Art,* and the pamphlet *Doom of Youth,* and as portraits in *The Apes of God.* In the place of the cultural ideal of civic manliness, the modern state offers a cultural norm of "babydom" infecting every institution, including the family itself, to render them all utterly infantilized, their language completely childlike, commonplace, mired in an ignorant slumber from which it is impossible to awaken.

> This is how it comes that the family once more occupies the foreground of our lives. With a new familiarity and a flesh-creeping "homliness" entirely of this unreal, materialist world, where all "sentiment" is coarsely manufactured and advertised in colossal sickly captions, disguised for the sweet tooth of a monstrous baby called "The Public", the family as it is, broken up on all hands by the agency of feminist and economic propaganda, reconstitutes itself in the image of the state. The government becomes an emperor disguised as Father Christmas, an All-father, a paterfamilias with his pocket full of crystal sets, gramaphones, Russian books, and flesh-coloured stockings, which he proceeds to sell to his "children." (*ABR,* 181)

What these rants reveal is that even before the advent of fascism, a critic like Lewis could identify the oedipal family with changing social norms and could locate in public discourses in the different domains of consumption, politics, and domestic life the shadow of a spectral kinship, conserving and preserving its racial character across several translations. Further, the affective and rhetorical force of his writing—his "blasting and bombardiering," to cite the title of his early memoir—are directly related to the cultural industry of race as a social proliferation of the *infans,* or one unable to speak, because, in the economy of the Lewisian phantasm, deprived of the means, the access, and the intelligence to protest the perverse social world of paternalistic political blandishments and emptied cultural values. When capital lays waste the republic of civic *virtus,* ranting substitutes the infamy of satirical invective and cutting demystification for the ethical work of *parrhesia;* from *infans* to *infama* and back again, the responsible work of reason's critique becomes shrill, repetitive, and all but unheard while the maddened modernist retreats into an ever more oppressive withdrawal from public life.

Lewis was not alone in this insight that family and state, private and public had exchanged their properties to proliferate a social type of youthful ignorance as the consumer citizen. Freud, too, remarked the strange "intellectual oppression" of modern public culture. As an example of the way that oedipal formations continued to exert normative force even in their erosion, Freud examined a pervasive cultural attitude toward child sexuality, one that Foucault references in his critical account of the repressive hypothesis. As argued in Freud's open letter of 1907 addressed to the medical community, "The Sexual Enlightenment of Children," the link between social consensus and repressive force emerges when we examine the traces of what is a faded lineage of ideality, from innocent language back to innocence itself. Describing puberty as both a second virginity and the social construction of innocence, Freud comments, "It is commonly believed that the sexual instinct is lacking in children, and only begins to arise in them when the sexual organs mature."[83] Linking the error—that physical maturation evident to the eye constitutes the threshold of a transformation from innocence to knowledge—with a willful social refusal to listen to the language and the discourse of childhood, Freud develops a theory of censorship from within the policing of normative language. Because infantile knowledge and practice of sexuality is taboo, childhood love and the culture of infantile inquiry are held captive by the social elaboration of innocence.

The idealization of childhood as innocence thus appears to be a social construction designed to banish child sexuality by disavowing a knowledge after the fact. Not only is this elaborate institution of virginity dependent upon a period of childhood ignorance, but the body comes to mark the threshold between an invisible virginity, that of a taboo on sexual knowledge, and a second, newly visible virginity giving rise to the "puberty rites that clutter this period of life." Peculiar visibility of an absence, puberty memorializes the loss of innocence through silence, through the rendering *infans* of an entire childhood culture of eros and investment. The virginization of childhood is produced in a hindsight that isolates and fixes it as image, but this is an image projected as a blocked sound or stifled speech. And this speechlessness is echoed in the ignorance of sexuality that is sought by the adult taboo in its multifarious forms of censorship that, as Foucault remarks seventy years later, "speaks verbosely of its own silence."[84] "One feature of the popular view of the sexual instinct is that it is absent in childhood and only awakens in the period of life described as puberty. This, however, is not merely a simple error but one that has had grave consequences, for it is mainly to this idea that we owe our present ignorance of the fundamental conditions of sexual life."[85] Such a cultural production of innocence as the origin of virginity reproduces the speechlessness of infancy in a socially enjoined forgetting of our archaic inheritance. And this social script has ramifications well beyond the treatment of children. Consider the pernicious effects of this innocence in the recent history of sex panics as detailed by Gayle Rubin's now classic essay "Thinking Sex," which argues that the inviolability of childhood operates as an alibi for the violent and disproportionate policing of sexual minorities, nonwhites, women, and immigrants.[86] This form of censorship through the production of a normative ideal that in turn enables the enforcement of social liminality on the basis of race and gender and through the troping of ignorance and knowledge is one example of how power stratifies the public in ways uncapturable in the language of the public sphere. For Freud the discourse of innocence proliferates well beyond childhood taking one of its most destructive forms in times of state warfare: "The state exacts the utmost degree of obedience and sacrifice from its citizens, but at the same time treats them as children by maintaining an excess of secrecy, and a censorship of news and expressions of opinion that renders the spirits of those thus intellectually oppressed defenceless against every unfavourable turn of events and every sinister rumour."[87] Through the alibi of innocence the state recasts its cosmopolitan citizenry as a mass public fit only for a mass media so tightly filtered that a new and indelibly modern form of oppression emerges almost accidentally in Freud's meditation. Intellectual oppression leaves us helpless, defenseless against the disorientation of social and psychic landscapes; or so was the view from Austria in 1918. For Lewis, war artist and veteran of the trenches, the culture that survived the Great War continued to bear the mark of that defenselessness so much so that "there is no longer any FAMILY, in one sense: there is now only a collection of children, differing in age but in nothing else. The last vestige of the *patria potestas* has been extirpated" (*ABR*, 167).

Adorno shares Lewis's and Freud's grim assessment of the link between mass culture and the strange communion of an oedipalized family narrative with its common tongue, and assuming this insight as a given, he takes it a step further to argue, from a wide range of sources, that culture, governed by taboo, has become sexualized, for "taboos can be reawakened because social suffering is . . . repressed and displaced onto sexuality."[88] Recalling Freud's formulation of a vast social project to assert the innocence of childhood, Adorno argues that this is the result not of blindness but of a guilty envy directed at that fabricated innocence, which comes to represent the supreme value attached to sex.[89] Yet overvaluation finds expression not in the celebration of childhood but in a twisted and inverted logic that, rather than protecting and upholding the ideal of innocence and purity, degrades and devolves into an infantilized celebration of transgressions and a cultural project to commodify even eros. "In the twentieth century . . . the erotic ideal has become infantilized."[90] This fascination and, in his view, regressive infatuation with figures of innocence is the result of a widespread damage to the culture of belief characteristic of the modern age, which can no longer mount its image of freedom nor project its own enlightenment:

> The taboos in the midst of the illusion of freedom cannot be taken lightly, above all because no one completely believes in them anymore, whereas they are still reinforced by both the unconscious of individuals and by institutional powers. In general, the more eroded repressive ideas have become, the more cruelly they are enforced: their application must be exaggerated so that the terror persuades people that what is so power-

ful must also be legitimate. . . . Sexual taboos in the age of at once both total and stymied enlightenment have an augmented power, since they no longer have a *raison d'être* even for those who obey them.[91]

Faded cultural residues continue to function as taboos but take on a new purpose: "they allow the accumulated ancient indignation to be redirected at whatever is timely and opportune, regardless of its quality: *otherness as such is the chosen enemy.*" Thus totemism, the sacrificial structure of belonging under the sign of the animal, the nation, the religion, and the ideological formation, returns in the refreshed energies of an aggressivity now set spinning in the public sphere by the illusion of freedom projected through mass culture's lure of consumption. Explicitly keying the Freudian terms that shape his observation, Adorno's analysis implicitly offers us an image of taboo gone hysterical, wildly lashing out at "otherness as such" to recharge the faded metaphor of kinship barely visible in cultural relics that outlive their usefulness, relics like the unconscious and our institutions of public culture.

Such a haunting return of totemism in the breakdown of taboo is not limited to infantile life but extends the family quarrel as discourse with the result that efforts to contain power—in its cultivated centers and through the terms and questions that produce discursive communities and characteristic intellectual idioms—become indistinguishable from an effort to break the bond of intellectual exchange absolutely. To relegate the other's discourse to infancy, a speechless space where paradoxically, his language becomes illegible and inaccessible, because it is all too clear or transparent, institutes as a normative condition of "discourse" the very refusal of difference, and this not only in the sense of discrete cultural difference. A peculiar institution of identity, this foreclosure on otherness marks a mutation in the oedipalized public, for the taboos that now secure the token of a community's belonging to itself (its totemic structure) are curiously diffuse and difficult to articulate while simultaneously their policing function enjoys a period of invigorated life. Adorno's conclusion allows us to understand the role that otherness is made to play when it is cast as unintelligibility and therefore forced to bear the burden of the public's disavowal of its own limits. The determination of intelligibility and its opposite emerges with new force. For this reason, sexuality, like race, furnishes the images and language for a displaced expression of suffering and subjection relegated beyond the limits of the human, where, as Balibar reminds us, universal humanism vigilantly preserves the human from decline; if otherness has been a watchword of postcolonial studies, it is in part because of this recursive logic that binds the speech of the other as unintelligible babble at a limit only retroactively reconstituted as the limit of the norm.

In this cocktail of innocence and regression, speech and writing are not easily separable from other social practices. Nor is the resurgence of normative ideals a neutral repetition of traditional forms. Rather, here is evidence of a further alteration in the structure of taboo itself, for, like all institutions, repression has a contingent and historically malleable life; as Adorno notes, it depends upon both institutional power and individual unconscious. The suggestion that change occurs in the fundamental taboo structure of modern life, not only in the expressions of oedipal kinship but in the forms of kinship possible, rebounds on those who would claim an access to "traditional" values, whether of family structure or community ideal, for a traditional value also has its historical and unconscious dimension. In a modern world that, as Adorno suggests, may be constituted by the very challenge to oedipality sketched here, the assertion of "traditional" oedipal kinship and the world it desires is itself altered by the fact of other, newly budding perhaps, claims to and of kinship not modeled on the blood bond but bearing within themselves an uncanny ghost of transmission. If Adorno is right to say that modern taboos are now policed most cruelly where they are least believed, does it follow that modern totemism also suffers this translation into weak belief accompanied by fierce assertion? Such a structure conforms to the emergent contradictions evident in Lewis's continual appeal to racial unity at a time when the very notion of commonality seemed so difficult for him to uphold. How might a psychoanalytic understanding of communal kinship enhance a discussion of the public? By reintroducing the themes of sacrifice and spectral kinship into our reading of social power, psychoanalysis exposes the trace of oedipal relations that continue to trouble the social fabric and precisely around the question of the norm. According to *Totem and Taboo* the oedipal structure of sacrifice and communion upheld in spectacle establishes the social network of exchange and inaugurates the trafficking in differences that consolidates communities of identity through the exchange of women, goods, and ideals. The patriarchal origin of sacrifice, and significantly for Freud a parricide, inheres in its abstract and dematerialized form as the metaphoric kinship made possible by totemic belonging, for communion in sacrifice cements the virtue of spectatorship as a powerful mode of participation in the community. In Freud's tale of ritual parricide and the totemic feast, it is not only the figure of the father that fades from view as the spectacle of sacrifice is theatricalized in social practices ranging from Greek tragedy to Christian ritual; kinship alters as well, through the mediations of violent sacrifice manifest in the changing forms of fate awaiting the hero upon the tragic stage or in the symbolic substitution of communion wafer for Christ's body.[92] These successive modes of sacrificial spectacle take on the character of what Foucault has described as a disciplinary practice that aims to reproduce a particular type or norm of conscience.[93] The seemingly disparate texts of Freud and Foucault are linked by this nearly identical observation inasmuch as the very notion of cultural transmission that emerges between them bears within it the trace of its spectacular origin. Whereas the psychoanalytic tale urges an understanding of history as the successive permutations of kinship's attenuation through the historical modalities of affect and supreme among affects, guilt, Foucault disseminates the possibilities of historical difference in the networks of disciplinary contact and relation that contour the present tense of power through the cultivation of forms of regulatory rationality. In short, whereas Freud proffers a mythic origin for a continuous process which repeats the same oedipal framework in each historical era, like so many historical and cultural variations on a theme, Foucault's understanding of practice forces us to consider the variations within a given context as resistances to a normative and dominant resolution of the range of particularity through the positing of a form of universality but with a crucial difference. Whereas Freud's myth of the primal father leaves us always resolving the universal through the exceptional status of fundamental taboos, on incest and parricide, Foucault's theory of the immanence of power and resistance is better equipped to examine and to expose the genealogy of exceptionalism in its tireless effort to resolve universality.

As an example of the shuttling temporality of decline and resurgence that Lewis, Freud, Adorno, and even Foucault observe in the modern development of subjectivity on the basis of cultural and unconscious taboos and investments of desire that are themselves channeled through concepts of race, *The Art of Being Ruled* (1926) is instructive. Although a work of sociopolitical theory, *The Art of Being Ruled* makes demands of its reader unparalleled in the record of modernist writing. It is not that the work is more difficult or esoteric than others; it speaks its message in direct language. Rather, this text rails, excoriates, and rages against the present and encompasses the reader in that raging demand. Masquerading as a satirical work of social theory, in many respects this lengthy and verbose text, which indulges its author's need to simultaneously exhibit and immediately master his own social panic, fails to do more than paint innumerable pictures of the public sphere in ruins. Half-abandoned but still tenaciously clutching at the social body, the civic moral of this work of public demystification and political hygiene cannot quite commit to seduction of its audience. Indeed, as the preface warns us, "a book of this description is not written for an audience already there, prepared to receive it, and whose mind it will fit like a glove. There must be a good deal of stretching of the receptacle, it is expected" (*ABR*, 13).

Despite its seemingly comprehensive cascade of topics, *The Art of Being Ruled* is never able to resolve itself into a coherent insight or argument; the form of the book resists totalization as social theory though it seeks it out as aim. Instead of a comprehensive synthesis, this social text identifies a series of contiguous degenerations that now constitute the national body under capital, and these variations coexist as a simultaneous but conglomerate social agon. Race war, class war, sex war, and age war, these are Lewis's terms for the proliferation of social inauthenticity that bedevils the public sphere and pollutes the civic ideal. Lewis's fascist insight allows him to diagnose the distinctly modern character of sexuality under the nation-state as a form of discipline that permits the state to regulate political and affective life through bland appeals to a vulgarized appetite. At a fifty-year remove, Foucault later clarifies this seemingly eccentric view of the imbrication of flesh-colored hose, crystal sets, and the state by observing that "sexuality . . . is a matter for individualizing disciplinary controls that take the form of permanent surveillance . . . but because it has procreative effects, sexuality is also inscribed, takes effect, in broad biological processes that concern not the body of individuals but the element, the multiple unity of the population. Sexuality exists at the point where body and population meet. And so it is a matter for disciplines but also for regularization."[94] This doubling of discipline and regulation at the gathering point, which is sexuality, means that individual identity is subject to power in at least two simultaneous directions. On the one hand, the individual is responsible for his bodily acts and desires; on the other hand, individual bodily acts reflect a social order and its potential for disorder. This basic mechanism of modern social relation could only be figured by Lewis as a corrupt social discord running through the social body entirely. From this perspective, the body of the subject is never his own, for he is always also a member of a larger population for which the threat of undisciplined sexuality holds open the possibility of crisis. Individual morality and collective health, these points of power's exercise demand subjective investment and reward it as well, for the smooth operation of the state depends upon regularization and the commitment of subjects ready and able to uphold its values as their own. As Lewis observed, discipline and regulation unite in the placid acceptance of state incitement to consume and perpetuate national ends as private desires.

Positioned at the crux of state control and individual responsibility, sexuality takes on a social function in modernity that supplements and intensifies the social purpose it may have had in networks of kinship, gendered spaces, and libertinage before the arrival of modern state regulation of movement, information, education, employment, and expression. Modern sexuality, then, cannot be divorced from the state even in subjective expressions and seemingly marginal practices; further, sexuality, when understood in its biopolitical entanglement with power as with errant subjectivation, must also be seen as one of several sites of the production of race as a major industry of state regulation and civic disciplinary reach. Racialization and the deployment of sexuality, the Janus-faced thresholders of modern subjectivity, become the major domains of a state exercise of regulatory scrutiny, disciplinary control, and demographic sciences, and as the objects of this obsessional interest, race and sex become the defining characteristics of the citizen subject to be regulated. Thus in Foucault's history of modernity, neither the exigencies of capital nor the inevitable march of knowledge alone can account for the development of modern subjection; these contingent historical forces required the cultivation of "war by other means" or the development of the human subject as exhibition space of power's signifying practice; race and sex come to dominate as the major axes of power's exercise, and, as such, supply the terms of resistance that are the defining features of the modern period. It is here that the link between what modernists thematize as the primitive coincides with the analysis of power. Whether imagined as native human essence as in D.H. Lawrence's *Fantasia of the Unconscious* or degenerate threat as by Lewis, the story of social wreckage and ruin inscribes the primitive either as antidote or as morbific cause.

As a counterweight to the modernist diagnosis of decline, even in such a marginalized one as Lewis's, we do well to recall the avant-garde and anticolonial writings of Césaire, Genet, James, and Fanon, who show that the imagination of an ideal public sphere now in ruins must scotomize histories of colonialism and capital to authorize its narrative of loss. Against this pattern of occulting history, the anticolonial ranters raise the specter of traumatic remembrance and knowledge gained in the spaces of abjection the better to address the future, including a future of the self. In the next three chapters we will examine three quite distinct negotiations with this legacy of the primitive phantasmagoria of modernity and its production of ranting excess in the modern speech of contestation.

CHAPTER 1

On Being Stubborn

Oscar Wilde and the Modern Type

The modernity avowed by the postcolonial avant-garde and twentieth-century modernist cultural critics is crosshatched by power and resistance in ways not captured by the center/periphery divide or an imagination of excluded otherness. To examine the paradox of foreclosed inscription from the very center of discursive relations, in this chapter we turn to London's fin de siècle inheritance of that midcentury Baudelairean ethos so crucial for the formation of modern subjectivity and to a figure whose social liminality derives from his complex relation to empire. The position of Oscar Wilde, Irish and Protestant, in London's fashionable society and intellectual world was not secured in advance by birth but earned through the brilliance of his performance at Oxford, the social connections he made there and later, the popular success of his light comic dramas, and, finally, the celebrity he carefully built through the cultivation of a public persona.[1] Successful seduction of the public was not proof, however, against the inescapable fact that being both Irish and queer, Wilde was doubly marginal to the norms of English empire and that, therefore, his fame exposed a vulnerability. As intimate alien, Wilde mustered all the resources of decadent aestheticism to his defense, and this included the legendary Wildean wit and sartorial elegance that has been his lasting image. Yet his vulnerability was borne out in 1895, when Wilde was indicted on charges of committing acts of "gross indecency" with another man. Serving two years hard labor in the Queen's prison, Wilde attempted to recuperate his legacy and to rebuke the laws that bound him by writing a letter, *De Profundis,* that, although addressed to his lover, was meant to circulate among a limited public until released for publication after a delay of fifty years. This carceral rant attests to a paradox central to fin de siècle cultural provocation and later twentieth-century concern over the degeneration of public sensibility; namely, that the ideals of normative sexuality derive from a "primitive" repression culturally induced in the present, as the price and thus the sign of being modern. This logic involves a temporal maneuver at odds with the teleologies of development that fueled rhetorics of empire and justified domination of colonial subjects, for decadence and modernism drew from metaphors of premodern history, figures to describe psychosocial facts regarding the nature of subjectivity and social power. In the same spirit, Wilde's rant reveals the intuition of a symbolic law of culture that he strives to challenge and hopes to change through the performance of a global sublimation of his imprisonment and the shame it brought; *De Profundis,* the result, registers a limit to its author's seemingly limitless powers of transcendence but performs this limit in a rebuke of the laws of kinship by which he is judged. As a failed strategy of transcendence, Wilde's rant nonetheless materializes the symbolic law of social intelligibility that dictates his crime and punishment.

Put simply, Wilde's career sketches an arc from censorship to foreclosure. As a queer Irish writer of the late nineteenth century, Wilde was free to express same-sex desire and love in a writing that is neither heavily coded nor illegible;[2] in saying this I differ from one thread of queer studies, which wishes to find, in Wilde especially, an erasure of gay male desire and a tendency toward censored abstraction. However, a large body of recent work in cultural studies that shows us an active culture of homosexual and homophobic expression in the London of the late nineteenth century corroborates my view that Wilde's explorations of subjectivity, psychic attachment, and homosexual desire are too bound together to be neatly disarticulated from one another, as I shall argue below.[3] What is clear is that Wilde's aesthetic ideology before imprisonment made full use of the "semantic mobility" of decadence,[4] and thus both exposed and relied upon social taboos to generate its aesthetic feats. The pleasure to be taken in a situation of double marginality is evident in his work before the crushing experience of social humiliation. In prison, however, the delicate synthesis of aesthetic culture and transgression that enabled Wilde to write with such precision about fantasy and gay male desire in *The Picture of*

Dorian Gray no longer functions; violently foreclosed from his popular audience and suffering bodily degradation, the decadent Wilde is recast as degenerate.[5] In essence, wit gives way to ranting because censorship, with which one can negotiate, was redoubled as social death and imprisonment.

The narrative I have just outlined moves from an aesthetic ideology capable of deviating around the norm without sacrificing its homosexual content to a shrill love letter that proclaims the interconnections between social scripts and family life in terms very like those of later modernists in what I have dubbed the diagnosis of the oedipalization of race. Wilde does not have this Freudian vocabulary at his disposal, of course; he does, however, share with the later modernists an intuition that the discoveries of the anthropological and biological sciences add up to something more than a survival of the fittest. For these thinkers, science was beginning to paint a picture of embedded social norms transmitted like the laws of nature and like our physical form, mutable and susceptible of change. Accompanying this new anthropological interest in the social tie was a faith in art's power to overcome primitive cultural residues through the ruses of imagination and fantasy, for, as we shall see in *The Picture of Dorian Gray*, fantasy triumphs over the normative order by setting to work the enigmatic message of the other, and thus "influence" rather than blood becomes the origin of desire and the means of novel subjectivation. Drawing on both Ruskin and Pater, Wilde's writings before his imprisonment amply demonstrate the power of influence or fantasy to create both desire and fear in the modern subject. As our discussion below will show, such writing displays an early modernist commitment to explorations of psychological motivations and an understanding of those motivations as socially induced. This chapter moves, then, from an aesthetic ideology of provocation and semantic slipperiness to an unmasterable social foreclosure before which the ranter risks collapse and unintelligibility in order to address the law of his own abjection. Let us not forget that the language of the recriminalization of sodomy in 1885 explicitly justified itself as protecting the youth of England from the corrupting influence of gross indecency.

This incipient social theory, which draws from such richly diverse fields as evolutionary science, anthropology, and aesthetics, connects the modernist explorations of psychological states and group mentalities that preoccupied writers and thinkers in the midcentury to a fin de siècle concern that social evolution could just as easily mean devolution.[6] For decadents like Wilde, the claim of art's ability to rewrite the primitive present and to resist the degradations of life fostered by relations of capital and by bourgeois morality is not to be underestimated. From within this aesthetic ideology fantasy was a primary imaginary resource against such realities. For this reason, I will dwell below on Eve Sedgwick's "Some Binarisms (II): Wilde, Nietzsche, and the Sentimental Relations of the Male Body," in *Epistemology of the Closet,* one of the most influential and significant readings of Wilde and centered on his only novel. A key feature of Sedgwick's reading is her argument that Wilde participates in a politics of abstracting the male figure with the result that homoerotic representation evaporates in a more socially accommodating narcissistic relation of self and mirror image. Reflective of commonly held attitudes, the accusation of modernist abstraction as against a literal representation of same-sex relations risks reinscribing as a form of liberatory critique a dismissal of decadence in modernism; as such, criticism that would demand mimetic style as a condition of visibility takes the added risk of repeating the repressive hypothesis that Foucault identified in our language of sexual liberation. A different relation to censorship is at stake in the case of Wilde, and therefore my reading must take a psychoanalytic approach to the excess of the rant and the politics of visibility. The speech act that emerges from this perspective, which qualifies psychoanalysis with a genealogical understanding of power and subjection taken from Foucault, is one that challenges the norms of intelligibility, the definition of the subject and the literary at work in the dominant readings of Wilde, especially those that would limit literary transgression to the breaking of taboos in the play of knowing and unknowing that has been called open secrecy.

I take my cue from Charles Bernheimer's opening reflections in *Decadent Subjects,* in which he examines a paradigmatic dismissal of "decadence" as a term—on the grounds that it means anything and everything—as a way of showing how easily attempts to define the meaning of "decadence" fall prey to the rhetorical strategies of dismissal and accusation.[7] For the literal minded there is no stable referent for the decadent habit of thought, which insists on confusing decay, historical mutability, and excess with aesthetic provocation. Bernheimer artfully shows that demanding meanings for an aesthetic ideology that privileges rhetorical ambiguity and liminal states as modes of a critical interruption of received ideas and conventional morality is itself a trap of decadence, one prepared in advance by aesthetic provocation.

> I would argue that the particular associations that a speaker may have with the concept of decadence are not what is important and culturally productive about this concept. It is not the referential content of the term that conveys its meaning so much as the dynamics of paradox and ambivalence that it sets in motion. Its meaning is the injury of the kind of meaning Gilman is looking for. Fundamental to the opening of this semantic wound is precisely the contaminating crossover that dismays Gilman, the slippage from poetic metaphor to historical fact, from aesthetic dream to real life. (*DS*, 5)

Bernheimer's approach invites historical research into the reading of decadence but not in the mimetic and empiricist terms that he claims are demanded by Richard Gilman. Instead of reducing decadence to a style of speaking about things, our task is to understand decadence as a cultural practice of the injury of meaning that results when the paradoxes and ambivalences of a world forged by subjection become the very means of writing and thus of new subjectivation. The injury of meaning is a powerful metaphor for the wounds of history that Wilde uncovers, endures, and turns into a way of life. Through Bernheimer's insight, we can see that Wildean aestheticism sought the social fact in the decadent acts of ruining rituals of thought. For when decadence put medical discourses to work alongside its insights into the nature of subjectivity and, we would add, the narcissism of colonial cultures, it set that subject and its desires within the discursive network of its engendering and, by doing so, decadence exposed both the real and the symbolic contours of subjection. In this chapter we follow Wilde in the 1890s as he took a path from fame to ruin that transformed his public address to train its newfound rage on the inexorable familial law that renamed him abject and degenerate.

READING FIGURES

> We can forgive a man for making a useful thing as long as he does not admire it. The only excuse for making a useless thing is that one admires it intensely. All art is quite useless.
> Oscar Wilde, preface to *The Picture of Dorian Gray*

By the time Oscar Wilde began writing *The Picture of Dorian Gray*, Théophile Gautier's maxim "l'art pour l'art" and its theatrical appeal to artifice were so well assimilated by London's cultivated elite that it hardly needed restatement. Only after the serialized version in Lippincott's *Monthly Magazine* was attacked in the press on the grounds of its corrupting influence on English youth did Wilde, with characteristic finesse, choose to preface his novel with an aphoristic aestheticist manifesto that repeats the main tenets of Gautier's provocative preface to *Mademoiselle de Maupin*.[8] Although to Wilde's admiring readers this was clearly legible as a defiance of conventional morality—the plot of Gautier's novel includes cross-dressing, male and female homosexuality, and mimed bestiality with a bearskin—the sexually transgressive nature of *Dorian Gray* was equally transparent to conservatives and perhaps the general readership. Exemplary of the sexual panic induced by *Dorian Gray*'s diffuse descriptions of indolence and artistic temperament, a critic in the *Scots Observer* said of Wilde, "If he can write for none but outlawed noblemen and perverted telegraph-boys, the sooner he takes to tailoring (or some other decent trade) the better for his own reputation and public morals."[9] Hence, the pride of place given to the admiration of uselessness in the novel's preface. As a response to the moralizing and all too evident recognition that his topic elicited, Wilde's blithe disavowal "There is no such thing as a moral book" operates a reversal that fails to deny the obviously homosexual content of his fable while parrying the more violent insinuations of his critics. Usefulness, however, was not a category to be entirely dispensed with, and there is a consistent play between notions of use and the license to engage in fantasy throughout Wilde's critical works, although reversal remains the primary weapon in his critical arsenal. Tactical polyvalence of oedipal provocation produces in Wilde's texts a characteristically defensive and disarming style that folds a serious aesthetic view into a more blatant social complaint, as when he says "It is the spectator, and not life, that art really mirrors," a maxim that collapses the aesthetic insight of perspectivism onto the denunciation of moral projection. Catachresis, the fundamental trope of his tactics, maximizes an oedipal posture of diffident rebellion, although critics have perhaps overstated this feature of Wilde's performance and forgotten his warning that "Most personalities have been obliged to be rebels. Half their strength has been wasted in friction."[10] The tactical force of catachresis and denaturalization, lurking behind deliberate paradox, provides Wilde with the resistant resources of the "new manner in art" and its potently useful tools: meaninglessness as topic, boundless and fanciful detail, cliquish humor, foppish dress, and wit.

Nothing is more characteristic of Wilde than the marshalling of wit in the service of a subtle but thoroughgoing social critique. Wilde's art of wit is one of seduction and transgression, disarming its challengers through humor, irony, scandal, and paradox. If Wilde's wit is an art of confrontation, it also parries the blows of the adversary in an ambiguous play of defiance, ostentation, elusiveness, pleasure, and persuasion. Where does one locate transgression in this complex scene of address? Wit, like jokes, seems to lift the bar of prohibition where laughter becomes the sign of a momentary victory over a censorious law. In a memorable line from *Jokes and Their Relation to the Unconscious,* Freud tells us that a joke is like news of a victory from the front; Freud's metaphor thus calls up a common enemy and a community vindicated as one, whereas Wilde's wit requires an understanding of the transgressive potential of his verbal challenges. Major resource of the avant-garde, wit possesses both the power of that community-binding good news from the front while retaining a less easily assimilated energy of disruption. In Wildean wit these energies commingle to produce the hilarity of incest, sly class cynicism directed at the aristocracy, bold indictment of the middle classes, and dangerous statements of homoerotic frankness. To approach the sexual politics as well as the critical interpretations of culture alive in the Wildean speech act, we will situate Wilde's rhetorical maneuvers on subjectivity in a reading strategy that takes its bearings from psychoanalytic notions of fantasy and a Foucauldian genealogy of modern subjectivity in the confessional subject. Beginning with an analysis of *The Picture of Dorian Gray* to establish Wilde's techniques of poetic intervention on social norming, we then read Wilde's prison letter, *De Profundis,* the text in which Wilde, at wit's end, rails against his accusers and the judgment under which he labors.

It would be a mistake to consider the aesthetic strategies essential to Wilde's emergent intervention on cultural normativity as uncritically assumed. Despite the critical panic that received the novel as a paean to hedonism, *Dorian Gray* was written largely as a criticism of the self-defeating narcissism that underwrites the aesthete's bargain. Thus, while aestheticism serves as a defensive posture in the preface, it comes under fire in the novel as a limited if exciting challenge to sexual normativity.[11] This criticism is spread out among the novel's characters and presents its object as a social rather than purely individual complex of ressentiment and shame. The novel's implied disavowal of oedipal resistance coupled with a moral that traces the injurious effects of repression and renunciation attests to the series of distances and qualifications that mediate between the pleasures depicted and the pleasures of reading and, through this very mediation, contributes to the visibility of a model of desire whose cultural terms were at that very moment in the process of being written. An important strain of misreadings of aestheticism in general, and Wilde in particular, paints the picture of shallow provocation and self-interest summed up in the phrase *épater la bourgeoisie*. Peter Bürger, for instance, claims that aestheticism is nothing more than an extension of romanticism in the arts, which he reduces to an expression of bourgeois subjectivity. In this account, aestheticism epitomizes the autonomy and withdrawal of the arts from political praxis. Wilde's work cannot fit such a narrow conception of literary history, one that scotomizes political intervention into the normative subjective investments of the arts. Not surprisingly, a dialectical model such as Bürger's inevitably folds upon itself so that what appeared as opposition in the past reemerges as appropriation by the dominant in the present. Nor can such a dialectical model attend to the gradations of difference presented by a queer Irish writer who sought to conquer the London stage. As a result, periodizing arguments like Bürger's, and other attempts to define the attributes of rather than to trace the genealogy of power and resistance in the discourse of the subject, have paid little heed to Wilde. Caught between a Marxist view of literature with no place for sexual politics and a formalist trend in literary criticism reticent to read the merely "thematic," Wilde has had to wait for the arrival of queer theory to be recognized as a major theorist and critic of modernity rather than a frivolous hedonist. Eve Sedgwick, whose study of Wilde and Nietzsche[12] has become a dominant reading of *The Picture of Dorian Gray*, offers an approach to this historical moment of emergence when she claims that signally in the novel and throughout his writings, Wilde invents or participates in the invention of a male/male desire governed by the circularity or specularity of sameness. However, in arguing for the condensation of homosexuality into the figure of sameness, Sedgwick misses the importance Wilde attributed to the evolutionary model in his imagination of specifically male-male desire, to the imbrication of fantasy with psychic repression in his figuration of the primitive and to the complex ways that his aesthetic ethos links sexual selection and embodiment to a cosmopolitan understanding of race. And by failing to attend to Wilde's political and critical investments in the interest of appropriating his work to a burgeoning model of sexual identity, this critical reception disarticulates the writer and the text from its political practice.

Sedgwick argues that this participation is at odds with Wilde's own pederastic preferences, where difference in age and maturity is essential to desire, and further that Wilde's literary advocacy of sameness substantially contributes to the poetics of secrecy and disclosure that, famously, she names alternately "open secrecy" and the "glass closet." While her analysis is both illuminating and foundational for certain kinds of queer reading, the central notion that Wilde's writings belie his practice, insofar as the writings explore forms of mimetic identification captured by the image of Dorian gazing at his portrait, requires that we accept the conclusion that Wilde's contribution to a wider cultural development of gay male sensibility lies with the mimetic plot of the novel rather than with the more dynamic and intersubjective staging of desire throughout the novel's descriptions, dramatic scenes, and avowal of style. Such a conclusion obscures the complex negotiation between prohibition and critical self-reflection, repression and the imaginative resources of sublimation at stake in the novel. This adherence is most palpable in the moments when Sedgwick distances herself from homophobic readings of the fable, readings that submerge or "finesse the novel's gayness out of existence" through a transparently motivated overreading of the portrait as an allegory of self-reflection. Sedgwick argues convincingly that an exclusive interpretive interest in questions of representation forms one strand of academic reception of the novella and as a result her own reading tends to deflate the significance of "self-reflection" as a central thematic pivot. Whereas Sedgwick deemphasizes the mimetic plot, Wilde conceived the book as a critique of aestheticist ressentiment, a reactive doctrine that figures its desire and thus its self-reflection only within the stalemate of mimetic transfixity.[13]

For Sedgwick, then, the circularity of Dorian's relation to his image, and the underlying argument that life indeed mimics art, is merely a camouflage for the open secrecy of the novel's gayness. Sedgwick polemically links what she calls the "disfiguring move to abstraction" to a modernist intuition that self-reflection implies a homosexual self-relation[14] and which she claims must be buried under the rampant, panicked invective against figuration that she locates in a series of critical receptions of modernism. But rather than seeing this as a censorious device for disguising the easily nameable, I understand the two registers of desire and self-preservation or influence and prohibition to be intertwined such that the first always comes into being at the price of the second; this is not to say that the Wilde of 1890 was advocating a repressive and homophobic moral, and still less that a novel as obsessively critical of figurality could do without figuration. Rather, there is an insistence, one characteristic of Wilde, on multiplicity, on the interminability of figures when desire is neither easily nameable nor entirely censored. This enabling stalemate between inventive expression and social proscription is tightly woven into the fabric of gay desiring as it appears and disappears in the characters' relations, in the classical reference through parodic invocation of Socratic dialogue, in decor, in dress, in the style of dinner conversation, and even in the orientalizing scene of gothic slums. His own remarks on the novel bear this out: for Basil, Henry, and Dorian are impersonations of Wilde. "Basil Hallward is what I think I am: Lord Henry what the world thinks me: Dorian is what I would like to be—in other ages, perhaps."[15] Sedgwick's reading appears to leave no room for Foucault's most important contribution to discussions of subjectivity, namely, the notion that power exacts its due in the disciplinary forms of subjection exactly where it provides the terms for unprecedented resistance in the form of new subjectivations. By dividing himself between the characters of his fables, Wilde knowingly sets to work a multiplicity of identification and erotic affinity while reserving the rights of critical reflection.

In short, I am arguing that the political usefulness of a reading strategy that employs a structure of emptiness against fullness or secrecy against disclosure runs aground in its encounter with Wilde. The novel splits its author in three and works that split for the tangled self-knowledge that a fictional text can yield without therefore staking its entire intervention on secrecy about its sexual content nor on full disclosure. The lucidity of Wilde's statement about his three identities seems to go unremarked not only in Sedgwick's account of knowing and not knowing, but also in a quick and admiring appropriation of Wilde as an emblem of gay liberation avant la lettre. What Wilde conveys is a predicament of desire and imagination. "Basil is what I think I am." What does his text show Basil to be? A self-censoring artist who conceives his desire as a lust for an ideal beauty and deposits that erotic capital on canvas. Against this model of censorship, Lord Henry performs himself as a public persona; provocative, indolent, stereotypical dandy, he seduces the raw beauty that is Dorian. Predatory and ironic homosexual, sublimating artist, and, finally, the utterly self-sufficient, ideal Dorian: these three "types" act out a series of relations that indicate Wilde's understanding of his own investments and limitations as clearly as they show Wilde at work to criticize the available terms of a socially constructed limit on male desire. From each position in the novel's fantasy Wilde has elaborated a figure of identity through and by limitation, and in doing so, he repeats the self-referential character of psychic fantasy, inasmuch as "fantasy represents not only a content in a scene but the way in which it is itself produced."[16] The fantasy itself offers to make the social bind of desire legible, and perhaps to alter that bondage by invoking the frustration of an example. "Give a man a mask and he will speak the truth."[17] The masks of fantasy allow the novel to explore the price of each path to and away from a desire, which was even in the moment of its publication visibly homosexual.

The Picture of Dorian Gray transforms its author, too. It establishes Wilde's reputation as an author by marking him publicly as a homosexual artist whose art explores and resists a normative heterosexism, and sets in motion a series of seductions on many levels. After a passionate reading of the novel, Lord Alfred Douglas arranged to meet Wilde in London. Douglas so impressed the author that Wilde not only gave Douglas a deluxe copy of the work, but he also offered to tutor him for his Oxford exams. So began Wilde's first long-term relationship with another man. If that seduction by a book exceeds the novel's narrative of a stalemate between art as a form of erotic censorship and artistic culture as an incitement to desire, it does so only because Wilde could so effectively convey both the fascination and the inhibition of his topic. It is here that the contradictory nature of sublimation as a concept can perhaps be productively introduced and reworked.

Laplanche and Pontalis's writing on fantasy is instructive in this connection, for their influential work "suggests that subjective dispersal across different figures is the salient feature of fantasy's *mise en scène* of desire and equally that such a dispersal repeats the structure of sublimation and its undoing."[18] As a psychic process sublimation derives from fantasy and shares with it an ambiguous relation to self-censorship. Ultimately *Dorian Gray*'s economic setting—luxurious abundance—is translated into a more diffuse, suggestive metaphor of seduction or sexual influence; this gesture is met by an equal and opposing tendency to disguise its sexual content with the opulent trappings of aestheticism and decadence. If the subject of the fantasy is dispersed throughout into differing roles, and if the object of the desire menaced by repression is preserved somewhere in the syntax of the fantasy, then fantasy becomes a privileged site for interpretive disclosure. Laplanche and Pontalis describe fantasy as a desubjectivized space of defensive preservation, but in this novel that defense preserves desire and its subject *as* diffusion and *as* figural opulence. Despite the translatability of fantasy, Laplanche and Pontalis also suggest that desubjectivization entails an equally nondisclosive possibility: the fantasy may never be sufficiently decanted down to a finite proposition. Fantasy's narratives are multiple; they aim to escape the repressive, watchful gaze of interpretation or prohibition. What the fantasy aims for is a kind of travesty that will resist absolute disclosure. A major weapon, then, in the deployment of fantasy becomes its stubborn, inscrutable, and sometimes meaningless nature, its tendency to produce decoys or, in Wilde's case, decor.

"The project of constructing the male figure is not made any the less central by being rendered as nonsense."[19] This "nonsense" is effected through the bald contradictions delivered by a definite poseur who insists himself not as himself but as an identifiable pacing and syntax. It is delivery that enables the suspense and the sometimes anticlimactic arrival of wit. This is not a disembodied spirit of mind but an inexhaustible capacity for impersonation, irony, and self-contradiction. It ensures the seriality of repetition. The workings of wit erode the dominance of paternal good sense, and so the male figure mobilized by nonsense becomes a resistant one. To seize upon color, decor, or smoke as essentials invents meaning as the capital of a subculture. The meaning of decor may be no meaning at all, but on a whim and in the service of unforeseeable contingency, it may be recycled as a total sense. Playing this game mimics the consumerism of capital,[20] but it also secures the future of any given discourse for the plunder of the speaker. This is the capital of "open secrecy" and the treasure of a play of surfaces; it is what is left for the sons when the semantic field has been overrun and overpopulated by the fathers.

Color is more than exemplary in this regard. To wit: the airy and masterful way Wilde explains *green* in his essay on the forger, Wainewright, who "had that curious love of green, which in individuals is always the sign of a subtle artistic temperament, and in nations is said to denote a laxity, if not a decadence, of morals."[21] Making meaning out of sheer nonsense, Wilde continued to use greenness in his public performances on the stage and in the docket. In 1892 at the opening of *Lady Windermere's Fan* Wilde invited friends in attendance to wear green carnations like the one worn on stage by the character Cecil Graham, and when Wilde himself appeared on stage to thank the audience, he, too, was wearing the flower. Asked, "And what does it mean?" Wilde replied, "Nothing whatever, but that is just what nobody will guess."[22] Later, when Queensberry read Robert Hichens's

The Green Carnation, which depicts the affair between Douglas and Wilde, and was resolved to punish Wilde, Wilde responded in some small way by wearing his green carnation to court. There are at least five potential uses of the ornament: 1) A signifier of homosexuality among French dandies,[23] 2) A local sign of fraternity at the opening of *Lady Windermere's Fan,* 3) A banner of Irish nationalism assumed under threat from the English court and aristocracy, and thus a nationalist version of oedipal resistance, 4) A symbol of "spirituality in individuals and laxity in nations," as Wilde explains in his essay "Pen, Pencil and Poison," and 5) A sign of artifice marking a resistance to the naturalization of imperial normativity. This loaded figurality represents an intensification of a signifier rather than its abstraction. It installs a certain semantic arbitrariness, which is limited and enriched by the will of the "artist" who wields it and the constraints of a society that surrounds it. If a green carnation can be the occasion of community, its influence has the virtue of installing imitation as a link of affiliation while it simultaneously sets spinning the imagined distinction between artifice and nature. This is a model of seriality and erotic multiplicity, one capable of breaking open the "economy of one" that is narcissistic isolation through the exacting mediation of an artificial nature.

Fantasy has three main connotations in psychoanalysis. Conscious fantasy, akin to daydreaming or imaginative play; unconscious fantasy deciphered by analysis; and primal fantasy, which has both unconscious and conscious dimensions insofar as the unconscious primal fantasy drives particular and individual expressions derived from bits of reality and woven into complex patterns that repeat in dreams, daydreams, and the text of free association. Freud was interested to draw out the similarities between unconscious and conscious fantasy, the transitions that take place between them, and their reversibility.

> It is the subject's life as a whole, which is seen to be shaped and ordered by what might be called, in order to stress this structuring action, "a phantasmatic." This should not be conceived of merely as a thematic ... for it has its own dynamic, in that the phantasy structures seek to express themselves, to find a way out into consciousness and action, and they are constantly drawing in new material.[24]

Wilde is particularly adept at weaving a conscious, creative scene (imagination) that reflects unconscious and primal scenes particular to homoerotic object choice. Insofar as fantasy prefigures and thereby frames one's choice of love object, fantasy can be said to provide the imaginative perception upon which depend love and identity. As an example, Dorian's captivated gaze before his portrait reflects one destiny of fantasy, but the novel provides us other forms of homoerotic desire and thus other fantasies and readerly perceptions, and it is this complexity of erotic investment that is lost in the critical readings that seek to historicize the novel, either through the teleologies of periodization or by narrating the development of gay male identity as a social type.

A commonplace notion of fantasy limits the psychic practice to a pleasurable and imaginative triumph over reality. Evoking such escapism, Teresa Brennan defines the term: "fantasy, in psychoanalytic thinking, is a mental activity that allows us to alter an unpleasant reality by making it into something more pleasurable."[25] While Brennan's formulation mistakenly attributes the commonplace notion to psychoanalysis, pleasure certainly exacts its due in fantasy; it takes many forms and has a far more complex relation to reality than wish fulfillment would suggest. The fictional quality of fantasy has little to do with avoidance of reality dictated by wish fulfillment and much more to do with the complex defensive mechanisms that enable prohibited feelings, acts, objects, and desires to be represented in the cultivation of wishes. These imaginary scenarios also represent the subject or, rather, they represent the subject in the context not of intentional aim or "something more pleasurable" but of desire itself where both the subject and his desire are articulated throughout the representations or scenarios of fantasy. Within fantasy, the subject "does have a part to play," for the imaginary sequences or scripts—not narratives, which would be already too responsible to cause and effect, consistency, and development of some kind—assign roles and perform actions that are, in themselves, the culmination of a subject's desire. Fantasy is as necessary for the creation or cultivation of subjectivity as it is for the satisfaction of desire; more to the point, the articulations of the subject in fantasy prefigure desire and determine the appearance and possibility of satisfaction. Originally derived from need, a wish is "fulfilled through the hallucinatory reproduction of the perceptions which have become the signs of this satisfaction" (*LP*, 482). A world dispossessed of such representations is a world emptied of desire by trauma or some other devastation akin to the maladies that Kristeva explores through the themes of abjection, revolt, melancholia and the borderliner; absolute dispossession that interrupts the capacity to generate the sign condemns the subject to an objectless world without desire and, equally, without the possibility of satisfaction because "the search for the object in the real world is entirely governed by this relationship with signs" (*LP*, 482).

Tracking Wilde's progress from fama to infamy, it is important to note that his ranting prison letter does not respond to social dispossession by relinquishing desire and its signs, by going silent; rather, like the literature of abjection, *De Profundis* sublimates dispossession in a form of writing that mediates between high art and low invective.[26] When Wilde confronts betrayal and imprisonment with fantasy and writing, he attempts to revive himself and to repeal subjection by resurrecting desire in the sign and according to his practice before imprisonment. The continuity, then, between *The Picture of Dorian Gray* and *De Profundis* lies in Wilde's practice of writing through, rather than working through, a particular kind of fantasy, one that could be recognized in the kinship of reading. *De Profundis* is a text of breakdown and ranting excess that cannot fulfill its own program; it promises to restore him to himself and pursues aesthetic strategies consistent with life before imprisonment; and yet, the conditions of social death and symbolic foreclosure that lend *De Profundis* its affective powers also prevent that lyrical work of sublimation from attaining its goal. And this is where the theory that Wilde's texts negotiate around the censorship of the day through indirection and open secrecy seems least convincing; explicit prohibition or implicit and heavy silence, censorship is always censorship of signs. One does not get around the fact that the satisfaction promised and achieved in *The Picture of Dorian Gray* or the stage plays is a satisfaction of the sign.

In his archival meditation on London's nineteenth-century gay subculture, Neil Bartlett pays attention to the fact that Wilde was engaged in the creation of a culture and a language of gay male desire; he observes as well that this culture was already underway by the time of Wilde's first forays into public celebrity, and citing the "Bow Street scandal" of 1870, which involved the arrest of two transsexual actresses, Stella Boulton and Fanny Park, who made a habit of living and appearing in public as women, Bartlett debunks the notion that queer life was in any simple sense invisible or absent.[27] Stella and Fanny become emblematic of the subcultural industry that produced a local queer argot (polari), social spaces (theaters and brothels), literature, an archive of letters and newspaper reports, memoirs, and pornography, all of which circulated through degrees of publicness. For Bartlett these forms are divided between those spoken in code to pass undetected in a hostile environment of gay male invisibility, and those whose modes of speaking, however explicit they may appear to a twentieth-century perspective and however shrill their attempt to draw notice in the nineteenth century, are so utterly foreclosed that they cannot appear as such; rather, these latter forms are met with a "heavy silence" and cultural denial. Wilde falls definitively, for Bartlett, into the first category of the uses of secrecy, where the public performative force of the green carnation and its social uses pales to a tepid nothingness when judged against the revolutionary, or, at the very least, more inclusive, possibilities of polari.[28] This narrative is in tension with other tendencies of his meditations on Wilde, but if we dwell on this aspect of Bartlett's reading, it is to note that "code" and invisibility are terms that stress the power of the censor and the story of secrecy at the expense of understanding how literary fantasy might signal, enliven, arouse, spark, and, indeed, influence desire through its cultivation of signs. Nor would Bartlett disagree; however, his own ambivalence about Wilde's elitism, evident in his assertion that one must be cultivated to read eros in Wilde's fiction, drives his reproach that Wilde, in a sense, left nothing for a specifically gay male posterity and that he did not aim to build a foundation of a gay male culture.[29]

There is some truth to this charge; certainly, Wilde's plan to publish *De Profundis* at fifty years' remove and to clear his name does little refute it. Wilde, like the rest of the gay male subculture in London in the 1890s, is far more interested in his own present than in founding a people. And what he does with that present is to establish the terms of a queer kinship that would be reproduced through reading, and thus through the very "elite" culture that Bartlett reproaches as a class obstacle. All of which is to say that the aims and rhetorical maneuvers of *De Profundis* can become invisible to a reader unwilling to attend to the stakes of fantasy and writing in Wilde's previous work, whether this attention comes in the form of a critical discourse or a passionate reading. Hysterical rambling and blame are certainly hallmarks of the letter; so is a highly developed ethos of reading and writing, which signifies participation in a homoerotic cultural industry of the sign that extends, in Wilde's perspective, over centuries and doubtless into a future. Destining his letter to a public both in the offing and underground, Wilde prepares to redress judgment and shame by addressing himself to any of many futures, including the near future readings by friends to whom he claims not to defend his actions but to explain them. In this *De Profundis* shares the kaleidoscopic address characteristic of C. L. R. James's prison rant and, as we shall see in the next chapter, Jane Bowles's incessant letters always promising that she was working despite her unrelenting writer's block. Promises impossible to keep are one feature native to all our rants; in Wilde's case the conditions of social shaming are so overwhelming, as we shall see, that no act of literary sublimation—despite all his faith in the aesthetic—could overcome the real and embodied circumstances of writing.

SEDUCTION'S INFLUENCE

Influence, then, initiates a series of admiring imitations, and on the authority of this repeatable, contagious model an origin that never was is abandoned in favor of seriality itself. A complex transferential theory of fantasy emerges in the discourse on influence and shares with psychoanalytic notions of fantasy both the psychic coding of social norms and the individual response, repression, and expression of desire effected through its unconscious transmission. Influence reveals the effect of one upon another ad infinitum, and in such a series, influence becomes the authorizing fantasy about one's homosexual origins. The circularity of the figure operates to seduce one's sexuality into being and to grant that initiation the status of an origin felt to be lacking and certainly unintelligible within the limited framing of normative causal relations. It takes the punitive force of a peer of the realm, of a Father, to intervene and isolate a singular figure as a scapegoat, martyr, or originary bad influence. In offering up Dorian's initiation into sex as a fantasy of origin, *The Picture of Dorian Gray* gives us two views of influence as desire. One corresponds to a pederastic model of initiation and the other to a form of mediation through reading or imitating the style of a work of art.

> Have you really a very bad influence, Lord Henry. As bad as Basil says?
> There is no such thing as a good influence, Mr. Gray.... Because to influence a person is to give him one's own soul. He does not think his natural thoughts, or burn with his natural passions. His virtues are not real to him. His sins, if there are such things as sins, are borrowed.[30]

In accordance with this shamed notion of influence, Basil protests, "I did not want any external influence in my life," and sinks his feeling for Dorian into the surface of paint; thus Basil models for a version of repression. Lord Henry, at the other extreme, is inflamed by the potent atmosphere of their unstated feelings and resolves to put himself between Basil and Dorian, to become the consummate influencer.

The dangerous sway of art and literature sets in motion a sympathetic mimetism, one that Lord Henry later denounces as mere imagination when Dorian reproaches him for passing on the "poisonous book" that so influences him.

"Yes; there had been things in his boyhood that he had not understood. He understood them now."[31] What Dorian imagines he now knows about himself has come to him through listening but only half understanding Lord Henry. "He was dimly conscious that entirely fresh influences were at work within him. Yet they seemed to him to have come really from himself."[32] The scene is Basil's studio. Henry has come to watch Dorian sit for a portrait, and though Basil is uneasy at the prospect, he buries his jealous foreboding under a preoccupation with painting while Henry successfully seduces the boy. Dorian's seduction comes in and through this statement: "We are punished for our refusals. Every impulse that we strive to strangle broods in the mind, and poisons us. . . . The only way to get rid of a temptation is to yield to it. Resist it, and your soul grows sick with longing for the things it has forbidden to itself, with desire for what its monstrous laws have made monstrous and unlawful."[33] Self-hindering, self-mutilating laws of the soul are the general rule for Henry, as his ethos of individualism cannot admit the force of a socially inscribed set of taboos. This emphasis on individual responsibility for one's own renunciations explains the effect his words have on Dorian. The trauma of Henry's speech lies in the blame he lays at the feet of the individual. Dorian is made to wonder, "Why had it been left to a stranger to reveal him to himself? . . . And yet, what was there to be afraid of? He was not a schoolboy or a girl." Though the scene clearly shows an initiation and a transmission of self-knowledge, that "knowledge" comes in the form of a recoil away from the possibility of self-mutilation and a sickness seeded in the body by the soul. "There was a look of fear in his eyes, such as people have when they are suddenly awakened." Awakened by a trauma, Dorian searches for some coherent expression of his emotion, but, before he can sum up the feeling, Henry returns to his disturbing tirade. "There is such a little time your youth will last—such a little time. . . . Our limbs fail, our senses rot. We degenerate into hideous puppets, haunted by the memory of the passions of which we were too much afraid, and the exquisite temptations that we had not the courage to yield to. Youth! Youth! There is absolutely nothing in the world but youth!"[34]

At this point in the scene, Dorian is rendered listless and nearly mute. He returns to his position on the platform while Basil, oblivious to the violent initiation that has just taken place, finishes the portrait. Painting and oratory are made equivalent across the mute and statue-like body of an enigmatic subject, not yet himself. This moment of suspension in the narrative allows the three principals to resume their paradigmatic roles in the fantasy's didactic thematics of the gaze. All eyes on Dorian, now blind with introspection, Basil sees only a formal beauty; Henry perceives only an opportunity to exercise his considerable powers of seduction. The tableau presents us with an allegory of Wilde's own identity refracted through three partial and blinkered views, but what seems to be organizing the scene's progress toward its ultimate conclusion in Dorian's diabolical wish is a relation to enigmatic origins.

This becomes clearer as the tension mounts toward its melodramatic release. Dorian approaches the finished painting in a series of bodily postures emblematic of the deviations toward the origin, which characterize primal fantasy. "Dorian made no answer, but passed listlessly in front of his picture, and turned towards it. When he saw it he drew back." Passing, turning toward, and recoiling detour around the self as around a first instance that cannot be reached. The fantasy of origin arises because its cause cannot be named, and into the blank space of that enigma the fantasy proposes its own solution to the question of its being. When that question is denied the terms of its own statement, for instance, when the name of desire falls under the sign of a social foreclosure, the origin of one's erotic investments, or so Wilde's fable suggests, takes on a figural intensity that redoubles the forces of fantasy.

> A look of joy came into his eyes, as if he had recognized himself for the first time . . . the sense of his own beauty came on him like a revelation. He had never felt it before. . . . Then had come Lord Henry Wotton with his strange panegyric on youth, his terrible warning of its brevity. That had stirred him at the time, and now, as he stood gazing at the shadow of his own loveliness, the full reality of the description flashed across him. Yes, there would be a day when his face would be wrinkled and wizen, his eyes dim and colourless, the grace of his figure broken and deformed. . . . The life that was to make his soul would mar his body. He would become dreadful, hideous, and uncouth. . . . As he thought of it, a sharp pain struck through him like a knife, and made each delicate fibre of his nature quiver.[35]

The quick passage from recognition to revelation to horror is a direct result of Henry's prattle about youth and the self-mutilating individual. On the basis of this seduction via a trauma, which is here dramatized as an "implantation," Dorian cannot assume his image as his own.[36] The scene enacts the principle that the "fantasy of implantation is the implantation of fantasy." He can only receive it already fractured by the desire of another, and so the fantasy, which tells the story of how he comes to desire at all, becomes the ground of an angry "self-relation."

That a book, a painting, or even a fresh aesthetic approach is capable of setting up a narcissistic economy of one, a self-relation in which dynamic contacts are internalized as static interior positions, is exemplified in Henry's account of his exciting encounter with Basil and Dorian. Henry relishes the future of his influence over Dorian; it is openly figured as a conquest, an appropriative desire, a seduction, and a violation. It is also aestheticized as:

> The new manner in art, the fresh mode of looking at life, suggested so strangely by the merely visible presence of one who was unconscious of it all; the silent spirit that dwelt in dim woodland, and walked unseen in open field, suddenly showing herself Dryad-like and not afraid, because in his soul who sought for her there had been wakened that wonderful vision to which alone are wonderful things revealed; the mere shapes and patterns of things becoming, as it were, refined, and gaining a kind of symbolical value, as though they were themselves patterns of some other and more perfect form whose shadow they made real: how strange it all was!

Through the extravagance of metaphor Dorian has become "Dryad-like," his "white purity of boyhood" translated through the aestheticizing fantasy into a "her." The alibi of the feminine pronoun camouflages the transformation of Henry's desire to be first between and then before a series of men. That he comprehends a clear choice between kinds of fascination in no way diminishes the nature of each possible choice as distinctly different from a love of the Same: youth or Art, this is the choice. Henry's musings begin to conflate Dorian's beauty "such as old Greek marbles kept for us" with Basil himself, who is here likened to "Plato, that artist in thought, who had first analyzed it," yet this conflation establishes a desire confounding both the inversion and the pederastic model of male/male erotics. These seemingly incompatible condensations are strung out at the end of the passionate reverie in a way that, without resolving conflictual modalities of desire, resolves Lord Henry to desire. "Yes; he would try to be to Dorian Gray what, without knowing it, the lad was to the painter who had fashioned the wonderful portrait. He would seek to dominate him—had already, indeed, half done so. *He would make that wonderful spirit his own.*"

Seriality and sameness collapse here, and with them the boundedness of mentoring and inversion. To turn the "heterosexuality" of pederastic mentorship into a series of mirrored desires is to reinscribe difference squarely within the alleged sameness of homosexual narcissism. He would make that queer spirit his own; he would devour, seduce, dominate, interiorize. At this moment when the repeated strangenesses are undeniably queer, hetero and homo are epistemologically equivocal. The internalization at work in this reverie would seem to belie the kind of literalism called forth in a "project of constructing the male figure," to cite Sedgwick again. To read for that construction demands that the text cease to elaborate the confusions and contradictions of a path to an identity in desire.

"As for being poisoned by a book, there is no such thing as that. Art has no influence upon action. It annihilates the desire to act. It is superbly sterile" (*PDG*, 181). The reproductive force of an influence upon action disappears when the subtle effects of passionate reading intervene; it is no stretch to link the bad, soul-killing influence of Lord Henry's so disclosive speech during the session in Basil's studio with this sterility. To see an aesthetic argument for the craftedness and against the naturalness of a book is only to restate the antimimetic manifesto that Wilde wrote as a preface to the book edition of the serialized story, but to find an aesthetic argument offered in the idiom of an ancient condemnation of homosexuality is to find that aestheticism braided up with a nineteenth-century idiom of sexual prohibition. It aestheticizes what had previously been pathological. This overcoding cannot be thought without the inmixing of different registers of practice and metaphor; the moral here lies in a reproach against the kind of reading and being that would find the sublime in sterility and, equally, in the limitation of desire to a self-serving oedipalism.

If Dorian is fascinated by the development of his own self-fashioning, and if the changes registered—not interpreted, but recorded—on the painting's surface spur him to more cruelties, Dorian's actions become a kind of poesis, which finds its sublimative power on the canvas. His narcissistic entrapment turns his very actions in the world into a work of sublimation. If a species of same-sex desire seeking not expression but displacement upward and outward is being linked to the more prosaic sublimations that art, society, and religion set up ready-made for the mutilated and self-hindering citizen, does it not become impossible to sieve out the good from the bad influence, the dull mimetism from the exciting homosexuality? The text braids these threads together because they prohibitively shape one another and lead to their own inextricability. Which is not to say that Wilde imagines same-sex relations to be inherently and melancholically narcissistic, but rather that he imagines the resentful avant-gardism of the tired if tirelessly confounding cry of *l'art pour l'art* to be a kind of psychological, aesthetic, and thus social atrophism.

In the crescendo of *History of Sexuality,* Foucault anticipates his critics' claim that he has sublimed sex from the scene of sexuality and replaced it with a series of ephemeral effects—not organs and functions, but organs of regulation and functions of power. To this delegitimating reproach he responds:

> Far from the body having to be effaced, what is needed is to make it visible through an analysis in which the biological and the historical are not consecutive to one another, as in the evolutionism of the first sociologists, but are bound together in an increasingly complex fashion in accordance with the development of the modern technologies of power that take life as their objective.[37]

This incitement to visibility echoes Wilde in important ways and sets up in Dorian Gray a conflictual exchange between the generality and the specificity of the salient image: body to image, face to face, the generality of a moral against the specificity of a character, or again the generality of the fantasy against the specificity of its embodiments. Wilde offers a body encrusted with pleasures, one that assumes mystery, rarity, and value with its hardy and melancholic narcissism. What some condemn as mere consumerism is in Wilde the license to manipulate, resignify, and forge communities of pleasure under the sign of ever-mobile objects. Where Foucault calls for the visibility of a body constructed, disciplined, and confessed, Wilde fixes the narrative gaze on a body both sublimed and frozen in a narcissism that is the product of influence, sublimation, and an erotic mimetology, leaving no room for a genuinely transformative template of homosexual desiring. Wilde both demonstrates the suffocating binding of the deployment of sexuality and suggests that what the triple bargain of Basil, Dorian, and Henry allows for is mere repetition of trivial sublations. What it utterly precludes is a genuinely pederastic mentoring of desire that could provide a lineage and a history; Henry's inseminating speech couples with Basil's brooding embodiment to produce in Dorian as in a child a self-knowledge already woven through by prohibition and disclosure, desire and desire's deflection, intense sensation and the secrecy of that intensification.

> It is apparent that the deployment of sexuality, with its different strategies, was what established this notion of "sex"; and in the four major forms of hysteria, onanism, fetishism and interrupted coition, it showed this sex to be governed by the interplay of whole and part, principle and lack, absence and presence, excess and deficiency.[38]

Accordingly, the riveting scene of Dorian's simultaneous birth as picture and self-disclosure as homosexual maps the double negation by which homosexuality is posited as both unnatural and narcissistic, excessive and deficient. The failure of the novel is its inability to distinguish between the productive incitements to visibility and its own making visible those incitements, and thus we are given the explosive scene of Dorian's birth, epiphany of self-disclosure from the outside and his jubilant assumption of his new imago. Is Wilde making the claim against repression only to undermine this intervention by giving us a version of Dorian unable to understand the code of homosexuality nested in narcissism? Is Dorian's damnation caused by an inability to negotiate the sublimations of aestheticism's attitude and, then, to wield those codes as the language of his sexuality?

Prefiguring the Foucauldian insight that resistance arises when power takes the body as its object, Freud's essay "On Narcissism" offers some possibilities for thinking through the ways that the psychic strategy of narcissism usurps or resists repression. Known as the metapsychological paper chiefly responsible for theorizing the internalization of social norms in the form of idealization and for illustrating the norm through the negative foil of pathology, the essay demystifies the allure of physical beauty and the vanity it occasions, as yet another form of subjection. Narcissistic "women have the greatest fascination for men, not only for aesthetic reasons, since as a rule they are the most beautiful, but also because of certain interesting psychological constellations."[39] The figure of the narcissistic woman looks astonishingly like Dorian himself, for whom beauty and self-sufficiency also "compensate [him] for the social restrictions upon [his] object-choice." Freud's insight into the power of self-sufficiency is little compensation for the fact that this potential, like that of anorexia or other forms of hysteria, is a fundamentally painful, self-destructive one. Nevertheless, like the "nonsense" of aestheticism's narcissism, self-absorption offends, excludes, demands, and inflames the exterior gaze. "It is as if we envied them their power of retaining a blissful state of mind—an unassailable libido-position." Curiously, Freud's essay, devoted to the double task of analyzing the abjectly feminine and the narcissistically homosexual, closely repeats the plot of Dorian's family romance, and through an oblique mapping of interconnections between these two forms of stubborn resistance, establishes a social affinity in restricted object-choice. The unassailably feminine and the homosexual converge at the point of their "self-sufficiency." From the metapsychological perspective, narcissism is utterly compatible with the inversion model of male/male desire, which again suggests that the alibi of homosexual similitude disappears when Beauty and self-absorption become the mark of difference. Freud's homology between male and female enabled by a shared resistance to a social limit is itself a cultural reading that complicates the narrative of "homo"-sexual, both in the epistemologies of queer theory and in the nineteenth-century deployment of sexuality. If the inversion model came to be essential, as Sedgwick claims, for conceptualizations of homosexual desire from the center of normative deployments of sexuality and ultimately contributed to the cultural construction of gay male desire, *Dorian Gray*, in its consistent confusion of these neat epistemologies, explores the psychology of a desire for the self born of a social limit, and does so through the cultural availability of cross-gender identification to do violence to the myth of Narcissus.[40] The novel's tactics, then, reinforce our observation that the social inscription of illegibility need not be lived as a ban on expression, but rather that *the foreclosed inscription of dissident sexualities and racialized identities resists social illegibility by elaborating a literary theory of primitive origins.*

Following upon this cross-gender homology, we might ask what the novel aims at by complicating the scene of Dorian's sexual origins with a family romance so grudgingly given. Dorian's mother fell recklessly in love with a young soldier of no means and eloped with him, only to be widowed a few months later by an "adventurer" hired by her own father. Coupled to Dorian's thwarted homosexual self is his mother's passion, and this is no incidental detail, for it is his mother's face that looks back at him in the mirror. Her beauty lives on in him and haunts the scene of initiation we witness in Basil's studio. If Dorian's self-disclosure amounts to an identification with the face of his dead mother, would this not indicate a form of inversion creeping up precisely at the site of the new definitional performance of homo/same/self? If we read Dorian's epiphany as a panicked flight from seduction by another more worldly man, that is, a flight from the classicism of pederastic pleasures, must this mean that his wish for eternal beauty and the contract it enacts should be read only as a self-relation, a self-relation navigated through the passage from homo to same? The scene, so loudly suggesting initiation, admits of more than one destinal plot and more than one site of identification.

Is this braiding of the maternal with the homosexual merely another oedipal strategy of resistance, this time through identification with the position and psychic tactics of the mother? Certainly, the novel proposes the theme of impossible identification as an explanation for Dorian's self-sufficiency. His "sins" allow the preservation of an identification with the effaced and rumerous maternal figure: her beauty, passion, scorn, her taste in uniforms, even her "voiceless agony." The split performed by his wish, always a double wish for another man and for himself, provides the fantastic space or scenario in which to act out a projective blame. This is one reason Dorian's image judges him so harshly: the wish for Basil/Henry/himself, threatened with repression, has been defended by being sublated into that "ruthless watching function," the ego ideal. One cannot be certain that the interiorized other, here projected as the portrait's judgment and its beauty, is not itself the product of a doubled identification with the mother's face, which is his own, the grandfather's incestuous incarceration of her and the grandfather's murder of the father. This is a family romance that reintroduces the inescapability of the feminine to strategies of self-imagining that would contain homosexuality within narcissistic sameness. At every turn the feminine reappears within the modalities that try to eradicate it, while narcissism and inversion reemerge within the very elaborations seeking to distinguish them.

By Freud's account self-preservation sexualized becomes narcissism, thus making narcissism an erotic reinvestment of material at risk of total repression or partial sublimation; however, a reading of Wilde requires us to restate the question of narcissism as a distinction between sublimation thought as the work of poesis and idealization as a kind of "ready-made object." Freud states that the formation of an ideal by which one measures oneself is the "condition of repression," a repression proceeding from the ego rather than an exterior oppressive force—which is to say that the efficacy of a social norm depends upon the internal production of consistent effects of measurement and shame from within the individual ego.[41] The ideal beauty Dorian possesses but Basil constructs for him on the model of his mother's haunting image sets in motion a series of objects full of the positivity conferred by a standard. Ideals mobilize personifications and lock desire into desexualized, sterile replication, whereas sublimations tend to preserve repetition as the creative energy behind self-invention. Freud further refines a theory of idealization by contrasting it with sublimation, which

> is a process that concerns the object-libido and consists in the instinct's directing itself towards an aim other than, and remote from that of sexual gratification; in this process the accent falls upon the deflection from the sexual aim. Idealization is a process that concerns the object; by it that object . . . is aggrandized and exalted in the mind. . . . Sublimation is a process that concerns the instinct and idealization, one that concerns the object.[42]

In the formation of ego ideals the accent falls on exchange; in response to the "criticism of others" one exchanges one's primary narcissism and the gratifications of self-absorption for an external ideal now internalized. "That which he projects ahead of him as his ideal is merely his substitute for the lost narcissism of his childhood." Precipitating into the future what was left behind, this is a near absolute exchange, for the price of idealization is in fact repression of other possible objects and the limitation of the standard by which one's actions are measured to a standard of one. Sublimation offers a shiftier promise of salvaging the drive supporting the object-libido and can allow desire to conform to the demands of egoical drives, idealizations, and repressions without absolute renunciation of the drive or its aim. Sublimative translation may be fully populated by objects, persons, figures, and ornament, but the force of such deployment lies in the syntactic possibility of fantasy's desubjectivating power. Idealization secures an origin of mimetic self-relation, whereas sublimation leads to an interminable series, one susceptible of resexualization. This may be an intolerable sequence, but it has the virtue of resurrecting desire for another object. Within the novel's staging of this difference, Basil suffocates desire in a sublimation, yet he preserves it for another use, leading to an open declaration of love that then prompts Dorian to murder. Dorian, on the other hand, cannot access his object outside of a mimetic relay of thwarted objects. If Basil and Dorian become extremist emblems of these two possibilities, didactic examples of how not to love, it must be obvious that they in no way repeat a drive for abstraction. The oxymoronic expression of Sedgwick's theory, that there could be a figure of abstraction, reflects all too neatly the impossibility of evacuating the homo or the hetero, the sexual or the nonsexual from the frontier that divides them. In this way, her notion of abstraction or antifiguration becomes another version of the repressive hypothesis that Foucault has taught us to question.

That the splitting off of idealization from sublimation, a splitting that resembles a modernist intuition of displacement—what Sedgwick would like to call abstraction—reflects a management of homosexual desire is undeniable. Freud makes conscience and the production of art dependent on the repudiation of homosexual desire and consistently delimits same-sex desiring to an absolute form of mimicry: "same genitalia."[43] Thus homosexuality comes forth in the psychoanalytic elaboration as a stunted juvenilism whose repudiation creates the necessary self-berating ground of civil society. What this maps is the poisonous contract of homosociality and its dependence on panicked self-censoring. The strength of the double bind is evident in the anxiety possible on either side of erotic bondage: hetero and homo alike share in the ample production of shame, which the novel literalizes as "a power . . . watching, discovering and criticizing all our intentions" that "does really exist; indeed, it exists with every one of us in normal life." It really does exist, but it is locked in Dorian's nursery; it judges him from the outside as if knowing all from the inside. This is no interiorized emblem but an exterior embodiment expressed in fantasy, and as such, it repeats before the fact a main tenet of Freudian theory; namely, that "the institution of conscience [is] at bottom an embodiment." In its terrible materiality the painting expresses and extends the theory of panicked sociality that Lord Henry explains so seductively to Dorian in their first meeting. "People are afraid of themselves nowadays. They have forgotten the highest of all duties, the duty that one owes to oneself. . . . The bravest man amongst us is afraid of himself. The mutilation of the savage has its tragic survival in the self-denial that mars our lives" (*PDG*, 17). To read only for the moral—be it the moral that condemns Dorian or the one that celebrates representation—requires that we sacrifice the insights of Dorian's condition; this is an especially risky reading practice when those insights contain the autotelic kernel of the novel and, indeed, of Wilde's living custom.

The Picture of Dorian Gray could be viewed as a fantasy of a particular subject, whose only recourse against desire's complete repression is defensive imagination. His interior landscape has been projected outward and literalized as a persecutory tableau, which develops over time and according to the law of implacable punishment. The stasis of the tableau, the aura of doom surrounding Dorian's fate, these act as warnings to us to manage our identifications well in this psychologized landscape that permits the statement of the prohibition on homosexuality in terms that present but do not authorize or legislate its law as Law. Thus the homosexual content and the struggle between different conceptions of a homosexual self are preserved and legibly set in motion. The liberties of fiction are amplified by the uses of fantasy, which cracks open the absolute closure of repression such that the unheard of, the inaudible, the unspeakable become the partially visible and the legible. "Fantasy is also the locus of defensive operations. . . . Such defenses are themselves inseparably bound up with the primary function of fantasy, namely the *mise-en-scene* of desire—a *mise-en-scene* in which what is prohibited is always present in the actual formation of the wish."[44] Laplanche and Pontalis claim that one's subject and object are preserved in the fantasy's syntax as each is dispersed or disseminated, both temporally and spatially, in the deployment of imagined scenarios. In this way fantasy becomes the sublimated support for a desire otherwise submerged by the force of repression. The subject, the "one" of this narcissistic exchange, is figured

> caught up himself in the sequence of images. He forms no representation of the desired object, but is himself represented as participating in the scene although, in the earliest forms of fantasy, he cannot be assigned any fixed place in it (hence the danger, in treatment, of the interpretations which claim to do so). As a result, the subject, although always present in the fantasy, may be so in a desubjectivized form, that is to say, in the very syntax of the sequence in question. On the other hand, to the extent that desire is not purely an upsurge of the drives, but is articulated into the fantasy, the latter is a favoured spot for the most primitive defensive reactions, such as turning against oneself.[45]

Taking this psychoanalytic understanding of Wilde's poetics as axiomatic, how are we to situate this late nineteenth-century poetic practice within the historical development of the modern subject of sexuality? Wildean sublimation put to dynamic uses looks very much like Foucault's fourth rule of the deployment of sexuality, "the rule of the tactical polyvalence of discourses," where discourse "transmits and produces power; it reinforces it, but also undermines and exposes it, renders it fragile and makes it possible to thwart it."[46] As an illustration of this double possibility to transmit but also to undo power, Foucault offers us the law's "reticence" and tolerance of sexual diversity in the eighteenth-century expression of sexual taboo, a tolerance that gave way under the pressure of the deployment of sexuality to increasing state control of sex; this deployment is also the chance for the homosexual community to come into public being, to speak in the discourse of the law using its terms no longer under cover of secrecy, and he notes that the terms newly taken are the very terms of the normalizing and punitive discourse. Such resignification allows for the translation of one's own need, desire, and self-description into a poisonous idiom and thence the infiltration of that nexus of power/knowledge with newly articulated, previously voiceless or marginally visible potentialities. The clear-cutting work of desublimations evident in Wilde's fable is made possible only at the price of an initial, and even collaborative, sublimation. Viewed from this perspective, diffusion and deflection are the necessary first moves in a genuinely political intervention on the norm. Without this capacity to speak the poisonous idiom or translate one's desires into the available terms of description, none of the voices foreclosed by normativity could ever be heard. Ranting, as we shall see in the discussion of *De Profundis* below, does not invent its language *ex nihilo* but speaks in the dominant discourse a new form of discord. This jarring and discordant speech arises as a surprising outburst or break with the expected terms of debate.

The ability of sublimative fantasy to generate signs for the uses of desublimation is most strikingly portrayed in the eleventh chapter of *Dorian Gray* under the alibi of a novel modeled on Huysmans's *A Rebours*. "For years Dorian Gray could not free himself from the influence of this book."[47] A scientific desire to catalogue his degeneration habitually seizes Dorian during his contemplations of the portrait; this is a desire cultivated by intensive rereading of Huysmans, by an extravagance of self-formation in the image of one who can tolerate with self-possession "the changing fancies of a nature over which he seemed, at times, to have almost entirely lost control. The hero . . . became to him a kind of prefiguring type of himself." Before the portrait Dorian exhibits all the signifying power of a bourgeois inventory or medical examination of deviance, but with the important difference that measurement and taxonomy are labors of love, a sickly displaced erotics of recording.

> He grew more and more enamored of his own beauty, more and more interested in the corruption of his own soul. He would examine with minute care, and sometimes with a monstrous and terrible delight, the hideous lines that seared the wrinkling forehead, or crawled around the heavy sensual mouth, wondering sometimes which were the most horrible, the signs of sin or the signs of age.[48]

What this betrays is an intensification of the body and the knowing apparatus; Dorian's self-contemplations are increasingly detailed, inquisitive, comparative, and knowing and lead to an appetite for power.

> In his inmost heart he desired to be something more than a mere *arbiter elegantiarum,* to be consulted on the wearing of a jewel, or the knotting of a necktie, or the conduct of a cane. He sought to elaborate some

new scheme of life that would have its reasoned philosophy and its ordered principles, and find in the spiritualizing of the senses its highest realization.[49]

From one displacement to another, Dorian desires to be more than a typification of sublimative talents, desires to be more than a model; he schemes to invent a system capable of inciting the senses and spiritualizing them at once. Incitements to ideality are not the "bodies and pleasures" that Foucault urges us to make visible; nevertheless, Dorian's confusion of form and ideality sets in motion a series of pursuits in the mode of sublative substitution that lead him inexorably back to bodies, pleasures, and things. That this circuit is utterly "illogical" or nonsensical viewed through the lens of a normativity capable of seeing sexuality only in nonallegorical deployments is not proof against Dorian's functioning as an arbiter of pleasure to an entire class of young aesthetes. That invisibility or diffusion is the condition of its desirability; Dorian offers a paradox of desire and identification insofar as he models for the glamorous mobility, artificiality, and transformability of the soul. His figure can become a site of erotic investment in change itself because the moralizing doom surrounding him incoherently suggests both identification with and distance from his posturing. This incoherence mimics the excess Foucault isolates at the heart of sexuality's deployment.

SURVIVING SCENES

> It is the confession, not the priest, that gives us absolution.
>
> Oscar Wilde, *The Picture of Dorian Gray*

In 1895 Oscar Wilde was sentenced under the Criminal Law Amendment Act to two years hard labor, the maximum sentence for the commission of consensual acts of "gross indecency" with another man. In the final months of his sentence and in a letter of 120 pages, intended for publication after his death, he undertook to convey his experience to Lord Alfred Douglas, his lover and son of the Marquess of Queensberry, who pursued Wilde to prison. *De Profundis,* written for a private reading yet intended for publication, is a trenchant indictment of English civil society and the institution of the father. Using an explicit rhetoric of race, Wilde likens English filial relations to that of Darwin's horde and launches a substantial critique of paternity in terms very like those of Freud's *Totem and Taboo*. The analysis of paternity and filiation spills over into a full-blown critique of modernity as a loss of the tragic function. In Wilde's terms, this amounts to a loss of the ability to identify with the other through the mediation of tragic empathy; in short, *De Profundis* announces the loss of loss.

Wilde's text presents its argument through a series of scenes that require reading to follow two distinct yet converging trains of thought. One track of this reading obliges us to situate his use of "race" within a psychoanalytic understanding of the phantasmatic scene, while the second track traces the affinities between Wilde's experience of the modern and Freud's analysis of modernity in the myth of patricidal sacrifice. Through this second reading modernity emerges as a drama of the violent inscription of national character. To counter such an inscription and its dependence upon a racial narrative, Wilde proposes an ideal model of a new kinship in amorous links of affiliation between gay men and founded upon a practice of shared reading. This imagined community is rooted in the letter by a resignification of the exemplary figure of sacrifice, Christ, and a Hellenic model of male friendship.

The letter's most significant meditations on kinship collapse the division between a private tragedy and a public scandal. In light of this tendency of the prose, it is essential to recall the statist nature of Wilde's abjection from the social sphere. Previous to the trials and even during them, Wilde is *the* important figure of the London literary scene. The Wilde trials take place mere months after the second Home Rule debate resulted in continued colonial occupation of Ireland, and the trials have been read as an effort to drive home that point. More palpable are the juridical effects of his imprisonment. His wife is obliged to divorce him. His sons no longer bear his name but that of a maternal relation. All his property, including his library and literary papers, are auctioned off by order of the bankruptcy court. He can never again profit from the sale of his own art. Wilde's only links of filiation are now determined through the ritual and legal subjection of imprisonment, and it is one task of *De Profundis* to forge new links and to relocate the source of belonging in the space of writing and reading.

The state set him to work breaking stones and picking oakum. For months Wilde spent his days prying apart fibers from tightly braided old ropes for recycling as stuffing in naval ship seams. This is hard labor, which tears the fingers, shredding them as they shred the tarry rope. It is tempting to find in this labor an emblem of the work of unworking that produces the disciplinary subject. The letter, too, takes its form from this emblematic shredding; it attempts to reweave its author but succeeds only in unraveling itself. Ironically, Wilde endeavors to make even humiliation yet another occasion for heroic sublimation.

In the opening chapter of *Discipline and Punish,* Foucault warns us not to consider the soul merely "an illusion, or an ideological effect. On the contrary, it exists, it has a reality, it is produced permanently around, on, within the body by the functioning of a power that is exercised on those punished."[50] Oakum picking is one element in the diverse network of this exercise. Confession is another axis of soul making. In *De Profundis* Wilde claims to find his soul after a series of humiliations, which teach him humility. The single most traumatic scenario he relates involves a public exposure at a train station, where he is held in chains and displayed to a jeering crowd. In response to this and other features of a total humiliation, Wilde engages a double strategy of reinscription. He attempts to project his humiliation outward through the letter onto the lover and by means of that gesture, to manically overcome the discipline to which he is subject. The first move of this procedure involves a peculiar trope of conversion.

THE QUEER CHRIST

Addressing Douglas for the first time in two years, Wilde begins by remarking the silence of his lover during which "my life had all the while been a real Symphony of Sorrow, passing through its rhythmically-linked movements to its certain resolution, with that inevitableness that in Art characterizes the treatment of every great theme."[51] Pain yields memory, and for Wilde only pain can mark the passage of time into discrete movements, can give time to life that otherwise consumes itself in a unity. "Had our life together been as the world fancied it to be, one simply of pleasure, profligacy and laughter, I would not be able to recall a single passage in it" (*DP,* 54). Suffering initiates Wilde into memory, and, more, it carries him through the sorrows of public shame and incarceration by phrasing his experience such that its singularity and its lesson are not obscured. *De Profundis*—what Wilde had preferred to call "Epistola: In Carcere et Vinculis"[52]—claims itself a confession and an entreaty in the form of a "terrible letter." The letter seeks not only to confess its author but also to purge its addressee of vanity, indifference, and silence through the movements of its own "symphony of sorrow." More explicitly still, the letter states as a conscious motive its intent to instruct: "You came to me to learn the Pleasure of Life and the Pleasure of Art. Perhaps I am chosen to teach you something much more wonderful, the meaning of Sorrow, and its beauty" (*DP*, 158).

Humiliation of this kind entails that one's kinship ties derive from their very lack, for it is into the breach created by scandal that the letter attempts to build up what a minute public exhibition of his private nature has torn down. As Wilde puts it, "everything needs to be a religion to be real" (*DP*, 98). He imagines for us a church of unbelievers, what he calls a "Confraternity of the Fatherless," thus signaling the necessity of ritual to make things real as much as it stresses the connection between fathers and faith. Prison has given him over to the rituals of sorrow and confirmed the reality of pain, but even pain needs its moods, its differing modes, and ultimately its meanings. This letter gives back to pain what prison steals away: a lesson's value. "There is only one thing for me now, absolute Humility: just as there is only one thing for you, absolute Humility also. You had better come down into the dust and learn it beside me" (*DP*, 96). It is only by virtue of the letter's pedagogic conceit that Wilde can begin to address the lover.

Wilde's demand that the beloved friend humiliate himself to learn humility repeats in its redundant form the central conversion experience narrated in the letter. He describes a two-year passage through "every possible mood of suffering," which makes him hear the voice of "something that tells me that nothing in the whole world is meaningless" (*DP*, 96). This thing he names Humility he finds in his "nature." It can only strike the reader that a humility arising from an extended and absolute experience of humiliation could not have the self-originating character Wilde claims for it, and yet it does. "It has come to me right out of me" discloses while disguising an utter lack of humility. More than failing its meaning, this "treasure" hidden away in the field of his own private nature gives rise to a series of boasts.

> Had anyone told me of it, I would have rejected it. Had it been brought to me, I would have refused it. As I found it I want to keep it. I must do so. It is the one thing that has in it the elements of life, of a new life, a *Vita Nuova* for me. Of all things it is the strangest. One cannot give it away, and another may not give it to one. One cannot acquire it, except by surrendering everything that one has. It is only when one has lost all things, that one knows that one possesses it. (*DP*, 97)

We might say that "it" exceeds its meaning, though meaning is the thing it serves to guarantee. What, then, is "it"? It is "in me" more than any other thing. It is the strangest, thus most foreign, yet most proper, not a thing but that which is rendered by a species of potlatch, for it appears only by virtue of a more than symbolic destitution. Something in me more than a thing, its possession gives me more than a life—it gives new life. This I take to be a poignant evocation of inscription as Foucault has theorized it, for the soul thus found cannot be acquired "except by surrendering everything that one has." Humility and humiliation are the path back to a name, Wilde's riven with scandal yet recuperable if these elements of the *Vita Nuova* can write the soul in its new modality. "My nature is seeking a fresh mode of self-realization." A mode of self-realization, this making real of the self, is also the making self of the real, what Wilde calls humility.

"There is not a single degradation of the body which I must not try and make into a spiritualizing of the soul" (*DP*, 99). Through the trope of humility, Wilde manages to translate the foreign, native object within from a language of conventional piety to a term of atheist self-invention. The humiliations of the mind and body transform the unbelieving soul and, by subjecting it to the rigors of an infernal passage where morality, religion, and reason fail to console, toughen the spirit. Wilde converts himself into a mechanism of perpetual conversion, transforming every harm into some spiritual capital. In so doing he impersonates a god. "Only that is spiritual which makes its own form. If I may not find its secret within myself, I shall never find it. If I have not got it already, it will never come to me" (*DP*, 99). Spirit makes in its own image. This making establishes a repetition, a mimetism of making, a conversion of conversion at the heart of confession and self-fashioning. It takes the lesson of discipline's humiliation and subjects it to a translation stripping penance from piety. Wilde elaborates the spiritualizing matter of the new life into a romanticizing portrait of Christ. Expanding ever outward, this transforming character gathers momentum as it gathers predicates.

The Christ emerging as central affective and tropological pivot of the letter is not the familiar, sacrificial figure. He is "the leader of the lovers" and the "supreme of Individualists," one who teaches by example that to be one's true self one must "get rid of all alien passions, all acquired culture, and all external possessions be they good or evil" (*DP*, 113). Through the force of Wilde's reinscription, Christ no longer stands as intermediary between a paternal god and a people, for the filial bondage of Christ has been broken. He does not require humility from his people but becomes an example of it, the author, even, of its most perfect expression and the originator of a "mode of manifestation." By emulating the modality of the savior, his "people" or lovers are no longer bound by a code of moral laws but are constituted as a kind by their self-expression. Christ, neither son nor sacrifice, incarnates the perpetual conversion of Individualist. Wilde makes this explicitly clear: "Most people are other people. Their thoughts are someone else's opinions, their life a mimicry, their passions a quotation. Christ was not merely the supreme Individualist, but he was the first in History" (DP, 114). This spectacular figure, endowed with the power to engender the self, turns the symbolic father away and substitutes himself in His place, thus effecting a shift toward bonds of affiliation and friendship where once there had been only lineage. In a gesture of prescient self-fashioning, Wilde converts Christ to the "Confraternity of the Fatherless," and in so doing, it is the new wild Christ who models for, by imitating, Wilde's legend.

The inversion at work has several turns. Wilde's passion converts him to himself, that is, he masters his situation through the trope of humility and finds his way back to himself by finding the "it" concealed within him. The conversion trope then gives way to a meditation on the necessity of sorrow to consciousness: "The remembrance of suffering in the past is necessary to us as the warrant, the evidence, of our continued identity" (DP, 54). Painful memory vouches for the future of an identity in the same way we would expect a name to justify our persisting as someone, the same one, "me." Remembrance of injury, trauma, or pain guarantees that repetition will perpetuate what is most proper to the individual, but there is nothing to say of suffering itself. It is nothing more than a means of consciousness, a moment in a series of equal moments; it is repetition itself. "Suffering is one long moment. We cannot divide it by seasons. We can only record its moods, and chronicle their return. With us [prisoners] time itself does not progress. It revolves" (DP, 83).

Sorrow and conversion repeat one another in a perpetual revolution, which, according to Wilde, resolves itself only in figures, identity, and forms. This is testimony to the necessity of art as the activity that gives form to sorrow's revolutions through the serial activity of sublimation. Art is sorrow's "warrant," for sorrow has now become the truth of Art. It "wears no mask"; sorrow is neither resemblance nor shadow nor echo. "Truth in Art is the unity of a thing with itself: the outward rendered expressive of the inward: the soul made incarnate: the body instinct in spirit" (DP, 105). Wilde links these phrases with colons as if to mark out the inevitability of the sequence—as if to say that the one who will survive and profit from the circularity of traumatic memory is the one who can most perfectly incarnate the repetitive character of pain in all its character-giving iterations. Christ will be the figure of conversion's incarnation; embodying the paradox of a model who models originality, the figure of Christ takes the paralyzed repetition of painful memory and refigures it as meaning, gives back its meaning. "The one thing I could not bear was that my suffering should be without meaning."

The tropes of humiliation and conversion are complicit with an understanding of confession as a powerful resource for self-invention. That Wilde alights on Christ for the emblem of his *vita nuova* indicates both his knowledge of traditions of *imitatio christi* and an awareness of a counterhistory of Christ's body as a site of heteroglossia and homoerotic investment.[53] In Foucault's elaboration of modernity confessional discourse has as its task the disciplinary individuation of a speaker as a "case," a compendium of practices and observations given over to a dominant and centralizing, because disappearing, audience. Writing, too, suffers a change, as "everyone becomes a case to be recorded.... Biography is no longer a monument for future memory but a document for possible use."[54] Wilde's letter is not naive in this regard. The letter constitutes a record of all that went unsaid or was misconstrued in the trials. In this way it subjects itself to the rigors of what Foucault calls individuation through discipline but directs itself against the claim that "this turning of real lives into writing is no longer a procedure of heroization; it functions as a procedure of objectification and subjection." The perverse aim of Wilde's letter is precisely a conversion of the abjected Wilde, who lies "in the lowest mire of Malebolge . . . between Gilles de Retz and the Marquis de Sade" (*DP,* 47), into a new and spectacular individual. The double task of the letter is to turn the means of subjection into the occasion of transcendence while also converting the addressee through a form of subjection. That confessional speech requires a withdrawn, unresponsive audience is a fact Wilde subverts by marking the silence of the addressee as that of a *lover.* Poisonous though the appeal is made, the pedagogic intent of the letter is to wrench that addressee from the silent security of an oedipal audition and a filiation that had publicly sacrificed the bonds of friendship. Wilde must join the disciplinary effects of the "case" to those of the sexual type, and he does this through the trope of the new Christ. For as humiliation becomes transferable it mimics the mobility of homophobic contamination, which legislates exposure as an exchangeable position. Confession is thus parodically reinscribed within an alliance of amorous friendship through the structural ironies of a Christ turned lover. An amorous Christ desires that one pass through the trials of "sorrow," learn humiliation's lesson, and join the confraternity of unbelievers.

Taking the metaphor of the lesson seriously, we must grant "humility" the status of a wrenching moment of reconstruction, one that is reassumed again and again as the newly fabricated subject turns toward his own conversion. From self to self the passage of humility returns the subject to himself. From this point of disciplinary refiguring of his private nature, Wilde sends forth a messenger in his own name. The queer Christ departs from the very center of paternal, juridical, and theological power to traverse the now impossibly imbricated public/private space emblematized by a love letter meant for publication. Wilde makes of Christ the precursor, the John the Baptist, of his posterity by forcing the "supreme Individualist" to body forth the ties of gay affiliation, ties that depend on influence and the sensible availability of figuration itself. The legend of Wilde will be by virtue of this letter the legend of Christ, lover and amorous friend.

RACE, THE EXORBITANT ORIGIN

Between the "neuropsychiatry of degenerescence"[55] that Foucault identifies as foundational for the bourgeois myth of self and the Freudian project to displace the naturalization of sexuality as a racial inheritance, Oscar Wilde participates in the effort to "reinscribe sexuality within the system of law, symbolic order and sovereignty"[56] by linking the arts, love, and civilization through a series of bodily and biological metaphors. More than this, he seeks to expand that order of ideality to show that the forms of biological inheritance are themselves subject to epochal and individual change.[57] His is a profoundly historical imagination of the symbolic and thus is open to perpetual renewal from within; it is essentially linked to aesthetic invention.

> Aesthetics, in fact, are to Ethics in the sphere of conscious civilization, what in the sphere of the external world, sexual is to natural selection. Ethics, like natural selection, make existence possible. Aesthetics, like sexual selection, make life lovely and wonderful, fill it with new forms, give it progress, and variety and change.[58]

Ventriloquized through Gilbert, who, in a series of small tirades in parody of Socratic dialogue, sets forth the principles of a new art of life, Wilde's aesthetics aims to free the sovereign subject from received ideological forms, to overcome resentment, and to establish a socially generative sexuality in bonds of male affiliation. The hellenized queer Christ of *De Profundis* is the preeminent new form; it is the emblem of a self-invention that does not depend on fraternal rivalry or oedipal violence to create itself. Aesthetics, like sexual selection, doubles here for love and departs from an ethical existence just as preference departs from nature. There is, however, a crucial reason to place Wilde's thought between the racial myth of degenerescence and a psychoanalytic myth of the primal father. Though Wilde was damning in his condemnation of the Victorian family, his subversion of sex entails a prior acceptance of the dynamic and virtually incoherent category of race, which is an essential feature of that domestic discourse. He weaves together a Hegelian cultural and aesthetic idealism with the Spenserian theory of the inheritance of acquired characteristics to arrive at a "modern" picture of the emergence of self-consciousness as the emergence of the "human race."

In an exhaustive annotation of Wilde's Oxford notebooks and arguing from textual evidence throughout his critical work, Philip E. Smith and Michael S. Helfand uncover sources for Wilde's synthesis of heredity and idealism. They argue that Wilde's

> assumptions about physical and mental evolution are drawn from Darwin's *Origin of Species* and *Descent of Man,* from Spencer's and Clifford's theories of the hereditary transmission of culture, and from the unity of the organic principle of life described by Huxley and Tyndall. Hegel's philosophy of dialectical spiritual progress drives [his] metaphysical assumptions: the realization of critical and imaginative self-consciousness in individuals gives humans the power to choose, to select on aesthetic and scientific principles, the course of their future development.[59]

While this description of the very best that Victorian education had to offer enthusiastically situates Wilde and, through him, aestheticism in the stream of sociological interpretations of biology, interpretations that provided the moderns with a steady source of metaphor to frame a modern understanding of history, little attention is paid to the fact that an Irishman and homosexual might measure the new sciences by the social consequences drawn from them. The human power to choose "the course of their future development" belies its origin in W. K. Clifford's theory of "tribal consciousness" and Darwin's fable of the horde. For in this late nineteenth-century synthesis, moral behavior develops through the historical inheritance of collective or "tribal" moral intuition, which in the best of worlds would, according to T.H. Huxley, lead to collective ethical evolution and uplift. The racial basis of the inheritance of acquired characteristics forces the body back into the historical progress of the Idea, but it in no way guarantees the perfection of national stock, and thus the moral progress of the human is shadowed by the possibility of decline and the social taint passed on in decadent times. A nascent psychology determined by racial belonging emerges in the worry over the devolutionary prospects of "fitness" unchecked, and this can be found in many works of the 1890s, from the scientific romances of the socialist H.G. Wells to Huxley's *Evolution and Ethics,* which warns the reader that "social progress means a checking of the cosmic process at every step, and the substitution for it of another which may be called the ethical progress; the end of which is not the survival of those who may be the fittest, in respect of the conditions which exist, but of those who are ethically the best."[60] For Wilde, who knew the work of sexologists and criminologists well enough to reference Lombroso from memory in *De Profundis,* the survival of those who are only "ethically the best" risks eliminating all "variety and change."

Nonetheless, social Darwinism lends Wilde a tool in the resistance to Christian chauvinism insofar as science refuses to lose the body in time. Where natural selection figures a primal horde of rival males competing for passive female mates, the secondary operation of sexual selection—selection according to individual, even arbitrary, and thus historically changeable preference—draws from a pool of successfully evolved and preening dandies. As Darwin puts it, the human male must "excite or charm those of the opposite sex,"[61] but as we know, the preeminent examples are birdsong and the ostentatious display of the "pied peacock." Sexual selection thus becomes the originary source of creative self-invention and of aesthetic practice within reproduction. Wilde's evolutionary aestheticism proposes a material and historical principal of change and invention against the heterosexualized body of ethical stock. Matching seductive conversation and the ability to charm with words, Wilde's affectations of style—right down to the peacock feathers he had fixed in the plaster of his Tite Street house—found a scientific basis.

Wilde's parodic yet earnest theory of aesthetic selection is emblematic of the rhetorical gesture at work in his aestheticist rescripting of race as the basis for a social transcendence. The analogy between nature and conscious civilization makes no mention of nature and opposes "the sphere of the external world" to the "sphere of conscious civilization." Aesthetics, through its authorization as a sexual principle and thus a principle of progress and variation, absorbs the other categories in a gesture that mimics the civilizing aim of a sublimation of appetite. By harnessing aesthetics to nature, Wilde again relies on the slippery technique of sublimation to subvert the stigma attached to "variety." Traversing Wilde's various theories of art and culture, a central paradox reappears in his rhetorical uses of the category of race. One tendency of his thinking contends that artistic invention carries the potential to invent the future as an ideal, to invent new ideals and new forms of expression, and to resignify the terms of the given. This power of invention and resignification is essential to a gay poetics of self-invention and accounts for Wilde's belief in the compatibility of family life with a homosexual and erotic culture.

In tension with this anarchic potential of art is Wilde's continual assertion of the efficacy of sublimation as a form of cultivation. For instance, later in the same dialogue cited above, Wilde has Gilbert assert that as long as war is considered wicked, man will be fascinated by it. The only way to render it repugnant is to make war seem something vulgar. Art can master violence by appealing to the aesthetic sensibilities of a properly trained and thus appreciative people. This is an extreme example and intended as a provocation, but in the rhetorical scheme of his work, the contradiction of art as an expressive potential and art as a form of transcendence holds firm. Aestheticism revels in the "progress" of new forms and assaults the stunted symbolic limitations of Victorian bio-power, but its reliance on race as a category of difference may merely repeat the ressentimental structures Wilde goes to such lengths to resist elsewhere.

In *De Profundis* the dominant figure of a synthesis between Wilde's notion of self-invention and his social aesthetics is, again, the queer Christ.

> He was the first to conceive the divided races as a unity. Before his time there had been gods and men. . . . He could bear on his own shoulders the burden of the entire world . . . oppressed nationalities, factory children, thieves, people in prison, outcasts, those who were dumb under oppression and whose silence is only heard of God. (*DP,* 110)

Here, race refers not only to nationality but also to the classical distinction between gods and men, making Christ a Prometheus who translates himself willfully between the two camps and embodies their unity. This is a figurative body that unites biology and spirit. Following from the embodiment of "racial" unity, oppressed nationalities and a string of abjected, subaltern classes join the "races." By making Christ model for Individuality, Wilde places the incarnation squarely within the field of aesthetic "life" where artistic expression constantly subjects symbolic forms to a species of sexual research. Aesthetic sexual selection renews, by rewriting, this body. Recall Foucault's insight that the object of the disciplinary regime of bio-power is to inscribe the self on a body, to write the soul into a subject in the mode of internalization.[62] Wilde, too, relies on a metaphor of inscription and reading to elaborate a theory of self-invention, yet his theory, as much as his example, asserts that art exceeds inscription. Wilde's self becomes the object of a series of inscriptions, which the artist translates into "expressions." The self's body becomes a virtual body because it becomes a beautiful one. The wily aim of an aesthetics that subsumes sexual selection is to push discipline and its writing through the body to arrive at a realm where the force of power serves the sovereignty of individual artistic expression. Foucault's map of the disciplinary techniques of confession that produce a body as the soul's body reaches an impasse in the parodic figure of aesthetic sexual selection when Wilde's parody absconds the body but leaves incarnation. Subversive incarnation, like the allegorical insubordination of parabasis, turns away from the dogmatic *telos* of discipline and church and toward a parody of that origin. If internalization has become the model of inscription on a disciplined body, sovereign incarnation sublimes the common sense.

"We are no longer in Art concerned with the type. It is with the exception we have to do. I cannot put my sufferings into any form they took, I need hardly say. Art only begins where Imitation ends" (*DP*, 128). The Victorian family, however, was preoccupied with type, heredity, and the visible signs of degeneration of the race. In the narrative of "tainted family," Krafft-Ebing's favored diagnostic tool, Oscar Wilde's homosexuality is immediately ascribable to hereditary disease. Exception is itself a site of considerable anxiety when the rule is breeding: hero or monster, any deviation exposes the line to question. The Criminal Law Amendment Act of 1885 under which Wilde is imprisoned for indecency clearly justifies itself through a panicked fear of "corruption of youth" and seeks to contain sexual contamination by incarcerating homosexual adult men. Sexuality, sickness, and race form a conglomerate object[63] that Foucault playfully names for us the "perversion-heredity-degenerescence system"[64] and which binds sexual instinct to eugenics and racism. Even the cultivation of this body through hygiene and the various forms of Victorian asceticism in marriage and child rearing

> attest to the correlation of this concern with the body and sex to a type of "racism." But the latter was very different from that manifested by the nobility and organized for basically conservative ends. It was a dynamic racism, a racism of expansion, even if it was still in a budding state, awaiting the second half of the nineteenth century to bear the fruits that we have tasted.[65]

Foucault identifies the unboundedness of the category "race," which in its very incoherence motivates a proliferation of forms of social management and a politics that "received their color and their justification from the mythical concern with protecting the purity of the blood and ensuring the triumph of the race."[66]

Against this background of "dynamic racism," Wilde asserts that the threat to the race comes not from an impurity of blood but from arrested cultural development and, further, that the decay of body and soul must be attributed to inhibition, repression, and race prejudice.[67] A passage from "The Soul of Man Under Socialism" fleshes out the hyperbolic, almost histrionic, annexation of themes in Wilde's synthesis of science, philosophy, and art. Savage regression and disease he links together by their common root in repression and the thwarting of individual development.

> It is to be noted that Individualism does not come to the man with any sickly cant about duty, which merely means doing what other people want because they want it; or any hideous cant about self-sacrifice, which is merely a survival of savage mutilation. In fact, it does not come to a man with any claims upon him at all. It comes naturally and inevitably out of man. It is the point to which all development tends. It is the differentiation to which all organisms grow. It is the perfection that is inherent in every mode of life, and towards which every mode of life quickens. And so Individualism exercises no compulsion over man. On the contrary, it says to man that he should suffer no compulsion to be exercised over him. It does not try to force people to be good. It knows that people are good when they are let alone. Man will develop Individualism out of himself. Man is now so developing Individualism. To ask whether Individualism is practical is like asking whether Evolution is practical. Evolution is the law of life, and there is no evolution except towards individualism. Where this tendency is not expressed, it is a case of artificially arrested growth, or of disease, or of death.[68]

In this anarchic individualism Wilde cites from his previous writings. The phrase "mutilation of the savage" appears at least three times throughout Wilde's oeuvre and again in his college notebook. In *The Picture of Dorian Gray* Lord Henry explains the dangers of renunciation: "The bravest man amongst us is afraid of himself. The mutilation of the savage has its tragic survival in the self-denial that mars our lives. We are punished for our refusals. Every impulse that we strive to strangle broods in the mind and poisons us" (*PDG,* 17). Consistently, he argues that self-sacrifice inheres in Victorian culture as a kind of mutilation that serves to construct the social world according to the dictates of duty and fear by persistently choosing the brute model of natural selection over the civilizing influences of sexual selection. Such a primordial self-sacrifice is uncannily similar to Freud's discovery of totemic taboos that organize the moral prohibitions of tribal life. Wilde's participation in the historical inscription of racial discourse through metaphors of "tragic survival" of "savage mutilation" permits him to argue against Christian asceticism, but at the great cost of complicity with the racial metaphor. For, despite the analytic and symbolic status granted this figuration of the primitive, despite its status as figure, Wilde consistently claims that primitive mutilation must be overcome for an actively and creatively homosexual subjectivity to come into being. The "primitive" homosexual transcends his primal link to natural selection by shedding the deforming, mutilating asceticism of medieval Christianity. Inhabited by a primitive vestige, the dandy can become fully himself only when he thwarts the repressions that traverse him, yet the very narrative of transcendence seems to authorize the mutilation it seeks to overcome. It is in this crossing of homoerotic and racialized primitives that aestheticism gave itself a compromised vocabulary for conceiving repression, one that is suspended over an anxiety about the deformities of the divided spirit rather than of the flesh.[69] What Wilde discovers is a paradox that becomes central for modernism—sexual morals and social taboos are nothing less than the survival of primitive self-sacrifice and thus constitute a form of heredity mediated by unconscious, socially inculcated limitation and taboo. This decadent intuition is not a clear-cut concept like Freud's notion of repression; rather, the narrative of self-transcendence and purging of interior limits incites fantasy to give it form and to find the imaginary symbols that reflect the human subject's bondage in the social script. In this way the insights of decadence begin an inquiry into the sexual nature of species and race and function as the denaturalization of these same ideas.

That Wilde authorizes the racial as an interpretive category is nowhere more evident or surprising than in his contorted championing of cosmopolitanism. "It is only by the cultivation of the habit of intellectual criticism that we shall be able to rise superior to race-prejudices ... [for] criticism will annihilate race-prejudice by insisting upon the unity of the human mind in the variety of its forms."[70] Worldly idealism will replace racism through the exercise of global self-consciousness because the notion of individual races will be superseded by a consciousness of human species united into one race. Continually in his essays, commonplace book, letters from at least 1889, and in *De Profundis,* Wilde lays the blame for race prejudice on nationalism. The analogy between national, imperial and individual character that subtends Wilde's use of *race* and the primitive he figures allows him to portray the British subject as stunted in his primitive and aggressive drives and characterized by vulgarity and violence. "The English mind is always in a rage. The intellect of the race is wasted in the sordid and stupid quarrels of second-rate politicians or third-rate theologians."[71] This peculiar annexation of nation by race owes something to Wilde's reading of Renan, whose *Vie de Jesus* was among the books he requested at Reading Goal. While his imagination of cosmopolitanism as the transcendence of nationalism is hardly unique, his belief that all would be united in a single race runs against the grain of another strain of cosmopolitanism exemplified by Freud in "Reflections on Life and Death in Time of War," in which he recalls a European cosmopolitanism laid waste by the Great War; there cosmopolitanism admits of difference, for it unites on the basis of a lack of racial unity.

For Wilde, social mediation of racial culture should have as its goal the control of primitive violence. Aggressivity inevitably passes to each succeeding generation, but this legacy can be halted by cultural intervention through criticism of that socially produced deformity. The stakes of art are only heightened by Wilde's synthesis of aesthetic idealism and heredity, for "the artist must intervene on the imitative and reproductive process to provide new ideals for life."[72] Accordingly, race, rage, and resentment configure modernity in the image of and as the heritage of Darwin's primal horde because the narrative of evolution always implies the possibility of a devolutionary telos and, equally, because Victorian values of industry and propriety promote such devolution.[73] In the vein of radical Darwinism rather than conservative social Darwinism, Wilde asserts throughout his aesthetic criticism that man is born with a specific creative potential, which is then brutalized by the shaming effects of Victorian morality and crippling poverty. He makes of aesthetics a challenge to the "perversion-heredity-degenerescence system" by using the founding concepts of that system in the service of autonomous Individuality. Indeed, the generative character of his intervention on reproduction has great social consequences, and Wilde's negotiation of morality and heredity in terms of an idealist aesthetics place his thinking uncannily close to the critique of family life and eugenics undertaken in psychoanalysis.[74] The idealist and utopian impulse in Wilde sets him apart from Freud, of course, but that should not blind us to the basic affinities in their shared use of Darwin to deconstruct what Foucault has called the "perversion-heredity-degenerescence system."[75] For this reason I have been stressing the necessity of placing Wilde, and this newly conceived aesthetics, between the racially marked family and the psychoanalytic interpretation of that family.

De Profundis extends the hyperbolic synthesis of aesthetics and sex that leads Wilde to devise a new form of criticism in the theatrical dialogues of *Intentions*. The shifting themes, errant logics, and exploded meditations of the letter are not merely mimetic of an obsessional state; the discontinuous volleys of invective and philosophical reflection have a totalizing aim. The letter wants to resolve its melancholy subject but succeeds only in tossing him from one association to another in a manic series, the other side of melancholia. Wilde's letter exhibits an inability to gather itself into a coherent structure of propositions or meditations on the modern, the individual, and the racial. Rather, the exigency of mania subjects the letter's voice to the errantry of the signifier. In an analysis of mania in Hamlet, Lacan examines precisely such an unhinging loss in the real, which subjects the now drifting subject to a swarm of images and voices. "Words, words, words," every sign is pregnant with potential meanings, and to the one unmade in Law, every usurping word stands in the very place where he himself should be. The structuring principle becomes accident itself; yet Wilde proceeds as if his synthetic powers were unimpaired. "As it stands . . . my letter has its definite meaning behind every phrase. There is in it nothing of rhetoric" (*DP*, 146). Blotted by his tears, covered with corrections and errata, the letter substitutes for his own body by escaping Reading Gaol. A body of pained rage, "my letter" means to reassert him in the symbolic register of exchanges, to resurrect him to the new life of a postprison notoriety.

"The Law has taken from me not merely all that I have, my books, furniture, pictures, my copyright in my published works, my copyright in my plays . . . but also all that I am ever going to have" (*DP*, 151). Not only has he been stripped of fame and fatherhood, but he can never again make a living from the sale of his art. This amounts to a complete destitution for which the writing of the letter substitutes an ineffectual "passion" and situates this rant as an impossibility to resolve mourning. "The maniac plainly shows us that he has become free from the object by whom his suffering was caused, for he runs after new object-cathexis like a starving man after bread."[76] In this case the new object is the old one subjected to a failure to convert, and mania's joy does not satisfy beyond the brief moment of its utterance. For precisely this reason, Wilde's text detours through allegories of modernity and tragedy because it cannot say what it is in the process of figuring: symbolic death leaves one no other tool than fantasy to rescript the timeless present. "Our own death is indeed unimaginable, and whenever we make the attempt to imagine it we can perceive that we really survive as spectators."[77] Spectator of his own death, he tries to fabricate a new life and new fantasy in the lines of this bitter letter.

"TERRIBLE LEGACY" AND THE MODERN TYPE

There is a race that even Christ could not unite nor redeem: the English aristocracy. Throughout *De Profundis* the passages of greatest venom are reserved for descriptions of the Marquess of Queensberry and his son, Lord Alfred Douglas. According to his own diagnosis, Wilde's tragedy is the result of a confusion of public and private brought about by the extension of the Queensberry clan's filial strife into the public sphere. "Through your father you come of a race, marriage with whom is horrible, friendship fatal, and that lays violent hands either on its own life or on the lives of others" (*DP*, 61). From all accounts his rhetoric is factual reportage.[78] What is interesting in these florid phrases, however, is the way they combine a classical trope of hubris with the newer vocabulary of tribal consciousness and inherited affliction, a vocabulary he gleans from his singular synthesis of Darwin, Spencer, and Clifford.

> Family instincts were strong in him. His hatred of you was just as persistent as your hatred of him, and I was the stalking-horse for both of you, and a mode of attack as well as a mode of shelter. His very passion for notoriety was not merely individual but racial. (*DP*, 70)

Family instinct comes to mean mutual hatred between father and son, which alone is responsible for unfolding the drama and which has the peculiar quality of flattening out the difference between a father and a son, leaving only the order of the horde. In the metaphor of Darwinian competition, Wilde figures himself as both a mode of attack and shelter, weapon and shield, but a few lines before he situates Douglas as the passive Darwinian female. "Indeed the idea of your being the object of a terrible quarrel between your father and a man of my position seemed to delight you" (*DP*, 70). Repeatedly, Wilde blames the entire course of events on that "mad, bad line" and persistently uses images of the hunt. Bosie "scents the chance of public scandal" and "hounds" his father to the "chase." Queensberry is a "bestial man" with a stableman's gait. Through these figures Wilde reconstructs the familial fantasy working to organize a legal battle in terms of a primal filial hatred with escalating rhetoric until, finally, "the madness of moods of rage that you were allowing to master you" causes public scandal. This "mood of rage" becomes in the letter as it already was in Wilde's critical dialogues, the devolutionary racial sign of English national character.

> Your quarrel with your father, again, whatever one may think about its character, should obviously have remained a question entirely between the two of you. It should have been carried on in a backyard. Such quarrels, I believe, usually are. Your mistake was in insisting on its being played as a tragi-comedy on a high stage in History, with the whole world as the audience, and myself as the prize for the victor in the contemptible contest. The fact that your father loathed you, and that you loathed your father, was not a matter of any interest to the English public. Such feelings are very common in English domestic life, and should be confined to the place they characterize: the home. Away from the home-circle they are quite out of place. To translate them is an offense. (*DP*, 147)

By projecting the commonplace onto the stage of history, this family miscegenates the genres of history and domestic life such that the primitive contest of the horde is misrecognized as the heroics of epic. The bad blood of Victorian family life makes room for filial resentment and infanticidal rage where the laws of symbolic behavior, kinship itself, ought to prevail. Suffering the violence of bad translation from the domestic to the public, the ethic of kinship has failed to drive the primal back into the horde, the English backyard, home to hatred. By accusing Douglas and his father of offensive translation, Wilde transcends the local scene to claim that such translations *are* the loss of the proper such that civility and public spectacle are transformed into monstrous public scandal. Neither father nor son cared to shield the public from a humiliating and unedifying display. Both shamelessly abused their access to public spectacle and destroyed the necessary mediations that laws of civility are designed to effect. The letter goes on to claim that Douglas's petty appetites are typical of the disorder afflicting modernity. An inability to comprehend the scale of social space and an insistence that patriarchal rivalry be played out in public robs the filial subject of any sense of proportion. Exactly as in *The Picture of Dorian Gray,* Wilde presents us with the portrait of men so locked in their narcissisms that they ignore the civilizing mission of sublimation and instead unleash a perverted violence on those around them. The "hard Hedonists," for whom every appetite is to be indulged, are separated by a thin thread of difference from this bestial nobility.

Wilde is able to read the unconscious fantasy native to both father and son. It is a fantasy that dissimulates its ambivalent longing for and hatred of law through a series of projections. As the letter puts it, "Whenever there is hatred between two people there is a bond or brotherhood of some kind. I could never understand why your father was to you an exemplar when he should have been a warning." The family discourse generated between Queensberry and his youngest son precludes any bond other than a fratricidal one, and thus, in a fatal mimetism, their shared relation to paternity exists somewhere before the rule of law, relegated to the horde. The racial metaphor becomes a means for Wilde to argue for the mediations of civility where actual fathers and sons by rights should be disciplined by a symbolic law. In this way race appears as a primal scene replaying an oedipal scenography that then scripts the tragedy of Oscar Wilde. I have been using a Freudian vocabulary to describe Wilde's rhetorical scheme because it clarifies the misfit that Wilde identifies in terms of offensive translation. Freud locates the advent of law in the mythological murder of the primal father by the Darwinian horde, who then, remorseful, institute law to protect their community from repetition of this murder. In *De Profundis* we have a depiction of a regression that translates parricide and infanticide into fratricide. Hatred creates a bond of brotherhood where difference ought to be. Whereas for Freud the social bond is tied over a double absence, that of the father and the act to be prohibited, here the bond itself is determined by the multiplication and transfiguration of absence—father and son into brothers, private into public, and public into monstrous, offensive translation. This identification of a regression is not made by Wilde in order to reassert the rightfulness of paternity and, thus, the fully oedipalized symbolic economy of the commonplaces of the Victorian family. Rather, against both the commonplace of English domestic life and this grotesque mistranslation, Wilde holds out a hope for tragedy.

The letter comes closest to the Freud of *Totem and Taboo* in its extension of the racial and familial fantasy to what is for Wilde a modern degradation of Greek tragedy. Tracing the persistence of an ambivalent relation to the father from the totem meal to Christian communion, Freud narrates a progressive abstraction of the paternal figure into a paternal function. The murder of the primal father at the hands of his sons "must . . . have left ineradicable traces in the history of humanity: and the less it itself was recollected, the more numerous must have been the substitutes to which it gave rise."[79] In tragedy this trace is manifest in the staging of the hero's suffering amidst the lamentations of the chorus. Freud says of the hero that "he had to suffer because he was the primal father, the Hero of the great primaeval tragedy which was being re-enacted with a tendentious twist; and the tragic guilt was the guilt which he had to take on himself in order to relieve the Chorus from theirs."[80] Sacrifice, historically the first attempt to atone for the primal crime and thereby grant a limit to guilty mourning, lies close beneath the surface of the drama. Tragedy marks a point of interiorization wherein the father and a singular subject are one, while the chorus figures the former fraternal clan. According to the Freudian narrative later Christianity extends the metaphorization of the father in its repetition of the totem meal such that ambivalence is ritualized. As Freud puts it, "The Christian communion is essentially a fresh elimination of the father."[81] For this reason Greek tragedy represents the theatricalization of an ambivalence, which in *Totem and Taboo* never ceases to haunt community. Inhibiting a "normal mourning" this haunting father relegates the social bond to a particular melancholic form, one that Oscar Wilde will parodically reinscribe in his emphasis on Greek friendship.

"You were a very complete specimen of a very modern type" (*DP*, 146), says Wilde after a detailed portrait of Douglas's unbridled appetite. That Wilde identifies Douglas's heroic fantasy with tragicomedy reflects the letter's argument for the loss characteristic of modernity in the letter. "The dreadful thing about modernity was that it put Tragedy into the raiment of Comedy, so that the great realities seemed commonplace or grotesque or lacking in style" (*DP*, 129). The modern represents a degeneration of tragedy, and with it the death of Wilde's delicate synthesis of aesthetic and sexual culture. Public space has become the zone of an undisciplined reign of oedipal feeling, which levels the fine architecture of the Greek *ethos* of public life and only parodies tragedy. The misrecognition of vulgar family dispute is a dangerous masquerade. For when the socializing effects of fear and pity no longer operate, when tragedy can no longer produce an identification between audience and spectacle, to what does one appeal as the ethical and sympathetic ground of culture? These are the exorbitant pressures Wilde brings to bear on an admittedly extraordinary and murderous mania that equates parricide and infanticide and no longer admits of essential difference. The knotted logic of this train of thought slowly accrues meaning precisely at the point where impropriety and public space intersect. While seeming to lament the loss of a rarified aesthetic form, the letter begins to fray the ethical limit of the law, for what law, he asks, can govern a time without proportion or a people with no sense of tragedy and, by the same token, no sense of history or the capacity to change it?

Social space, then, is lost in an offensive translation reducing tragedy to a hybrid species. To illustrate the global social harm wrought in the public sphere, Wilde reveals the trauma behind his aversion to tragicomedy in a dramatization of disciplinary power, a training in the discharge of catharsis itself. November 13, 1895, Wilde was being "brought down" to Reading Goal from Wandsworth prison, where he had lain sick with an untreated ear infection. While waiting on the platform at Clapham Junction, he was "shown under conditions of unspeakable humiliation to the gaze and mockery of men" (*DP*, 93).

> From two o'clock till half-past two on that day I had to stand on the centre platform of Clapham Junction in convict dress and handcuffed, for the world to look at. I had been taken out of the Hospital Ward without a moment's notice being given to me. Of all possible objects I was the most grotesque. When people saw me they laughed. Each train as it came up swelled the audience. Nothing could exceed their amusement. That was of course before they knew who I was. As soon as they had been informed, they laughed still more. For half an hour I stood there in the grey November rain surrounded by a jeering mob. For a year after that was done to me I wept every day at the same hour and for the same space of time. (*DP*, 130)

Taken abruptly from prison, he finds himself suddenly in a strange and crowded zone of asociality where spectacle is all, but where the discipline of aesthetic spectatorship is suspended. This public dumb show exposes him to a literal enactment of abjection, one that he experiences as sacrifice. What could more palpably dramatize his outcast state than to have a crowd, united only in their transience and alienation, band together in a spontaneous show of mockery?[82] In that moment of collective sentiment the ethical discharge of fear and pity is itself discharged, evanesced. It is a trauma so horrible as to originate its own mechanical and fantastic replay in a daily memorial. As an event taken up by Wilde's own fantasy, this scene shares with modern drama the impossibility of transcendence and the grotesque character of empty repetition, a repetition that represents nothing but the insistence of its return void of any cathartic release. If Wilde is haunted by the scene in which he and all modernity become "zanies of sorrow," it is also important to note that the haunting itself does not take the form of a re-presentation of the scene. He does not revisit Clapham Station in memory; rather, he cannot escape the revisitation of the time and spacing of the original. The empty ghost of that traumatizing pause between two prisons returns as a blank space, a voided image. This return constitutes the memorializing of a scene in a repetition, which marks the time and duration of the play. From two o'clock to half-past two, at exactly that time and for the same space of time: these details become the tangible substance of rites of mourning. For exactly one year, the length of time commonly held to be appropriate for mourning the dead and mentioned by Freud as the duration of normal grief, he repeats "with sickly iteration" the empty "space of time" that now masquerades as social space.[83]

The tragic comedy of a collective indifference to another's suffering leads Wilde to say, "Everything about my tragedy has been hideous, mean, repellent, lacking in style" (*DP*, 129). The barbarism of a socius given over to visual appropriation of another's pain consigns modernity to the same analytics of decadence and decay echoed in the diatribes of conservative social Darwinists and other theorists of mob mentality.[84] Whereas they lay the blame for the degeneration of the state in phantasmatic figures of racial, sexual, and class miscegenation and enfeeblement, Wilde rebukes the indifference of the crowd and the shameless extension of primitive passions into social space and with it the rescripting of sociality by a phantasmatic racial unconscious that here and, in every letter he will write again, remains resolutely English. The usurpation of tragedy by primitive sacrifice follows a logic of contagion similar to that which Freud finds at the origin of punishment.

> In order to keep the temptation down, the envied transgressor must be deprived of the fruit of his enterprise; and the punishment will not infrequently give those who carry it out an opportunity of committing

the same outrage under colour of an act of expiation. This is indeed one of the foundations of the human penal system and it is based, no doubt correctly, on the assumption that the prohibited impulses are present alike in the criminal and in the avenging community.[85]

However, the difference between the foundation of the penal system here elaborated by Freud and Wilde's experience lies in the assertion made by public laughter, an assertion of the impossibility of identification between these spectators and their "hero." Wilde is rendered wild, a species of totem animal substitute for the primal father, who goes unacknowledged and thus unmourned in the scene. The laughter signals the complete foreclosure of Wildean aesthetics and with it homosexuality, from the social field; significantly, the crowd is primed for such laughter, primed to respond to the spectacle of disciplinary power with the social foreclosure demanded by their savage ethic. By sacrificing Wilde, this public loses its essential relation to tragedy as a civilizing mediation of the paternal function. In this way they lose their loss to gain a primitive regression.

Wilde strives to bring his mourning to an end but can only resolve his melancholia in fits of manic recuperation. The racial scenography is one such manic speculation. Queer affiliation is another resource of a fantasy that seeks to suspend interminable grief. Elsewhere he invokes the narrative of a Celtic racial imagination as the only cure for English barbarism. "It is the lack of imagination in the Anglo-Saxon race that makes the race so stupidly, harshly cruel. Those who are bringing about Prison Reform in Parliament are Celtic to a man. For every Celt has inborn imagination."[86] Extending Mathew Arnold's claims for Celtic character, Wilde annexes the source of resignifying potential, imagination, as the essential property of the Celts.

In light of this sacrificial economy it is little wonder that Wilde reasserts the importance of a mediating and transmuting imagination. The conclusion he draws from his training in abjection points in the direction of a classic resolution to the Oedipus complex through the transcendence of frustration and aggressivity by careful development of ego ideals in sublimation. The Greek and the Celt become figures of such ideality inasmuch as they are *already* for him figures of imagination. There is a deep connection between the Greek theme and that of fantasy's powers of transformation. The two are linked by the terms of amorous affiliation, which give one over to one's sexual nature but also to one's cultivated nature. Wilde discloses this in a passage devoted to his discovery of things "Greek" through the influence of a cultured college friend. "Greek" encodes eros and ethos, sex and cultivation, love and appreciation of the arts. This Oxford friendship brings out his nature as a lover of men who is a lover of aesthetic ideals, and thus friendship brings the friend back to himself by drawing him out. The sublative detour prospers the "soul" by returning to it that which is most proper to it, the sensation of its own presence. Fantasy—in Wilde's idiom *imagination*—is then a necessary detour through imaginary constructions of play, influence, and shared reading. In this realm of the imaginary, objects, impressions, and learning are dignified as expressions of a cultivated, erotic nature; from out of the bonds of friendship, the imaginary produces the terms of the symbolic, a manifestly and newly signifying gay identity. It is friendship to which Wilde appeals as a cure for Douglas's savage family values and imagination that will restore him to himself. "To understand it you will have to cultivate your imagination. Remember that imagination is the quality that enables one to see things and people in their real as in their ideal relations" (*DP*. 153). Transcending the law of the father only to restore him to a symbolic realm, the queer Christ moots the unhealable trauma and extends himself to the renewable bonds of affiliation. Reading and writing, like the "causerie intime" of Rob Ross's frequent letters to Wilde, are the binding and visible signs of friendship's links, identifications, Freud tells us, based on shared ego ideals.[87]

Despite the intervention of a parodic incarnation, by the end of the letter it seems that Wilde would agree with Lacan's assessment of modernity as

> a vast community . . . at the limit between the "democratic" anarchy of the passions and their desperate levelling down by the "great winged hornet" of narcissistic tyranny. It is clear that the promotion of the ego today culminates, in conformity with the utilitarian conception of man that reinforces it, in an ever more advanced realization of man as an individual, that is to say, in an isolation of the soul ever more akin to its original dereliction.[88]

These effects forming "our" derealization of others and our social space are exactly those endured by Wilde at Clapham Junction, but whereas Wilde had hoped for the evolutionary development of the individual—indeed, had believed this to be an inevitability of historical development—the terms of his own abject "derealization" come to signify a dereliction of the modern. Wilde approaches a theory of alienation that envisions a continuity between unbridled appetite and egoic tyranny, and for which the offensive translation of the Douglas family is one instance of this "promotion of the ego." Lacan speaks of a loss of "all those saturations of the superego and ego ideal that are realized in all kinds of organic forms in traditional societies," from "rituals of everyday intimacy to the periodical festivals in which the community manifests itself."[89] Where Lacan imagines an organic traditional society according to Freud's vision in *Totem and Taboo*, Wilde insists, again uncannily presaging Freud's identification of the Christian redeemer as the father of tragedy, on a revived Christ who can embody the religion of the sons without the father, forgetting the father. Lacan's fantasy of organic traditional origins, like the Freudian fantasy of the primitive, seeks a moment of premodern saturation that can act as a state-of-nature fiction masquerading as a natural ground. Likewise Wilde proposes to turn back the clock to a moment before November 13 and thus before the loss of tragedy. Before our modernity, before we were alienated, neurotic, or merely vulgar, tragedy's spectacle produced the natural ground of ethics, which is to say, ethics finds its natural basis in an aesthetic form. Wilde and the two psychoanalysts share a mixed appreciation of primitive premodern festival and spectacle that contrasts sharply with what they diagnose as a modern devolutionary impulse to revert to sacrifice. In each of these writers the modern is so for having fallen from a historical past configured as an ideal of community and sensibility around a tragic negativity. What stumbles and falls in Freud, relegating the subject to infinite irruptions of regression, moves without purpose in Wilde. Disgorged upon a platform the modern socius degrades itself in its moments of idleness where freedom becomes waiting, and time and space have lost their meaning. Lacan will recast that idle social activity as projection and in doing so will link the stumbling and staggering of modern neurosis to Wilde's perception of a violent purposelessness turned to violent repudiation. It is this legacy of decadence and psychic misfit that marks Lacan's vision of dereliction as modernist and decadent, a legacy predating the surrealism with which he is usually associated. Both Freud and Wilde use the term *race* to denote a psychically embedded stratum of symbolic behavior and constraint, while Lacan's anthropological conceit carries over the earlier sense of a symbolic structuring of kinship and thus a racial binding of forms of life while infusing it with a nostalgia that Freud resists. If for Lacan the primitive life of the premodern soul retains a tie to a primordial fusion in community—before the "realisation of man as an individual"—for Freud as for Wilde this modern primitive is both repellently resurfacing and piously civilized; whereas the ancients respect the formality of ritual and achieve an identificatory rapport with tragic subjection, modern primitives are united in and identified by the mob rather than by a sympathetic union with the abstract values of tragedy, but it is only in the newly howling context of a loss of tragic sympathy that those values can reappear as abstract. This difference is underlined again and again as a necessary demystification of the present in the Freud of *Totem and Taboo* and Wilde alike. Their texts sit precariously at the frontier of a modernity still salvageable if their warnings are heeded; thus *race* is accessible as a term of critique—"you come of a race with whom marriage is horrible"—but malleable enough to also accommodate "Celtic imagination." The multiple devolutions of the modern individual, his social world and venerable origins, whether Greek or Celtic, share the same rhetoric and discursive occasion, *race*. For Wilde the vast community of *De Profundis* is now the tomb of the real Individual whose evolution had seemed so inevitable in "The Soul of Man Under Socialism," yet he invokes the confraternity of the fatherless as a signal of hope, of a filiation without sacrifice. Even this hoped-for new kinship is imagined in relation to the racial terms of Wilde's excoriation of modern family life, for there cultivated development will preserve the Individual as the carrier of Celtic imagination. Even in his turn away from the family, Wilde inscribes his ideal community with the sign of race, thus making of race the productive scene of cultural activity and connection to human history. As the word is stretched to a point of almost meaningless elasticity, it enables yet another fantasy of social life.

Against a backdrop of persistent and pervasive denigration of the Irish, Wilde invokes a mythic Celtic race throughout his writings. As recent research into conceptions of race in nineteenth-century Britain shows, *race* when applied to the Irish is not a concept but a fluid and malleable term fixed within an overwhelmingly racist, imperial discourse. As a term it traverses several disciplines to confer a deceptive substance upon itself. In short, *race* is a recurrent fantasy that serves the interests and ends of a particular regime of power; as a fantasy, it is resistant to reasonable modes of demystification and can be harnessed to tactical advantage by a counterdiscourse mounted to dislodge its most pernicious effects. Wilde's is one such counterdiscourse, which, rather than eschewing the term altogether, translates it to new purpose; however, the form of the letter undermines its claim to reason. Thus the counterdiscourse stumbles into ranting.

In Michael Banton's *Racial Theories,* an account of the useful imprecision of the term in nineteenth-century science and humanities, *race* emerges as the name of difference variously coding a host of other issues: social class, animal species, sexuality, nationality, biology, genetics, lineage.[90] Corroborating Foucault's argument in the *History of Sexuality, Volume I* and the lectures published as *Society Must Be Defended,* Banton argues that *race,* as a phantasmatic category, infects, through its very ambiguity, the discourses of human science to grant the appearance of empirical reality. Progressively, and especially in Anglo-Irish relations, the term becomes analogous with nation, religion, and empire such that by 1895, the year of Wilde's imprisonment, the British Secretary of State for the Colonies, Joseph Chamberlain, can with impunity proclaim, "the British race is the greatest governing race that the world has ever seen."[91] Banton shrewdly points out that by the end of the century the category of *nation* authorizes a fabricated assertion of racial homogeneity and ascendancy for the English, a people of mixed ethnicity. Attending this graft of nation onto race, a well-developed stereotype of the Irish as an uncivilized, atavistic rabble in need of British government is infused with the quasi-scientific strain of the new racial classifications.[92] The "wild Irish" of Spenserian lore become by way of science the missing link between our common ape ancestors and modern "man." Anthropologists like John Beddoe (president of the Royal Anthropological Institute, fellow of the Royal Society, and fellow of the Royal College of Physicians), Robert Knox, M.D., and David Mackintosh all provided scientific justification for Britain's bayonet justice in their Irish Colony. Beddoe, author of *The Races of Man* and the inventor of the "index of nigrescence," which, building upon previous cephalic indexes of race, purported to quantify the degree of racial impurity and inferiority of humanity through statistical presentation of eye and hair color, was inspired by the revolutionary nationalisms of 1848 to develop a racial theory of unchanging cultural habitus that we might label "essentialist" today; Beddoe's empiricist and antihistorical methodology reflects the growing dominance of physical anthropology at midcentury, which in turn prepared the way for a backlash in the modernist fascination with the primitive by the century's end and best exemplified by the immense popularity of *The Golden Bough.*[93] In the same anthropological vein, Mackintosh measured and catalogued the "prognathous" features of the Irish, while Robert Knox, whose *The Races of Men: A Philosophical Enquiry into the Influences of Race over the Destinies of Nations* ran to a second edition (1862), favored a form of historical typology to argue that "race is everything: literature, science, art, in a word, civilization, depend on it."⁹⁴ Knox's writings denounce the Irish as deficient in every sign of culture and shamelessly ascribe these putative defects not to the brutalities of occupation but to race:

> The source of all evil lies in the race, the Celtic race of Ireland. There is no getting over historical facts. . . . The race must be forced from the soil; by fair means, if possible; still they must leave. England's safety requires it. I speak not of the justice of the cause; nations must ever act as Machiavelli advised: look to yourself. The Orange club of Ireland is a Saxon confederation for the clearing of the land of all papists and jacobites; this means Celts.⁹⁵

As Banton explains, Knox was no fringe figure but was a respected anatomist whose medical school lectures, by which he supported himself, were responsible for popularizing racial notions of national and religious difference. "Previous to his time, little or nothing was heard about Race in the medical school; he changed all this by his Saturday's lectures, and Race became as familiar as household words to his students, through whom some of his novel ideas became disseminated far and wide."⁹⁶ Scholarly works such as these laid the ground for a further twist in the development of Celtophobia. Since the beginning of modern European contact with the New World, the Irish had been likened to the new colonial "savages." With the development of anthropology as an institution, this comparison expanded to comprehend "mutually derogatory comparisons between Irishmen and the Chinese, Hottentots, Maoris, Aborigines, Sudenese and other 'barbarians.'"⁹⁷ During the 1860s and '70s, however, the substitutability of premodern peoples was truncated as the comic press undertook a massive propaganda campaign, underwritten by the most advanced sciences of the day, to portray the Irish first as African and then as apes, thus demonstrating the development of a popular Darwinian imaginary. By 1885 the political climate was felicitous for Beddoe to suggest, via his index of nigrescence, an African origin for the "Africanoid" Celts. Simianization of the Irish was only one step further down the racist evolutionary scale, and by the 1880s depictions of "Caliban in revolt" or "Mr. MacSimius" become as commonplace as the assertion that the Irish represent the missing link between apes and Africans. This association of foreign "savages" and domestic colonies became a watchword of anthropological science with different consequences both scientific and ideological and extended domestic and classed cultural values to the racial theories of empire. "For Englishmen at home and abroad, domestic class and overseas colonial society were linked by the 'internal colonialism' of the Celtic fringe. Thus Ireland, especially, had since Elizabethan times provided a mediating exemplar for both attitude and policy in relations with 'savages' overseas."[98] If dominant discourse sought the derogation of Irishness and, indeed, all Celtic culture via the new sciences of evolution and anthropology, a counterdiscursive trend allied to colonial drives but developing resistant potential was also at work in the modernist obsession with things primitive. It is this development of a primitivism that is alternately and incoherently represented as brutish barbarism or untapped psychic and creative potential that we have been following in the elegantly controlled *Picture of Dorian Gray* and in its polar opposite, the ranting collapse of *De Profundis*.

CHAPTER 2

"The Bar Was Not Very Gay"

New Kinship and the Serious Writer's Block

At the conclusion of Jane Bowles's only novel, *Two Serious Ladies*, published in 1943, the two ladies of the title meet for the last time at a swanky hotel bar. Possessed of "the desire to tell someone everything that had happened," each hopes that her newly found seriousness will find means for the telling. A break in the text announces the coda before the final scene resumes the narrative with the stark phrase "The restaurant was not very gay," a phrase emblematic of the surprising ways that Bowles's life and writing struggled to name her most profound intuitions in the most naive language. Yet the very moment when readers might reasonably expect a climactic end, the hope of confessional kinship is dashed by a real scene, an embarrassing spectacle, as the sober religious zealot, Miss Goering, speechless and stiffly transfixed, watches while the other becomes seriously, publicly drunk. Having entered with a "scream," Mrs. Copperfield sinks and pitches through the scene as she "walk[s] a crooked path to the bar," where she sits "gulping down her drink, occasionally spilling a little of it over her chin." By the end "terribly gay," Mrs. Copperfield orders a round for the house, an extravagance punctuated by equally extravagant outbursts waveringly aimed at anyone within earshot. When finally Mrs. Copperfield, supported between her girlfriend and the girlfriend's fiancée, makes her stumbling exit, she does so only after speaking her piece. "I *have* gone to pieces, which is a thing I've wanted to do for years. I know I am as guilty as I can be, but I have my happiness, which I guard like a wolf, and I have authority now and a certain amount of daring, which, if you remember correctly, I never had before."[1] Abject speech at its core, her message misses its mark to call forth only more blank speech, for this little rant breeds incomprehension and lack of connection in the place of sovereignty and self-mastery, here perceptible only in the negative space surrounding the failed speech act. Modeling for the bar of abjection in Bowles's fiction, the meeting between stiffness and bodily dislocation, between silence and tirade, between the sobriety of incomprehension and the intoxication of speaking one's piece, fails to explain or offer a theoretical discourse for what it displays: or as Pacifica, Mrs. Copperfield's Panamanian lover, puts it, "She is like a little baby. I tried to explain it to my young man, but I can't explain it really to anyone." In the very place of a failure to name its meaning, this little drama raises a series of questions about meaning, specifically the possibly gay meaning of its own invocation of confession, impossibility, self-description, and regression.

We learn from reading Bowles that if the bar is not very gay, this is because, within the epistemological framework of the novel, being terribly gay means returning speech and its body to a primitive state like drunkenness or being a baby, states or conditions that risk losing authority in the very claim that one has won it. Losing it does nothing to secure these women as sovereign subjects of their speech; rather, the scene allegorizes the sexual politics of containment, irrelevance, and incomprehension pursuing the characters, despite their wanderings in Latin America and New England. Each is barred from speaking the nature of her predicament because to speak it would mean to be it, and each suffers that failure of naming as a perpetual repetition consigning her to the fate of "piling sin upon sin" or "going to pieces" again and again. The indeterminacy of this unspeakability, as much as its overwhelming presence, exerts a constant pressure on the narrative, so much so that by the time we enter the bar we are prepared to witness the dramatization of obstruction, not its transcendence. The signature mark of Bowles's fiction, its most instructive point of obsession, lies in its powerful ability to materialize the law of its own abjection through the dramatization of failure rather than sovereign triumph. The law appears because the characters fail to manifest its accomplishment. The project of materialization is connected in Bowles not only to a restrictive economy of gender, but also to a broader, less distinct work of aggression that overflows the borders of her fiction and ties the aesthetic to her biography in ways that demand a reading of key aspects of her life. Aggressivity working its way through complaint and recrimination is one stylization of the rant in Bowles. Silence is another, for between Bowles's fiction, plays, and letters, the address of ranting persistently aims at the law, but without the sound and fury that characterizes Wilde's understandable breakdown. Consistently, Bowles's fiction strives to manifest the regime of symbolic organization in order to enact fictively an address to that law; thus scenes of breakdown, pathetic and infantile declaration, and vertiginous speech have as their function the positing of a symbolic law and the simultaneous upbraiding of that law. When orchestrating such moments of nonarrival and nonappearance, Bowles's narrative art conducts its own study of power and subjection by attending to the least capable, most dependent personalities.[2] These failed denunciations manifest in their failure the symbolic prefiguration of power by a prior act of social erasure and foreclosure, yet Bowles's insistence on *figuring* the law prevents her text from isolating a consistent, single image, instance, or object as the absolute, and masterful, origin of symbolic exclusion. This simultaneous positing and rebuke of the law is basic to ranting and something we notice in a wide range of rants, for instance, as a feature of Valerie Solanas's *The S.C.U.M. Manifesto,* which hammers away at its fundamental insight, that men cannot call a thing by its name nor feel a genuine emotion so addicted they are to sublimating all truth in their cultural fictions; this denunciation reaches a crescendo in the claim that "even sex is sublimation" for a man. A mad assertion, perhaps, but Solanas knows that when even sex is sublimation, a major rejection of the body and its primitive history is underway.

In the previous chapter we followed Wilde's rejoinder to the social foreclosure of his desire and read his rant as the attempt to reenact the sublimations that enable fantasy to transfigure abjection. The stubborn refusal to lose the beloved, and with him the means of loving, expands the self-berating character of melancholia in *De Profundis* to an impossible act of reproach against the law that enjoins loss itself as the abyssal ground of love and culture. Although intending to write his own *vita nuova,* Wilde produces instead a form of melancholic speech unable—indeed, unwilling—to complete mourning and thus finally and definitively to lose the ideal object of desire; to renounce Bosie would amount to renouncing Wilde's desire entirely for the simple reason that Bosie had come to embody an ideal imperfectly realized in life. This circularity has no resolution apart from its continuation on another plane, aimed at another, and thus manic recuperation becomes a fictive resolution. *De Profundis* ends with the articulation of a new kinship lived in defiance of what the letter describes as a barbaric symbolic law of family life, yet this is a resolve that Wilde could not put into practice.

Bowles's characters suffer the bar of foreclosure differently, in part because they inherit the queer legacy of Wilde, but as drifting, rootless women, wives, tourists, and runaways. They are the great unnoticed, the trivial, the insignificant. No aesthetic movement hangs on their words; they set no fashion and have no influence. The bar is in full force at this point of seeming freedom, for they suffer the lack of attention as a lack of possibility in their lives. The lesbians in her fiction are frustrated and dowdy butches or dreamily wounded femmes who lament their failure to be adequately butch; the Latinas and mixed-race women are stereotyped sisterly prostitutes. What these characters share is their relation to a primitivism that equates psychic states of inadequacy or regression, deviance, low social class, and "foreignness," all viewed from an imaginary perspective of the norm. The repeated figuring of this primitive equation symptomatically reveals the implicit theory behind Bowles's scenes of ranting dislocation. Ranting in Bowles is the last resort of a fearful and failing subject. The resulting speech projects subjective aggressivity outward and reflects an intensity of humiliation, hyperbolizing the weakness of the speaker. Of the many abject figures in her repertoire, only the melancholic, collapsing American femme possesses the power to launch an address at the law whose silent audition is always "dubbed" by a relation or friend. Because the rant's address is an allegorical one, rantical outbursts directed at the law always miss the ear they aim for and find instead a substitute hearer who metaphorically and structurally represents that law. Ranting in Bowles is the melancholic speech of someone suffering the bar of foreclosure where speech itself will fail to authorize the speaker as authorized to speak.

In this chapter we leave behind nineteenth-century aestheticism to track the ways that Wildean wit and the dandy's provocations are stigmatized when decadence is performed by a modernist woman writer in the 1940s. The figure of Bowles's feminine dandy has been largely ignored, and the modernist innovation she forged during World War II has not been part of the canonical tale of Anglo-American modernism. Despite substantial stylistic overlap between Bowles's formal innovations in light satirical style and the primitivism of American postsurrealists (Charles Henry Ford) or the spare narratives of the early Beckett, Bowles does not figure in the story told of the rise and fall of high modernism. Nor can her sentimental and primitivist fiction be assimilated to an early postmodern cool. We will examine Bowles's practice of ranting through two interlaced optics: through the historical context of her literary production, which includes both a Parisian modernist expatriate milieu and a Moroccan domesticity, and through a psychoanalytic engagement with the notion of a symbolic law, lived as taboo and foreclosed inscription. This discussion of a psychic law that produces social foreclosure prepares the way for chapter 3's discussion of Lacan's theory of foreclosure, while our consideration of Bowles' complicity with colonial and racial narratives paves the way for Meddeb's explicit and critical recall of colonial violence and postcolonial normativity. Where decadence breaks down into primitive fragments in Bowles, it is resumed in Meddeb's masterful poetics of ranting, which weds the primitive and the decadent into a new synthesis to be wielded as a powerful anti- and postcolonial critique. Unable to sublimate her social marginality, Bowles negotiates it by ranting from the space of foreclosed inscription that recalls both C.L.R. James's abject appeal and Genet's insight that he must use the master's words to forge his own unique expression.

In Bowles's case the rants are split between letters appearing in the fiction and moments of descriptive intensity and drama conveyed in dialogue or as the narrating voice itself. This tendency to animate and literalize the ranting voice in fiction is complicated by Bowles's writing practice in the years following the onset of her writer's block in 1947. She did not cease writing entirely; rather, she began an epistolary career that lasted until her death in 1973. These letters, for which she had her own generic designations, are often amusing but always stuffed with complaints, brimming with self-reproach and obsessional details. They are full of self-reflective commentary on their own style and content: "I am being vague and half cocked about plans because I'm trying to fool myself out of an 'agonizer.' I can feel this letter slipping into one."[3] "Agonizer" is Bowles's own term for a letter that veers off into self-reproach and almost does not make it to the post: "I am going to walk to town and mail this before I throw it away. I have as usual gotten too wound up about some remark which you have by now forgotten."[4] The rant form dominates nearly all the letters as they upbraid the addressee for a minor infraction and neglect or obsessively work over some deficiency in their author. The overwhelming epistolary strategy is to turn the addressee into a substitute authority, a misplaced ear filled to brimming with her plaints.[5]

Bowles called these letters "literary exercises in precision," a description that authorizes them as a literary form of autobiography intended for interpretation. The letters show an appetite for self-exposure that extends to her piecemeal discussions of her writing block and the struggle to find a way back to writing. It is in the letters that she fosters a link to writing, first surprisingly and then with finality foreclosed to her. This epistolary ranting chronicles the decline of her writing powers as it stubbornly registers her paralysis and marginality. The letters exercise her right to be read even in the absence of a writing that might authenticate that reading. Thus her inability to write becomes another strategy of hyperbolic self-abjection painfully displaying her being-for-the-law even as its ambition is to scatter light off the law and thereby make it glancingly visible.

Into the gap of a suspended writing Bowles introduced a theme binding the biography to the fiction. One of the plots of *Two Serious Ladies* follows the erotic career of a weary femme, Mrs. Copperfield, as she travels unwillingly behind her adventurous husband to Panama. Because the husband refuses the lures of the tourist town with its colonial hotels and expatriate bars, she finds herself in the parallel "native" town with mixed-race prostitutes as the only source of feminine company. She becomes attached to Pacifica, a carefree and practical survivor whose charms inspire in Copperfield fantasies of protection and shelter. Interestingly, this plot prefigures, at a remove of more than ten years, Jane Bowles's pursuit of Cherifa, a Moroccan grain seller whom Jane spied in the Tangier marketplace. In the letters that chronicle one side of their relationship we find Bowles at pains to establish a domestic economy of difference and order—kinship—which would enable her to "believe" in herself as a serious writer, grounded in a place and a world of practices. By setting up a household with Cherifa, Jane establishes a realm of desire that is separate from her mission as a writer and that seeks to literalize the primitive as something materially apart from herself; in this way, becoming hostess absorbs the injury of infantile femininity and disseminates it within another register, one of defined social practices and limited but legible power. Cherifa is for Jane an irreplaceable link to a stable identity and one that continues to shore up the gap of absent writing. My reading of one side of their relationship suggests that while Bowles's fiction may labor to materialize the law of foreclosure on her desires, in her life she strove to shift the burden of that primitive outside onto another.

Jane Bowles was often struck by blockage in the middle of writing fiction, asking, "How can I write it if I can't see it?"[6] Caught between the demand of writing and the failure of vision, which shifts unstably in her texts between meanings suggesting both perception and imagination, Bowles describes the impasse of her blockage with the question "how?" How, we might ask in turn, are we to read such a statement? Not quite a question, neither is it an accusation. As with all the rantical moments in her fiction, this fragment of her literary effort at precision appears torn out of a heated dialogue on the possibility of writing at all. Addressed to an imaginary taskmaster, it aggressively dodges the harsh injunction to write, but considered from another angle she seems to ask for a way out of an impasse. Rhetorically, the *how* is both too full and too empty, for if she beseeches the listener merely to witness her arrested progress, the affective fullness of the *how* empties it of its semantic contents. On this reading the *how* turns toward the hearer and entreats a hearing. Read another way, the question begs an answer, a map, directions through the impasse of the end of sight. The emptiness of this *how* demands to be filled in with the sensible substance of imagination: *this is how you write when you cannot see*. Servile and insubordinate by turns, the *how* of vision fails to be the end of writing by reducing down to an infinitesimal particle the drama of writing to which Jane Bowles is subject. Vision, still the warrant of her writerly aspiration, undergoes a change as it passes through her frustration to give evidence in the fiction that writing is born in the failure of sight. What is foreclosed to Bowles subjects her to writing where she pursues the themes of impasse, failure, and exclusion in tiny irruptions of ranting address.[7] This paradox, which brings foreclosure to a standstill, offers our consideration of ranting a difference of scale, for bombast is not her mode; rather, ranting in Bowles is a persistent, stubborn, and relentless agonizing punctuated by an occasional flamboyant upsurge of noise.

The impasse she continually stages derives, at least in part, from her failure to find a readership. Despite the good reviews that welcomed the author of *Two Serious Ladies* as a delightful new voice, Bowles dismissed her small and devoted readership and her career as nothing more than "writing for one's friends," while ten years later the largely uncomprehending reviews of her stage play *In the Summer House* corroborated her growing sense of marginality and failure. Characteristic of her literary reception is the inability of her critics to distinguish a consciously "primitivist" style from the author's unorthodox personality and openly lesbian relationships.[8] This conflation constructs a "primitive" figure of infantilized femininity to substitute for a reading of the same subject depicted in her fiction, while her writing explores the motivations behind figurations of primitiveness, marked as "oriental," and shows that such figures become the fractured language of feminine subjection. If the feminine appears passive, indolent, infantile, and psychically regressed, this is because such moods and modes are the language available. As we shall see, Bowles's reception shows that her peers consistently mistook her subjects for her character, her literary style for her person. This collapse of personality into style suggests that the femininity she explored was in some way imperceptible to her audience or illegible as an aesthetic. Such a conflation works to circumscribe the range of allowable topics and styles of writing through a refusal to understand naiveté or exaggerated femininity as modes of fiction. Again and again, stories like "A Stick of Green Candy," "Camp Cataract," and even the puppet play explore a complex theory of gender through the naive language and narrative fantasies of women and girls. In the same era of de Beauvoir's first feminist publications and Levi-Strauss's study of kinship and the gender system, Bowles returns to the primitive arcana of domestic scenes to restate the law of feminine abjection in other terms, yet this twist of the norm passed largely undetected by her contemporaries.

In her failure to write Bowles stumbles upon the paradoxical structure of the symbolic law of gender, which dictates that gender appear as the utterly natural, fully known, and thus complete, total system, despite the challenge to that transparency revealed by the difficulty Jane Bowles experiences when she tries to "see it." The same instability between literal and figural meanings, which brings her to the pitch of her rhetorical questions, commits her to write about femininity, especially lesbian femininity, as a realm of symbolization foreclosed. This, then, is why she chooses a primitivist style and why she returns to childhood and infantilized femmes to demonstrate a socially enjoined loss. What Bowles cannot see guarantees her writing; this powerlessness to see the thing she must depict or to know the things she must know captures the ambivalence at the heart of primitiveness as it is imagined by modernism and theorized by psychoanalysis. Freud's primitive builds up a picture of the world by throwing out his ambivalences onto objects. Spirits then animate the objects, granting them life and an unsteady but predictable place in ritual practice. The primitive on this account is both too full—filled with ambivalent love and hate—and too empty for having jettisoned his affective property to accomplish his desire in totemic objects. The primitive is thus the very antithesis of Wilde's tempered man and much closer to the appetite-driven modern type. By this account, primitive achievements derive from a belief in the omnipotence of thought, of which there remains, for Freud, only one cultural vestige in modern societies: "Only in art does it still happen that a man who is consumed by desires performs something resembling the accomplishment of those desires and that what he does in play produces—thanks to artistic illusion—just as though it were something real. People speak with justice of the 'magic of art.'"[9] Bowles's increasing inability to realize her desire in writing is matched by her insistent foregrounding of that impossibility in the letters that substitute for writing. Yet, like Freud's primitive artist, she learns to accomplish magically desires unmet by writing. The genre of the letter exempts her from her blockage, and in the place of a less "authorized" writing she manages to express what is denied to her in fiction. This magical art substitutes readers for a readership by enabling her to deviate around the criticism or indifference that her fiction elicited. Whatever else the epistle might be, as practiced by Jane Bowles, it is not a manly art, for it participates in the schema of address evoked by her rhetorical questions.

Before we turn to Bowles's use of the overlapping figures of the primitive, the regressed feminine, and the oriental, all ways of alternately manifesting and resisting foreclosed inscription, an example from *Two Serious Ladies* offers a context for the peculiar and harsh literary reception of her work. This 1943 publication, her second novel but the only one to be published, was described as "incomprehensible" by some, celebrated by others in the literary press, and largely ignored by the critical press.[10] Poor reception among friends and family added to Bowles's disappointment; she reacted by repudiating the work as "not even a novel." If by 1943 the experiments in stream of consciousness, the antics of surrealism of the 1920s, and resurgent American interest in the gothic amply suggest a complex literary genealogy for *Two Serious Ladies,* the strangely subtle frankness of Bowles's explorations of sexuality proved more resistant to critical understanding. The plot of the novel, like that other largely unread erotic masterpiece *Mademoiselle de Maupin,* details the erotic life of children, female sexual license, prostitution, cross-racial sex, complications of kinship, masturbation, erotic religious fervor, and lesbian love and obsession. The opening scene of *Two Serious Ladies* involves a series of sadomasochistic children's games, justified as religious play, and introduces us to one of the novel's two protagonists, Christina Goering, who suffers from "mental struggles—generally of a religious nature" (*MS*, 4). Growing up to become a "religious leader" without a religion, Christina later seeks out poverty and prostitution as her own private forms of saintly mortification, as she delights in "piling sin upon sin" rather than the sin itself, but in this early scene her religious passions are clearly aroused by her older sister's favorite playmate. Provoked by her jealousy that Mary "belongs" to sister Sophie, the sadistic games reflect the "desire to have Mary to herself of an afternoon" (*MS*, 4). In the first of these saintly games Christina performs for Mary a sun dance that conflates pagan ritual with a species of monotheism.

> "Now don't take your eyes off me," she said. "I'm going to do a dance of worship to the sun. Then I'm going to show that I'd rather have God and no sun than the sun and no God. Do you understand?"
> "Yes," said Mary. "Are you going to do it now?"
> "Yes, I'm going to do it right here." She began the dance abruptly. It was a clumsy dance and her gestures were all undecided. When Sophie came out of the house, Christina was in the act of running backwards and forwards with her hands joined in prayer.
> "What is she doing?" Sophie asked Mary.
> "A dance to the sun, I think," Mary said. "She told me to sit here and watch her."
> Sophie walked over to where Christina was now twirling around and around and shaking her hands weakly in the air.
> "Sneak!" she said and suddenly she pushed Christina down on the grass. . . . For a long time after that, Christina kept away from Sophie, and consequently from Mary. (*MS*, 5)

The very simple language intensifies the farcical character of Christina's improvised ritual performed here only in a flimsy slip. Christina's attempted seduction proceeds entirely in this ponderous style, and, quite undeterred by Mary's slightly deflating "Are you going to do it now?" Christina will continue to try to get next to Mary, herself always positioned between an only slightly believable conceit of ignorance and a complicity. In other stories Bowles will repeat this coupling with adult characters, in scenes in which one woman inexpertly desires another woman who smoothly but unaccountably shifts from real or feigned ignorance to reciprocation.[11] Given Bowles's psychic and literary investment in depicting, dramatizing, and living out the limit experience of impediment, it should come as no surprise that the erotic situations she most often writes about also reflect an impasse. The dynamic between a self-conscious lesbian desire and a mysterious because shifting interest and repudiation of lesbianism repeats throughout the novel and Bowles's stories, where the barrier between two women is always figured as something definitive and irrefutable. At times the barrier emerges as the specter of a violation of the incest taboo or as unspeakable murder; in her puppet show "A Quarreling Pair," child's fare serving up adult longing and thwarted desire, it is figured by a prop, "a rod or string dividing it down the middle to indicate two rooms" (*MS*, 414).

Awkward and unprecedented children people her fiction to strain the conventions of realism as they pursue unnamed but palpable desires. Later Christina and Mary strike a gaming bargain in the "tower where the children often gather." This is another of Bowles's joking references to the carceral spaces allowed for childish play, spaces that run the gamut from the tower's place of tortures to the Kinsey Memorial Playground in "A Stick of Green Candy."

> She asked her if she would not like to play a very special game with her. "It's called 'I forgive you for all your sins'," said Christina. "You'll have to take your dress off."
> "Is it fun?" Mary asked.
> "It is not for fun that we play it, but because it's necessary to play it."
> (*MS*, 6)

Mary agrees to this necessity. They prepare Mary's costume. She is tied into a sack with holes punched for her eyes. In a state of high excitation, Christina fumbles for purpose, and in the landscape of the wooded stream she hits upon the mud as another necessity of the ritual.

> "Come to the water," said Christina; "I think that's how we'll wash away your sins. You'll have to stand in the mud."
> "Near the mud?"
> "*In* the mud. Does your sin taste bitter in your mouth? It must."
> "Yes," said Mary hesitantly.
> "Then you want to be clean and pure as a flower is, don't you?"
> Mary did not answer.
> "If you don't lie down in the mud and let me pack the mud over you and then wash you in the stream, you'll be forever condemned. Do you want to be forever condemned? This is your moment to decide." (*MS*, 6)

Feigning control, Christina obliges the other girl to obey. These commands must be seen, she says, as obvious facts emanating from the world as naturally as the stream at the end of the wood, and nature is called upon to verify the facticity of her own fantasy's order. The only sin attributable to Mary is that of inciting desire, yet hers is the sin elaborated by Christina's ritual. Between the first spectacle of the sun dance and this game of expiation, Christina has learned that Mary can be manipulated and, equally, that she responds to Christina's older sister largely because Sophie dominates her.

> "The mud's cold," said Mary.
> "The hell fires are hot," said Christina. "If you let me do this, you won't go to hell."
> "Don't take too long," said Mary. . . .
> "Oh, please no, not the water—I hate to go into the water. I'm afraid of the water."
> "Forget what you are afraid of. God's watching you now and He has no sympathy for you yet."
> She lifted Mary from the ground and walked into the stream, carrying her. . . .
> "Three minutes will be enough," said Christina. "I'm going to say a little prayer for you."
> "Oh, don't do that," Mary pleaded.
> "Of course," said Christina, lifting her eyes to the sky.
> "Dear God," she said, "make this girl Mary pure as Jesus Your Son. Wash her sins away as the water is now washing the mud away. This black burlap proves to you that she thinks she is a sinner."
> "Oh, stop," whispered Mary. "He can hear you even if you just say it to yourself. You're shouting so."
> "The three minutes are over, I believe," said Christina. "Come darling, now you can stand up." (*MS*, 7)

A series of masks comes into play: concealing Mary in the sack, covering her with mud, holding her down, declaiming and enjoining her to pray. These acts signal that the prohibition on touching Mary will be circumvented by covering, suffocating, purging her. After the ceremony Christina's energies are spent; she has no further interest in the younger girl. The girls' play converts from pagan dance to Christian mortification, from theatrical ritual to humiliation and expiation of sin, from spectacle offered to the god to sadistic ritual enjoined by him, yet both the pagan and the Christian are equated in their ritual aspect. Christina accomplishes her desire to touch Mary by means of a game that looks like the antithesis of desire and that is justified in terms of antithesis: "It is not for fun that we play it, but because it's necessary to play it." And this becomes key to the character's desire throughout; even as she prostitutes herself to a cartoonish gangster or watches impassively an almost incomprehensible act of masturbation, Christina Goering revels not in the sexual but in the degradation that she rains down upon herself. Self-mastery through abjection is the twist on sovereignty orchestrated through unmotivated plot turns and flat, unembroidered characters in a narrative that refuses to ease the reader's confusion through a masterful authorial voice. These bathetic qualities offer little to the salacious imagination as the eros depicted is both mysterious and utterly singular; neither moral emetic nor merely obscene, these scenes demand a reading of desire as both enigmatic and vulnerable to naming.

Unstably located between the magical arts of primitive religion and the desire-driven play of the artist, Christina's rite follows a logic similar to that outlined in "The Antithetical Sense of Primal Words," in which Freud reflects on the "strange tendency of the dream-work to disregard negation and to express contraries by identical means of representation."[12] Reviewing K. Abel's recent book on the origin of antithetical meanings in "the Egyptian language, this unique relic of a primitive world," Freud champions the philologist's argument that "every conception is ... the twin of its opposite," for "Man has not been able to acquire even his oldest and simplest conceptions otherwise than in contrast with their opposite; he only gradually learnt to separate the two sides of the antithesis and think of the one without conscious comparison with the other."[13] Christina plays in the space of this antithesis by reversing the order of faith and expiation just as the antithetical words *altus* and *sacer* enact both high and low, sacred and profane. "We remember how fond children are of playing at reversing the sound of words": To render Mary "clean and pure as a flower," she will pack her in mud, cold as hellfire is hot. To address Mary as "darling," Christina will contradict every expression of desire and dread the other girl offers. "Wash her sins away as the water is now washing the mud away," she urges her god, but how did Mary get so dirty? What exactly is her sin? Mary's sin is Christina's desire, the very thing that goes unnamed and unavowed throughout the ritual game.

It is through recourse to the primal sense of "primitive" words and rituals that the thing foreclosed by the law, that second meaning of *sacer*, can return to the scene of its evacuation. These allegorical children reflect back upon the putative immobility of kinship laws and sexual prohibitions that would circumscribe their desire in their play. Scenes like this one track the "origin" of lesbian object choice as a lost object and reflect a sophisticated understanding of the place of play, religious rhetoric, and prohibition in the sexual fantasies of children. For Bowles the price of choosing to return to these "oldest and simplest conceptions" to explore what Freud rather cavalierly refers to as "a lack of social possibility" in women's lives and object choice was misrecognition and obscurity, as the slippery antithetical sense of primitivism worked against her to stigmatize her person and her writing. The following pages sketch a context for understanding this (non-) reception and for situating it within the Freudian analysis of contagion occasioned by the extension of blood ties to kinship ties, where the latter are understood to be fundamentally those of metaphor. The writing block that ensued from this cultural misrecognition caused the moments of fictional ranting to blossom into a living practice, manifest as an epistolary discipline. From foreclosed speech to ranting, Bowles found new ways to secure her modernist project of self-invention.

LESBIAN MODERNISM AND THE ORIENTAL JANE

> The strangest fact seems to be that anyone who has transgressed one of these prohibitions himself acquires the characteristic of being prohibited—as though the whole of the dangerous charge had been transferred over to him. This power is attached to all *special* individuals, such as kings, priests or newborn babies, to all *exceptional* states, such as the physical states of menstruation, puberty or birth, and to all *uncanny* things, such as sickness and death and what is associated with them through their power of infection or contagion.
>
> Sigmund Freud, *Character and Culture*

In the fall of 1949 Jane and Paul Bowles passed through Paris, paying a visit to Alice Toklas, who had, along with Stein, adopted Paul into their household in the '30s. The Toklas-Stein household occupied a place of great influence in the lives of the American literati living in Paris both before and after the war, and the opinions of the widow Toklas carried a certain authority even in 1949. Toklas and Stein provided Paul with a domestic mentorship of a somewhat tyrannical nature. It was Stein who encouraged, even ordered, him to Morocco for the first time, and she who announced that he should give up writing, going so far as to chastise him for publishing his poems, which she found laughable and, indeed, laughed at in front of him. He obeyed her in both cases, laying down his pen until the 1940s, when, under Jane's influence and after Stein's passing, he resumed writing. The encounter between Alice and Jane, beginning with this first meeting and lasting until 1964, is a significant one for tracing a lineage in lesbian modernism both as a literary and a broader cultural history. Their meeting draws a fault line within lesbian modernism, one that figures a generational shift in the terms of a wider cultural derogation of the primitive as against the adult and the civilized. In essence, this generation gap marks Jane as a failed femme, while her failure to live up to the lesbian femme ideal is coded in Toklas's letters as a racial and psychic difference.

Though Jane belongs to a generation of expatriate writers who inherit the legacy of modernism, she is distinguishable from them by the fact that, unlike many of the "women of the Left Bank," she was fluent in French. Not only did she write her first novel in French, but she was also well versed in French modernism. In fact, her literary vocation was forged in a Swiss sanatorium at Leysin, where reading became her most passionate and essential link to the world, and where her French tutor made sure that she read Gide, Proust, Céline, and Montherlant, among others; her letters tell us that she was reading Sartre and de Beauvoir before the major translations. Writing for her was mixed with a fervent adulation of the avant-garde, and she liked to be seen in Paris and New York with a volume of Simone Weil or Kierkegaard under her arm. This worshipful attitude is borne out by one of the many fables she would circulate about herself. Returning to New York on the liner *Champlain* in 1934, a man interrupted Jane reading *Voyage au bout de la nuit,* with the comment, "I see you're reading Céline." "He is one of the greatest writers in the world," she said. "Céline, c'est moi," he replied.[14] Such brushes with fame, told and retold by a young woman determined to be a writer, in advance of any actual writing, betray a desire for the celebrity of authorship, but it was her misfortune to be most famous for being the *wife* of a noted writer. The crushing misogyny of this scenario was policed from "within" the expatriate lesbian cultural milieu of Paris by Alice Toklas.

Toklas's letters are completely unabashed and indiscreet in their judgment of Jane; peppered with censorious declarations, the letters are emblematic of the responses Jane drew from the sophisticated establishment that now controlled modernist fashion. These letters to friends, among them Paul, paint the picture of a severe femme working to enforce femininity in the Bowles marriage, at the price of Jane's writerly reputation.[15] Things begin nicely enough, with Toklas writing that Jane's novel is a delight, though unwisely published at the beginning of the war, "obviously not a propitious moment to present gaiety and insouciance."[16] Even here, however, Toklas announces that Jane is "like" her novel, a claim that Toklas will later expand into a wholesale condemnation of the fiction as a form of nonfiction. As we shall see, Jane will end up in the Toklas account not an author at all but merely someone who "projects" her view of the world onto the stage of fiction. Her fiction will be "like" her, an unmediated and artless emanation of a peculiarly primitive character.

"She says she is working regularly—but is she. Has she any intimate acquaintance with either work or regularity—can and should one introduce them to each other."[17] So begins the myth of an undisciplined Jane, too self-indulgent to adhere to the rigorous schedule Toklas imagines to be key to writerly life. The condescension is all the more surprising in a letter addressed to Paul Bowles. In a world ordered by a strict code of feminine refinement and elegant hospitality, Toklas's condemnation is couched in the language of that domestic order. "Can and should one introduce them" pits the power of a feminine world of teas and lunches against the unruly childishness of play and impulses. Throughout the letters she struggles to sum Jane up in a single pattern or type. "Jane Bowles' play never came off in New York—someone told me—it may even be true—that she messed things up by falling in love with the actress who was to be the leading lady—who wasn't interested. Dear Jane . . . she is to her misfortune true to type."[18] Well in advance of any misfortune, Toklas has already cast Jane in the role of the badly behaved child, monster of eros, lacking the basic structuring regularity of a lady who does not allow emotions to make a "mess."[19]

This tendency to cast Jane in a tragic role she had yet to play in life is evident in nearly all the testimonials upon which Millicent Dillon's biography of Jane is based. Ned Rorem claims that Jane was a childish and "impossible person" who thrived on pointless complications; Edouard Roditi, though more sympathetic, fully embraces the narrative of squandered talent bound to a self-destructive drive and doomed from the first. None of these minor modernists consider the effects of their judgment or the possibility that the queer "establishment" of postwar literary circles might have been creating the little monster they were so eager to lament after her tragedy. On April 4, 1957, she suffered a stroke, leaving her with permanent brain damage affecting her vision and language skills. As we will see, the experience did not impair her literary drive; she continued to write—in one form or another—until her death in 1973. Interesting for a literary and sexual genealogy, these testimonials—there are hundreds of them, comprising a modernist compulsion to remember Jane always within the clear outline of a particular "type," the abject femme of wasted talent, childish charm, and complication—conspire to build up an image of Jane as everything a postwar modernist would not want to be, especially if she were a lesbian. This compulsion to typecast Jane reveals a disavowal of an identification at work in the loose social body of queer modernism in the aftermath of the war. Abjecting Jane is a symptom of the social activity of foreclosure with which queer, especially lesbian, modernism sought to define its boundaries.

Toklas's irritation at Jane's uniqueness grew with the reputation of the author. Even her way of being lesbian came under fire. After seeing Jane with a lover, Toklas concludes, "Jane is strange as an American but not as an Oriental—especially an Oriental D.P. It was to this conclusion that seeing her with Libby Holman brought me. If accepting this makes her more foreign it at least relieves the strain—that morbidity—she originally seemed at first to be consumed by."[20] This judgment, though unique in the record, expresses a common thread of the reactions to Jane Bowles. She is said to be morbidly on her way to destruction, strangely foreign in a way that ruffles and strains because she threatens to infect her companions with disorder and death. Her presence evokes oriental chaos and laxity at a time when sexual dissidents and artists were denounced as decadent impediments to national unity. To see Jane with the even more feminine torch singer, Libby Holman, throws up a projection of that which can become legible only on the condition that it first be rendered foreign. The Orient, signifier and carrier of a decaying, dying culture, an incoherent trope of primitive decadence, provides the anchor for this mobile morbidity and explains away what could not be understood. Within the logic of this commonplace orientalism, seeing Jane with Holman provides Toklas the harem tableau of two feminine women together from which she can then reconstruct an understanding. The unoriginality of Toklas's commonplace prejudice authorizes the American as the model of a vital yet stable eros to ground a sexual identity and from which one might engage in the artifice of fiction without risk of self-exposure. An entire theory of the relation of life to art and race to life lurks behind the trivial gossip; the effects of that theory were not so trivial, however. That Toklas, a Hungarian American Jew, says this of another Hungarian American Jew only confirms the projective logic working to distinguish between them by invoking a figure of failure and regression. Toklas finds it less of a strain to willfully imagine Jane as an "Oriental"—signifying neither a geography nor a people so much as a way of death.

Like every policing activity, this one thrives in company. A letter to Mercedes de Acosta offers up a comprehensive judgment of Jane, complete with pathologizing pseudo-psychoanalytic assessment. It is instructive for the way an aesthetic judgment is linked to a psychological diagnosis that relegates Bowles's writing and her character to an abjectly juvenile status, and it reveals the extent to which Freudian models and vocabulary were naturalized as common parlance by the late 1940s. Telling, too, is the way Toklas prevaricates around the question of her own substantial preoccupation with Jane. Incapable of admitting a fascination with the younger woman, she will relish the portrait of Jane in another woman's words.

> When I asked you to tell me about Jane Bowles' play it was not to ask you to take time to analyse it in detail as you did but what you had to say fascinated and interested me beyond words—for it was an exact portrait of Jane herself and as I suspected the play is nothing but a projection of herself—ergo neither she nor the play are adult. As you so very clearly saw. What in her seemed based on fear—her strongest realist emotion—you have put your finger on—fear of taking an adult attitude to her weakness—more particularly even fear of facing adult responsibilities. If mistakenly I mistook the reason of her fears the moment you gave the right one we were agreed. And I was relieved for it had worried me a bit—of course it diminishes one's interest in her to have the answer.[21]

How do adults play? Evidently, they are not to play with projections—and still less with children. Here we see nothing if not the collusion of two women at the expense of a third. That this looks more and more like a baroque erotic intrigue bears out the staginess of the disavowal at work in the exchange. Casting Jane as the craven child sacrifice, Toklas preserves for herself the space of adult femininity uncontaminated by the queerly childish threat. The letter moves from excitation to disinterest through the spectacle of Jane's failure to write a play sufficiently infused with the bracing airs of adult renunciation. This genre of collaboration to exclude another effectively performs the law's cut where it throws up the symptomatic representations of projection. "As you so very clearly saw" is perhaps the most important link in the chain that binds the correspondents together, for it will be on the basis of a shared perception that they will decide Jane's character and her literary worthlessness—"perception" will set the stage for the fundamental disavowal of fascination and similitude. To see Jane's primitive projections staged is to know her for a narcissistic child who can do no more than repeat herself where the rigors of artifice ought to be. Toklas adds to this an assertion of her own adult, feminine character by invoking stock poses of the delicate femme, worried and disturbed by the disordered irruption of a regression and paranoid projection where there should be serious art. "If I wasn't shrewd enough to find it out for myself—I do thanks to you know now what worried me and why there could be no real pleasure in knowing Jane."[22] No "real" pleasure: but substantial investments of time, words, fantasy, and violent judgment culminate in the knowledge that all that came before, those false pleasures of scrutinizing Jane, are now at an end. With Mercedes' help Alice can now disavow the evident desire aroused by Jane where knowing "why" means knowing that there can be no pleasure in knowing Jane. The girl who was "a delight" a few years before has *become* a child and is thus banned from the stately regime of lesbian desire.

The twinned logic, binding together the decaying, primitive Orient and the regressed, psychically primitive child, flows consistently through the testimonials, yet the more approving portraits give us something closer to a witty, feminine dandy. In fact, the personality so often remarked as childish, hysterical, impulsive, and enigmatic is a cipher largely because it is that of a dandy, self-consciously using the gestures of the dandy: feckless and transcendent self-construction, mediated through and by the poses, phrases, and tantrums of a precocious young aesthete. Picturing her personality becomes almost an object of obsession for every critical essay, every bit of biographical memoir published about her. Essential to this depicting-drive is her eternal, fixed character.

> Jane, with her dahlia-head of cropped curly hair, her tilted nose and mischief-shiny, just trifle mad eyes, her very original voice (a husky soprano), her boyish clothes and schoolgirl's figure and slightly limping walk, is more or less the same as when I first knew her more than twenty years ago: even then she had seemed the eternal urchin, appealing as the most appealing of non-adults, yet with some substance cooler than blood invading her veins, and with a wit, an eccentric wisdom no child, not the strangest wunderkind, ever possessed.[23]

One camp of those who survive her holds that she is regressed, fixated in a regressive state, falling away from adulthood through a lapse of will: in a word, decadent. If she is unchanging it is because she has always been limping away from the destiny of a complete and full development. Preserved by that "substance cooler than blood invading her veins," she is half-dead in life, eternally surrounded by flowers. Capote's description of Jane here casts her as the eternal urchin but locates her appeal in the promise of something beyond the "adult." In the husky soprano of an original voice, Jane's hybrid gender captures something at the threshold of boyish clothes and a girlish figure, where the adult world simply fails to appeal.

The contrast between the responses of Capote and Toklas represents a cultural and generational divide that might be understood as two reactions to the same threat. If Capote relishes Jane's "thorny wit," which he drinks up like a "newly tasted, refreshingly bitter beverage," it is because the gamble of wit does not terrorize him, and the figure of desire only draws him near. Toklas, on the other hand, seems consumed by fear of Jane's alluring oddity and sees her inventiveness only in terms of excess and eccentricity. Capote's pleasure in knowing Jane relates, in part, to the fact that that pleasure is not captured and trapped within a rigidly gendered schema. He can join in her games, playing with this "most appealing of non-adults" without risking the edifice of his desire, because play *is* that desire and because his openly gay identity takes its refreshment in the play of wit.[24]

Toklas is quite another story. A brief sketch of Toklas's expectations of lesbian gender norms fleshes out the terms of the cultural policing she attempts to enforce. In Shari Benstock's history of Left Bank lesbian modernists, gender role-playing comes to the fore as a primary activity of community and cultural life. "If class status and economic privilege allowed women of the Paris community to act freely on nontraditional sexual choices, these privileges also bound women more closely to the institution of patriarchy."[25] The Toklas-Stein household was run strictly along the axis of a butch-femme casting, where "his majesty the baby" was distinctly, and only, male. "As a couple, they followed the conventions of nineteenth century Victorian domesticity, and their coupling reproduced an entire cast of family characters: Stein, who at first was 'husband,' also played 'Baby' to Toklas' role as 'Mama,' while Carl Van Vechten—one of Stein's most steadfastly loyal supporters—played 'Papa.'" Benstock describes a domestic economy where Toklas reigns as the maternal femme, called alternately "Mrs." and "little Jew," who

> occupied a position with respect to (and in respect of) this same law: her "husband" and "baby" may have been biologically female, but "he" acted as a male, leaving Alice to take the female role. She feminized this role intensely—from her choice of beaded jewelry and lace handkerchiefs, careful manicures, and love of perfumes, to her fondness for rich pastries and sweet desserts. Toklas paid an enormous price for the role she created for herself in Stein's life, and this suffering was made worse by the self-imposed law that prevented her from ever admitting—even to her closest friends—that Stein was often unkind to her.[26]

While Benstock's narrative of the abused and masochistic femme follows rather too easily from the few details she quickly outlines, the portrait of strictly enforced—and pleasurably enforced—gender performance within the relationship reveals a systematic culture of gender that determines Toklas's discomfort with Jane Bowles. If the feminine is rigorously delineated as caretaker, and if babydom belongs exclusively to the masculine position, is it any wonder that Toklas reacts with venom to the spectacle of a baby-dandy who is fully femme but not richly bedecked, one who hates sweets and rebels against feminine finery with all the energy of a teenager? Jane is resolutely femme but just as resolutely indifferent to the specific markers of feminine gender that were so productive and vital to an earlier generation. The stakes of the animus Toklas palpably felt and communicated to others only mount if that seductive baby-femme were to arouse her passions. If there is something like a generational schism between these two ways of being lesbian and performing femininity, there is certainly no way to posit one as more "closely tied to the institutions of patriarchy," as Benstock argues.[27] Rather the example of Toklas and Bowles's relationship shows the impossibility of being "untied" from the institutions that shape one's desire and identity. Equally, the relationship reveals the operation of foreclosure and repudiation in a lesbian setting, for they are not equally and stably situated at the border of heterosexual normativity but are in their interaction traversed by the same bar that would seek to foreclose their desires, their identities, and their appetites. The weapon Toklas levels at Bowles is the apparatus of a hyperfeminized lesbian culture—which is to say that Toklas has found a way of shaping and delimiting a being-in-culture that reworks, displaces, and consolidates the ideality of norms. Bowles, who within this strict regime fails to be "adult," becomes the abject whose company no cultured person could or would enjoy. Toklas, who cannot not-be the scolding maternal figure in this pairing, stakes out a set of norms culled from the antique world of modernism's early negotiation with sexuality and gender and rigidly holds Jane to a standard of gender decorum that is for Jane the very figure of the law she consistently resists in her life as in her work.

If the narrative joining of the theme of the regressed child to that of the mad and the primitive seems familiar, it is so perhaps partly because of an earlier attack on Gertrude Stein by Wyndham Lewis. In the pages of *Time and Western Man* Lewis advances his critique of modernism as a mere "cult of childhood" that "uses the forms of infantile or immature life," making an art of technical imperfections and exploiting "natural ignorance," which he views as evidence of a desire to be a child.[28] According to Lewis, the child cult in Stein extends beyond her work to characterize the period of "revolutions of sentiment or of ideologic formula today." Further, "the cult of the savage (and indirectly that of the Child) is a pointing backward to our human origins, either as individuals (when it takes the form of the child-cult) or as a race (when it takes the form of 'the primitive')."[29] Such primitivism or infantilism is no more than a form of romantic affectation, deriving from a sentimentality that Lewis characterizes as morbid, "mournful and monstrous, composed of dead and inanimate material. . . . Its life is a low-grade, if tenacious, one."[30] His dismissal of Stein bears an uncanny resemblance to Toklas's denunciations of Jane. "My general objection, then, to the work of Miss Stein is that it is *dead*. My second objection is that it is *romantic*. . . . It is the personal rhythm, the obvious bias, that of a peculiar rather than a universal nature . . . all this excess, this tropical unreality, I find . . . in Miss Stein."[31]

It is precisely Jane's peculiar rather than universal nature that comes under fire. She elicits and absorbs the cultural baggage of what must be functioning as a queer unconscious among a certain generation of modernists.[32] How else to explain the eerie rematerialization of these terms of odium? "This excess, this tropical unreality" is not so far from an "Oriental D.P.," simultaneously languorously morbid and compulsively overemotional. Lewis neatly links the metonymic series, child-primitive, to its metaphoric capital conceived in terms of an exploration of personal and racial psychic prehistory. That Lewis advances the theory of the child-primitive in the genre of literary criticism does not make it either more or less significant than its reemergence as gossip in Toklas's letters, but it does signal that his criticism of Stein finds its way into the discourses of queer modernism under the sign of a taboo that will work to decide the proper and the improper. As we know, "a taboo is not a neurosis but a social institution,"[33] and it is the social institution of the taboo on regression that we see exercised in Toklas's letters about Jane. Modernism consigns Jane to the status of the abject, excessive, modern problem child, who, always making scenes and inventing complications, returns the new to the old, revives the child where the adult should be. To situate Jane within the context of lesbian and gay modernism after the war is to engage with the active exclusions of that social institution.[34]

Jane Bowles seems caught between insult, envy, and dependence in her own letters about Toklas. She clearly found her isolation as a writer unbearable and consistently compares Paul's fame to her own marginal obscurity. "Your literary success is a fact now and it is not only distinguished but widespread. I think to have [Cyril] Connolly and Toklas and a host of other literary people, plus a public, is really remarkable and wonderful."[35] Equally clear is the significance of Toklas's judgments, as is evident in a vignette narrated to Paul in 1950.

> I see Alice Toklas now and then, but I'm afraid that each time I do I am stiffer and more afraid. She is charming and will probably see me less and less as a result of my inability to converse. This is not a result of my shyness alone, but of a definite absence of intellect, or should I say of ideas that can be expressed, ideas that I am in any way certain about. I have no opinions really. This is not just neurotic. It is very true. And Alice Toklas gives one plenty of opportunity to express an idea or an opinion. She won't serve me those little bread sandwiches in different colors any more because she says I like them more than the cake, and so eat them instead of the cake. I do like them better. And now I must go there and eat only sweets, which makes me even more nervous. Maybe she'll never speak to me again.[36]

Toklas's charm seems to lie in her ability to conjure away Jane's powers of speech by simply sitting and waiting expectantly. This terrifying expectation leads to the mortification and passivity identified by Toklas as Jane's essential personality. The severity of her audience finds further expression in Toklas's condescending enforcement of food taboos. Teatime becomes an ordeal in which the victim must navigate the hard and angular surfaces of completely unaccountable hostilities and forbidden zones. "I am stiffer and stiffer" describes the effect of superegoic injunctions conveyed as a senseless and magical silence. When an explanation is ventured it is also senseless: "She says I like them more than the cake." Toklas appears to embody in Jane's enflamed imagination a panoptic discipline, one that Jane had already written about in "A Stick of Green Candy," a story detailing the enforcement of femininity through gift exchange and a market in unwanted candy. If sweets were a signifier of feminine rigidity for Jane, the signifying potential of food is no less conscious and deliberate for Toklas, whose only claim to authorship rests with her cookbook. One detects, too, the ghost of Gertrude Stein and her equal obsession with food as a mobilizing reference conveying both wit and a silencing disavowal of complication. Urged to leave by the American consul after the fall of France, Stein claims to have decided the matter by saying to Toklas, "Well, I don't know—it would be awfully uncomfortable and I am fussy about my food. Let's not leave."[37]

"You shall like cakes" encodes for Bowles only the worst and most constraining form of femininity. A distaste for sweets represents in her fiction, too, the distaste a girl feels for the deflection of her imagination into conventional and gendered, thus allowable, regions and forms.[38] While Bowles will repeat some of the aspects of the Toklas regime of the feminine in her relationship with Cherifa—turning Cherifa into the irrational and tyrannical butch-baby who must be obeyed or humored—Bowles's writing and her mythology of the writer's burden prevents her from taking up the selfless, sacrificing drag of the hyperfemme. Some part of Bowles's very public self-berating and melancholia is in the service of resisting what was for her a mortifying law of the feminine.

Cringing and indulging her appetites by turns, Jane could never be mistaken for a "model" modernist woman. What's good for Jane is not good for all; it is this that makes her such an irritant, that and the fact that in "refusing to grow up" she poses a temptation in fantasy. Not only does she seem to allow herself all, to live in the most abject state of dependence on fate and the charity of others, she is constantly making plans that have no real objective restraints. She seems to go where and to do what she pleases. She throws up a specter of what life could be if every little appetite and sorrow were indulged. She mimes the neurotic regression as an avowed one, willful and fun, nervous and tortured.

The charge of projection—"the play is nothing but a projection of herself"—leveled at Jane Bowles is yet another variation on the Lewisian theme of the child-primitive, for it claims to identify a form of literalization in an aesthetic failure. As such, "projection" becomes a feature of the abjecting discourse that isolates Jane as an exception to be excluded. "What is in question is fear of an infectious example, of the temptation to imitate—that is, of the contagious character of taboo. If one person succeeds in gratifying the repressed desire, the same desire is bound to be kindled in all the other members of the community."[39] To be exceptional is always to be vulnerable to censure, as Freud's analysis of the social institution of the taboo shows. Jane's failure to conform to an outmoded standard of the feminine as well as her naive attention to "trivial" details of women's lives in her fiction situates her on the frontier of the social world to which her marriage introduced her. Jane's letters of this period tell the story of being ignored in society until someone discovers that she is the wife of Paul Bowles. Invisible unless bound to a man, she finds her marginality remarked over and over by this negative form of attention. She was, however, not living with her husband during her many visits to Paris;

she usually lived with many different women. One thing is made clear through her relationship with Toklas, however; Jane unsettles like and through her play. She conjures up ambivalence and then must live it out in the nowhere of abjection. Too like "them" to be dismissed, she is too unlike them to be suffered; thus, Toklas and others conspire to teach her place—dictating that she is bound to them only through the metaphoric tie of marriage.

METAPHORIC RELATIONS

The possibility of incest would seem to be a temptation
in phantasy set in motion through the agency of
unconscious connecting links.
> Sigmund Freud, *Totem and Taboo*

At the outset of Freud's elaboration of the analogy between "primitive" and neurotic man we find the psychoanalyst digressing to explain the curious fact of hostility between a son-in-law and his mother-in-law. This relation of irritability and malevolence has its roots, according to Freud, in an unconscious temptation emanating from the always already repressed incestuous desire for the parents, lost somewhere in the prehistory of the son-in-law's object choice. That first, incestuous desire falls under the bar of repression, learns the law of substitution, and, in doing so, leaves behind a trail that Freud has no difficulty identifying as primarily "genealogical" in nature. "Because of the barrier that exists against incest, his love is deflected from the two figures on whom his affection was centred in his childhood on to an outside object that is modelled upon them.... His horror of incest insists that the *genealogical* history of his choice of an object for his love shall not be recalled."[40] The mother-in-law "offer[s] him a temptation to incest," defended against through the expression of hostilities that are only the consciously felt aspect of a long-standing unconscious ambivalence. Freud thus derives a genealogy of unconscious investment from the evidence of irritability and petty hatred produced by the metaphoric extension of kinship to the "in-laws." The metaphoric relation of being-in-law finds its analogue in "the agency of unconscious connecting links," which distort, displace, and suggest the disturbing genealogy that must remain beyond any recall. The metaphoric relation so predictably produces this effect of the "in-law" that a cultural norm arises to name or contain the fact. The danger that the metaphoric relation evokes is one that Freud repeatedly describes as "an infantile feature," for it bubbles up out of the genealogical past as though the careful labor of reinscribing abandoned object choices had never occurred, as though that work could be undone.

The being-in-law of the metaphoric relation reveals the havoc wrought by an association that is both too close and not close enough, an association so familiar that her mere presence calls up that which should remain beyond recollection. Her proximity to the parents, here specified as the mother but increasingly throughout Freud's text identified as the father, retrieves a souvenir of unconscious infantile fantasy that has been laboriously worked over, lost to good purpose. On the basis of the loss of this original object, the subject is inaugurated into the regime of gendered order, for the first loss creates the propulsive play of identification and, finally, avowed object choices.[41] The irony of the metaphoric relation lies in its ability to show the fragility of that normative order, which teaches the subject, here resolutely male, to compensate himself with allowable objects. That it should be a "metaphor" that evokes the unconscious, repressed object in the mode of fantasy is no accident. The mother-in-law is like the desired original object but not like enough to be assimilated by the subject's practiced arts of repression. These ready-made defenses founder precisely where the genealogy ceases to produce substitutions and threatens to take its object unmediated. Unlike a blood relation with whom Freud says the "possibility of incest is an immediate one and the intention to prevent it may be conscious," the metaphoric relation of being-in-law remains a threat to the subject's very constitution, a threat all the more menacing for being established in fantasy.

From this speculative detour Freud deduces a key difference between the so-called "primitive" or "savage" peoples and the pitfalls of neurosis in modern man. Primitives handle their horror of incest by securing ritual as the measure of avoidance and installing a social vocabulary to take up the burden of individual defenses against the desires of fantasy; according to the Freudian reading of anthropological findings, their social world assumes the responsibilities of unconscious ambivalence; the social institution of taboo, Freud's earliest definition of the term, is lived as a collective and thus learned practice. Because "modern" man lacks the "saturations of the superego" that color the social landscape of primitive life, he must reinvent the wheel of his earliest repudiations once a metaphoric relation has worked its destabilizing magic.[42] Or so goes the fable shared between Freud and Lacan in their modernist narrative of a sickly and broken modernity that has shattered the fine networks of traditional relations. Not so much a narrative of disenchantment as a story of misfit and bad casting, the projection on the body of the mother-in-law is a faded and weak substitute for primitive ritual; but for the modern son, friction with the mother-in-law is the next best thing to genuine peril. In arguing for infantile fantasy as a common ground of psychic life between primitives and moderns, Freud inserts a developmental model into the account where a genealogical one had sufficed to describe the trajectory of fantasy and desire in the son-in-law.

> Psychoanalysis has taught us that a boy's earliest choice of objects for his love is incestuous and that those objects are forbidden. . . . A neurotic . . . invariably exhibits some degree of psychical infantilism. He has either failed to get free from the psycho-sexual conditions that prevailed in his childhood or he has returned to them—two possibilities which may be summed up as developmental inhibition and regression. Thus incestuous fixations of libido continue to play (or begin once more to play) the principal part in his unconscious mental life. . . . It is therefore of no small importance that we are able to show that these same incestuous wishes, which are later destined to become unconscious, are still regarded by savage peoples as immediate perils against which the most severe measures of defense must be enforced.[43]

The temporal logic of this move is counterintuitive, for, rather than arguing that the primitive is less aware or less conscious of his fantasyscape, Freud maintains that the primitive is more aware and suffers consciously from the terrible potentiality of fantasy's temptations. Superstition is merely the symbolic cultural evidence of a knowledge of fantasy, proof of its inescapability. The primitive will continue to exhibit his knowledge of collective temptations, mediated by rituals of all kinds; as the primitive proliferates taboos in the landscape he will have to multiply knowledges to cope with the increasing pollution of his environment by the psyche. By contrast, the neurotic suffers from a fixation of libido in an infantile play that relegates his psyche to perpetual servitude to the unconscious. What has been "overtaken by repression" fails to be sufficiently taken over by the mediations of the later object choices that substitute for the earliest incestuous ones, now lingering like tyrants in his psyche, and so the neurotic himself lingers somewhere between return and fixation. He suffers from a "developmental inhibition" analogous to the lack of repression in primitive life on the basis of their shared relation to the "temptation in phantasy."

Freud posits a lack of unconscious repression in the primitive only to effect a speculative retraction of that putative lack at a later point. The primitive is said to be lacking yet replete in ambivalent projection, and so the historical trajectory of development becomes legible in *Totem and Taboo* as an increasing internalization of ambivalence under the bar of repression. What is primitive in the primitive is a certain kind of knowledge or know-how. What is modern in the neurotic and normative subject alike is a haunting inhabited by temptations and figures of fantasy that find only partial, compromised outlets. As Freud unweaves the genealogy of this primitive/modern relation, his text shows, in an oscillation not entirely under its author's control, that the social function of projection in the primitive community is not so far removed from—and, in fact, is metaphorically related to—the social function of sacrifice and abjection in modern man.

When Freud says that "a taboo is not a neurosis but a social institution" he shows the "social" becoming the sexual as hostile impulses fall under prohibition and are displaced inward. The law itself becomes displaced inward: "This impulse is repressed by a prohibition and the prohibition is attached to some particular act, which, by displacement, represents, it may be, a hostile act against the loved person."[44] And later, "The instinctual forces that are diverted and displaced in neuroses have a sexual origin. In the case of taboo the prohibited touching is obviously not to be understood in an exclusively sexual sense but in the more general sense of attacking, of getting control, and of asserting oneself." Repression of aggressivity thus preserves the aggression against the other within the psychic terrain of self-relation. This activity of prohibition and retrieval of aggressivity is to be distinguished from the regulations of foreclosure. Repression and its compromised expressions are ways of continuing to live within a landscape that has utterly banished other possibilities. The repressed desire and hatred felt toward a representative of the incest taboo does not express a compromised array of feeling and symptoms toward the *law* of the incest taboo, but toward the *representative* of that law. The law lurks behind the figure that raises the specter of desire and hatred. Thus, the ambivalence felt toward the law's representative gives only indirect clues about that law; it cannot speak the law itself.

Freud speaks here of "taboo conscience," or a taboo sense of guilt, and takes this to be the prehistoric, primitive version of the conscience. If Toklas's venomous assessment of Jane is evidence of the installation and maintenance of a taboo, projection seems all the more present on both sides of the judgment, for projection is not merely a defensive

"The Bar Was Not Very Gay" 147

mode of dealing with emotional conflict. Projection also functions as a means of perception, and as the citation below indicates, the structuring effect of perception conceived on the model of projection is analogous to the activities of abjection—always in relation to a law foreclosed—illustrated by Toklas's letter about Jane.

> The projection outwards of internal perceptions is a primitive mechanism, to which, for instance, our sense perceptions are subject, and which therefore normally plays a very large part in determining the form taken by our external world.... Internal perceptions of emotional and intellective processes can be projected outwards in the same way as sense perceptions; they are thus employed for building up the external world, though they should by rights remain part of the internal world.[45]

The text argues for a second sense of projection, as that which is both the mechanism by which we jettison the troubling noise of ambivalence and the means by which we perceive the world. We are not very far away from Wilde's lighter formulation, "Life imitates Art far more than Art imitates Life," for here it is the phantasmatic interior of feeling that manifests the world. To build up the world on the basis of internal emotions and thoughts, to build that world in the image of all that you hate and love, this is the primitive psychic process upon which psychoanalysis hopes to shed light.

> It was not until a language of abstract thought had been developed, that is to say, not until the sensory residues of verbal presentations had been linked to the internal processes, that the latter themselves gradually became capable of being perceived. Before that, owing to the projection outwards of internal perceptions, primitive men arrived at a picture of the external world which we, with our intensified conscious perception, have now to translate back into psychology.[46]

Where the primitive derives a picture of the external world, psychoanalysis will arrive at an analytic text offering descriptions of the internal world. This would imply that the translation effected by abstract and analytic language is one from the image to the word. The image is, yet again, the literal ground of a direct transmission—something lacking in mediation, supine before the projections of theory. Like the Muslim patient in chapter 3, below, Jane will find her writing relegated to a pre-scriptural picturing activity where the work of foreclosure seems to be most evident in the text produced by her interpreters.

The metaphoric relation of picturing and writing is something her own writing refuses to repress. She stubbornly insists that the written must derive from a reality granted by vision. Her persistent pursuit of vision is certainly one mode of frustration, but it carries with it the essential and common feature of all Jane's frustrated and productive endeavors. This is among the reasons that her literature always lapses into the "analytic" language of the agonizers. She turns the explanatory narratives of psychological states into ways of picturing the world from the point of view of obstruction.

TURKISH LADIES AND THE WORLD PICTURE

During the thirty-year period of her writing block, Jane Bowles completed sections of a novel, *Out in the World,* which was to be a "Balzacian" work detailing at length the lives of a gay soldier, a lesbian working-class couple, and a middle-class wife coming to consciousness about her lesbian sexuality late in life. Fragments of the novel have been edited and published as very short stories in the volume of Bowles's complete works. Two of these, "Emmy Moore's Journal" and "The Iron Table," suggest a quasi-autobiographical writing that highlights the rhetorical necessity of joining writing to picturing as the conscious thematic content of plot.

"Let there be no mistake. My journal is intended for publication. I want to publish for glory, but also in order to aid other women." "Emmy Moore's Journal" is a first-person narrative written by Mrs. Moore for the purpose of "justifying" her withdrawal from marriage and her desire to transform herself from the dependent and excessively feminine woman that she is. "I must justify myself every day. On some days the need to write lodges itself in my throat like a cry that must be uttered" (MS, 445). Into the journal Emmy Moore copies a letter addressed to her husband, a man she describes as "sympathetic towards me, and kindly. He wants very much for me to be happy, and worries because I am not. He knows everything about me, including how much I deplore being the feminine kind of woman that I am. In fact, I am unusually feminine for an American of Anglo stock. (Born in Boston.) I am almost a 'Turkish' type'" (*MS,* 444). The text wanders from grandiose declarations of her desire to publish to pathetic attempts to describe and justify feminine failure. Combining a very shabby discourse on "Turkish" femininity with a dogged attempt to convey in analytic language her "secret picture of the world," these efforts at clarification and communication fall short of their aim, and in the final lines of the story Emmy Moore despairingly registers her failure to speak. "She had been so happy copying this letter into her journal, but now her heart was faint as she scanned its scattered pages. 'I have said nothing,' she muttered to herself in alarm. 'I have said nothing at all. I have not clarified my reasons for being at the Hotel Henry. I have not justified myself'" (*MS*, 449).

"Sometimes I feel certain that I exude an atmosphere very similar to theirs (the Turkish women's) and then I despise myself. I find the women in my country so extraordinarily manly and independent, capable of leading regiments. . . . If possible before I die, I should like to become a little more independent, and a little less Turkish" (*MS*, 444). This explanation of her emotional predicament explodes in the letter into a full-blown theory of Turkish dependence that identifies the Orient as the place of abjection and conveys this in a parody of political discourse.

> As for the Turkish problem, I am coming to it. You must understand that I am an admirer of Western civilization; that is, of the women who are members of this group. I feel myself that I fall short of being a member, that by some curious accident I was not born in Turkey but should have been. Because of my usual imprecision I cannot even tell how many countries belong to what we call Western Civilization, but I believe Turkey is the place where East meets West, isn't it? I can just about imagine the women there, from what I have heard about the country and the pictures I have seen of it. As for being troubled or obsessed by real Oriental women, I am not. (I refer to the Chinese, Japanese, Hindus, and so on.) Naturally I am less concerned with the Far Eastern women because there is no danger of my being like them. (The Turkish women are just near enough.) (*MS*, 446)

Striving to represent her views in all their minute detail, Emmy Moore rambles from thought to thought, incoherently but persistently drawing the contour of her vision. Her admiration of Western women can only be stated through the detours of sight and distance; she admires from afar because she is not of their kind, but a misplaced person. The "real" Orientals are so far away and so "different from the way [she] looks" that only the middle ground of an Orient "just near enough" can serve as the territory of her dependent femininity. Her treatise on her Turkish nature is offered as a map of "my secret picture of the world" that will explain why she fails to be a member of "Western Civilization"; this secret picture derives from other pictures and vague murmurings about Turkey. The mania for the visible in the passages from this letter comes through as the word *picture* appears again and again, culminating finally in the statement that "I know full well that you will consider the above discourse a kind of joke . . . yet I assure you that I see things this way, if I relax even a little and look through my own eyes into what is really inside my head" (*MS*, 446). The spatial distortion of this remark has Emmy Moore entering her head from the exterior via the eyes in search of her own property, her own "discourse." Oddly resonant with Wilde's map of his soul, this picturing discourse is Emmy's figure of the self and must substitute an unseen geographic fantasy for the bodily image that dissolves as she approaches it. No mirror reflects an appealing form of self-mastery for Emmy; instead, she must use the materials of her own insufficiency—her dependence, her soft, flabby body, her lack of drive—to construct a phantasmatic materializing origin. Discourse, here heard only as a joke, will construct an argument for identity where the pictures have failed; thus the absurd geometries and literalization of insight into the self become the discursive terms of a self-description. The world picture she holds, a secret because her "vision" cannot be "seen," is not accountable to a logical or comprehensive argument, for "the fact of having forgotten utterly to consider them [logical arguments] has not altered the way I visualize the division of the world's women" (*MS*, 447).

Though the story echoes Toklas's fantasies about women of the "Orient," and though it dramatizes the abject speech of a hyperfeminine woman despairing of her own nature, the tone of the text smacks not of distant irony but of a struggle to communicate—just as Emmy Moore's effort to "justify" herself exhibits a genuine and painful longing to say something rather than nothing. Bowles's text prefigures a key tenet of feminist thinking when she dramatizes the inability to speak from within the terms of abjection. That Emmy Moore cannot speak is proved by the failure of her writing to do more than mimic the discourses of feminism and politics or the essay/memoir genre. "Because of my talent for mimicry I am able to simulate looking through the eyes of an educated person when I wish to" (*MS*, 446). Such an awkward aside dismisses her from consideration as a theorist of woman's condition. Her letter, addressed to the husband but grandiose in its aims and its pretensions, attempts to reach beyond the local audience to a wider one, for glory "and to aid other women." Bowles does not relish Emmy's failure but depicts it to throw light on the inexorable law of failure and exclusion. Like her own letters to the superego, this fictional journal and letter mark out the scene of failure as the very materialization of the law. Emmy's inability to confront her desire for

"American women" as desire dooms her writing to perpetuate the generality of "saying nothing," and thus the specifically lesbian character of her longing remains inexpressible and out of reach.

Emmy Moore's raw and ridiculous inarticulations are more than matched by those of the wife in "The Iron Table," a story confected from a fragment of Bowles's last and never to be finished novel. The scene is a patio at a Moroccan hotel frequented by Spaniards rather than "Anglos." The husband, whose conventional orientalist fixation leaves little room for his wife's opinions, holds forth on a familiar theme: "the whole civilization is going to pieces." The dialogue sums up a key feature of the tourist's drive to seal the Orient in its moment of death while preserving a claim to authenticity as the tourist's private possession. If the "whole civilization is going to pieces," that collapse will be rancorously recorded by a touristic delectation in loss, disguised by a ressentimental hatred of the West.

> Her voice was sorrowful. "I know it." Her answers to his ceaseless complaining about the West's contamination of Moslem culture had become increasingly unpredictable . . . he knew she had no desire to go to the desert, and that she believed it was not possible to continue trying to escape from the Industrial Revolution. (MS, 465)

She plays along, intent on avoiding argument or outburst, when finally, with savage condescension, the husband says, "You'd go to an oasis because you wanted to escape from Western civilization."

> "My friends and I don't feel there's any *way* of escaping it. It's not interesting to sit around talking about industrialization."
> "What friends?" He liked her to feel isolated.
> "Our friends." Most of them she had not seen in many years. She turned to him with a certain violence. "I think you come to these countries so you can complain. I'm tired of hearing the word *civilization*. It has no meaning. Or I've forgotten what it meant, anyway."
> The moment when they might have felt tenderness had passed, and secretly they both rejoiced. Since he did not answer her, she went on. "I think it's uninteresting. To sit and watch costumes disappear, one by one. It's uninteresting even to mention it." (MS, 467)

What the wife remarks in her husband is his pleasure in the uninteresting prospect of cultural decline. He does come to these countries to complain because his complaint must have as its literal ground the matter of a "past" civilization enacting its own death before him. The wife more than knows his deepest pleasure and counters it, saying that civilization itself is meaningless and that traveling to relish loss is a very expensive form of disavowal. "My friends and I don't feel there's any *way* of escaping it" tells us again that the West is everywhere but not in the form of civilization and only as a mode of industrialization. If the word *civilization* is meaningless, this is in part because she cannot see it demonstrated; if the West is everywhere, it is because it follows them everywhere they go, especially in his complaints.

Piercing the self-inflated discourse of the husband's tired orientalism by insisting on the language and conclusions of her experience, corroborated by the fragility of friendship, this wife does not dispute in conceptual terms; she rebukes. That it is uninteresting to "sit and watch costumes disappear one by one" only implies that travel ought to be interesting, even pleasurable, but she is unable to mount her argument or argue for her own pleasures. Like the prose of Emmy Moore's letter, the language of this fragment from the unfinished novel insists a series of images and dramatic exchanges in the place of an analytic discourse that is shown, through the vague posturing of the husband, to be but a conventional mask for a very particular desire. The husband's obsession with contamination obscures the fact that even in the remotest region, the thing he tries to escape has come within him because he travels only to witness his own lack of desire disguised and projected again and again. Where the husband beholds failure and corruption as a tableau before him, the wife's remarks attest to an insight that the putative concreteness of a decaying culture is a kind of wish fulfillment constructed on site and in the moment of vision. Childish and self-indulgent, the wife is nevertheless enabled by the incompleteness of her rhetoric to deliver up a deflating barb to unmask the ploys of mastery without herself taking on the master's voice. Each of these fragmentary works links this yielding but thorny femininity to a figure of the Orient, either bluntly, as in "Emmy Moore's Journal," or through the more circuitous route of a resistance to the paternalistic orientalism of the husband's tirade. In each case writing constitutes a third pole of investment around which the feminine and the primitive are composed.

The weak speeches of these thwarted characters represent a femininity that cannot rise to heroism; instead, a species of compulsion comes to stand for the resolutions of a final, heroic instance, and this repetitive, persistent quality keeps everything, even the author, afloat. "I started to 'write' when I was about fifteen and was obliged to do composition in school. I always thought it the most loathsome of all activities, and still do. At the same time I felt even then that I had to do it."[47] Called to writing, Bowles was able in these early days to defer the duty by writing in another language. Her first efforts culminated in a French novel; later she left it in a taxi as if it were just another incidental possession. Despite this substantial ambivalence toward her own texts and her avowed hatred of the process, the duty to write remains unchanged for the entire period of her writing block. Although she arrives in Morocco already blocked and sending off interminable letters of lamentation, the early years of her life there witness the creative energy of writing, its ability to invent myth, as it is fostered by her relationship with Cherifa. Yet, increasingly, her erotic arrangements take on the frustrated character of her writing process and seem to compete with writing.

Her isolation in Morocco makes letters more than fiction the perfect staging ground of an offensive address to the law, for it is the first feature of such speech that it is addressed to an absent other who is nevertheless bound there in his most "abstract" form. The oscillations of the rhetorical question can be felt here as we engage with the difficulty of deciding what is figural and what is literal in the epistolary form. In the specificity of their addresses, the letters would seem to correspond more closely to the "metaphoric relation" uncovered in Freud's analysis of the mother-in-law. For Freud it is the figural representative that inspires hatred, not the abstract law of the incest taboo. In the generality of their similitude, the figural singularity of each letter is blurred, for each does little more than paint the picture of Jane's symptoms and her relation to that abstract law. Compelled to go further, to the furthest reaches to send for the law, she sends forth her own scattered light on things. Repetitively alternating between assurances that she is working and meditations on her own isolation, the letters of the early period of her writing impasse chronicle the noisy self-hindering of someone whose "experience is probably of no interest at this point to anyone." One accomplishment of the letters, however, is their ability to transmute her complaint from a kind of "natural" state, that of femininity, to a serious and engaged investigation of what writing requires.

> It has been hard enough for me to get on with my novel here (italics) because of four or five tremendous stumbling blocks—none of them however due to the circumstance of my environment. (My novel is entirely in this laborious style.)
>
> The more I get into it, which isn't very far in pages but quite a bit further in thinking and consecutive work the more frightened I become at the isolated position I feel myself in vis-à-vis of all the writers whom I consider to be of any serious mind. because I think there is no point in using the word talent any longer. Certainly Carson McCullers is as talented (italics) as Sartre or Simone de Beauvoir but she is not really a serious

writer. I am serious but I am isolated and my experience is probably of no interest at this point to anyone. I am enclosing this article entitled "new heroes" by Simone de Beauvoir, which I have cut out of town and country, at least a section of it . . . It is what I have been thinking at the bottom of my mind all this time and God knows it is difficult to write the way I do and yet think their way. This problem you will never have to face because you have always been a truly isolated person so that whatever you write will be good because it will be true which is not so in my case because my kind of isolation I think is an accident, and not inevitable. . . . not only is your isolation a positive and true one but when you do write from it you immediately receive recognition because what you write is in true relation to yourself which is always recognizable to the world outside. With me who knows? When you are capable only of a serious and ponderous approach to writing as I am—I should say solemn perhaps—it is almost more than one can bear to be continually doubting one's sincerity which is tantamount to doubting one's product. as I move along into this writing I think the part I mind the most is this doubt about my entire experience. this is far more important than feeling 'out' of it and 'isolated' I suppose, but it also accentuates that guilt a thousand times . . . I am working and I am diligent and faithful about it but I feel it's such a Herculean task that I shall not finish for years! on the other hand it may, if I can just get over having myself in a book, it may go quickly.[48]

This letter was written to her husband in 1947 during the period that marks both the onset of the writing block and the completion of her two most important short stories, "Camp Cataract" and "A Stick of Green Candy." The citation above is less than one quarter of a letter that moves in and out of the anxious mood seen here. Diligent and faithful to writing, she is nonetheless isolated in a way that reflects neither choice nor character. Her isolation, she tells us, is "accidental," and like Emmy Moore's mistaken birth, it lays her open to an all-consuming doubt about the validity, interest, and worthiness of her experience. The terror she feels upon realizing her isolation is no exaggeration, for she continues to feel it whenever she approaches the threshold of writing. This doubt never ceases to open her to the trauma of her position—in the world, as a writer, as a woman. Whatever she may have understood or identified as important in the article she clips to send along with this letter, the division expressed by "God knows it is difficult to write the way I do and yet think their way" suggesting again the accidental and misplaced character of her project and her means. Solemnity, faith, and diligence are the only proofs she has against an overriding guilt that attends her doubt, and she offers them up to the addressee as feeble proofs. The question "With me who knows?" reveals that to be isolated in this misbegotten way is to live and write without witnesses, and so the letters call up an audience for what would otherwise remain unheard.

The combined effects of a seriousness pressed to the point of inexpressibility and a lack of recognition by the literary establishment result in a writing melancholia that Jane tries to contain in letters. As her writing finally devolves into guilty remonstration, proffering evidence of her obedient attempt to write, we can see that it takes up the place of a systematic anti-cathexis, which, as Freud says, keeps her revolving in the pleading position. Always confessing her failure and a groundless faith in continued effort, she becomes the writer who cannot write, whose "experience" will then be the only point of consistency within her writing. If the ceremonial ordeal of the prohibition on writing becomes writing itself, she does manage to preserve the world from falling under what Freud calls the "embargo of 'impossibility.'" Jane will "save" the world by sacrificing writing to the rituals of painful effort and incompletion. It is writing, not life, that becomes impossible.

Jane Bowles presents a writing self that writes itself into the impossibility of being "had." "If I can just get over having myself in a book" names the having linked to the self of writing. The loss of self that marks the "serious writer" as one who must always lose herself to writing colonizes the writing vocation as the place of her self's destruction, a public exposure that she seeks to overcome in the ranting letters that fill up the void opened by the failure to write. "I have got back on my work again with unbelievable difficulty and continue crawling alone. I am so slow it is almost as though I were going backwards. . . . I keep forgetting what writing is supposed to be anyway . . . Perhaps you can write me what I mean" (*OW*, 39).

The pleas to her husband to find the key to her impasse accumulate and vary their form over the next three years as she carves out a life for herself in Tangier. Increasingly she comes to resent his success and to identify her blockage with her isolation.

> 08/47 I am enjoying my Sickness unto Death throughout the summer . . . Please write to me. It is much easier for you to write than for me, because I always feel that unless I present a problem in a letter I have not really written one. (*OW*, 41)
>
> 09/47 I am desperate however at all this time passing and have done little more on my novel than you have in spite of not moving around. I am terribly discouraged and of course the fact that you get these letters from publishers complimenting you on stories is no help to my morale as far as a career is concerned . . . this does not concern me deeply but I realize that I have no career really whether I work or not and never have had one. You

> have more of one after writing a few short stories than I have after writing an entire novel. (*OW*, 46)
>
> 10/47 no distinguished magazine has ever written me and complimented me on a story, or asked for a contribution, nor have I certainly ever won an O. Henry award. I seem to be completely ignored by the whole literary world just as much as by the commercial one. (*OW*, 59)
>
> 12/48 it was a terrible strain and just last week I thought maybe this time I really was going to crack, but I made a very big effort and I'm working again. (*OW*, 128)
>
> 01/17/50 my work went well last week. I had got into a routine, but this week it's all shot to hell again . . . I have decided not to become hysterical, however. If I cannot write my book, then I shall give up writing, that's all. Then either suicide or another life . . . I mean, to continue as I am, but not as a writer. As the wife of a writer? I don't think you'd like that, and could I do it well? I think I'd nag and be mean, and then I would be ashamed. (*OW*, 144)
>
> 01/50 Yesterday the whole thing dried up on me again . . . It happens too often really and I'm afraid that it is the physical expression of sterility. I go on trying though it is a terrible fight . . . . I do feel very strongly that I should I give up writing if I can't get further into it than I have. I cannot keep losing it the way I do, much longer. (*OW*, 149)

As this sampling shows, the writerly collaboration between Jane and her husband, which had transformed him into an author and helped her complete the novel, slowly degenerates as his career takes off. The realization that she is ignored by the literary world increases her dependence upon him at precisely the moment when he no longer seems to need her writing companionship. The marriage, which from the outset had been imagined in terms of writing, was now transformed into a relationship of financial dependence as she ceased to earn royalties from her published works. Her anxiety and guilt over money push the writing block to a pitch of shame and forces her to the choice of "either suicide or another life." As the writing impasse and dependence converge to make her say, "I don't exist independently," she finds another solution to her insecurity, directly related to the sense of being shunned by the literary world.

"I MUST CLOSE MY FIST TO SEDUCE HER"

For Bowles, the accusation of primitive uselessness, coupled with her superfluity in the literary world, becomes the ground of a new set of preoccupations as she attempts to "find another life," one that will not consign her to obscurity and poverty. Though she will maintain her economic dependence on her husband for the rest of her life, she finds a way to consolidate that dependence as power by displacing it within her relationship with Cherifa. As her self-construction and the aesthetic are fused in her vocation, it comes as no surprise that her erotic adventures take on the same frustrated character as her writing block; she passes from one obstacle to the next until she manages to find a steady state just as her writing settles into letter writing. Seduction on every level becomes the new object: a woman, a way of life, a country, a people, a language, a novel—it is all the same to her. Each is a potential conquest, each an impossibility. All those lures and provocations add up to a kind of sexual tourism and prostitution, which she transforms into stable family life. These alternative affiliations represent efforts to alter kinship nominations in ways that simply prevent the ordinary uses of the words *wife, husband, lover, lesbian,* or *straight* from operating at all. It is not as if Bowles were empowered to subvert and transcend the categories that she puts into play. Rather, she brings them to a halt by bringing them up short against the multiple forms of their mutual exclusions. Whereas her marriage to Paul Bowles was enabled by a mutual comprehension of gay and lesbian identity—there is ample evidence of this, not the least of which is the fact that she spent her wedding night with a girlfriend, to Paul's dismay, and if he had not understood the terms of their engagement, he soon learned what it meant to be married to this lesbian writer—her courtship and eventual domestic arrangements with Cherifa depended on a mutual incomprehension of their desire.

"I wish to hell I could find some woman still so that I wouldn't always be alone at night. I'm sure Arab night life would interest me not in the slightest. As you know I don't consider those races voluptuous or exciting in any way, as I have said—being a part of them almost" (OW, 55). Jane's conquest of North Africa begins inauspiciously with an indifference to "Oriental" women that she marks as a "racial" indifference. Her tastes tended toward "Scotch-Irish" women of decidedly independent demeanor, and to complicate matters, Paul left Tangier soon after she arrived, leaving her to fend for herself. She was to spend most of the next three years apart from him, and it is during this time that she met Cherifa. Adding to all the complications was the continual problem of the language. Eventually she came to speak the Moroccan Arabic dialect, but her facility with the language has been much exaggerated in the accounts of her life there.[49] The early letters written while Paul was still there are sprinkled with resentment of the place, the people, the language. "I don't of course know about the Arab town of Tangier (I refuse to use that Arabic word)" (OW, 962). It is only after her husband leaves and she is thrown back upon her own resources that her attitude changes. This change comes about through her growing preoccupation with the local grain market.

"There seems too much really to write about—I mean Fez and money and Africa altogether and my failure to like in it what you do and to like what you do at all anywhere. I love Tangier—the market and the Arab language, the Casbah" (OW, 78). A rare feeling for her anywhere at any time, this optimism about Tangier and the hope that it will continue to give her something, even too much, to write persists as she penetrates more deeply into the market where she first meets Cherifa and an early rival, Tetum. For once her sense of place, writing and romance coalesce into a hoped-for synthesis that might become a genuine alternative to the frustrating stalemate of her literary exploits. And yet the sense of optimism derives from an experience of exclusion and difference that has taken on a very material form.

> I continue to love tangier—maybe *because I have the feeling of being on the edge of something that I will some day enter.* This I don't think I could feel if I didn't know Cherifa and the "Mountain Dyke" that yellow ugly one [!?]. It is hard for me to separate the place from the romantic possibilities that I have found in it. I cannot separate the two for the first time in my life. Perhaps I shall be perpetually on the edge of this civilization of theirs. When I am in Cherifa's house I am still on the edge of it, and when I come out I can't believe I was really in it—seeing her afterwards, neither more nor less friendly, like those tunes that go on and on or seem to, is enough to make me convinced that I was never there. (OW, 85)

The place abides in its romantic possibilities, which, though static, are enough to refresh her interest continually. Quite suddenly she has moved from the petulance of her initial racial indifference into a phase of perpetually heightened awareness. Sadly, these are the happiest passages in her epistolary career. Being on the edge of something she may someday enter is, for her, the most exciting place of her romantic imagination. Tellingly, too, she prefers the stasis of the interminable, here figured as a tune that anyone else might find monotonous or maddening. Having or not having hardly seems to matter in these early accounts, because living at the frontier of hospitality holds the promise of continuation. But not for long:

> I wrote to you how exciting it was to feel on the edge of something. Well, it's beginning to make me very nervous. I don't see any way of getting

any further into it, since what I want is so particular [as usual]; and as for forgetting them altogether, it's too late. For me Africa right now is the grain market and being obsessive . . . it is not any personal taste that I'm obliged to fight but a whole social structure, so different from the one you know—for certainly there are two distinct worlds here [the men's world and the women's], as you've often said yourself. (OW, 93)

The very fact that so entrances her, that there are two distinct worlds structured along a gender divide, is turned into the annoying source of obscurity. In this letter to Paul as in others she explains carefully that the techniques of lesbian seduction in Morocco do not follow the simpler rules of sex between men. Because she has no Moroccan friends outside the peasant class, and because her Western friends are either short-term residents of Tangier or not lesbians, Jane has no map of how it is done. Between the nervousness of the continual stasis of her seductions and the seemingly infinite possibility implied by working and traveling without a map, she can experience her particularity—as both anxiety and titillation—and her own freedom to invent what she wants.

The differences that she finds simultaneously so frustrating and titillating extend from class and sexuality to ethnic identity. The erotic charge she gets from penetrating into Moroccan rooms is always a curiously general one. For quite some time, her letters reflect only the charms that Moroccan women display as a group. They are always "them" in her descriptions, whether gushing or grudging. This faceless generality stands in contrast to her own mobility of identity. Though American and Jewish, she is in Tangier a "Nazarene" and usually taken for European. Her foreign identity is both absolutely fixed there at the "edge" and malleable. This allows her access to a range of experiences, which her letters never show before her arrival in Tangier. The difficulties she faces in her attempts to enter into Moroccan life expose her to a morphological shifting that dislocates her identity as she seeks ways of characterizing her experience. So consumed by the feeling of being outside, she seems unable to confront the class character of her difference from the urban workers she pursues, and instead she glosses that dislocation as a racial one. The racial scene of the fantasy she proffers to explain her failure to seduce is a heterosexualized one. Here she becomes a "Negro man":

The average American woman would be revolted I suppose by a Negro man, and I think I suffer from the disadvantage of being "different"—all of which made your success years ago. Naturally, I admire the women

> for being this way, so much more dignified than the men, or are they just more conventional? I don't know. I suppose I could banish all hope from my heart and get it over with but I hate to and I never regret being with them. I can't quite explain to you or anyone what it is like to be in one of those rooms—I mean how I feel about it. . . . the women look wonderful in their homes. (OW, 108)

"The disadvantage of being 'different,'" which she imagines to be a lure for men, only works against her in the "world of women." She refuses to consider that class differences also play an enormous role in separating her from the women she wants to possess, despite the fact that the only women who manage to capture her attention are drawn from a suburban merchant class. "What it is like to be in one of those rooms" suggests that the object of fascination is not a woman but that spatial frontier itself. Being on the edge has given way to being in the room, in the private realm of a life to which she does not belong. The women are represented as decor completing a tableau rather than as active inhabitants of their homes. Everything is designed to be pleasing to the eye in an interior world capacious enough to exclude "the Negro man." At no point do her letters register the inadequacy of such a comparison between Morocco and America, nor do the letters take on the more likely equation of her presence and her dollars to the colonial presence and the persisting legacy of that colonial moment. Rather, content to ignore this historical context, she registers resistance to her attempted conquests only by complaining in her letters. The final and most lasting impression she has of her own shifting identity and sensibilities suggests that the indecision and "nervousness" native to her is all too easily discarded under the authority of money and the residue of colonial rule. "If I live in a house here I insist on a harem. There is no other way of doing it. They cope with all the details and keep one company [I am quite happy with them without any kind of romance]" (OW, 125). Though she complains that her entry into Moroccan life is not as easy as was Paul's, she clearly imagines her future domestic and erotic successes on the model of the foreign man of means.

Jane's delight at being on the frontier of a world so separate from her finds its limit in her courtship of Cherifa, who begins to signify Jane's contestation of this border. At first Cherifa presents only the more attractive choice of two different and, to Jane's eyes, available women, despite the former's obvious efforts to avoid Jane.

> Cherifa, I'm afraid, is never going to work out. I think she's very much in love with Boussif. She's in a rage because she expected that once his wife

"The Bar Was Not Very Gay"

> left he would marry her, and instead he's taken some woman to cook for him whom he also sleeps with. . . . They are definitely confusing people. I think Cherifa is afraid of me. I saw her sneak behind a stall yesterday when I appeared so that I wouldn't see her. Nonetheless I am determined now to learn Arabic. It is good exercise for the mind in any case and there are more chances that I will get pleasure out of it than not . . . . I said my first words yesterday after Cherifa sneaked behind the stall and I suppose I said them in desperation. The older dyke was there, thank God [she comes to the market irregularly], so I walked over to her and somehow spoke. Just a few words actually, but immediately some old men gathered around me and everyone nodded happily. (OW, 81)

She enters into the life of the market to some extent, and for a time this satisfies her. Her resolve to content herself with mental exercise and apply herself to her Arabic lessons is, however, short-lived. She is enormously frustrated with the language barrier, for it deprives her of her most winning charms of seduction. She simply cannot make her way into Cherifa's heart by wit, and this deficiency in their courtship outlines her increasing impatience with the whole process. Her former hope that she might traverse the edge of Moroccan life to actually enter into it is now flagging and no longer figured as an opening threshold, but as a violent rejection.

> Either she is ashamed to be seen with me alone or, quite sensibly, doesn't see the point because I cannot really speak to her. I don't know. I am merely trying to know her better socially [having given up hope as far as anything else is concerned]. I can't bear to be continually hurled *out* of the Arab world. . . . Perhaps you have never been in this inferior position vis-à-vis the Arabs. I can understand how if one could get all one wanted here and were admired, courted, and feted, that one would never never leave. Even so, without all that—and you've had it—I have never felt so strongly about a place in my life, and it is just maddening not to be able to get more of it, (OW, 93)

Goaded beyond her limit, she cannot endure the repetition of inferiority that she knows all too well at home. Having entered into the marketplace with a completely self-serving conception of her role there—that *she* is the "Negro man" and Cherifa is the American woman—she balks at the obvious conclusion to which her (non-) reception would lead her. Her desire to possess a "harem" but her unwillingness to pay for it presents her with the conundrum of stalemate and avoidance. The substitute pleasures of language and small accomplishments are brief, and as the relationship progresses or stalls, her understanding of "their" expectations becomes more calculating and even desperate. Jane finally breaks down to confront the economic framework of desire that she has entered. If it is sex that she wants, she is going to have to pay for it, but this payment causes her no end of guilty rationalization and constant reevaluation. She learns quickly how and when to pay: "By offering a present at the right time I keep my oar in" (*OW*, 103). This discovery reveals that there is, in fact, a map and set of rules to be learned; Jane is not particularly happy about this, as it tends to erode her own sense of romance and uniqueness, but the new life enabled by the dollar raises her up from the "inferior position vis-à-vis the Arabs," which had cast her as a purposeless hanger-on. Now she has capital enough to override her foreignness. She begins to give bribes of all kinds.

> I do see and I refuse to all at once. Still socially I am making some headway, particularly in a new role that started last week—that is of a procurer for Cherifa. I procure Boussif for her when he disappears, which he does for days at a time. . . . She's trying to get one [a sheep] out of me already. . . . I expect to have to invest a little money in the Arab part of my life—the only reason for being here, at least the most important one. I have to buy Cherifa a djellaba and shoes eventually. Also I am taking her to the doctor's right now which is ruining me. She has a skin disease from grain. (*OW*, 104)

Seeing and refusing to see that the source of her sudden and considerable attraction for Tetum and Cherifa lies in Paul's pockets, Jane embarks on a path of seduction in which she pays for the attentions of her two favorites. She coyly portrays herself as the procurer when the facts are quite otherwise. What she buys with Paul's money she thinks of as an investment that verges on plain gambling, as she cannot foresee the outcome of so much expenditure. Soon she begins to feel the limits of her latest strategy, but by now it is too late to withdraw her funds without losing face and possibly losing all contact with Cherifa.

> They have all my scarves, most of my money, my watch, and I am now taking Cherifa to the doctor's twice a week. . . . I don't mind being liked for my money one bit. Being the richest woman in the world has certain disadvantages but I accept them. I feel that I have done everything absolutely everything wrong, but perhaps something nice will happen anyway. . . . Cherifa wants me to buy her a taxi. . . . She is getting quite plump because of my affluence and every now and then instead of looking like a boy she looks like a complete Oriental woman. (*OW*, 131)

As the demand for goods in exchange for services rises to the level of a taxi, Jane risks destitution but manages to transform Cherifa from the cute boyish figure in "dungarees and haymaker shirts" to a "complete

Oriental woman." Effectively, she has acquired the harem she thought would confer power, comfort, and freedom from care, but, in fact, her own existence is more harried than ever as she is constantly attending to the ladies she has "created." Still, she complains about the rate of progress even in this new economy: "Our relationship is completely static: just as I think that at least it's going backwards [on the days when she sneaks behind the stall] I find that it is right back where it was the next day. Nothing seems to move" (*OW*, 88).⁵⁰ The stasis of her advance upon Cherifa's virtue is stated in language identical to an earlier description of her writing, "I am so slow it is almost as though I were going backwards . . . I keep forgetting what writing is supposed to be anyway." Whereas pleading for writing would tend to show up the language and structure of a symbolic foreclosure upon writing specifically and upon speech more generally—at least upon the position of "speaking out"—here she pleads for sex and comes up against an incomprehension to which she cannot quite admit. Perhaps Cherifa is willing to "give all" if adequately compensated, but if she cannot imagine what that "all" might actually be, then Jane's hope for a harem that would exceed the exchange of money is a forlorn hope. Jane runs up against what she calls "that awful, hard-to-get virgin block," which she has trouble imagining as sincere despite her continual frustration with the "sleeping," the euphemism that she and Cherifa share for sex. The progress of her seduction stalls on the question of knowing and not knowing, authentic and inauthentic desires, where the possibility that "they do not know" what lesbian sex is amounts to a resolution of the moral challenge to her self-image. Caught up in a tangle of autoerotic motivations and unwilling to content herself with prostitution, she holds out a hope that love, desire, and affection might emerge given time.

> I love this life and i'm terrified of the day when my money runs out. The sex thing aside, it is as if I had dreamed this life before I was born. Perhaps I will work hard to keep it. I cannot keep Cherifa without money, or even myself, after all. Paul told Cherifa that without working I would never have any money so she is constantly sending me up into my little work room. A good thing. Naturally I think of her in terms of a long long time. How one can do this and at the same time fully realize the fact that money is of paramount importance to one's friend and etc., etc.—that if there is to be much sleeping it will most likely be against their will or something they will do to please one, I simply don't know. Possibly, if it came to that, I might lose interest in the sleeping part, possibly why I keep putting off the bargaining—but the money I know is paramount. Yet they are not like we are. Someone behaving in the same way who was not an Arab I couldn't bear. (*OW*, 180)

Jane hesitates to bargain because the knowledge that "it will most likely be against their will" disrupts her own erotic investments. She clings to the belief that "they are not like we are," and it is on the basis of a reified conception of Arab womanhood that she will persist in the relationship. Out of the contradiction of knowing and not-knowing, Jane plans for the long term as if the problem posed by Cherifa's motivation were something that might be resolved in a mode other than servitude. "Someone behaving in the same way who was not an Arab I couldn't bear" tellingly situates the limit of her tolerance for "being had," as she finds it just as aggravating to pay for sex that she is not having as she would to pay for sex at all. More disturbing, her desire to portray Cherifa as utterly ignorant of sex by dint of her culture situates culture as the tantalizing obstacle to consummation; and this need to produce their mutual incomprehension and tentative movement toward one another as the primitivism of the one frustrating the pocket of the other will resurface as the dominant theme of their association.

For Jane it would be devastating to admit that "they" are like "us" inasmuch as this admission would force her to confess that her desire abides in, even thrives on, a scene of purchase—she is always eager to show that the constant demand for money is either taxing or comic rather than invigorating. She can cast the economic exchange as a comedy as long as "their" behavior marks them as other, foreign and ignorant of the ultimate object of her desire and, further, as long as their wants mark them with the sign of their class status. What do they demand? Food, medical care, clothes. These demands are easily assimilated by the comfortably comic tone of Jane's condescension: that they ask for the material means of city life brands their desires and values as more primitive than their benefactor's. Jane shifts between a candid assessment of her role as "the richest woman in the world" and her desire for something more romantic; her letters evince a strange juxtaposition of knowledge and disavowal on this point. When she finally runs out of money, she writes, "Now I do have an upper hand that I never had when I spent more money. What is it? I suppose one must close one's fist and allow them just the right amount of money to make it worthwhile and not shameful in the eyes of the neighbors" (*OW*, 185). Cherifa, too, learns that the source of her newfound wealth lies in Jane's "work," and she has no trouble taking up a commanding role as Jane's taskmaster. Between them they establish a domestic routine that accommodates both their needs, but Jane, still at a loss to characterize the relationship, chafes at the bluntness of their modes of exchange.

Having struck a balance between "having" and being had, Jane and Cherifa move into a different phase that leaves Jane wondering what the limits of her own power to force the issue or "clamp down" might be.

> I waited and waited before writing because foolishly I hoped that I could write you: "I have or have not—Cherifa." The awful thing is that I don't even know. I don't know what they do. I don't know how much they feel. Sometimes I think that I am just up against that awful hard to get virgin block. Sometimes I think they just don't know. I—it is difficult to explain. So hard to know what is clever maneuvering on her part, what is a lack of passion, and what is fear—just plain fear of losing all her marketable value and that I won't care once I've had her. She is terribly affectionate at times and kissing is heaven. However I don't know quite how soon or if I should clamp down. I simply don't know. All the rules for the playing the game are given me by Paul or else Temsamany. Both are men. T. Says if you don't get them the first two times you never will. A frightening thought. But then he is a man. I told Paul one couldn't buy desire, and he said desire can come but only with habit. And never does it mean what it means to us—rather less than holding hands supposedly. Everything is very preliminary and pleasant like the beginning of a love affair between a virgin and her boy friend in some automobile. Then when we are finally in bed she says: "Now sleep." Then comes either "Goodbye" or a little Arabic blessing which I repeat after her. There we lie like two logs—one log with open eyes. I take sleeping pill after sleeping pill. Yet I'm afraid to strike the bargain. "If you do this, I will give you all of the money, if not—" it is very difficult for me. Particularly as her affection and tenderness seem so terribly real. I'm not even sure that this isn't the most romantic experience in a sense that I have ever had—and it is all so miraculous compared to what little went on before. (*OW*, 177)

These letters shift unstably from disavowal to frank assessment of the economic basis of their relation. Jane's disavowal of Cherifa's status as her employee or even as a prostitute—and it is the specter of prostitution that she finds so disquieting, for what does that make of her own desire?—complexly works to veil the trajectory of money. The letters continue to work through the contradiction of the "rules" and her own experience, and each effort to contain the ambiguity of her relationship with Cherifa brings with it a consistent thread of reification that culminates in the suspicion that Arabs do not mix love with sex.

> I hesitate to rush it, to be brutal in my own eyes, even if she would understand it perfectly. I think love and *sex*, that is tenderness and sex, beyond kissing and les caresses, may be forever separate in their minds, so that one might be going toward something less rather than more than what one had in the beginning. According to the few people I have spoken to—

among them P.M. (the Englishman who wrote the book)—I hate mentioning names—they have absolutely no aftermath. Lying back, relaxing, all that which is more pleasant than the thing itself, if one is in love (and only then) is non-existent. Just quickly "O.K. Now we sleep," or a rush for six water bowls to wash the sin away. I'm not even sure I haven't in a way slept with C. because I did get "Safi-naasu."[51] ("O.K. Now we sleep.") but it does not mean always the same thing . . . since I cannot seem to bring myself to the point of striking a verbal bargain (cowardice? delicacy? love?) I don't know—but I simply can't—not yet. I shall have to wait until I find the situation more impossible than pleasant, until my nerves are shot and I am screaming with exasperation. It will come. But I don't believe I can say anything before I feel that way. It would only sound fake. My hunch is she would go away saying "Never." . . . last night . . . I kissed her just a little. Later downstairs she said . . . she wondered whether or not God had seen us. I wonder. (OW, 178–79)

To maintain a confusion over whether the Arab women she pursues are capable of feeling love or capable of connecting tenderness to sex would secure her own machinations in a suspended state of indecision. In this way Jane can continue to shield herself from the obvious fact that her wealth is the essential link between herself and her lover. In a work exploring colonial and touristic queer sexuality, Michael Lucey analyzes this problematic in terms of disavowal and naming, writing, "This problem of naming is one of the main supports of the repressed fantasmatic content of this scene for a European who would like to be convinced that sex paid for with money in North Africa might be called something different than it would be called in Europe."[52] The difficulty of naming her desire a desire for "prostitution" is not so much a matter of repression in Jane's case. Rather, she is fully capable of an extended discourse on the means of exchange and the modes of sex while maintaining the suspense of "seeing and refusing to see." Jane profits from this "indecision," which admits fully of the knowledge that she pays for sex but confounds that knowledge with a simultaneous insistence on the "romance" of frustration. The "problem of naming" resurfaces in Jane's sexual adventurism already resolved by the Arabness of the women whom she pays for sex. Thus, it is in her interest to propose a complete disconnection between the two registers of feeling, sex and love, and to project that disconnection onto the unruly object of her affections. This disconnection is, in fact, a greater feature of Jane's approach to Cherifa, who by Jane's own account is in love with Boussif, for it is Jane who cannot decide anything, least of all whether the aftermath of sated desire is worth risking the foreplay of frustration, a form of desire familiar from its elaboration in other areas of her life. The possibility that love and sex are inherently split, divisible, threatens her, and as she recoils from this shadowed image of her own disconnection she projects it outward on the lover. The more disturbing fact revealed in the letter above is that within her milieu of expatriates in Tangier, the commonplaces of sexual lore are so rigorously, racially abjecting.[53] This belief that Moroccan women and men (for it is only on the basis of an analogy from the experience of men that she comes to bed armed with a theory) cannot derive love from or attach it to the sex act becomes the ground of her elaboration of Cherifa's primitiveness.

Without a common language and in the absence of a common expectation of the form that their relationship can take—whereas marriage is always a possibility with a man—neither woman has any sense of security. Cherifa has only her value in "not being had" to guarantee Jane's interest; Jane has only the warrant of her money to ensure Cherifa's presence. Without a socially prescribed form for their coupling they are both exposed to a host of haunting and fearsome possibilities; each is potentially the humiliated and the subjected, and these effects are heightened by the differences of language, class, and cultural experience. That Cherifa wonders "whether or not God had seen" them is not to be taken as evidence of the inherence of sacred law or the fundamental literalism of her symbolic; it is a fragment verifying the presence of a dematerialized law, here God-the-father, between them. Cherifa's uncertainty, her invocation of God, these add up to a way of speaking the presence of the law, suddenly and so easily run aground by their own unnamed desire: can he see the unspeakable? Are we invisible or very exposed? "She wondered whether or not God had seen us" is evidence that Cherifa knows something of what Jane wants from her and, equally, that there are dangerous consequences to this knowledge. As a result, they move toward each other through progressive scenes of stalemate where each can test and measure the terrain. Unlike the marriage bond, the symbols of which confer a ceremonial mystification upon the traffic in women while simultaneously celebrating that exchange, the bond between Cherifa and Jane has to be built up from the exposed facts of exchange. There is no way to disguise the element of prostitution so troubling to Jane and so disruptive of the affection she fears to trust. Jane's efforts to create a livable social world by replicating the bonds of kinship otherwise are constantly strained by the lack or absence of a culturally sanctioned disavowal of kinship's constructed nature; when marriage can appear as a natural destiny of love, disavowal has prepared the ground of love in advance. No such sanction of forgetting welcomes these lovers, and as a result their domestic arrangement can never shield itself from the suggestion of prostitution, colonial appropriation, or domestic servitude. As she writes in a different context, "One is never quite totally in the world: It is intolerable to be in this world without a myth" (*AL*, 299). In the case of her courtship of Cherifa, the bones of the structure are too bare, so bare that each has reason to distrust the other. When Jane writes of her power to bargain and "clamp down," a power she holds in check, she toys at the edge of the overexposure lurking between them. Like the characters of her unfinished novel, she is dangerously destitute of myth and desires one, especially a myth that might authorize her sexual encounter with Cherifa as love. At the same time, Jane is so habituated to high degrees of frustration that she finds herself in the contrary position of saying, "I'm not even sure that this isn't the most romantic experience in a sense that I have ever had." Knowing and not knowing, seeing and refusing to see are the oscillating terms of an excitement that she will draw out until the final moment of "exasperation," yet one cannot help wondering if that ultimate exasperation describes not a limit but the pinnacle of excitement.

If the colonial setting enables Bowles to reinscribe her own resistance to the law of gender and to the rule of lesbian "invisibility" along the lines of a faltering but original affiliation with Cherifa, it also sanctions a form of contempt for her lover that would be, perhaps, more difficult to express as such anywhere else. She reproaches Cherifa for her primitiveness and constantly writes to far-flung friends about her childish and ridiculous ways. These tales have the same value as the incessant doings of the cats, Berred and Dubtz, and Paul's parrot. Cherifa "looks like a child," lives in a "bordello," eats "like a monkey." Her efforts to secure the important meals from Jane during the holidays of Ramadan are constant fodder for Jane's epistolary amusements, and it is by extension of this ridicule that Jane criticizes the rituals attending the holiday. At one point Jane writes to Paul, "I get hysterical about Cherifa the way one does about a child" (196). These signs of contempt betray the working of difference within the relationship. The "hysteria" she feels about Cherifa's safety and her health and the pleasure that she takes in little differences of their habits always secures the adult and the sensible as properties of Jane's "parenting." Cherifa is made a child by Jane's intense scrutiny, and this stable edge of an absolute difference becomes the basis of Jane's commitment to the relationship.

Such a web of disavowal and derogation extends the problem of naming to the stasis of fetishism, which resolves the initial disquiet through a detour of belief.⁵⁴ "I do see and I refuse to all at once" speaks the structure of her desire as a disavowal echoing Mannoni's formulation, "je sais bien, mais quand même." In the essay of the same name, Mannoni argues that the fetishist suffers from a crisis of belief in the very matter of his desire. He knows full well that, say, women do not have penises, but even so he will persist in the belief. The fetishist, however, does not present his desiring scenario in quite these terms. "He knows that women do not have a phallus, but he cannot add any 'even so' because for him the 'even so' is the fetish."⁵⁵ The fetishist says instead, "I know full well that women do not have a penis, but, oh, the shoe." Thus, the fetish is announced as the practice and object that excites the preserved desire, saved from repression by the detour of the fetish. As Mannoni notes, the fetish is the cause of the circuitous statement, "I know full well"; it is not appended as a justification. It precedes the statement of which it is the extralinguistic cause. This sequencing of fetishistic cause and effect secures a realm of belief apart from the domain of facts that might challenge the fetish with repression or demystification. Neither unconscious nor simply conscious, the fetishistic statement defies logical contradiction by securing something outside the mode of facticity. The shoe, to take up a common example, cannot be contradicted or demystified. Its invincible strength lies precisely in its dumbness. To be as dumb as a shoe is to endure as a monument of something saved from change, time and pernicious attacks of knowledge; it is to be preserved as belief.

In Jane's path to and from Cherifa, this belief structure will invent the cultural differences between them as the literal fact of the fetish. Cherifa's Arabness will become the childishness necessary to sustain the disavowal of prostitution so troubling to Jane's fantasy of romance. That "they do not know" the ways of loving between women serves to support the imagination of an absolute difference in the place of a fairly ordinary economic exchange of money for sex. This invented and absolute difference, so rigorously policed in the bravado of the letters, will come to play a decisive role, guaranteeing the uniqueness of Cherifa in Jane's erotic landscape. Urged by Paul to leave Morocco for Mexico, Jane will refuse by saying simply, "There will be no Cherifas there." It is essential that Cherifa be unique and that she be legible to Jane according to a mobile thematic of primitiveness: Cherifa is alternately the infant, boy, thief, premodern, tribal, Muslim, pagan, Arab. Jane can later anguish over her leave-taking and claim that it is a shame and a fault to abandon Cherifa, who, had she not known Jane, "would not have become used to European ways." Jane positions herself as European, having European ways in contrast to the primitiveness of Cherifa's Arab ways—odd, considering that an upper-class Moroccan woman might be more European than Jane. Jane jettisons the primitiveness of an American identity by displacing deficiency and lack onto Cherifa—now doubly lacking for having become a hybrid of Europe and Morocco, child and whore. The substance of Jane's disavowal might be translated as "I know full well that this is prostitution, but, Cherifa, Tangier . . . "

Significantly, Mannoni also notes that the figure of the child is key to an understanding of the fetishistic structure of institutions of belief and to an extension of the fetish structure beyond the preliminary analysis of fetishism as perversion outlined in Freud's brief essay "Fetishism." Tracing an analogy between the belief structure of a religious institution and that of a demystified secular culture, Mannoni argues that the child underpins the peculiar pairing of disavowal and fixation in relationships of mentoring or initiation.

> We have yet to adequately investigate what goes on exactly when an adult feels the need to mystify a child—about Santa Claus or the stork, etc.—to the point, in certain cases, of fearing that throne and altar, such are Freud's words, would be in peril if one were to demystify the victim. . . . From a synchronic perspective, the child, as an exterior and present figure, can play a significant role in assuming our beliefs after repudiation. . . . He does not know the secrets of adults, which seems to go without saying, but we know that for certain perverts, it is the normal adult who becomes the believer and who does not know the child's secrets. In other words the situation is not so natural, and if psychoanalysis has rid us of the myth of infantile innocence and purity it has not gone very far in the analysis of the function of this myth. . . . If we acknowledge that to invoke this innocence of children is but a way to show their credulity, the picture changes considerably. As among the Hopi, but less clearly, infantile credulity helps us to repudiate our beliefs—even if we are not dealing directly with children, of course, their image is enough. Many adults would admit—sometimes the absurdity of the thing holds them back—that they are not religious for themselves but for the children. And the important place children hold in the organization of beliefs cannot be explained by the rational concern for their spiritual development alone.[56]

The child shores up an adult realm of belief and fetishistic disavowal by functioning for that ephemeral adult world of ideas as if childhood were the literal ground from which it sprang. The burden of belief is carried by the child, making childhood a cultural fetish. In fact, as Mannoni shows, the concerted effort to fill up childhood with mythic characters and theological rituals—from secularized myths like Santa Claus to the elaborate childhood rituals of organized religion or even the commercial incitements to believe in a natural heterosexuality embodied in toys—serves as the material support for a staged transmogrification as the child who believes in the fetish becomes the adult who believes in ideas and understands the difference between the literal and the figurative. The adult life of the mind requires a ritualized alibi in the lies told to children. This fetish culture of ritual and discipline sets a standard for childhood—a standard of belief as of practice—quite apart from the dematerialized faith of the adult realm. Such a normative fetishism is to be distinguished, in Mannoni's argument, from that of the "pervert" who departs from normativity but whose trajectory is still shaped by that point of departure. If we take our distance from the pejorative language of this so-called "perversion," we can still acknowledge with Mannoni that there is a shade of difference between a fetish, which must be privately held and refreshed by a particular psychic history, and the structure of disavowed fetishism that inheres in initiation and parenting. Like the muteness of the shoe, a fetish, once established, sets apart the one who adores it.

> The fetishist does not seek a believer. For him, others are in the dark, and he leaves them there. No longer a question of making believe, at the same time, it is no longer a question of believing.... We see that the place of the believer, that of the other, is now occupied by the fetish itself.... After instituting fetish, the domain of belief is lost to sight.... If with disavowal the whole world has entered the field of belief, those who become fetishists leave the field in that which concerns their perversion.[57]

The burden of Bowles's fetishism is twofold. It must establish Cherifa as the irreplaceable beloved by signifying her the absolutely other, the complete child. Once the link is established and Jane can believe in Cherifa's affectionate dependence, so different from the ruses of prostitution, Jane no longer needs to invest her energies to force the issue. She creates a myth to live by and then exits the scene herself. This structure of exiting the field of belief once the fetish is secured to perform that task for one is borne out by the letters following the consummation of their relationship. The tone is set and Cherifa pops in and out of the letters for comic relief—she ceases to develop in any way at all. Jane's life with Cherifa is a fetish culture securing belief: the house, the chickens, the medical appointments. Cherifa, arrested in a state of perpetual presexual adolescence not unlike the household pets, remains fixed as the stable pole of Jane's domestic life for years to come. In this way Jane rids herself of the sting of primitivism and childishness that clouded her rapport to Toklas, but she must remain always near the object of her fetishistic devotions for the ploy to work its magic.

Cherifa is notorious for practicing a Moroccan form of medicine and magic.[58] Do her fetishes absorb desire, her own, or do they absorb her ambivalence? Charms for warding off evil and granting wishes invade the house. These signs of "primitive" ambivalence are not so different from Jane's relation to writing and domesticity. As Jane's writing suggests, to perform a regression is one way to manifest the structure of the law as a mythic one. The self-perpetuating fetish culture carries the burden of creation because the structure must become the "natural" ground of desire. Cherifa's charms provide the same service in a different mode as they absorb hope and anxiety. That Jane understands her own life in Tangier, as well as the life of those around her, on the model of a magical, fetish culture of faith rather than "planning" is evident in her attempts to explain how the "dream world" of Arab life manages to function.

> Somehow in this peculiar world where nothing is arranged there is a sudden miraculous junctioning, a moment of unraveling when terribly complicated plans—at least what would be a complicated plan anywhere else—work out somehow as if in a dream, where one has only to think of something for it actually to appear [your novel]. It would take years to believe in this and not to see it merely as an amusing mirage—I meant to believe that such things do work out for the Arabs when they do, not because there is a law of chance but because such a lack of concentration on even the immediate future would allow all sorts of mysterious rhythms to flower, which we are no longer in possession of. (*OW*, 185)

Familiar as an orientalist trope—the phantasm of a passive and fatalistic East—this "lack of concentration" on the future is a reflection of Jane's exclusion and incomprehension. That she must "give in" and learn to live there becomes in her own eyes a kind of magic, once possessed by the West, now lost everywhere but Morocco. Living *there*, a living that must be learned, enables living at all, for the fetish embodied in the place, the woman, and the culture materializes a world. Her home life with Cherifa provides her also with the time to "believe" that her own complications can find a resolution. Here we see her confusing her own psychic blockages with Moroccan "time" but the profit to her is a way of life.

Life with Cherifa will guarantee for Jane a playmate, one who validates and verifies the materializing character of her obsessional wants. If the primitive, in Freud, possesses the power to manifest his ambivalence in the material world, this will be a lost art that Jane Bowles recovers at her own expense; hence the inconclusive yet repeated symptom of her contrariness. The reversals of fantasy—turning prostitution into family life, turning a writing block into an enormous corpus of letters, turning "out" to "in" as in the title of her never-to-be-finished novel *Out in the World*—expose the norm that constitutes her as outside by refusing that foreclosure and the death sentence that goes with it. Fantasy will also provide the necessary element of "belief" that can allow her to regain a measure of "mystification." "It is impossible to live without a myth": evidence that she wants more than to demystify the law of her abjection. She wants another myth, and the way to get it is to establish a firmament of ritual, a fetish. The exchanges with Cherifa that guarantee Jane's power do so in the mode of helplessness, much like the animist imbues his environment with energy and intention.

According to Mannoni, the literal realm of the festival is but a prop for the metaphysical realm of invisible realities. Children are required as the alibi for adult belief in the ideal as that which cannot be "shown" and thus cannot be demystified. The adult passes through his demystification to arrive where? The adult "real" world of true faith in the guise of nonbelief in the fetish. The fetish is the place of childish things, for children must have things "proved" to them. To revert, then, to childish things is: 1) to demand that the imaginary yield up its magic; 2) to fight the symbolic function with the symbols of its transferability; 3) to demystify an appearance of systematic totality without ceding the myth-making function. If one's world of adult belief has totally denigrated the imaginary only to deny its own foundation, there is much value in regression, for it returns belief to the imaginary and wreaks havoc on the static order of the symbolic. If one must believe it is only by virtue of having made something visible, legible, and audible.

Bowles's writing escapes to the place of her "real" practices for, when she writes, she travels to the most traumatically imbricated place of her psychic gaming. If she always turns her addressee into the law, she always steals away from that law by sending it postcards and letters. Magical thinking, like the primitive rituals of the shaman, has the power of materializing a "here" and a "there" to anchor her psychically on a map. Bowles's deviations around the laws of kinship enable her to establish her own little province of domesticity with its rules of order and laws of exchange and thus, in the "language" of class and ethnic difference, to establish an island of privilege that mimes by reworking the notion of difference. These same deviations around the law of kinship and the rule of the economic order, however, cannot sustain her. Every effort to thwart the terms of her abjection seems to leave a residue of guilt in her "new order." While she constructs the law of her own exclusion and then rebukes it in her letters, something prevents her from finding in her writing or in her domestic arrangements with Cherifa true respite from her anxiety and manic self-doubt. More attached, it seems, to the scene of her own abjection than to any dream of "being out in the world," her novel of the same name remains unfinished, because being-out-in-the-world would mean for Bowles being without pain and, finally, being-before-the-law as a final and irrefutably material instance; there can be no being sufficiently material before the laws. Thus she continues to circle around the guilty failure to be out-in-the-world and the equally guilty failure to be-before-the-law. Instructively, the case of Bowles contaminates the clean division between empty and full just as she undoes the hoped-for clarity of "in" and "out" in the world. Bowles is most full in her speech when she chatters and most empty when she tells the "truth."

"TORTURED LETTERS ABOUT TINY DECISIONS"

I don't expect to earn money on my book, but anything to forestall a bad reception . . . I could go on forever about all this, the pros and cons of going or staying here but I fear that the letter would turn into a fifteen page *ganze magilla* of "if's and but's" which I shall never send and then more months will go by and I will never write; but the letter could be used as a document for some doctor who specializes in states of anxiety

I shall certainly write you again now that I've started but you may come to dread these tortured letters about tiny decisions. I am famous for them or I was when I was famous, with a few friends (most of whom are dead) . . .

Jane Bowles, in *Out in the World:*
Selected Letters of Jane Bowles 1935–70

In 1957 and after squabbling with Cherifa over the cost of the Ramadan feast, Jane Bowles at the age of forty suffered a debilitating stroke from which she never fully recovered. Some blame a lethal combination of drugs and alcohol, others accuse Cherifa of poisoning Jane, and at least one close associate suspects an untreated epileptic fit as cause of the attack.[59] After the stroke her physical handicaps provide yet another source of meditation on her writing condition. The brain damage caused by the stroke does not alter the way that she speaks about her writing block, despite the fact that now the body mirrors the psychic conflict that so reliably brought her to impasse in the past. Blind in the right field of vision, suffering the linguistic side effects of a brain lesion that consigns her to say the opposite of what she thinks, she continues to imagine herself in and through the terms of writing. In their harsh reality, these complaints of the body cruelly parody the elaborations of disorderliness evident in her life leading up to the stroke. She has no control over her own speech, yet the disability becomes the site of extreme effort as she musters all her mental resources to overcome the massive obstacle in its most minute forms. Substituting "hot" for "cold," "blue" for "yellow," she regains some control over her linguistic failures by organizing the symptom into another way of meaning what she says; it is the task of those around her to learn to comprehend her exertions.[60] Her doctor said of her shortly after the stroke and during the early days of her rehabilitation that "She was aware of her power within her head, particularly in terms of language, but she was unable to exert that power. She was a hand-wringer, I remember. She seemed to know what she wanted to say, but she couldn't get it out."[61] As an added irony he prescribed for her linguistic malady a kind of writing and set her the task of writing compositions. In these brief texts, of which only one tattered and much-handled example survives among her papers, we find the clearest articulation of the writing dilemma that frustrated her, perhaps to the point of mixing drink with epilepsy medication, and that posed the choice of life or suicide every day.

> I don't know whether or not I understood you corectly —But is seems if I am corect -you asked me to write compositions for you. I can not. Please try to find some other way. I cannot write a composition. If I could I would. I don't think I have been able to for years anyway-and a this time it is completely impossible. If it is a failure of the will-then my will is sick-it is not lazyness. I am trying to read and I must say that I am doing well in that. If I could write a composition I would find my way out. But there is such a thing as a failure of the will which is agony for the person who suffers from it. I did not suffer a stroke for nothing at my age at age-and I have gone far away down the path   of no return. I must have started down that path when I was very young. I know that you want me

> to write something different-but I can't. I know that there are years of suffering ahead and that nobody can look into my brain. I know that they keep basket cases alive and that you don't choose to express your opinion on this—because as you said it a unresolved-a religious or philosophic unresolved—problem—Are we to take our lives or anyone elses—to save ourselves or anyone else from unindurable pain. Is torment pain—the final the purest offering we have to make to a supreme being because if it is not them why is it concidered   a   sin to relieve
>
>   one is alone finally and there is no doctor for the soul. I   one can find the strength to bow to the soul and accept it as existing beyond the ego—and beyond pain—perhaps the torment would ceise.[62]

She does not explain her inability to write in physical terms but in spiritual ones. The reasons she gives predate the stroke, as she clearly states with the phrase, "I did not suffer a stroke for nothing at my age." The body, signified by "brain" and "looking" inside the brain, occupies the enigmatic interior of her self, whereas her soul has become a harsh master beyond the pain and torments of the body and strangely exterior to the spatial metaphor she seizes upon to describe it. "I cannot write a composition. If I could I would . . . there is such a thing as a failure of the will which is agony for the person who suffers from it." These attempts to justify what for us would seem to be physical obstacles to writing—at this point she can neither see the text she has written nor can she be certain that she is hitting the right keys on the keyboard because of the visual disruption on the left side of her brain—are conveyed as failures of the will. She takes pains to distinguish the will from the ego's body, and further the soul from the pathetic self hiding in her brain. Still arguing with her doctor over the prognosis and her right to die, she catches him in a commonplace sophism as if to say that his own belief is both cruel and unreflective. She seems to have argued him into a corner by saying that his demand that she get well is contradicted by the very reason he offers against suicide. "Is torment, pain, the final the purest offering we have to make to a supreme being?" If not, then why would it be a sin to relieve the pain of someone who cannot be well, through a sickness that attacks the will and the soul? Does the last sentence read, "I, one, can find the strength to bow to the soul and accept it as existing beyond the ego and beyond pain," or does it read, "if one can find the strength to bow to the soul"? How has the soul become the exterior judge of her body separate from her inner being, the suffering in her brain? "I read. . . . I can in no way tell whether I have really read the sentence or not. If I could really describe this to you I would be alright—because then I could write."

This writing would save her, but she cannot read the sentence that she is to describe. And so she writes, but only that she cannot read her sentence. Thus she manifests what was always for her the death sentence of writing, from and through the writing of that place. Writing is the place she manifests her death, and always only through an address to another particular person—not the abstract other of writing but the local other of the address. If there is a "politics of address" here it is the politics of a standstill or demonstration of how she is the one caught, arrested in the development of her writing. There is a kind of genius in this stubborn refusal to pass on to "life" where life is understood as the other's myth, not your own invention. "It is impossible to live without a myth"; for Bowles this means that it is possible to die for lack of one. And die she does, indestructibly, until the end.

CHAPTER 3

"A Long Tirade for a Direct Interjection"

Talismano *Rebukes the Oriental Tale in Jacques Lacan's* Séminaires

> Thus we are nothing, neither you nor I, beside burning words which could pass from me to you, imprinted on a page for I would only have lived in order to write them, and, if it is true that they are addressed to you, you will live from having had the strength to hear them.
>
> Georges Bataille, Inner Experience

The second and final volume of Elisabeth Roudinesco's history *Jacques Lacan and Co.: A History of Psychoanalysis in France, 1925–1985* ends with a curious appendix. Trailing in the margins of this masterwork, a page of *The Interpretation of Dreams* in its Arabic translation appears without citation, though the book's title is noted.[1] As if torn out of its binding the text begins abruptly *in medias res;* to the reader of Arabic, no attribution is offered. Only an almost accidental recognition will serve those to whom the script is a language. This oblique citation transforms written Arabic into empty ornament—legible as an untranslatable emblem of otherness—and converts the now occulted writing into a kind of rebus, a form of calligraphy, that is, script. Within the framework of this common gesture, Arabic writing becomes a figure for the unconscious and, as the writing of the Other, a figure that raises to a suddenly derogatory degree the metaphoric character of Lacan's maxim, "The unconscious is structured *like* a language," for that likeness will also guarantee that the difference between the terms in play, language, and unconscious, French and Arabic, will be a distance unbridgeable by kinship.² In this appendix, there is no possibility of a metaphoric extension expanding the family relations of psychoanalysis; rather, the gesture of inclusion becomes a gesture of exclusion.

Moreover, this gesture is not unrelated to the history of Europe's encounter with the Orient, for the passage in question narrates an anti-Semitic incident that befell Freud's father and to which the son responded by cultivating a passionate interest in the story of Carthage and Rome. Hannibal, the imaginary figure of a heroic paternity, is summoned in this passage from *The Interpretation of Dreams* to shift the young Freud's identifications away from assimilation within an anti-Semitic boys' school culture and onto a legibly Jewish figure.³ Thus the story of his father's failure to embody the virtues of Hannibal is not only the story of Freud's own experience with the paternal function expressed in the form of a national fantasy; it is also the tale of Freud's decolonization of himself. It is no less significant that the work's Arabic translator is himself an African, like Hannibal, and has thus inserted himself obliquely as a follower in the appendix through a representative displacement into the history of Lacan's return to Freud. This calligraphic troping functions like a dream image, condensing a complex history of psychoanalysis's colonial reach. For if the fragmentary Arabic text seemingly heralds the successful conquest of oriental lands, it simultaneously signals the need for psychoanalysis to reflect on its complicity with colonial histories, whether in the guise of a colonial psychoanalysis graphically illustrated by Octave Mannoni's *Prospero and Caliban: The Psychology of the Colonized,* or in the form of a revolutionary practice as exemplified by Frantz Fanon's *The Wretched of the Earth.* Such a double bind structure, promising extension and inclusion but only at the threshold of the text and only as a supplement, legibly transcribes in a figural form the ambivalences of psychoanalysis, duty bound to illuminate universal structures of modern subjection but unable read the rebus of modernity in all its inflections.

The calligraphic trope of *Jacques Lacan and Co.* symptomatizes what it does not explicitly address; it appears a regressive move to contain otherness in a representative example, even as it aims to figure the otherness of the unconscious in the social inscription of subjectivity. This representation of the exotic other demands what Althusser, avid reader of Lacan, called a "symptomale" reading practice that "divulges the undivulged event in the text it reads, and in the same movement relates it to a different text, present as a necessary absence in the first" in order to uncover the "paradox of an answer which does not correspond to any question posed."[4] In keeping with this paradoxical structure of reading's unbidden answers, *Lacan and Co.* does not question the politics of translation and address that is set to work by its citational practice, nor does it comment or provide a mediating rationale for its appendix. Reading for the symptom, we might ask why, in a historiography attentive to the institutional development of the "dynamic psychiatry" of the 1920s, to the influence of surrealism on analysis and to the exchanges between psychiatry and psychoanalysis for the next sixty years, no mention is made of the relation or nonrelation between French psychoanalysis and Fanon, who is surely a part of that history and whose works cite amply not only surrealists like Césaire, but Leiris, Mannoni, and Lacan? Such a question and its politico-historical concerns are rigorously foreclosed in this account, a fact that doubles the uncanniness of the calligraphic trope, which simultaneously inscribes and erases the image of language as language and in so doing expels any knowledge of its own origins in a history of orientalism. At once an imaginary representation of language as such, and therefore of the symbolic order, and an image of a foreclosure, this first page of the appendix enforces a law of othering by which the one who reads the symptom is interpellated as the outsider within.

A figural collision of erasure and inscription, the Arabic fable of Freud's Hannibal in Roudinesco's appendix emblematizes the presence of "necessary absences" that this chapter pursues through a symptomatic reading of two texts that defy generic ascription. Lively, obscure, scolding, and seducing by turns, Lacan's second seminar, delivered over the course of 1954–55, is a kind of endless monologue in the form of an oral teaching. Just as difficult to characterize, the Tunisian novel *Talismano* by Abdelwahab Meddeb, published twenty-five years later and heavily influenced by psychoanalytic writing of all kinds, throws the monologue form into a vortex of harangue, tirade, reverie, and haunted writing that can be read as both a retort and creative reuse of the major Lacanian formulations found in the seminar but also in the essays of *Ecrits*. The two texts share as well their attention to a repeated trope of writing, specifically the invocation of an orientalist fantasy that attributes to Arabic the qualities figured in *Lacan and Co.* and which I have been calling the calligraphic trope. But whereas Lacan's seminar invokes a commonplace orientalism to illustrate a crucial theoretical innovation in the development of his theory of foreclosure, Meddeb's novel responds to this lapse by embroidering what might have remained no more than a retort into a major literary challenge to psychoanalytic normativity; that the novel does so while also advancing psychoanalytic speculation is the least of its feats.

Indeed, *Talismano* reworks Lacanian psychoanalytic theories into an effective literary tool of postcolonial critique that is then trained upon the failures of the postcolonial state. Public space is exposed for the psychic and symbolic violence that contours its modern boundaries as a series of limits on subjectivity and expression and centrally, as a repression of the body, for which there is little autochthonous precedent in a regional culture that has historically been hospitable to a wide range of religious, ethnic, and linguistic identities and certainly, to a more elastic definition of bodily propriety than has Western modernity. Resisting and refiguring both the pieties of a postcolonial shame of bodily and subjective difference and a psychoanalytic overvaluation of normative kinship and the symbolic laws that uphold it, *Talismano* declares that writing, which it privileges as a domain of imaginative refashioning, "reflète le désordre du corps plus que la loi primordiale."[5] If the body becomes the disordered agent of a political critique in the novel, it is only by dint of its prior inscription within a psychoanalytic imagination of address, and this commitment to the psychoanalytic scene of speech and careful listening prepares the narrative ground for a trenchant indictment of the postcolonial public sphere and the speech it forecloses.

The analytic model of speech and address that provides *Talismano* with one of its richest sources of reflection on subjectivity and community is set forth at length in "The Function and Field of Speech and Language in Psychoanalysis" and especially in the distinction, and often conflict, between a register of imaginary idealization and the slow, clinical emergence of symbolic truth in the unique speech situation of the talking cure. As was discussed in the introduction and taken up again in the last chapter with Jane Bowles's "empty chatter," Lacanian psychoanalysis locates the labor of analysis in a form of listening that brings the subject out of imaginary fixation and into a symbolic assumption of responsibility for his own truth. Lacan opposes full, symbolic speech to empty speech, "where the subject seems to be talking in vain about someone who, even if he were his spitting image, can never become one with the assumption of his desire."[6] The emptiness of such egoic speech contrasts, too, with the analyst's disciplined listening, for the analyst "takes the description of an everyday event for a fable addressed to whoever hath ears to hear, *a long tirade for a direct interjection,* or on the other hand a simple *lapsus* for a highly complex statement, or even the sigh of a momentary silence for the whole lyrical development it replaces" (*Ecrits,* 44). The address of full speech aims, through the syntax of empty chatter, at the other's understanding, but this model of address does not entail a knowing and intentional subject; rather, the symbolic truth of his speech emerges in the repetitions of address where the analytic scene enacts the division between the symbolic and the imaginary so that the painful symptoms of chatter can be lifted in the service of a subjective restructuration. The latter occurs only through the intercession of his own full speech which "reorder[s] past contingences *[sic]* by conferring on them the sense of necessities to come" (*Ecrits,* 48). To facilitate this reordering, the analyst must learn the patient like a song: "analysis consists in playing in all the many staves of the score that speech constitutes in the registers of language . . . in order for the analyst's message to respond to the profound interrogation of the subject, the subject must hear and understand it as the response that is particular to him" (*Ecrits,* 79).

Although Lacan speaks of the fullness of therapeutic realization as an opening onto negativity from out of the closure of empty, egoic, and imaginary constructions, at times his handling of the three registers of the Imaginary, Symbolic, and the Real reifies their distinction. This can be seen in the care he takes to delimit the imaginary from the real father, who threatens the subject with the law in cases of disrupted filiation. The normative pressure exerted by this conception of true and false, full and empty, stabilizes the triadic structure and creates more questions about the relation of image to word, surface to depth, and social norm to social exception. Literature poses particularly difficult problems for the Lacanian theory of language when it is displaced from its clinical setting, insofar as literature produces fantasy, image, and hallucination in the symbolic register of words addressed to the other. Capitalizing on the disruptive and generative quality of literary language and image, Meddeb's writing, by privileging the disorder of the body rather than the primordial law of oedipal kinship, illustrates the efficacy of the Imaginary to contest the putative closure of the Symbolic, which if it were recast within the Lacanian idiom might be something like a reading of that direct interjection that is the long tirade. The novel is able to produce such an intervention largely by harnessing the rant as symptom and turning it into the source of a poetics of resistant writing that is theorized in the novel under the sign of calligraphesis, which we will discuss at length below; thus the ranticle irruptions in Meddeb's text reflect the progressive intensification of the critical function of ranting and differ from the rants in Bowles and Wilde insofar as for Meddeb psychoanalysis has provided a literary set of reflections to read ranting and thus to subject it to a poetic manipulation; this self-conscious poetics of ranting allows a generative speaking to occur from the space of foreclosed inscription, and for the first time in our consideration of ranting, the aesthetic ideology of ranting takes on a genuinely utopian cast in the avowed fusion of writing and embodied subjectivity that the novel pursues.

In this way, *Talismano* both assumes and reorients a Lacanian theory of clinical transfiguration toward a social critique that mobilizes abject and repressed speech to political ends. The attention to language functions on many different levels but always foregrounds subjective processes and operations articulated through dreams, reveries, excessive ornament, fevered tirade, fantastic dialogue, and delirium. Key to the novel's critical portrait of postcolonial Tunisian public space and the speech that is foreclosed there by the tropes of modernity, *Talismano* literalizes derogation and profanation in its narratives and images to convert the detritus of national exclusions into the terms of subjective renewal.

DECADENT ORIGINS

Injecter sang, déverser pleurs, ne serait-ce qu'en ces heures partout mourantes ; et l'idée qui traîne et vacille entre les berges : l'idée qui parfois s'emprisonne et paralyse les doigts ; et l'idée qu'on jette éclatée, transbordée, atomisée et réfugiée rosée matinale qui dégoutte douceur des plantes aux abords de tant de villes. Histoire qui n'est que mots et morts, coït restreint ou dense, mobile en toute hâte, rebords réconciliant les mythes d'un soi fuyant.[7]

                  Abdelwahab Meddeb, *Talismano*

Decadence, not a concept or project so much as a field of speculative and literary obsessions, has also been the name of modernity, especially for writers from former colonial states. The lines of the exergue above might easily be mistaken for a prose poem of Huysmans; they are in fact from the opening of Meddeb's *Talismano*. This moribund modernity, figured here as an open wound, burdens the writing subject with the history of words and corpses, a coupling as irrefutably figurative as it is manifestly material. Mired in a traumatic history, the writer of decadent modernity might suture the edges of his fugitive subject into a delusory wholeness or, as in the case of Abdelwahab Meddeb, he may choose to maintain the painful opening, attempting to represent the flux and instability of his own situation. Meddeb's text explicitly avows the latter task of modernism and would welcome the association of Huysmans's writing with his own, for *Talismano* seeks to attach the many haunting "vivants" that traverse the narrator's writing "je" to the experience of reading.[8] The modernity of this author is one that makes a virtue of the loss of faith in the law ("s'édifiant désespérance de loi") by incorporating the mixed blood of his own literary lineage.

The Maghrebian extension of modernism does more than add yet another province to the map of modernist expansion; North African literature is distinct for its engagement in contemporary discourses on writing and the body as well as for its deep investment in psychoanalysis and the avant-garde. The result is a body of literature uniquely equipped to interrogate the symbolic fixity of discourses of modernity. One key element in this project of revaluing the present without forgetting or suturing over historical facts of trauma derives from the unique predicament of Arabic literature. Writing in Arabic is overshadowed by the sacral nature of the language—not because of the inherent primitivism of the sacred book, but because of an explicitly linguistic basis of modern Arab claims to nationhood. Without seeking to reduce the complex history of nationalism in the region to a simple one of linguistic choice, it is, nevertheless, tremendously important to understand the pressures brought to bear on questions of language and, equally, to reflect on the nature of that language. The Algerian writer Assia Djebar, echoing a sentiment shared by many writers of the region, has claimed that Arabic has never been secularized and that the nationalism of the postindependence era has been characterized by a scholastic Arabic masquerading as a nativist return to the authentic language of the nation.[9] Although the colonial history of Algeria differs remarkably from other Arab states, making it a special case, Djebar's observation hits upon a general feature of Maghrebian writing in Arabic, for the written language differs markedly from the spoken, and that difference immediately creates a breach between the local and the written. Because of the unique stratification of diglossia in Arabic, and, equally, because the Qur'an is the source of the classical lexicon and thus still exerts a strong pull on questions of language, Maghrebian authors are faced with a unique constraint on literary practice. The choice of writing in French or Arabic has preoccupied the field of Francophone studies from the beginning, but Djebar makes a different point when she claims that nationalism, far from ushering tradition into the public space of the secular state, instead instituted a new sacred with the project to re-Arabize the state. By this account, engagement in avant-garde formal innovations is already participation in the desacralization of the language of state, which has been so historically resistant to using vernacular as the official language.[10] The choice to write in French can be as much a retreat from this historical burden as it may be a pragmatic or political decision. And while re-Arabization projects are differently pursued in the North African states, criticism of re-Arabization has become a cliché of postcolonial studies in the United States while other nativist projects to restore or invent a language of state are celebrated elsewhere. In the international market of idées fixes Algerian re-Arabization symbolizes the evils of postcolonial modernization, yet the project of linguistic and cultural restitution continues to play a role in regions where the colonial state's lingua franca is neither native nor a majority language, as was the case for Algerian French. For all their differences even the South African solution of maximal inclusion through the translation of state discourse into eleven languages owes a certain debt to the earlier Algerian efforts to renaturalize the lost language of colonized peoples and thus to repair the damage of colonial predation through language therapy.

Writing in both French and Arabic, Meddeb consciously seeks to infuse each of these languages with features of the other and to incorporate the literary archive of each in the other. The impetus to desacralize the writing of Arabic is also present in his French poetry and prose, in which he is consistently preoccupied by the theological assumptions and underpinnings of the symbolic organization of his culture, as Abdelkebir Khatibi recognizes when he writes that the French Meddeb invents represents a violent transformation of the former colonial language.[11] Meddeb infuses this prose with local sounds, words, and rhythms while incorporating the poetry of Ibn 'Arabi and al-Hallaj as well as a host of other figures, both orthodox and heretical, from Arabo-Islamic literary history and beyond, but this is no labor of folkloric transcription. His writing always debunks the conceit of an unlettered "tradition," but it does so from a position of substantial knowledge, and in doing so, the novel *Talismano* performs what

Khatibi has also called a work of decolonization, carried out at the level of the word and critiquing continuing Western hegemony as well as the idealized forms of Arab nationalism and public piety.

Talismano begins with only the barest conceit of a subject, less a protagonist than conduit of textual flow, and follows his itinerant wanderings through the streets of Tunis.

> Me voici de retour exprimé ville à dédale, ému à me distraire d'enfance : à retrouver des saveurs anciennes à travers les déduits de Tunis. Les portes, bleu doux tendre, clous noires, repères où s'inscrustent les ébats incertains de la mémoire. A percer le secret des rues et impasses qui ne furent jamais foulées, n'était-ce itinéraires anciens d'une enfance que je ne fabule pas paradisiaque perte.
>
> Bab 'Asal, porte, puis rue sentimentale : je savais enfant que tel menuisier était un parent vague. Il ne me reconnaissait pas. Mais à le voir à l'oeuvre, mètre en main, crayon à l'oreille, j'étais fasciné et au mépris : n'est-il l'unique manuel de la famille à dénombrer notables, théologiens, commerçants aisés, féodaux, bureaucrates, médecins, notaires, avocats, juges?[12]

Breaking with grammatical norms, the text places itself in a modernist lineage of fictional autobiography by returning to errant infancy to tell its tale. The characteristic modernist fusion of primitive regress and decadent history is also tellingly established in these first lines. Beginning in a ruined language, the novel collapses a regression to a scene of infancy atop a parodic genealogical observation, itself the story of a decline in class and a ruined history. The ancient routes of childhood are not the stuff of nostalgic fable but become the materials to be worked by hand, to resist the abstract repetitions and family repressions of his lineage. The text's refusal to translate *bab 'asal,* a place name derived from an old fortification, graphically condenses the linguistic intimacies that *Talismano* exposes. Untranslated but transliterated, the name is reworked in its new context, achieving an afterlife in "French" where the ambiguity of the letters permits additional wordplay in Arabic—honey gate or primal portal (*bab 'asal* or *bab aSal*).

Shifting from "me voici" to aerial views of Tunis, the prose alternates between sweeping panorama and jerky, quick images conveyed in cameralike shifts of perspective and point of view. We survey the city, its streets, schools, and prisons, before resting to dwell on the burial preparations of Safia, whose death introduces the theme of ritual pre-Islamic practices that secretly persist despite orthodoxy. Dominating this montage of themes is the text's persistent approach to figures of the body, in pain, in death, in motion, as it descends through the many institutions of growth—the school, the mosque, the uncle's study containing a gloriously falsified genealogical tree proclaiming exalted Bedouin origins—and thence, on to institutions of decline in the prison and graveyard. Accompanying this circling motion through Tunis are descriptions of Halfawine, the old medina, as a nautilus, a labyrinth, a spiral. It is clear that despite its lapses the "ville à dédale" (labyrinth) can and does motivate a psychic, bodily, textual progression.

The reader must supply the punctuation to make sense of these complex phrases. He does so by lending his voice to the text, much of which calls to be read aloud. Playing off the recitative traditions of the Qur'an, *Talismano*'s intricate and imagistic writing spirals out of narrative control, yet there is a reliable regularity to the rhythm, allowing one to track and recognize the patterns of sound. This regularity of beats infuses even the text's formal aspect with the persistent theme of the primitive, for the novel invites the senses as modes of reading. Thus a formal innovation at the level of sound and pattern represents in yet another way the thematic, rhetorical, and political content of its meditations. These techniques not only signal the text's participation in a modernist avant-garde, but they also point to a resistant effort to ruin any seamless ideological fiction that might come ready-made between the author and the reader. At one point the text praises a madman for abiding in a madness: "qui ne divise pas le réel, qui le préserve flou exact et atomisé poudroiement." Such an evocation of a reality in flux that breaks apart the screen of received wisdom owes much to the insights of the aesthetic movements of decadence and modernism, and in particular to the setting to work of transgression in the unworking and reworking that the literary text enables.

Opening with a scene of boredom bred of a history both personal and impersonal, *Talismano* ends with an excessive, impassioned appeal to a future of writing that would be the future of a heterogeneous Maghreb, unashamed of its paganism, its dialects, and its popular religious practices and knowledges. In this text that navigates the complexity of Maghrebian speech and Arabic and French literary conventions, Abdelwahab Meddeb attempts to bridge the chasm between the speech of women, "maîtresses de la tradition orale"; written Arabic, radically different from the dialects spoken in the Maghreb and the official medium of national life thus "gendered" male; and the language of the law, always negotiating between the sacred text, legal precedent, and local instance. He conducts this complex literary representation of the symbolic space of his own writing in a fractured French like no other, but because Meddeb foregrounds the symbolic and linguistic situation of his writing, his interventions upon the inherited themes of decadent history and primitive ritual allow for a reinscription of those themes such that the dangerous lassitude and inflexibility of modern Maghrebian normativity must confront the frustration it creates. Primitive traditions, local ritual, and dialect become sources of an unromantic and critical reuse seeking to affirm an archaic encyclopedia of acts, objects, and speech against their ideological repudiation, indeed abjection, in the official discourses of the state. Both inheritance and invention, this evocation of traditions pointedly refuses the hegemony of national forms of culture that repudiate abjectly feminine speech, pre-Islamic social organization, foreign influence, folk medical practices, and pagan ritual by representing them as excessive, regressive, and otherwise dangerous to modern sensibility. The text's rhetorical swerves and encyclopedic layers attempt to assemble the experience and imagination that would otherwise be rigorously eliminated by orthodoxy. Between the rhetorical emphasis on form and the politicized insistence on gender and cultural heterogeneity, the modernist themes of the primitive and the decadent as modes of resistance and invention resurface in Meddeb's project of decolonization. These formal and rhetorical interventions on the ideological norms of the colonial residue and nationalist dogma seek to manifest the psychic, social, and formal figure of a dematerialized paternity everywhere in crisis yet always reasserting itself.

Talismano stubbornly registers the deadlock between poetic excess and censorship, historically a by-product of the impulse to decolonize, to purge Arabic culture of colonial residues. Meddeb's fiction and melancholic ranting thus dramatize his own involvement with the law of foreclosure by always taking as his subject a speech that disarticulates conventional modes of reading and transmission. At a critical point in the novel, and to illustrate the foreclosure of excessive transports by orthodoxy, Meddeb has his protagonist and alter ego narrate a memory. Attached to an ad hoc band of pagan sorcerers the "je" is about to participate in an idolatrous ritual, and, shaken by his own audacity, he meditates in an essayistic fashion on the different character of Maghrebian cities, dilating on their tribal pasts, the waxing and waning of dynasties, all of which evokes a history too complex to fit the uses of nationalist epic. Suddenly he is seized with the memory of his early religious instruction.

> Tel père a enseigné en cette profitable mosquée : ses paroles de maître, savant parfait du hadîth et des sources du droit . . . Père érudit honnête combien modeste en sa manière de transmettre sans prétention l'exactitude de son savoir . . . Mais comment imposer la précision des chiffres là où la fable aurait mieux exprimé ce qui se refuse à la mesure? Ma première querelle avec le père éclata mélange des mots pendant la transmission récitative du texte : je ne supportais pas, rebelle, reproduire par coeur les versets coraniques; . . . Tel père ne jouait pas le sens du texte; . . . par la leçon, il aurait voulu favoriser une discipline. Et j'étais moins rebelle au sens qu'à la soumission par devoir. J'ai rencontré le père par la pratique du texte. Il m'était pénible de m'adapter à sa mnémonique fruste.[13]

Careful to distinguish the law from its servant, Meddeb mobilizes the scene of instruction as an edifying fable of his own textual excesses, of his intolerance for the automatic and thoughtless repetition of tradition. Unlike the father, this son refuses to submit to the law of discipline and so, faithful to another law, he dwells upon the enigmas of the fanciful sacred text. The scene is offered as an explanatory prelude to the final section in which a blasphemous public sacrifice scandalizes the pillars of the community and that is clearly marked as a literary attack on national epic. The love of violent excess is produced, Meddeb argues, by the idealization of a tradition conceived not as living but as the rote transmission of duty. This is why it would be an error to understand *Talismano*'s investment in transgression as an anthem to the powers of sexual, textual, and political subversion, although such an interpretation colors the most important readings of the text.[14] Indeed, the textual intricacy falls out from a fundamental psychoanalytic insight woven through the postcolonial scenography; namely, that what is foreclosed by and from the Imaginary of nationalism returns as the foreclosed social Real. The rhetoric of this decadent relation is essentially that of the law understood as an irresolvable tension or double bind between two opposing understandings of the symbol and its law.

The notion of the law that I am invoking borrows from Lacanian vocabulary to identify a realm of symbolic organization, which is determinate but not totalizable and characterized by a form-granting negation legible as an institution of foreclosure. Whereas Lacan defines foreclosure within the context of his work on psychosis as the repudiation of the paternal function, a more useful extension of the term takes stock of the discursive production at the heart of any evocation of the law. Such a reworking and negotiation with this concept is undertaken by Judith Butler in "Arguing with the Real." There the link between foreclosure and the law emerges as a contingent "act" of power, one that institutes foreclosure as generativity, as the generation of socially possible and socially impossible subjects. "The subject is produced in language through an act of foreclosure. What is refused or repudiated in the formation of the subject continues to determine that subject. What remains outside this subject, set outside by the act of foreclosure which founds the subject persists as a kind of defining negativity."[15] Produced in language, the negativity that haunts the subject will persist as a linguistic and discursive negativity, as that which establishes the limits of representation. Resignifying the notion of foreclosure, Butler clearly states that the regulatory mechanism of foreclosure can be understood as the law and, equally, that this law is itself subject to historical contingency. Thus the law makes appear by making disappear, yet the activity of foreclosure is itself subject to the movement of materialization that is its mode of power and that exceeds its own grasp. In this way the notion of a symbolic law is productively qualified to highlight the phantasmatic character of the theoretical postulate and to situate it both as an institutional effect and as the effect of instituting subjects. The law is no more real and no less a product of fantasy than are the hysterical symptoms or melancholic lamentations produced in relation to the law and as its "real" effects. "To the extent that this law engages the traumatic production of a sexual antagonism in its symbolic normativity, it can do this only by barring from cultural intelligibility—and rendering culturally abject—cultural organizations of sexuality that exceed the structuring purview of the law."[16] Thus a retaliatory act would undertake an impossible task of speaking from the place of cultural unintelligibility to highlight the ongoing delimitation of the law's "purview." To point the finger at the activity of the bar is to engage with the phantasm of the law at the frontier of symbolic norms. Such speech is in some sense empty speech. It points to the "place" of its own abjection by stubbornly abiding there. It is a deictic speech uttering a repetitious message that cannot fill up the "contents" of the bar's demarcation.

If we return, then, to foreclosure as a regulatory mechanism that appears in the guise of the law, it is not with the intent of substantializing that law as a timeless psychic fact but rather with the expectation that the theory of foreclosure can shed light on the twin structures of exclusion and idealization.[17] In an early formulation of foreclosure as censorship, Lacan evokes the dynamic of the enabling constraint, which is the law.

> La censure, c'est ça, en tant qu'il ne peut jamais y avoir de rapport avec la loi dans son ensemble, puisque la loi n'est jamais assumée complètement.... Censure et surmoi sont à situer dans le même registre que celui de la loi. C'est le discours concret, non seulement en tant qu'il donne à l'homme son monde propre, que nous appelons, plus ou moins exactement, culturel. C'est dans cette dimension que se situe ce qui est la censure, et vous voyez en quoi elle se distingue de la résistance. La censure n'est ni au niveau du suject, ni à celui de l'individu, mais au niveau du discours, pour autant que, comme tel, if forme à lui tout seul un univers complet, et qu'en même temps il a quelque chose d'irréductiblement discordant, dans toutes ses parties. Il s'en faut d'un rien, de rien du tout, que vous soyez enfermé aux cabinet, ou que vous ayez eu un père accusé à tort de je ne sais quel crime, pour que tout d'un coup la loi vous apparaisse sous une forme déchirante. C'est ça, la censure.[18]

The law is defined as that which cannot be fully comprehended, assumed, or made one's own. Censorship or foreclosure determines and delimits the subject's relation to the law as one characterized by excess and a failure to fully inhabit and be inhabited by that law. There is always more to the symbolic organization of kinship and its "concrete discourse" than the particular face of foreclosure shown to and in an individual subject. For this reason, censorship inheres in the full universe of discourse as that which can interrupt the discourse to bring the subject up short against the nothing ("very little"/"rien"), which exposes him to the appearance of the law. If foreclosure works through the appearance of the law it nevertheless appears "to you" in a "lacerating form." The law appears as a tear or rip in one's integrity: for Meddeb thematized as the destrudo of textual form itself, for Bowles the "falling to pieces" so insistent in both her fiction and her letters, and for Wilde the terrible scene at Clapham Junction that only serves to seal his failure to circumvent the courts by a fully theatrical confession that would transport and transcend, even sublimate, accusation, judgment, and punishment. Yet the law as cut abides in its disguised form as a discord in the "concrete discourse" of cultural abundance. Ranting speaks this discord but directs its speech at the tear in substance, which projects the terrible appearance of the law.

This formulation of censorship equates it with "concrete discourse" through the claim that discourse possesses unknowingly the element of discord that Lacan names the law. If it is the destiny of discourse to be haunted by a discordant element, one that a subject can experience only as trauma, how are we to speak of this law? Where is it to be located? Is it before, within, or beneath discourse, as one tradition of psychoanalysis imagines the id to be beneath the ego, buried in the primordial depths of the unconscious? The text seems to gesture in the direction of a distinction between the chance appearance of the arbitrary, "everything that happens, everything which constitutes discourse," and the calculated gift of the proper, "it gives man his own world." The French text reads "en tant qu'il donne à l'homme son monde *propre*," as if to say that the distinct and clean outline of a given discourse depends from a fragile consistency "which we, more or less accurately, call cultural." Censorship "is" the concreteness of the cultural discourse and abides there because the apparent self-sufficiency of the discourse is undermined by a discord flowing through it entirely, which is to say that censorship is not the cut, but the consistency appearing only in the violent and sudden visibility of its own absence. Censorship flows through "everything that happens, everything that constitutes discourse," where the appearance of self-sufficiency derives from the ability of a discourse to form, "all by itself," a full universe. Significantly, the French emphasizes the properly poetic dimension of discourse when Lacan describes it as engaged in an activity of *forming* itself in the mode of completion. The translation offers *constituting* as an equivalent.[19] Where the former emphasizes molding by instruction or discipline, embodying and constructing by derivation, the latter brings with it the sense of assigning a legal form. The two words converge in the single meaning: to frame. Embodiment and assignment at once describe the institutional framing of discourse at work in Lacan's text on censorship. Together they suggest the antithetical meanings bound up in Lacan's conception of discourse. If discourse forms autonomously a cultural universe, it does so only "after" the legality of its particular forms have been judged. This twisted logic finds censorship both before the law and after it, manifest in discourse as a strife "dans toutes ses parties." These parts collapse the putative wholeness of the form that is discourse and without which the particularity of discourse would never be apparent. The emphasis on a form haunted by the noise of discord and threatened with dismemberment is familiar as the imaginary gestalt of the mirror stage. Whereas the mirror stage conceives form in terms of the subject's identity and bodily integrity, here the threat of dismemberment is reinscribed as a split between the completeness of discourse and the antagonism within it, appearing as a desublimating tear. The analogy between discursive integrity and bodily form reveals the priority accorded the singular form of the symbolic as much as it exposes the ghostly need of the law to find its bodies, to arrive at its own incarnation.

"A Long Tirade for a Direct Interjection"   193

What status do symptoms have within this emerging model of foreclosure in language? How are these bodily representations connected to the law? Lacan details the role of the superego as an agency that produces symptoms charged with the responsibility of figuring the law.

> La censure, c'est ça, en tant que chez Freud, à l'origine, ça se passe au niveau du rêve. Le surmoi, c'est ça, pour autant que cela terrorise effectivement le sujet, que ça construit en lui des symptômes efficaces, élaborés, vécus, poursuivis, et qui se chargent de représenter ce point où la loi n'est pas comprise du sujet, mais jouée par lui. Ils se chargent de l'incarner comme telle, ils lui donnent sa figure de mystère.
>
> C'est tout autre chose que le rapport narcissique avec le semblable; c'est le rapport du sujet avec la loi dans son ensemble, en tant qu'il ne peut jamais y avoir de rapport avec la loi dans son ensemble, puisque la loi n'est jamais assumée complètement.[20]

"La censure, c'est ça," the sentence points, and the gesture is repeated: "le surmoi, c'est ça." The blunt language constantly highlights censorship and the superego through these few pages, while simultaneously it plays upon the doubling of "ça" as deictic particle and Lacanian code for the unconscious. This hyperbolic deixis is itself a symptom of the law, which the text seeks to reveal, for the law, itself, cannot be revealed. The law is performed as that which is put into play by its own symptoms, carried out by the subject in the grip of incomprehension. The superego terrorizes the subject with the constructions of what will become the subject's own property, the blockages that move and develop while being burdened with the task of representation. Charged with figuring the place where the law is neither contained nor understood within the subject, the symptoms' task of embodying the law exceeds the singular, subjective psychic "acts" of repression foundational for any subject, and, yet, it is here, in this performance of the law in symptom formation, that one's singularity lies.[21] Because the law is not only the law as written, it cannot be seen or known in its totality from any single position within its "concrete discourse." In the case of foreclosure, the superego's activity is not joined to the production of ego ideals but to the incarnation of the law as that which cannot be fully known. Accordingly the symptom develops at the point of nonknowledge of the law where refusal is commanded by that which exceeds the subject in the subject, and so the coherent outline of the discourse is cut by a relation to nonknowledge, refused in the subject with the consequence that this repudiated knowledge becomes the wellspring of the subject's negative attachment to the social "world." When foreclosure ceases to haunt discourse as a kind of discord "in all its parts," it springs itself upon the subject as the law incarnate in a lacerating symptom. The difficulty of this figure lies in its dual character as a social foreclosure, guarantor of the generic type, and as a singular, subjective effect. Being locked up in the toilets by mistake and having a father wrongly accused are accidents that assert the generality of the law as a traumatic, personal appearance of exclusion.

Lacan's text edges toward an account of discourse as that which grants the "world" in the activity of foreclosure where that form of discursive unity is phantasmatic and thus unmasterable, open to its own potential for resignification against the grain. Yet there is an equal pressure to forestall the logical extension of the theory of foreclosure. The world emerges on the condition that something in its "totality," "as a whole," "dans son ensemble" falls under the bar of censorship only to be resumed in superegoic productivity. The subject, then, performs the law at the limit of his grasp of it, in a blind spot of unconscious repudiation. The lacerating tear in one's substance, which is the advent of the law's appearance, is itself another place of uncomprehending performance. This exhibition of the law, what I called earlier the materialization of the law, differs from a narcissistic relation to the image, and implicitly to idealization, insofar as this materiality exhibits the absenting of an idealization or image. These are the pictures that must remain unseen, the signifiers that cannot be spoken and thus are signified as lacking in the place where they are made to fall away, fall to pieces. The symbolic register of the law can only function as fixed and thus legible as one law in and as superegoic symptoms of the law. The law appears as complete only in the place where foreclosure works its magic to produce incarnations of the law. Embodiment of the law is the mode of power and the mechanism by which it can be said to be dematerially present—as a haunting absence of the father in Freud's formulation—in the place where it is throwing out its "own" materializations.

There is a tension within Lacan's treatment of the law. As the absent origin of a materialization, which itself grants the law "its face of mystery," the law is defined in profoundly theological terms. This seems to be a temptation throughout the various formulations of censorship and foreclosure, one that is finally resolved in the third seminar in the figure of the oedipal and symbolic father, guarantor of the law. There the functioning of the nom-du-père shores up the difficulties within the theory opened up by the malleability of the earlier notion of a "concrete discourse." Where the latter threatens to permit a genealogical tracing of the cultural instances of foreclosure, the theory of a psychotic threat summons a panicked endeavor to fill in the variability of discourse with the figure of the father. A second tendency of this early theory of the law locates it in discourse and does not require that the law be limited to the law of the incest prohibition or any other paternal closure to symbolic normativity. On this account the law stands as normativity in discourse and as the policing of the boundaries of discourse. It is on this second potential of the theory of foreclosure that we lean when we seek to show that what the law forecloses cuts a symbolizable figure of exclusion.

The passage above ties foreclosure to symptoms, incarnation, performance, and form and in doing so suggests that the activity of foreclosure always strikes a signifier by producing another signifier. Symptoms, in their relation to that which is foreclosed—whether it be the law itself that is foreclosed, as in the case of psychosis, or a realm of symbolization—signify the performative realm of the law and as such give rise to a culture of the negation of some morsel of symbolization. "The notion of foreclosure offered here implies that what is foreclosed is a signifier, namely, that which has been symbolized, and that the mechanism of that repudiation takes place within the symbolic order as a policing of the borders of intelligibility."[22] The relationship between foreclosure and the superego in Lacan's text is clear evidence for Butler's account of foreclosure as the administration of the border of intelligibility inasmuch as the censorship of discourse issues commands to the superego and determines what will be obstinately signified as unsymbolizable, mysterious. The superego builds up a discourse on the foundation of a repudiation and thus legislates the incomprehension and unintelligibility of certain signifiers by generating others. In these early seminars, Lacan has not yet marked out that which refuses symbolization in symbolization with the stamp of psychosis, nor has he limited foreclosure to the paternal signifier. Hysterical and neurotic symptoms produced within the discourse through the workings of negative representation or "defining negativity" continue to dominate Lacan's considerations and his choice of examples. However, a closer look at his text reveals a determinate register for that which must be foreclosed. As such, it constitutes a prehistory of the concept of foreclosure in Lacanian psychoanalysis and conditions that conceptual framework by enacting a foreclosure at the origin of the theoretical articulation. Such an archaeological approach to the theory is key to understanding the combined thematics of Meddeb's work, for in these early Lacanian elaborations, as I am about to show, the psychoanalyst mirrors the novelist and poet by showing symptomatically that what must be refused to symbolization must become the primitive. Here psychoanalysis and fiction share in the construction of the primitive in the place of cultural difference; as such, this construction marks both the theory and the literature as modernist endeavors. What is foreclosed in Lacan's speculation will return to the same place renamed, remade as the primitive.[23]

THE MUSLIM PATIENT

At the end of the passage above Lacan's text refers obliquely to "a father wrongly accused" in the course of explaining the sudden materialization of the symbolic law in all its violence. "It takes very little, very little at all, being locked up in the toilets, or having a father falsely accused of lord knows what crime, for the law all of a sudden to appear to you in a lacerating form. That is what censorship is." The text refers to a twice-told tale of a "Muslim" patient suffering from a writer's cramp.[24] Lacan recounts the story in both his first and second seminars, and through this repetition, it holds a singular status with respect to the articulation of the symbolic law and foreclosure as key concepts. The "Muslim" patient comes to Lacan to be treated for a writer's cramp that had persisted unabated through a previous analysis.[25] Lacan uncovers, behind the patient's symptom, a childhood history of an accusation of theft against his father, a civil servant who lost his post as a consequence, and deduces the figure of a Quranic commandment dictating that the punishment for theft be the removal of the hand. He then asserts that the patient lives his relation to *the* law—the symbolic law of kinship in language—as a suspension of this Quranic law that subsequently reappears to him in the lacerating form of a disabling writing cramp that effectively and symbolically cuts off his hand. Consistently in each mention of the tale, Lacan links the suspension of law to the superego and its representations; thus, the child's resistance to a cruel juridical form becomes inscribed in the psyche as the superego's productivity. In each telling of the story the Quranic law is relegated to a "tradition" with a "totalitarian character" as if there were not an equal tradition of civil law in the patient's country of origin. "In the Islamic sphere, on the contrary, the law has a totalitarian character which will on no account permit the isolation of the juridical from the religious plane."[26] It is significant that at the point where

Lacan argues for the discursive nature of the law and thus, implicitly, its institutionality, he makes the "culturalist" error and insists on the totalization of the Muslim law as a closed cultural system, in short, *tradition*. Such an understanding of tradition undermines the potential to read discourse in the Foucauldian sense of the discursive production of institutions of power; thus the possibility, for Lacan, of reading the psyche as historically mutable and institutionally constructed through the mechanism of foreclosure is itself lost at the threshold of its own theorization. This reifying ethnocentric move isolates the putative tradition as completely knowable, because primitive, over against a modern complexity exceeding "our" grasp. "Now, the law is something infinitely more complete than we can imagine, in our cultural sphere, defined as it is by *Render unto Caesar that things which be Caesar's, and unto God the things which be God's*. In the Islamic sphere, on the contrary . . . "[27] The complexity of "our" civil code against the completeness of "their" totalitarian religious law: the rhetorical gambit of such an opposition has ramifications for both laws. "Our" cultural sphere will be defined as the negation of theirs, and in that gesture, cultural difference will be sealed off as a temporal, geographical, and religious totality. As an alibi for a textual refusal to engage with the possibility that there might be more than one law even among "them," modern complexity can only be determined against a simplicity imagined to reside elsewhere.[28]

What Lacan attempts to identify is an implicit connection between a being-blocked—here, aptly, a writing block—and the written law. Further, he argues that a law that is "written" can substitute for the symbolic law "as a whole" and thereby stand in for "the law" by being foreclosed in the subject—which is to say that the law, being prior to the subject, is symptomatically and negatively present in the subject by being refused there. Textually we are witness to a slippage between the activity of writing, its inhibition, and the speculative notion of inscription under construction in the argument. This is evident in the clumsy way Lacan qualifies his characterization of Islam: "To be sure, for a long time now the prescription has not been put into effect . . . But it does not remain any the less inscribed in the symbolic order which founds interhuman relations, and which is called the law." Again his text aims to place the subject in a psychic and discursive context that exceeds him while it tries, simultaneously, to show the defining negativity of that social bond. Lacan finds the example of the Muslim patient, who provides an instance of resistance to the law lived out symptomatically, so useful so often because in identifying the "Islamic sphere" Lacan can then claim "his history is unified by the law, by his symbolic universe."[29] The example poses many more questions than Lacan takes on board. What will count as a representation within the "concrete discourse"? What can appear as the law? How are the many laws adjudicated within a single subject? What are the boundaries between "the universal symbolic system[s]"? How are they evident? Within Lacan's account, the example functions to shore up the twin project of arguing for the immutability of the symbolic law and substantializing that law through recourse to another, simpler, primitive culture. The developmental model of historical progress is fundamental to the argument, but history is the thing most rigorously foreclosed from the speculation.

There is, one might say, a symptomatic lack of concreteness and complexity in Lacan's handling of the example. It is a fact of no small importance that Lacan gives us no information to locate the patient geographically or nationally; obviously, a subject's relation to religious law would be substantially mediated by his relation to civil law. Equally obvious, in the French colonies where there might be French-speaking Muslims in 1953–55—the period of the seminars—the status of indigenous legal systems and their entanglement in colonial administration is both complex and nationally variable. The intricacy involved can be illustrated by two diametrically opposed and, for that reason, paradigmatic examples of French policy toward the institution of law in its Muslim colonies. However cynically, the French characterized the difference in French colonial management between the protectorate of Morocco and the province of Algeria as a difference between assimilation in the case of Algeria and association between France and Morocco. In Morocco, the indigenous division of the court system into Muslim courts, rabbinical courts, and consular courts, where the consular courts exercised jurisdiction over foreign nationals with consulates in Morocco, was substantially changed under the rule of Resident General Lyautey. The place of religious courts—both rabbinical and Muslim—was circumscribed as a subcategory of the French court system under the control of Lyautey, himself under the authority of the Ministre des Affaires Étrangères de la République Française. However, this bureaucratic refinement of the tripartite court system did not affect the fundamental divisions of the kinds of law, religious and secular, nor did it cease to tie the purview of the law and the jurisdiction of the courts to the civil status or identity of the complainant or accused. If a crime were committed by a Moroccan against or with a Frenchman or other European, a French court would hear the case. Crimes between Moroccans and cases of property dispute or inheritance were heard by the Muslim or rabbinical courts, each of which had, in turn, a religious and secular court; whether a case was heard by a religious or a secular court depended upon what aspect of law was touched upon by the charge. Thus the impression of a "traditional" law of "totalitarian character" that cannot recognize the separation of church and state, to which Lacan alludes upon first mention of his patient, cannot be borne out by the example of Morocco, because the institution of law, before and after colonial intervention, had built into it a "traditional" division between the purview of the secular and the religious, and further, because the court system institutionalized religious difference, a key feature of a secular imagination.

Algeria is an entirely different case. There, France simply declared Algerians French without thereby granting them citizenship. Algerians were required to commit apostasy by renouncing their Muslim civil status in order to become citizens of the French province of Algeria and thus to vote in their own country. Apostasy would then become the guarantor of one's legal status as citizen under the French *code civil*.[30] Thus, it is the French civil code that has the totalitarian character of a failure to distinguish the powers of church from those of state.

In the example of Muslim writer's cramp, the symptom is alleged to stand in for a foundational repudiation of the sacred law. Lacan treats his patient not for an "orthodox" Freudian masturbatory resistance to prohibition—which would then be bound up in the compromises of repression and a different character of symptom formation, said to be the compromised expression of a repressed wish—but for a foreclosure that has shaped his being beyond any particular family scene of prohibition. In fact, Lacan emphasizes his own resistance to orthodox excesses by noting the painful costs to the patient of such an approach.[31]

> An analysis conducted along classical lines did its utmost, without success, to organise, at any cost, his various symptoms around, obviously, infantile masturbation, and the prohibitions and the repressions that it would have brought with it in his environment ... One of the most striking elements of the story of his subjective development was his estrangement from, his aversion to the Koranic law.[32]

Lacan's analysis of the patient differs from orthodoxy by proceeding from an "understanding" of the general social scene of his childhood milieu. Still, what might an estrangement from, which is then qualified as an aversion to, Quranic law mean? Might not the misrecognition of the sacred law actually be evidence of the incompleteness of the law, of its proliferating and changeable form? In the course of analysis, the patient is not enjoined to learn to love the law as a condition of cure but to recognize that the law is performed in and through the symptom as the guilty incarnation of what he refused to swallow so long ago. Thus the analyst would seek to seal the patient's singularity in a cultural fetishism originating in the analysis. This would be the analytic mirror image of what Lacan claims to happen in the primordial past of the patient: the literal letter of the law is sealed away from the spirit, a gesture that never fails to transform that which must stand as literal into a fetish, in this case, a fetish of psychoanalysis. How does learning to "know" the place of incomprehension of the law effect a cure? And when a "Muslim" patient is told that the source of his hysterical symptom is the foreclosure of the Quranic law, when he is told this by a Frenchman whose knowledge of things "oriental" comes casually, even in the form of an academic discourse, are we to assume that this telling of the "law" is something that can or ought to be heard? Should the patient gratefully swallow this crumb of orientalist knowledge whole? Might there not be an equal, even overwhelming, discomfort, a shifting on the couch as the patient is forced to protect the analyst from the ocean of knowledges that he does not know? And how might the knowledge that the analyst is blind, even an idolater, curtail or enhance the function of a symbolic regime? At what point might embarrassment inhibit the functioning of the law, the assumption that the analyst's word is law? In this scene of analysis it is in the analyst that we see the operation of foreclosure, for the possibility of a secular, Muslim relation to the sacred law appears only as something censored. Lacan's discourse is a symptom of this act of rendering culturally impossible the very real possibility of a "nontraditional" involvement with "tradition."

In the context of French colonial history in Algeria, the writer's cramp could easily be a vestige of an insistence *on* and an assertion *of* the priority of the Quranic law over against the colonial, bureaucratic French *code civil*. As Lacan says, the patient's aversion to religious law is so great that "this subject manifested a failure to recognise the Koranic law."[33] How Lacan deduces a failure to recognize the law in a patient who manifestly says that he does not like it is a mystery. No evidence is presented for the global claims made on behalf of a distaste formed early on and cultivated throughout the subject's development.

"The whole of his relation with his original milieu, everything solid, the judiciary, order, the basic coordinates of the world were barred, because there was one thing he refused to understand—why someone who was a thief should have his hand cut off."[34] By Lacan's own account of the activity of censorship, offered in the second seminar, the patient's noticeable aversion to the Quranic law, presented symptomatically in the analysis as "the most striking elements of the story," ought to be legible as a symptom of the foreclosure of something else; after all, the symptom is held to perform the law in the subject as the nonappearance of the law; therefore, the aversion, along with the writer's cramp, should have as its task the incarnation and performance of the law within the subject. Yet Lacan tells us that

> this proposition [that the punishment shall be severing of the hand] was for this subject thus isolated off from the rest of the law in a privileged manner. And it became lodged in his symptoms. All the other symbolic references of my patient, all these primitive arcana around which such a subject finds his most fundamental relations to the universe of the symbolic organised, were forfeited on account of the particular emphasis that this prescription had acquired for him. For him it lies at the centre of an entire series of inadmissible, conflictual, symptomatic unconscious expressions, linked to this primal childhood experience.[35]

The foreclosed aspect of the law breaks off from the body of the law to become the body of the patient's symptom where the symptom relinquishes the "primitive arcana" of "such a subject." This model of foreclosure as a primal loss suggests that before Lacan theorizes foreclosure with respect to psychosis and as the foreclosure of the paternal signifier, he has already theorized this cut, "at the centre of an entire series of inadmissible, conflictual, symptomatic unconscious expressions" in terms of cultural dislocation.[36] In keeping with his early emphasis on social alienation and the loss of "saturations of the super-ego" in modern space,[37] cultural dislocation might provide a basis for an extension of the theory beyond the confines of a Parisian metropolitan subjectivity, but Lacan fails to profit from the patient's cultural malaise; instead, the analyst sublates this difference within the patient as a difference between a secular civil state and the nebulous Muslim domain. The exoticized basis of this theory derives in part from the assumption that the culture of the patient is both primitive and sealed by the boundaries of faith. The "primitive arcana" of "such a subject" effects a collapse of "primitive" as a designator of early, childhood psychic structure onto "primitive" as the name for any culture where the law might be revealed in its completeness and as the literal letter of the law. This gesture, repeated in each telling of the tale, concretizes the law, with its symptoms, in the place of the Muslim patient such that the cross-cultural situation of his present, as much as the discursive complexities of his childhood milieu, are made to stand in for a primitiveness that psychoanalysis requires in order to authorize the symbolic as the oedipal law.

Lacan will go on to qualify the complexity of what he calls Western civilization as the discordant clashing of the law's many planes. These planes conspire to render up a "uniform point of intersection" from their clashing demands. "In as much as the different languages of civilisation gain in complexity, its tie to the most primitive forms of the law come down to the essential point—this is Freudian theory at its purest—which is the Oedipus complex."[38] The primitiveness of Muslim culture, here rigorously distinguished from and, on the basis of the ethnographic gesture par excellence, foreclosed from the modernity of the West, will serve to anchor the claim of unity for that West.[39] This rhetorical move will link the primitive sacred law to the theory of the symbolic law, and in doing so it secures the primitive as that which shall grant psychoanalysis its primordial foundation in the "place" where it, the primitive, shall be foreclosed. As if a character in the bildungsroman of old, the Muslim patient will live the history that the modernist invents to absent him.

As the *Seminar* argues, the inhibition of writing in the Muslim patient is exhibited as a somatic symptom because his childhood refusal to "swallow" the written law returns that law to the body. Such a return to the body encodes one thread of the psychoanalytic use of the primitive and mirrors Lacan's rhetorical drive to situate the Islamic law as a literal, primitive, and embodied law exacting its bodily punishments in the lines of its sacred text.

> By definition, no one is taken to be ignorant of the law, but it is never understood, for no one can grasp it in its entirety. The primitive who is caught up in the laws of kinship, of alliance, of the exchange of women, never has, even if he is very learned, a complete vision of what it is in this totality of the law that has a hold over him. Censorship is always related to whatever, in discourse, is linked to the law in so far as it is not understood.[40]

If the primitive, like his Western counterpart, cannot fully comprehend the essential point of the law nor see what it is that captures him in the cut of foreclosure, the analyst claims to have a wider view. Lacan tell us that the patient's father, a civil servant, lost his position when falsely accused of theft, but his failure to situate the family culturally seems calculated to disarm any attempt to bring to light more than the narrow slice of the Symbolic that the analyst identifies as pertinent. This civil servant: was he an apostate in the Algerian government or a functionary of the Moroccan protectorate, and thus an agent of a colonial project to preserve quaint native practices? In both cases the son's avowed hatred of the Quranic law might be evidence of an aggressivity toward his own assimilation of French civil status, of a French civil code that failed to exonerate the father; for it is not irrelevant that the civil servant is dismissed from his post rather than punished according to the dictates of a religious law. The writer's cramp might well stand in for the sometimes more abstract tactics of civil and penal codes, which punish through a loss of status, and in doing so it would represent an ambivalence that seems tellingly absent from Lacan's account. The pain in his hand might then be the incarnation of the law that dictates the repudiation of Muslim law by the civil code and as its guilty symptom. The hand that failed to ward off an evil befalling the father would be, in this reading, the hand that fails to write in French.[41]

Lacan's primitivist notion of the totalitarian character of Islamic law is offered as an example of "concrete discourse," the concreteness of which obtains from its simplicity, completeness, and derivation from a primordial past. The "primitive arcana" becomes primitive in its theoretical elaboration because it is made to stand in for simplicity and "totalitarian completion." This is a fundamentally colonial trope inasmuch as it represents its object with the rhetoric of arrested development and regressed proximity to primal, sacred forms while simultaneously justifying the colonial civilizing mission of the analyst's intervention. More than this, the imagined completion of the Islamic law is legible as the emergence of an aestheticized version of the law having implications for any use of the concept of foreclosure. The law's completion is the condition of its aesthetic power. Lacan introduces the example by remarking the genre of his usage: "Ce que je vous raconte a l'air d'être un petit apologue."[42] This annotation condenses apologue, in the sense of moral fable with apologia, a defensive speech—and thus a writing in relation to judgment and law—but does so by highlighting its status as a genre. To name the genre of one's speech is already to situate that speech within aesthetic and rhetorical categories. The genre named by Lacan's text is explicitly that of the fable illustrating a prior claim where the beauty of the example derives from its perfect adequacy of the concept of the law. The use of this particular example demonstrates a vacillation between a romantic notion of the beautiful as completion and adequation and a modernist investment in alteration and destruction as a mode of the aesthetic where the completion of the sacred law is matched by its demand for bodily mutilation. The example concentrates several analogic moves contained by fable because they cannot be ordered into logical subordination, as can be seen in the list of characteristics condensed in the crabbed hand: primitiveness, completion of the sacred law, overvaluation of scripture, literalization of scripture, exotic spectacle.[43] Lacan's evident attraction to the example derives from its cultural distance, its aesthetic completion, and its scriptural investment capitalized and literalized as inscription on the body. Writing in its many inflections resounds here, for the cut the analyst finds in his Muslim patient is a profoundly allegorical one, charged with the responsibility of representing the law foreclosed, itself the occasion of an edifying parable of development. The Muslim patient's fractured relation to Islam and to his own body replays, within the script of the theoretical fable, the history of assimilation and "association" as the profoundly unknowable, for the foreclosure of his "primitive" mysteries will effectively inaugurate the modern, split subject of French philosophy on the condition that colonial trauma continues to dwell beyond the law. In seeking scriptural evidence for a speculative "fact"—that the law inscribes itself within the concrete discourse of the subject by subjecting him to scripted lacerations of symptomatic performances—Lacan occludes the properly historical dimension of his patient's cultural dissonance and instead capitalizes upon the patient's trauma to present a "concrete instance" or little fable of the arrested development of a Muslim into a Frenchman; such a *formation* initiates the subject into the law of the self foreclosed, a modern alienation already theorized as a mode of abstraction and specularization in Lacanian psychoanalysis and thus always hungry for a literal ground or instance from which to depart. The severed hand enjoined by sacred law reiterates in the cut a theory of the split subject, divided by ambivalence.[44] And by these means, *a modernist ontology is manufactured in its universal form through the foreclosure of colonial history.*

This move is no mere idiosyncrasy of Lacan's thinking but reflects a persistent feature of orientalist attempts to describe the modernity of Islamic cultures. *Tradition* is held to be the evidence and emblem of historical stasis, indeed the antithesis of history, while it is said to reflect as well a particular form of historical completion, one aestheticized for having reached its potential long ago. On the one hand tradition is the name of arrested development, and on the other it is the fulfillment of a historical destiny, a finished project. At once too full and too empty, Islamic history is always staged by this staggering logic as an oxymoron.[45]

It is striking that Lacan's reading of foreclosure locates it in the subject's refusal to swallow the law while the evidence that he offers in the apologue, scant though it is, would suggest a likely alternative, namely, that the subject is himself refused by the law(s). The theory of foreclosure, embedded as it is in this orientalist formulation of the law, exceeds its fabular origin to open up the cultural dimension of symptoms as well as that of symbolic exclusion. Lacan's efforts to formulate the law as the mechanism of a foreclosure that haunts discourse produces the insight that one's cultural capital might operate most potently where it is most irretrievably refused. Cultural dislocation would be one manifestation of a "dissonance" between the differing symbolic registers that organize the patient's symptoms where that dissonance captures a form of repudiation more final than disavowal, more liable to be figured, symptomatically in the Muslim patient, as an impotence or an impasse.

If Lacan's orientalism allows him to theorize a defining negativity by performing a foreclosure of his own, *Talismano* argues that the ready-made modernity of a "presentable" middle-class Arabness is also dependent upon a phantasm of timeless oriental tradition. "Mais l'ère des indépendances s'est souvenue de l'édifiant précédent cairote.... Une ville comme Tunis, honteuse épousée, se défit de ses places populaires en même temps que de ses statues coloniales. Elle se para pour célébrer sa liberté neuve de squares made in Cairo, modernité assumée, reconciliation avec une présentable arabité" (*T*, 234). Meddeb identifies the demise of public space in a negativity that renders all but the most ideologically sacrosanct socially impossible. This culture of negativity and foreclosure he names decadence. In the pages of his *La crise des intellectuels arabes: traditionalisme ou historicisme?*[46] Abdallah Laroui explicitly applies the term "decadent" to the Maghrebian situation when he narrates the career of the *Nahda*, or renaissance movement, begun in the nineteenth century with the intention of modernizing Arabic intellectual life by translating and assimilating European works, ideas, and practices and by reviving the great texts of Arabic literature, philosophy, and science. *Nahda* consciously equated the period of foreign domination with decadence but sought to sift out the exciting modernity from the corrupt and degrading effects of colonization. According to Laroui, the *Nahda* movement is instructive for the way it incorporated liberal Western tastes and preoccupations without pushing its own political critique of colonialism beyond the moral and even sentimental repudiation of decline and decadence. Developing a narrative that moves from early nineteenth-century intellectual circles to the 1970s, Laroui critiques the revisionist attempts to "update" Arabic culture, exemplified by *Nahda* but pervasive long after, without also adopting a specifically Marxist conception of history and historical development. This failure to understand modernist notions of time relegates the post- and neocolonial cultures to what he calls "historical retardation" and decadence. While every preoccupation and technical advance of European modernism can be found, and is repeatedly, tirelessly, defensively found by revisionists to exist already as essential features of Arabic philosophy, poetry, logic, linguistics, literary criticism, and political and religious philosophy, Laroui argues that it is crucial to resist this species of Arab revivalism. Instead, he urges the Arab intellectual to break out of the internalized forms of liberal culture, which he classifies as culturally retarded. Rather than simply arguing that Arabic intellectual culture has been colonized by the West, he claims that it was always already liberal and is now caught up in an unwillingness to criticize its own forms. Laroui extends his criticism to nationalism when he points to the chilling effect that nationalist movements have on their own members and, equally, when he calls for a persistent and radical critique of the state. Decadence emerges in Laroui's work as the name given to the gap between intellectual aspirations and economic and political realities. Meddeb responds to this paradigmatic position by refusing to allow a statist version of history to dominate his imagination, and, more specifically, by insisting upon the complexity and plurality of history as it unfolds in his fictional Tunis. The city's decadent doldrums are one figure of the historical predicament he grapples with.

It may seem odd to couple a text as vertiginous and deliberately difficult as *Talismano* with a Marxist critique, which could easily be read as an indictment of that very text, and a psychoanalytic theory with orientalist origins. Where Laroui claims that tradition is a phantasm, that only works to foreclose the historical dimension of modernity, Lacan sets in motion a phantasm of traditional culture in order to argue that foreclosure is the mechanism of rendering existing cultural forms unintelligible. Part of the value of Meddeb's writing lies in the fact that it confronts these theoretical questions poetically, seeking out the figurative sinew of such claims. If Laroui turns to the term *decadence* as a derogation and to conceptions of historical evolution and Marxist critique for remedy, Meddeb chooses as his battleground the symbolic, for he observes that gender, language, inspiration, and the state—indeed, national identity—are not so easily separated in the local context. It is a fact of life in the Maghreb that language is linked to questions of the state. The history of this linkage owes as much to the status of the Qur'an as the standard of a sacralized language as it does to the legacy of French colonization and the postindependence policies of Arabization.[47] This emphasis on the symbolic allows him to intervene textually upon what he himself names the decadent and ossified forms of a misguided modernity.

The suspicion that Meddeb found Lacan's second seminar compelling in its argument but deliriously off the mark in its reading of the Muslim patient is suggested strongly by another instance of writing. In 1985 the Parisian weekly *Libération* carried the following text by Abdelwahab Meddeb, one of four hundred authors asked the question, "Why do you write?"

> I write haunted by the hand amputated in my former life, when I was scribe to a Persian Governor; one inspired night . . . insomniac, I stole from the Table the mystery of the letter. I invented a style in which form and number accorded perfectly. My jealous master accused me of plagiarism and denounced me to the law. He had my hand cut off. A thousand years later, returned to life, I grew up on the shores of Africa. I initiated myself into the arcana of occidental exile before settling under darker/somber skies, where I translate from memory the angel's voice which I transcribe in a foreign tongue to ward-off that primitive amputation and to retrain my hand, stirring like a restless graft,[48] at the memory of the block clotted with my blood, the sharp blow of the executioner[49] that threw me into unconsciousness, arm in mourning, orphaned morsel of that hand which strikes, claws, grasps, scratches, gives, caresses and which, when it writes, gathers into a single gesture all the exchanges of which it is capable.[50]

The Muslim patient's family narrative supplies the reverie with its motifs, right down to the westering exile and the denunciation of a metaphoric theft. The Lacanian themes are also pronounced as Meddeb embroiders the gift of language into the exchanges of writing. Strikingly, the narrative answers the question posed by *Libération* with a story. As an explanation of writing's motive, traumatic haunting demands further interpretation; if the hand, violently severed and on suspicion of theft, engenders writing, it also literalizes a theoretical trope by heightening the orientalist imaginary to an extravagant degree. More striking still is the almost mockingly dense accumulation of orientalist tropes that speed up to a crescendo in a series of affects of the violated hand, replacing the tongue as writing's body. If a single figure could condense the movement from ranting excess to ranting poetics, it is this hand that gathers all the exchanges of which it is capable.

This short and emblematic text evokes some of the features of rant found in the novel. Key to the project of materializing and manifesting the symbolic law in *Talismano* is its characteristic staging of vertigo. One is constantly brought up against a disorienting scenario, phrase, or word. The text reads as if maddened or deliberately confounding understanding:

> texte poussière à recevoir comme Livre à l'envers, un texte rassasié, où quatre ou cinq idées se répètent, dans le jeu clinquant de la différence, s'édifiant désespérance de loi, s'insérant à l'expérience où des vivants à travers mon je se reconnaîtraient : *écrit couché, à l'envers rêvé dans le Livre feu allographe qui désorigine la sensibilité,* rassasié, de gauche à droite transcrit alors que le corps et les yeux suivent leurs cours méditatifs à lire dans le texte de droite à gauche, dans la même continuité horizontale s'éclaire le sens renversé : paroles d'exil, soleil qui se cache, homme qui disparait, de l'ici à l'ailleurs on erre entre le cachant et l'émanant, couchant et levant, *à privilégier le moment sanglant plus que la naissance illuminante,* genèse de l'ephémère, cacher, couche : maghreb ; et par-delà voiles réapparaître au oui païen par le texte tant que les jours accourcissent, afin d'affirmer sa présence sur les traces de l'abandon, par anti-thèse et graphie au physique inversée, *par retour aux thèmes qui ne supportent pas mots : corps, jouissance, mort, désert ; tant d'indicibles à transformer moments du dire en passant par le langage de la métaphore, à rendre archaïques à soi-même, séculaires,* pour répéter que ç'est de femme que viendra lumière à éclairer nos territoire : par l'astre Jupiter, par la pierre chrosolithe, par Vénus, pare hématite, la féminité fecondera les lits foulés par la disponibilité mâle ; et que cette nouvelle ingérence ajoute au corps divisé sa parcelle orpheline.

"Dreamed backwards in the fire book, a stratified dead writing writes itself otherwise to uproot the senses." To read this sentence one has to concede to the sharp turns of the phrases and keep the many meanings of the words afloat. The *"écrit couché"* refers both to a stratified writing of different languages and to different registers within the same language; it is also the "literal" orientation of letters, for *couché* can refer to a twist of axis that shifts a normal vertical orientation to the horizontal plane. Dense and vertiginous at once, this pair of words encapsulates the rhetorical gesture operating throughout the novel as the layering of meanings opens out onto increasing fixity and literal references. We are not offered an open-ended multitude of meanings; instead, the very action of sedimentation is enacted in the lines. "*Écrit couché*" is itself the allographic writing of that sedimentation.

"*Retour aux thèmes qui ne supportent pas mots : corps, jouissance, mort, désert ; tant d'indicibles à transformer moments du dire en passant par le langage de la métaphore, à rendre archaïques à soi-même, séculaires.*"[51] Echoing an earlier evocation of writing as the body's disorder rather than the primordial law, this making secular by making archaic has become by novel's end the purpose and predicament of writing. By writing in French Meddeb proposes to uproot, to "désorigine" the sensibility of the letter, whether French or Arabic, while the text moves from the local instance of a particular history only to "secularize" language, forcing it to take up difference. The move toward the secular is a move away from the theological model of the symbolic Law and toward the heterogeneity of his own expression, where "making archaic" translates a double return of infantile, primitive subjective traces along with fragments of occulted regional histories. Secularity, no longer product of the modern and therefore creature of the state, hosts the simultaneity of many pasts in the present and many cultures at odds with one another. If such a westering/*taghrib* is to be no exile/*ghurba* as the closing passages insist, it is only by virtue of a rhetorical materialization of the law of one's own disappearance. Or said another way, the tireless theater of the rant's empty speech.

THE FADED BOND

If you really wish your country to avoid regression,
or at best halts and uncertainties, a rapid step must
be taken from national consciousness to political
and social consciousness.
        Frantz Fanon, *The Wretched of the Earth*

At the height of nationalist struggles for decolonization in 1961, Frantz Fanon wrote this warning against too great an attachment to the rhetoric, images, and energy of what he calls national consciousness. Almost twenty years later, *Talismano* directly confronts the issues raised by Fanon's prescription for a genuinely postcolonial cultural imagination.[52] The "rapid step" finds its ironic rejoinder in the itinerant arabesques of the narrator's path through the postcolonial cityscape. Reconstructing a personal history, the narrator revisits the sites of his childhood by traveling the map of Tunis; in so doing, the wandering narrative composes a portrait of a heterogeneous city over and against the totalizing modernist claims of a postcolonial national consciousness. Circulating through the spaces held captive by the idée fixe of the modern state, the text capitalizes on the itinerant step to imagine an alternative species of writing—what the novel calls *allography*—that could mark difference in the public spaces of identity. Through this invocation of the graphic trace of locale, of particular and singular histories, *Talismano* seeks to reconnect that singularity to the network of its broader historical relations, and in so doing, to intervene in a postcolonial imaginary that would be done with all the "noise from below." This tracing of the constrained contingency of locale opens onto a series of larger questions linking postcolonial literature to the project of articulating an understanding of history when that history is irretrievably marked by imperialist intervention. The problem first posed by Fanon remains a question for *Talismano:* how do we narrate the story of traditions breached by violent intervention without falling into the trap of a reconstructive error that represents the time before colonization as a homogeneous whole and relegates the seemingly unassimilable residues of that past to the netherworld of abjection?[53]

In response to this question, Meddeb's text establishes a theory of writing that emerges from the postcolonial situation of a broken tradition. This is especially significant in the case of Islamic societies where, prior to colonization, the legitimization of power derived from a juridico-theological domination of writing. In shorthand, the graphematic character of writing's challenge to the presence of speech is acted out: 1) on the historical plane as a historical shift from "tradition" through occupation to postcolonial modernity; and 2) in the social dispensation of space where another form of writing reflects the haunting relation of tradition to modernity. Further, *Talismano,* like many Maghrebian novels, borrows from the psychoanalytic notion of the symbolic to frame its critique of the postcolonial state. In what way does the conception of Symbolic law offer a tool for understanding the affective and political relations of the postcolonial nation?

The modernity of the postcolonial state cannot be projected as a mere matter of translating the modernity of the West into native idioms. It is the insight of Maghrebian writers and critics that the complex of power and the discursive space of knowledge must be rethought in conformity with the material transformations of writing, urban space, class, language, and gender already underway in the postcolonial scene. The exigency forced upon any writer of Arab origin, who must of necessity confront the clash of a long discursive tradition that derives from written and interpretive practices with a modernity that draws its discursive power from the standardization of knowledge, has become in the hands of some Maghrebian authors the occasion for a complex meditation on the relation of language and writing to power. In the case of Meddeb we find that the move away from a habit of translating the Maghreb into French has led to a writing practice of *transgraphing* that effectively shifts the emphasis from a concern with semantic meanings toward a search for new terms, that is, new forms of writing that might materialize the social transformations of kinship evident in the modern postcolonial state. Transgraphing is not the equivalent of translation, for rather than transporting meaning from one site to another, the novel relocates the ideological impasses of the national imaginary within the unraveling contexts of the linguistic, historical, and religious complexity of Maghrebian culture. A productive literalism has taken hold in Meddeb's writing—one that retrains the eye, refocusing it on the shape of writing and the ramifications in social space of these forms hitherto ignored. His text leads us to consider calligraphy, not as an autochthonous and esoteric theological arcanum but as a practice that has deep roots in the languages and life of the region and from which one might extract a performative model for producing new forms of social connection and critique. This transgraphing practice we might call a *calligraphesis* in the service of his more ambitious undertaking, allography.[54] Taking his bearings from psychoanalytic conceptions of the unconscious, the symbolic matrix of normative order, and the vertiginous character of linguistic self-constitution, Meddeb has crafted a literary style that reinvents the narrative *"je"*/"I" to re-create features of an "Islamic" calligraphic textuality within the confines of the French and, one might add, "Western" writing system.

In his study of Yemeni epistemologies of power, *The Calligraphic State,* Brinkley Messick traces the shift in the dominant form of authority from a system based upon handwritten documents—what he calls the regime of the spiral document, which derives from the literal practice of turning a page to continue the writing of a contract or other official document—to a modern system of abstract and generic forms that Messick identifies as a Western-style "grid."[55] Building on

Messick's work, we shall see that Meddeb's writing practice highlights the linkage between seemingly disparate elements: writing technologies, subjectivity, urban space, national ideology, kinship, and futurity.

CALLIGRAPHIC TIES

In the Egyptian city of Aswan, an elderly Nubian café proprietor talks of the colonial period. This not so distant past he calls a time of trickery, when his people, vulnerable to the deceptions of the English, lacked vision and the confidence to rebel. His long discourses on the colonial past and the future destiny of the postcolonial nation are addressed to our protagonist, a foreigner and an avant-garde writer, who, fascinated, soaks up the memoirs of the octogenarian. The two share more than their mutual history of traditions lost in the ignominy of colonization, British and French; they are both marginals as well, for the one is Nubian, a minority within an Egyptian majority, and the other is a Tunisian writer, exiled by the language of his craft: he writes in French. They share one last thing: their skepticism of the present worship of modern nationalism. As their chance meeting draws to a close, the Nubian makes a surprising request. His café is polluted by spirits, poltergeists, and bad magic. He asks the writer to compose a talisman to banish the ghosts and return the gathering place to its former peace. Incredulous and speechless, the writer, knowing no magical arts, no powerful words of faith to offer as talisman, succumbs to a night of sleepless, anxious resistance, bodily collapse, and, finally, revelation. He writes despite the blinding hesitations that inhibit belief in the sacred words he transcribes. Waking from his writing he confronts "la totalité révélée, croyez-le ou pas, du talisman, mots et figures à délivrer au solliciteur nubien sans que moi-même j'en comprenne tout le sens" (T, 136).[56]

The talisman appears in the penultimate section of Meddeb's novel. Spiraling on three edges of a rectangular sheet, it contains a series of mottoes that derive from stock Quranic phrases (figure 1). Translated in French within the narrative, the "bottom" line reads "no sword like truth, no aid/protection like truth/sincerity" (T, 137). On one side and in a series of conventional lines praising god, the author has cleverly encrypted his own name, Abdel-Wahab-Meddeb, in a series of synonyms. To read the lines one must turn the page. Thus, the parody that surfaces in a talisman inscribed by a man of no faith is both structural and rhetorical—the latter because he does not believe; the former

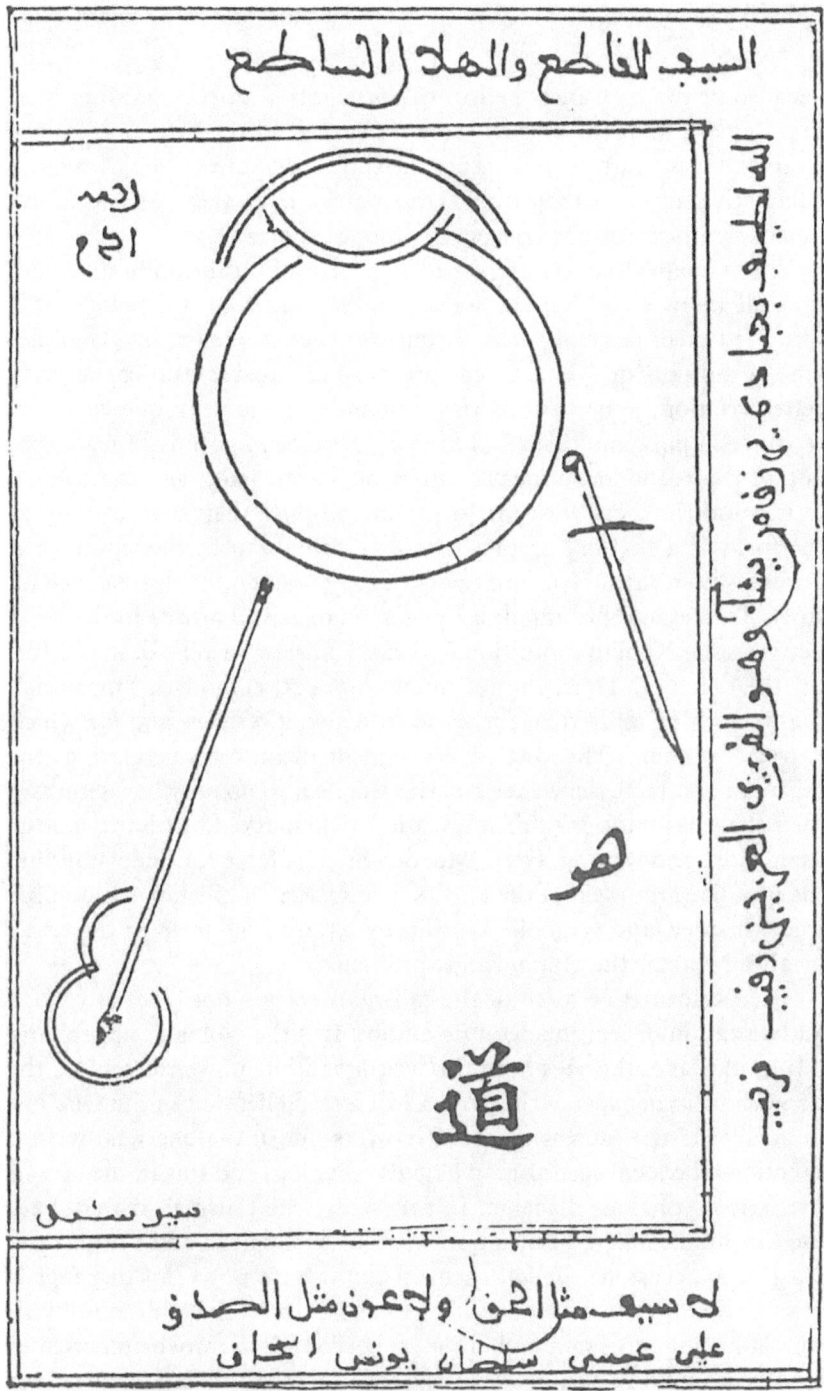

Figure 1. Meddeb's Talisman. From Abdelwahab Meddeb, *Talismano* (Paris: La Bibliothèque Arabe Sindbad, 1987), 137.

because of the turn inscribed in the orientation of the spiraling lines that demand that the French book be turned to read the lines of the Arabic text. In this pivotal scene, the spiral turn of the book becomes a narrative structure that unfolds the logic of textual events and simultaneously illustrates the concept of embodied meaning.

The Nubian's request arrives in the form of an intuition and with the full knowledge that the writer has no supernatural powers: "Je sais que tu n'es pas compétent à concevoir des œuvres prophylactiques mais je suis sûr que dans ce cas précis tu es capable d'efficacité; sans cette intuition, je ne t'aurais rien demandé. . . . je veux que ce séjour retrouve sa paix antérieure" (T, 136).[57] Neither in parody of tradition, nor in the ready-made identification of like to like, here the foreign writer and the local with the long view produce their own affinity in the form of a textual, graphic bond. In other words, this spiral produces its own form. The emptiness of the talisman, its dependence on stock phrases and meaningless images, enables and attests to the bond between the Nubian's intuition and the Tunisian writer's desire to fulfill the demand. Thus, the talisman comes to embody a "meaning" that is nothing more than the bond to which it testifies and for which it was "written." The written instrument of an ethical relation, the talisman contracts the writer and the recipient to no duty but witnesses their shared situation within a historical field marked by tradition, loss, aspiration, and writing. Here, Meddeb offers a fable for understanding the peculiar argument of the book's meditation on kinship, the graphic trace, history, and symbolic kinship by altering the form of the text's meaning outside the graphic logic of French.

The performative force of the talisman derives not from any prior authorization or legitimacy of its author. It is the Nubian's appeal and intuition that authorizes both the writing and its power to rewrite the tie of kinship between writer and addressee. Belief, not in the One nor in a supernatural access to occult powers but in the one who writes, sanctions the local scene of a particular writing, and this in the face of the writer's obvious disbelief. In this sense, the talisman materializes the kinship between an intuition without foundation and the surprising gift it occasions. Belief, then, in the other's power of disbelief is graphically inscribed in the written image as the very condition of kinship, a kinship disseminated in the scene, for the narrative orchestrates a field of embodied meanings irreducible to a single language or the symptoms of a single character. It is worth noting that the talisman cannot be reduced to a meaning—cannot be translated—for its effects far exceed even the narrative configuration of the gift just sketched. Instead, the image and text materialize a historical predicament with ramifications well beyond the subjects of the story being narrated. In effect, the appearance of the image and words transgraphs—transposes in their graphic form—a series of discursive elements characteristic of Maghrebian modernity but always already subservient to a normative hierarchy. Simply by infiltrating the French book with Arabic and Chinese writing that demands a physical motion for reading—the book must be turned to decipher the sideways text—*Talismano* reshuffles the dominant hierarchy of value by redrawing the map of reading.

Scholars of Maghrebian Francophone literature have long observed the bilingualism characteristic of this writing, and in so doing they have followed a fundamental claim of Maghrebian writers, which holds that the colonial period marks a traumatic rupture in the symbolic structures of institutional life: paternity, the family, subjectivity, and, more obviously, the state. The very fact of writing in French initiates the Arab writer of "Francophone expression" in a moment of "arrest." The problem of linguistic affiliation, exhaustively treated in the debates surrounding Maghrebian literature, continues to function unconsciously as a cipher for a series of intertwined relations within the postcolonial state. My own approach departs from this convention to focus on the *analysis* of such symbolic violence found, often in allegorical form, in postindependence literary works by reading the issue of filiation and kinship that underlies this so-called linguistic arrest.[58] For it is in the interpretation of the symbolic character of historical transformations that we find Maghrebian literature participating in a wider discourse of modernity, one that dwells on the limits of normativity and the potential of local and linguistic practices to alter the contour of those limits. Reading along these lines, one encounters a persistent national fantasy of a modern restoration of authentic traditions, represented in fiction as an object of criticism and desire. This phantasm of "tradition" continually haunts modernist narratives of decolonization, both liberal and radical, and in turn gives rise to an enduring literary fantasy of addressing that symbolic law in imaginary terms. Accompanying the thesis of a breach within psychic and family codes, many Francophone authors of the Maghreb imagine social life to be organized according to the dictates of a symbolic law now no longer legible in the institutions that ought to reveal its form. From this literary perspective, modern Maghrebian kinship derives from a prior breaking of kinship bonds that continues to reproduce the social as a space of rift. Within the domain of the literary, this conception of social order as unconscious and unpresentable, because unlocatable, law opens up questions about the interaction of postcolonial literary appropriations and permutations of psychoanalytic theory within contexts of social foreclosure. Yet, a larger question concerns the efficacy of the symbolic as a framework for understanding histories of violent disruption as well as for understanding the illusion of seamless tradition.

Insofar as Maghrebian authors cultivate the conceit of the symbolic they participate in a more general phenomenon identified by Freud and Foucault as the signature mark of modernity, which can be seen at work in the pervasive fantasy of social and psychic cohesion under a single figure of authority, never fully embodied or legible. Modernity appears in the Freudian account as a culture perpetually dematerializing its law through metaphoric substitutions. Famously, the final chapter of *Totem and Taboo* tells the story of a ghostly father whose presence vanishes, first in an original totemic feast where the Darwinian horde devours his body, then in metaphoric substitutions for the original primal feast.[59] Progressing from primitive sacrifice to Greek tragedy and thence to Christian communion, Freud's fable of the advancing mystification of ambivalence—its transmutation into practices that highlight the phantasmatic, theatrical nature of the symbolic—erodes the mythic father figure to leave only his functioning as law. His ghost saturates the forms of ambivalence and the very renunciations of instinct that are held to be signs of progress. Increasing rationalization of this paternity in institutional forms, Freud seems to say, only produces private subjects as already subjected to the regime of ambivalence and repression.

In the opening scene of *Discipline and Punish* Foucault echoes this Freudian structure of increasing power devolving from decreasing presence when he identifies the generative character of a desire to "dematerialize" the effects of punishment by shielding the public from the scene of execution.[60] Reading Foucault in a Freudian register, we might view *Discipline and Punish* as the story of a peculiar, modern fabrication of the superego whereby the father figure is perpetually erased in the proliferation of forms of social control according to the rituals of purification and punishment that Foucault renames for us as hygiene and discipline. Freud's text, too, moves from an account of individuals within a totemic system that confers being as a being subject to the community—one that embodies in "external" forms the ambivalence of the sacred and the profane—to an account of individual "subjects" troubled by the burden of having to bear in their own bodies the effects of a law felt to operate independently of any subject. Where Foucault insists on social practices that exceed the articulation of any "law," Freud proffers a dichotomy between "primitive" external prohibitions and a neurotic system of obsessional compensations devolving from an internalization that reproduces repression and substitution as the inevitable effect of having taken in the law. Foucault's identification of the deployment and discipline of sexuality effectively qualifies the Freudian myth of the primitive, for in his analysis of the fetishistic play of normativity and deviance, Foucault enables us to question the metaphysical manufacture of subjects by recasting the subject as a species of modern fetish sustained by a network of power that subjects to the extent that it seduces.

Maghrebian authors have taken up psychoanalytic theory, and discussions exploring the differences between Freudian doctrine and the Muslim cast of Oedipus are far from rare. Within this discursive frame, psychoanalytic vocabulary and theories become the material of fiction, and Meddeb is more than exemplary in this regard. Narrating the coming into being of the writing *je,* his texts abruptly shift from the thin layer of narrative to discuss the merits of the talking cure or to tell the story of his first encounter with a paternal function fully separable from the characters that set it in motion. The slightness of the picaresque narrative, which leaves Tunis for reveries of other cities (chiefly Cairo) or for meditations on writing, subjectivity, and social commentary, acts as an alibi for the staging of philosophical reveries. However, the philosophical compulsion of the text is never satisfied with a purely analytic discourse because the text so needs its images to exhibit the relations explored. The repeated reference to the hand throughout the entire work invites us into a network of relations between the hand and its writing instruments: pen, pencil, crayon, chalk, brush, quill, frond, needle, chisel, hammer, pins, any incising tool; a series of spatial locations: the banks of the Nile where the hand is washed, the charnel house where it gathers body parts to compose a blasphemous idol and image of man; and scenes of unaccountable affect: the trembling hand, the pained hand, the commanding hand leading the loving hand. The network of images, spaces, instruments, and affects exceeds the psychoanalytic framing of these very images. In its stubborn coupling of story with theoretical meditations that break down the coherence of the pronominal voice, Meddeb's writing mobilizes the fantasy of the law while depicting the failure and gift of attempts to resist the rigidity of that symbolic order in literary terms; in this way the writing is experimental in the sense that the text projects more than it can deliver. What follows reflects on the regulative foreclosures of the postcolonial nation-state that emerge in the calligraphic motif of *Talismano,* a work that prescribes a particular kind of writing, what Meddeb calls *allographie,* as a utopian cure for the scripted stalemate of normativity and abjection.

TRANSGRAPHING THE SOCIAL SPACE OF WRITING

Before exploring the complexity of the calligraphic conceit as a figure for an alternative imagination of nation and self in *Talismano,* it may be useful to invoke some features of calligraphy as an instrument of state. In his study of epistemic shifts in Yemeni legal writing, specifically the modern transition from an economy of handwritten and notarized contracts to print media and modern official forms, Brinkley Messick analyzes what he calls the "calligraphic state," which he describes as both a political entity and a discursive condition in Yemen and, by his own extension, in the Maghreb. He examines this textual domination by tracing connections between the literary processes behind the constitution of authority in legal texts and the social and political processes involved in articulating the authority of those texts. Messick seeks out the cultural system that can be said to precede and produce modern forms of nationalism in the region. With the Qur'an as paradigm, the genealogies of textual transmission were anchored in a recitation, a leitmotif of this "written law" tradition. Coupled with a distinctive emphasis on the efficacy of human presences, recitative methods recurred throughout key domains of textual practice: instruction, court witnessing, the conduct of state affairs, and the creation of property instruments.

In a 1937 commentary written by Zaidi imams, the *pharmakon* of writing is elaborated in the service of justifying greater reliance upon written evidence while detailing the complex history of the law's relation to writing (CS, 213).[61] Writing emerges as a "safeguard" preserving the life of witnessing and with it memory, speech, event. Yet it also harbors within it a threat, as Messick puts it, "As a protection against death ... writing was itself predicated upon a kind of death. It is both a remedy and a poison ... and so, the writer and his writing then are associated and equated with the witness and the oral activities of giving dictation and testimony" (CS, 213).

How is this paradox resolved in the problematic of legal documentation? Through redoubling the process of representation such that the document that represents fairly and justly is itself represented in the handwriting that writes it. Handwriting becomes the "representation of the legitimizing act of the human notary-witness" (*CS*, 215). This redoubled, spiraling mark of authenticity is not active in scrivening or copying; its proper place is the one opened up by the threat of misrepresentation and forgery possible only within a framework that demands of writing that it be an unbroken chain (figs. 2 and 3). As Messick puts it, "The power and mystery of the legal document resides in the nature of writing as human signature" (*CS*, 215).

In this attempt to replicate the authority of law in every present moment the stakes of writing are very high, for "through his document text, the writer mediates both the reproduction of the law and the incorporation of the world" (*CS*, 227). These documents all begin with the *bismillah*, the phrase "in the name of God, the merciful and the compassionate," as exergue above the body of the text. The invocation not only reminds the participants in the scene of legal writing that they are sworn to bear true witness; it functions also as an index of the whole of the Muslim textual tradition. The invocation attaches a simple bill of sale to the opening lines of the Qur'an, and within it to the beginning of the Qur'an's first *surah* (chapter), and on and on. "The genealogical connection to the authoritative original text is explicit" (*CS*, 228).

"In recent legislation of the Yemen Arab Republic, however, a template is provided for a new world of document writing, one in which the weight of authority shifts from the notary to the state" (*CS*, 215). The spiral text of embodied presences and true witnessing is superseded in a historical shift of episteme, where the new regime of state/signs/writing/truth becomes a generic form whose own space delimits, prefigures, and even scripts the information and knowledge used to fill in the abstract form. This epistemic shift is graphically represented as a movement from handwritten texts to the production of knowledge through templates, what we understand as forms. This shift betrays a fantasy in the construction of legal instruments and the state; namely, that the generic form demands only the contents that fit the space.[62] Thus the mediocrity of the generic template that now masquerades as singular truth signals a modernity defined by the conferral of identity through the intercession of a template. Knowledge and its space are radically determined in the new regime by the form of the form. In contrast, the spiral text of the older regime produces its own form, from the act of

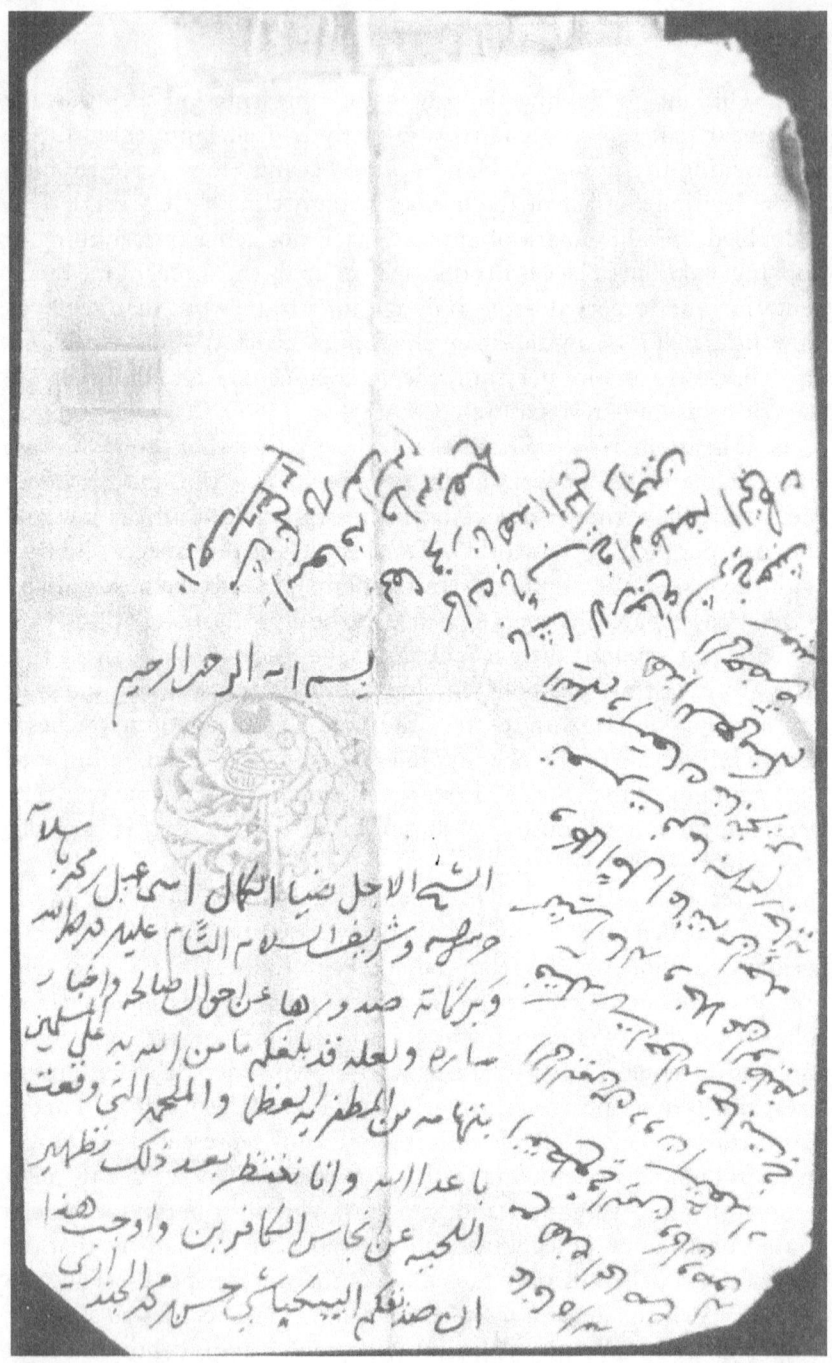

Figure 2. A spiral letter, 1917. Reprint permission University of California Press. Originally in Brinkley Messick, *The Calligraphic State: Textual Domination and History in a Muslim Society* (Berkeley: University of California Press, 1993), 232.

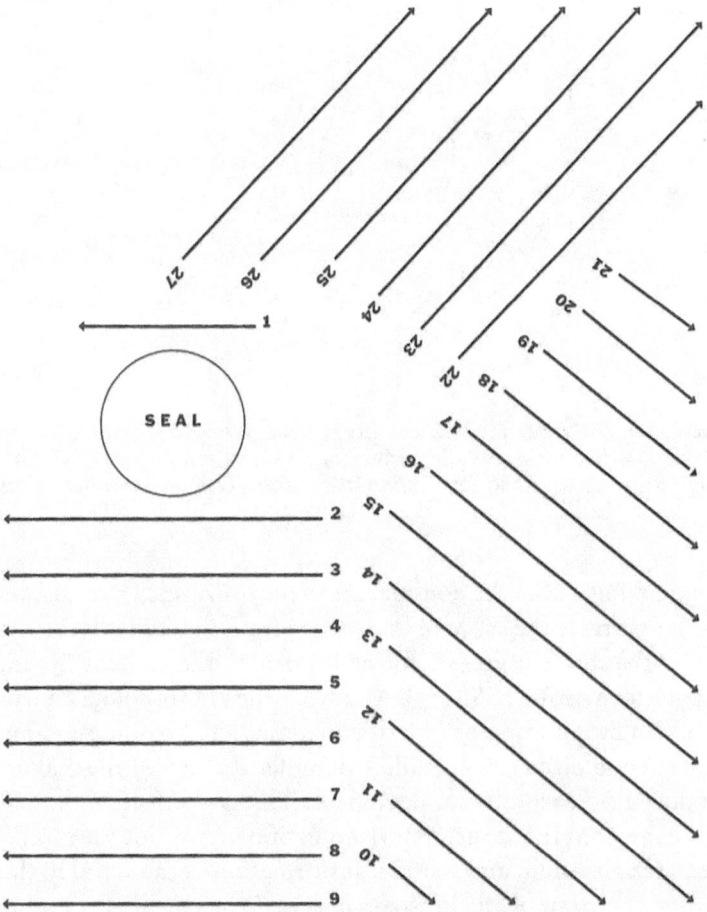

Figure 3. Brinkley Messick's schematic of the spiral letter. Reprint permission University of California Press. Originally in Brinkley Messick, *The Calligraphic State: Textual Domination and History in a Muslim Society* (Berkeley: University of California Press, 1993), 233.

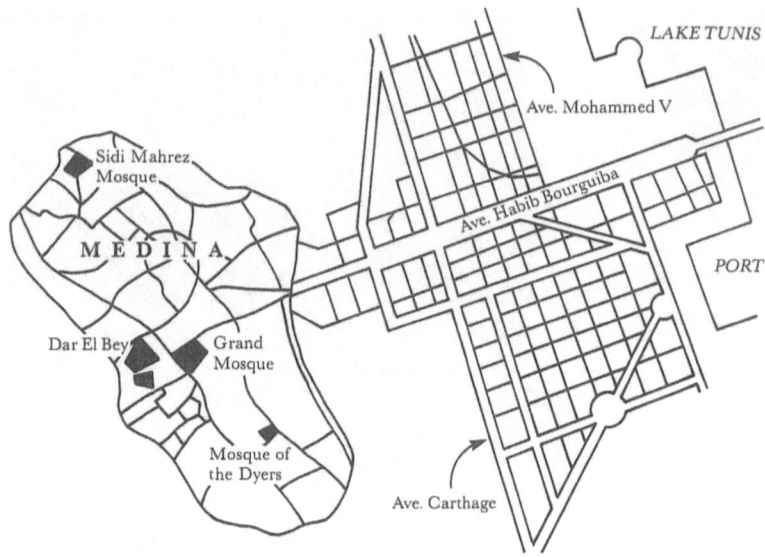

Figure 4. Map of Tunis showing old city spiral and new city grid. L. C. Brown, ed., *From Madina to Metropolis* (Princeton, NJ: Darwin Press, 1973), 29. Cited in Brinkley Messick, *The Calligraphic State: Textual Domination and History in a Muslim Society* (Berkeley: University of California Press, 1993).

writing and as befits the contract enacted. In Messick's terms, the old spiral texts create the space of knowledge from the contents themselves, whereas the modern generic forms determine the content by limiting the space for writing (*CS*, 237). And what the anthropologist records is the sudden evaporation of reported material and attributes; names are shortened and discourse curtailed all under the sign of the seal of state reproduced on each official document. The grid effect of these forms seems analogous to the metaphorization of paternity, or the mechanism of dematerialization, and so the transformation of the spiral to the grid within the writing of legal instruments and the construction of public space is legible through the same set of questions that are raised by Foucault and in the context of developing an analysis of modernity (figure 4). In the language of kinship, as it might be rethought through this historical model of writing, the subjectivating power of the grid operates by virtue of a forgotten lineage. The prior form of embodied authority, alive in the hand of the notary, dematerializes and becomes diffused in the form of the form.

Through the calligraphic trope, Maghrebian literature engages with the rhetorical discourses of the Arabo-Islamic tradition. This engagement seeks to critique the apparent fixity of ideologies of writing and the sacred and is thematized in the works of Abdelkebir Khatibi, Rachid Boudjedra, and Meddeb. As a figure for the writing of a modern Maghrebian literature, the calligraphic trope raises the pragmatic questions of who is empowered to write, in what language, and according to what balance of lucid reason and a wilder creativity. The calligraphic trope enables also a questioning of the more subtle forms of censorship that menace the modern Francophone writer with accusations of pandering to a French or assimilated readership, or charges of having assumed a hieratic distance from popular discourses and realist fiction. One of the more compelling claims consistently made in texts that use this figure links the decorative excess of calligraphy to imaginative invention and argues that such invention exceeds the limitations of normative religious transmission as well as the equally blinkered versions of modernity and history apparent in the rhetoric of the modern postcolonial state. Calligraphy becomes a reference point for these avant-garde projects of decolonization, critiquing both the continued hegemony of French and France as well as the forms of autocolonization at work more generally in Maghrebian culture. Thought of as an embodied writing that vacillates between sound and sight, the calligraphic conceit works within the diverse network of this literature as an intermediary form, a writing equipped to negotiate between the discontinuities of a history of foreign manipulation and native dogma. In the work of Meddeb and Khatibi, calligraphic writing is directly allied with tattooing to emphasize the lithe and embodied character, the importance of the form of writing in the texts that are needled into flesh.[63] *Talismano* explicitly frames this linguistic performance in terms of the body: "Je ne force pas l'analogie si je me résume écrivant d'une manière proche, décrivant en langue autre le délire d'une ville. . . . Cette langue qui me prête un corps sur quoi j'appose la marque de l'appropriation, cette langue à symboliser métropole" (*T*, 125).[64]

    The calligraphic character of this writing describes the space of the narrative and of the city and occurs within a tracing on the borrowed "body" of French. Indeed, the title of Khatibi's autobiography, *La mémoire tatouée* (Tattooed memory), figures a writing that can acknowledge the retroactive character of self and attempts an autocritique suspicious of egoic self-construction. Recovering tattooed memory redresses the harm of a colonizing deadlock between normativity and the deviants it requires—or so the reading of calligraphy as subversion would claim. As Khatibi puts it in the final lines of the book, "Se décoloniser de quoi? De l'identité et de la différence folles" (Decolonize oneself of what? Of mad identity and difference).[65]

The calligraphic conceit, then, is a means of tying a classical Muslim discourse of self-examination to writing, for the calligraphic word comes to stand in for the mysteries of a writing unfettered by absolute meanings; however tempting it may be to understand *Talismano* as a manifesto of subversion, my reading challenges this tendency of the critical reception—one consistently found in every anthology of Maghrebian literature that admits Meddeb into its canon; in the serious attempts to grapple with this most difficult novel; and in the passionate devotion the novel inspires among left intellectuals such as Tahar Djaout, who proclaimed that *Talismano* manages to do what no Arab novel has done, namely, to embody *the* Maghrebian transgression.[66] Against this claim I contend that one encounters the growth of the subjective *je* as a theater within which to stage the dynamic manifestation of the law—conceived as a deadlock represented in imaginary forms by nationalism and theological dogma, that is, tradition—by dramatizing the conflicts internalized according to the model of subjection we find in Freud.

In her consideration of *Talismano,* Ronnie Scharfman argues that the metaphors of writing provide a subversive alternative to the dead letter of sacred law and sacred writing.[67] This early reading, while attentive to the filial tie linking Meddeb's avant-garde experimentation to a Euro-American literary modernism, proceeds as if unaware of the specifically postcolonial character of Meddeb's literary inventions. To tie this author to Franz Kafka is not an error of judgment; it has the uncanny effect, however, of binding Meddeb there as a follower, as at best a fellow traveler. As another unwitting consequence of such reading, the specifically Arabic, Islamic, and Tunisian intervention on the notion of "tradition"—the substantial political critique of nationalist rewriting of that written tradition—is lost as well. For calligraphy does not represent for *Talismano* a revolutionary dynamism opposed to the orthodoxy of Islam or the rationalism of the state. In the work of Meddeb and Khatibi calligraphy is not identical with all Arabic writing. It is the figure of difference and nonknowledge in the space of legibility—it is an embodied form of a haunting structure. As Khatibi puts it: "Entre le pouvoir et la lettre s'inscrit notre histoire récente (personelle et nationale). Si cette blessure traduit une actualité trop aveuglante, elle masque en même temps la difficulté, l'immense difficulté, de penser le concept d'histoire."[68] Talking about the logocentrism of Islam, he says this of calligraphy: "C'est dans un lieu interstitiel que se joue le tracé calligraphique comme une fête sacrée du signe. Loin d'être un simple supplément graphique ajouté à la parole, le tracé calligraphique est une composition intérieure au texte, une production cristalline du corps linguistique lui-même."[69] These remarks set out the link between power and writing within the history of the Maghrebian nation-state as one of a wound that inhibits the thinking of history. *Talismano* attempts to translate the modality of calligraphy, its gift of nonknowledge, and its capacity to make illegibility appear in the very space of reading/ knowledge production. Translating calligraphy is an impossibility, but this seeming limit becomes for *Talismano* the scene of writing's promise as calligraphesis restores the problem of embodied meaning to the aspirations and proscriptions of the nation-state figured there. Far from being an ancillary effect, the illegibility of the calligraphic line is interior to legibility itself. The obvious and the obscure, the clear speech of state dictum and the unspeakability thus legislated, are intertwined in any writing that will acknowledge the calligraphic character of its own inscription. This is why it is untenable to simply situate avant-garde writing in opposition to a phantom of tradition in the Maghreb and why readings that stress only the revolutionary dynamism of Meddeb's text miss the mark.

While both Scharfman and Khatibi dwell on the text's autotelic character, their exclusive focus on the metaphysics of writing obscures the substantial and specifically postcolonial politics motivating the novel's discourse on writing. Khatibi's treatment of Meddeb takes on more of the novel's political stakes in his concern to reiterate the bilingualism of the Maghrebian situation; however, Khatibi's own text on bilingualism tends to reduce the political implication of allography through the uncritical invocation of the calligraphic trope. For Khatibi, the calligraphic conceit is renamed "bilingualism" in order to argue for an irreducible encounter between a "mother tongue" and other forms of standardized language, where the mother tongue represents an unwritten because "unwritable" oral dialect. *Talismano* shifts this binary relation to challenge both the unwritability of dialect and the reification of abject, prosaic, or subaltern language as the feminine. Unintelligibility is shown to be a disavowed property or possible destiny of all writing. By redrawing the outline of a repeated invocation of norm and abject, *Talismano* shows that this oppositional "structure" is constantly being constituted. The social analysis of transgression and normativity available in the novel presumes the unconsciously operating, performative dimension of an insistent relation: norm/abject, man/woman, piety/blasphemy, word/image, French/Arabic. Calligraphesis marks the appearance of difference as it is simplified, represented as a difference between two, caught within a hierarchy of value, as a kind of social wish fulfillment, but it proliferates these distinctions beyond that hierarchy in a performative textual network that exceeds the narrow intention of a known transgression. Thus, never simply the mother's tongue or the father's law, writing—allography/calligraphesis—exceeds the structuring intent of structure.

In this way, *Talismano* does not stop with profanation or new orthodoxy; it continues with writing in the social spaces mapped by the modern nation, and it takes up the calligraphic conceit from the very beginning by detailing the cultivation of a first person in a fluid series of reveries that are explicitly described as the gyrating movement of the calligraphic line. As the text's arabesques grow denser and more difficult, the "talking cure" *(la cure du dire)* becomes the model for the self-fashioning of the text, yet this turn in the development also leads back to calligraphic forms.[70] The text reads,

> En ce je, les idées qui poussent mauvaises, j'entends d'une négativité qui ne participe pas au perfectionnement, sont à chasser; la cure du dire n'appelle pas à t'accepter comme tel, mais à t'admettre énigme irréductible au sens, à la loi, à la mesure; le je engage avec lui l'histoire: ces ans qui ont imprégné ma naissance, mon origine, mon enfance pénètrent les fondements ébranlés d'une classe à trahir moribonde; je représentatif d'une génération arabe qui a à se débattre image fêlée, marquée monstrueuse par Europe et France, à vivre d'expérience l'exil, ... à corriger son corps social par une démarche à l'envers. *(T,* 57)[71]

Meddeb takes up the decline and decadence of the postcolonial Maghreb to suggest in this passage that the psychoanalytic cure can "correct" the social body by moving backward through the self in a progress that accepts the discontinuous time of psychic history. Undivided flow of a gyrating line that knows itself to be devoid of meaning, this calligraphic figure becomes, as the novel progresses, the figure of the self suspended between the law and its others.[72] One among many such moments, here the text commands the obedience of the *je,* which it treats as object in a battle over the possession of its marked image. Again the calligraphic conceit enters to disrupt the readings of meanings.

Throughout the novel calligraphy performs multiple tasks. It is at once the medium of a word made image and the means of a total loss of meaning, as one learns in the passages of the second chapter where the narrative alibi is but the occasion of a long meditation comparing the Christian art of painting to the Eastern arts of calligraphy. This thin plot—a "nighttown" picaresque through an underworld of blasphemers and those whose arts, once magically alive with the power of the culture, now linger on in bitter acrimony (Sufis, storytellers, sorcerers, alchemists, psalmists, seers, notaries, and calligraphers)—is itself imbricated in the calligraphic trope structuring the book. The conventional character of the night passage, with its expected orgies and familiar scenes of rebellion, performs the same function as the stock phrase embellished by the flourish of the calligrapher's pen. The same function, yet with a difference, because in these seemingly disconnected scenes and reveries the convention of rebellion is performed as an evacuation of piety, emblematized by the pious phrase, the *bismillah,* which is then reiterated in different contexts, wordplay, and gratuitous extension. The thread of narrative is thin, indeed, largely because it is so heavily embroidered with digression and interrupted by generically different forms. This linguistic adornment situates the chronicle of the various transgressions as but one code among many in a narrative intent on marking the locale, Tunis, with the significance of its social imaginary. Thus, the events leading up to the final conflagration that consumes the city are the lines between which the work's arabesques are written.

After a prolonged development of the first-person voice, the embodied *je* becomes a character and falls in with a band of sorcerers, calligraphers, and tattoo artists who plan an idolatrous rite and absorb him into their throng. The interminable night ensues interspersed with reveries, a theoretical disquisition on calligraphy, and the memory of his creation of the talisman, which then appears as a punctual end to the second chapter. A key scene reveals that the calligraphers, chanting their prayers, have expelled the name of God from every prayer invoking him by expunging the *bismillah.* The calligraphers replace the word "Allah"—which is given in the text in its roman transliteration and in its French translation as *dieu,* and given in the talisman in Arabic—with a blank in their Hallajian motto and in the *bismillah* that conventionally opens every prayer.[73] Rather than uttering the name, the calligraphers pause in the chanting of their prayer. In writing, they graphically mark the absence by inscribing a blank where the name ought to be. This textual and narrative maneuver allows Meddeb/the narrator/the textual *je* to thematize the blank as *"le vide"* (void) and to recompose his own relation to mystical writing and ritual along the lines of a desacralized calligraphy. In this way the writing that is *Talismano* regraphs the roman alphabet through transliteration and thematic reinscription in the direction of two distinct contents: 1) the blank opens a space within which French and Arabic, "popular" ressentiment and modern avant-gardism, tradition and the postcolonial, circulate as complicitous; and 2) the blank becomes an occasion for a meditation on the meaning of writing that diverges narratively into a series of fantasy interviews with a host of great authors (Dante Alighieri, Muhyiddin Ibn 'Arabi, Constantine Cavafy, Jean Genet). Rather than the single name, the name of God, we find a series. The list of names is itself an index of a transgraphing already underway in so many details of the novel, for it is a roster of mixed locales, authors who signal Europe, the Maghreb, and the Middle East in their writings. Crowding the text with short resumes of their writing ethos, these reveries of dead authors frame the final scenes and add their names to the mob processing toward the great mosque at the center of the medina. The blasphemous popular parade culminates in an animal sacrifice in the heart of Halfawine and the erection of a pagan idol made of corpses. The city fathers watch aghast, say their piece, and finally the town is sacked, left in ruins. No account of the novel can ignore the way that critical meditations on form are bound to events in the story, for the text narrates the link between the two. Like the cultivation of the writing *je,* the chronicle, the romanized narrative, binds the story of a social space to the space of a social writing. Consistently, the text calls this a relation of embodiment in a work of desacralization.

This tendency of the text toward narratives of desacralization is a constant. Khatibi has made much of the fact that *Talismano* removes Allah from the *bismillah;* yet he neglects to notice the way in which Allah returns in the avowal of otherness and a different species of writing in the book's coda.[74] There calligraphy gives way to allographesis, that writing of the other that cannot become an object of faith and belief as the nation and its promise of modernization have already become. Calligraphic writing emerges at the end of the novel as itself a limited tool of resistance that can promise so much largely because it means so little—like Walter Benjamin's revolutionary image whose very inscrutability is the guarantor of a future vision. Or as Meddeb says, "Ceux qui s'islamisèrent calligraphient . . . ou plutôt dissolvent le sens de l'écrit par le geste ample et jouissif du calligraphe. . . . Et l'écriture devient monumentale perte du sens" (*T,* 112).[75] The allographic writing invoked in the final lines draws its laws astride the voice of the tale, on the back of the calligraphic conceit itself.

The calligraphers' dematerialization of God's name repeats in a different register the move to an abstract grid form and away from the spiral of authoritative presences represented in the written instruments of the law. *Talismano* maps the traces of older discursive arrangements of power as the narrator wanders through the city, but this tracing of disappearing forms argues that disappearance is, itself, something orchestrated and manifest even in the dispensation of architectural relations within the city. As Messick writes, "This poetics of written space then can be extended to general domains of spatial organization: towns, architecture, and the space of the state" (*CS*, 123). In Meddeb's rhetorical universe the most valuable attribute calligraphic writing possesses is the loss of meaning because such loss desacralizes the sacred, even if the calligraphic conceit cannot then secularize that loss.[76] Messick shows that the calligraphic state hedges the loss or risk inherent in writing through the spirals of representation and the redundant doubling of authoritative oaths of truthful presence. But even the imams were aware that a witness can lie before God, that an entire edifice constructed upon the shifting faith in a just witness in a chain of equally just men can falter on a broken link.

By inscribing the shape of the narrative, Meddeb's wanderings insist that form, sound, the spelling of words, the rhythm of sentences, and the sweeping aerial views conform to, rather than overdetermine, the content of his text. The rhetorical scheme of the inscription metaphors that carry the novel forward and that compose its subjective body suggests that his is a spiral text. Such a speculation alters our view, then, of the text's narcissistic obsessions—its singular focus on a writing *je*—for this voice is necessary to authorize the justness, the sincerity *(sadq)* of the text's purpose. The narrator's sympathies are fully engaged with the rabble of witches and blasphemers who profane a mosque with pagan and invented rituals. He accepts the duty to stray from the order of the straightened modernity that disorders the social imagination of his hybrid Tunis. Yet the distance of the narrative and the example of the *je* force one to confront transgression's devotion to the very law it hates. If the grid structure of modern discourse and power stands in for the evaporating rule of law and if the grid of the modern postcolonial city comes to mean the law of foreclosure[77]—in this case a foreclosure of history as well as of pagan practices—then these very transgressions would be no more than the symptomatic writing of that law, taking its dictations and repeating them in a negative form.

Talismano moves us toward an understanding of the mysteries of writing that demands we do more than celebrate the abject. The parody of revolutionary rhetoric among the sorcerers juxtaposed with the scandalized outcry of the professional classes represented in the final scene add up to a dynamic portrait of the interdependence of positions, subjects, and acts. The novel's critique lies in the framing of this depiction as we begin to understand the unmastered effects of the grid's reproductions in the present, for the primitive regress of rebellion and the refinements of a modern state avowed to development and progress generate one another.

Over the labyrinthine map of Halfawine, where popular cultural practices still gather a following, the text's reverie of Asbekya, a formal French-style garden in the heart of Cairo, superimposes the grid of Egyptian modernity and the nationalism that Egypt represents on the spiral of Halfawine, saying explicitly that the formal square aims at nothing other than the destruction of vernacular social formations. These passages on the simultaneity of flux and order, Halfawine and Asbekya, suggest that the latter haunts the former because flux is always being produced by foreclosure as its abject other. Thus the poetics of subjectivity argued in the novel, what Scharfman has called the *thanatography* of this text, is itself constantly produced by the work of the grid and so is uncomfortably similar to the futile rebellions and transgression depicted.[78] The modernity imagined by *Talismano* consists not in the juxtaposition of the grid next to the ancient, precolonial spiral; rather, the one haunts the other with the failure of their shared aspirations. This is a haunting that suggests the ghost of foreclosure, for we are no longer dealing with a map but with a negativity that generates writing.

The readings of *Talismano* that emphasize the narcissism of poetics at the expense of the nation-state plot neglect the substantial link between the state and the textual politics of Meddeb's aesthetic excess. To reinscribe the state within the novel's meditations on writing, meaning, and the body leads inevitably back to the question of kinship understood as an uncannily faded bond. The calligraphic trope offers a way of reading this entanglement as an identifiable figure, a model for the prose style and for an imagination of the self beyond the limited forms of the grid's template. Calligraphesis emerges as the condition of allographic writing in the book's final pages. The calligraphic movement of Meddeb's text enables the simultaneous presentation and representation of exactly those elements of social, individual, and religious life held to be unspeakable, including the analysis and depiction of the kinship of abject to normative modes of life. Thus, allographesis presents the unspeakable limit that borders life without reconditioning or restoring that foreclosed limit of speakability in a newer form, that of subversion. To write the other otherwise is to refuse the religion of modernization and the state.

WRITING BEYOND IMPASSE

The procession of the mummified idol ends in a rite unleashing a conflagration of history on the doubled map of Tunis and Cairo. Invaders from the many epochs of colonial occupation descend upon the square: Spaniards, French, and Turks reduce the city to nothingness only to be countered by a tribal resistance that proves incapable of stirring the remaining population to rebellion. Finally, *les matraqueurs* (thugs), trained by foreign powers, enter the ruins to stamp out the lingering weeds. But these latest invaders come armed as well with vague slogans, this time aimed at history itself and in the service of what Meddeb calls "la caution nationale qui légitime une logique politique asservie à des normes de pouvoir prétendues universelles!" (*T*, 237).[79]

The epilogue returns us to the idolatrous celebrants, now fugitives from the ruined city and wandering bedraggled through the desert, their purpose and vision diffused in their errancy. They divide into two groups: One takes up the pagan thread of their previously blasphemous devotions and disappears into the desert and a newer orthodoxy. The other group, that of our narrator, goes toward the Occident, as he puts it, *"taghrib non ghurba,"* which in the idiom of the *Talismano* comes to mean "going West but not in exile." I take the westering theme of these final passages to mean writing itself, a writing freed from the constraints of piety and given over wholly to the string of infinitives and imperatives that trail in the book's coda. And in the series of these promises to himself and his reader he announces his thwarting intention: "à nous livrer par l'écrit sans vous donner prise, à vous fatiguer l'oeil par l'arabesque des mots, à vous proposer les réseaux du voyage" (*T*, 243).[80]

In its final fable, the digressing text asserts its desire "to reorganize space" after the total destruction of the city. The text has no subject at this point, though the *je* is reasserted once more only to say that "I join those who aim for the Western roads" and only as the necessary precondition for the "we" of the last paragraphs. Explicitly, then, the text allies the graphic dispensation of social space to the dissolution of the politics of melancholic history and the ideological stalemate of normativity and abjection it inaugurates, including its abject forms of (hand)writing. But this is not all. For, by referencing the necessary redistribution of spatial relations in the same finale where the novel prescribes the "networks of travel" *(les réseaux du voyage)* as a generative alternative to the law, *Talismano* suggests that allography may well be analogous to the labor of this network. The implications of this figural shift from the hand's body to the network of allography reclaims a circulatory system of symbolic relations, connections, or graphic codes. Such an understanding of the symbolic as containing within it the possibility of a different path through the same space, a reorganization of space through the medium of the graphic trace, is itself a performative resignification of the calligraphic conceit. Hardly a movement from bondage to freedom, the networking metaphors instantiate a series of passages legible as the constrained contingency of writing.

Calligraphesis forges the link of beauty in the network of metaphoric travel, in the perpetuation of movement and the continuous "tradition" of change. If writing is always cut off from its origin, then writing in French of Arabic calligraphy may well be a mode of transporting Maghrebian writing from French to an elsewhere. The network of travel to which writing is conferred by the final "calligraphic" passages produces the image of the newly conceived tradition that the novel proposes. By retraining the eye, native or foreign, on the graphic form of writing, even when presented in French, *Talismano* relocates the Maghrebian symbolic within the network of power and power's representation as something that can and does traverse the boundary between French and Arabic. Representing these relations in French has the effect of turning French into the graphic medium that hosts both the writing of the Maghreb and the Arabic writing in its literal form. Such a turn on the norm mediatizes the French *verbe* as a calligraphic script that ornaments and vehiculates a meaning, here the meaning of its own embodiment of difference.

Notes

INTRODUCTION

1. Michel Foucault, *Fearless Speech*, ed. Joseph Pearson (New York: Semiotext(e), 2001), 170–71.
2. The exergue comes from "Society Must Be Defended," his seminar of 1976.
3. Hence Foucault's effort to situate Kantian critique not in the sovereign exercise of reason but in the obligation of independently formed opinion free from tutelage. See "What is Critique?" in *The Politics of Truth*, ed. Sylvère Lotringer and Lysa Hochroth, trans. Lysa Hochroth, transcript by Monique Emery, revised by Suzanne Delorme et al. (New York: Semiotext(e), 1997).
4. Michel Foucault, "The Subject of Power," in *Power: Essential Works of Foucault, 1954–1984, Volume III*, ed. Robert Hurley, James D. Faubion, and Paul Rabinow (New York: The New Press, 2001), 326.
5. Foucault identifies three types of struggles, all of which are immanent to power: "1. against domination (ethnic, social and religious); 2. against forms of exploitation that separate individuals from what they produce; 3. or against that which ties the individual to himself and submits him to others in this way (struggles against subjection, against forms of subjectivity and submission)." Ibid., 331.
6. Foucault, "Preface to Transgression," in *Language, Counter-Memory, Practice* (Ithaca, NY: Cornell University Press, 1980).
7. Theodor Adorno, *Minima Moralia: Reflections on Damaged Life* (London: Verso, 1987), 151.
8. Aimé Césaire, *Discourse on Colonialism*, trans. Joan Pinkham (New York: Monthly Review Press, 2000), 54–55. Hereafter cited as *DC*.
9. Gathering the signs of colonial demise, Césaire's *Discourse on Colonialism* expresses a sentiment later to be repeated by another postcolonial Franco-

phone writer, Assia Djebar, who in a gesture of serious irony thanks General Pélissier for the remorseless and detailed record of his murderous exploits in the conquest of Algeria, which provides her the most complete picture, down to the numbers of corpses and their genders, of the suffering enjoined upon the Algerian people by the French conquest. Djebar, *Fantasia: An Algerian Cavalcade* (Portsmouth, NH: Heinneman, 1993).

10. Césaire was soon to break with the Communist Party, thus, according to Robin Kelley, even the "comrades" of the discourse are ironically invoked. See Robin D. G. Kelley, "A Poetics of Anticolonialism," in *DC*.

11. See "The Fact of Blackness," in Frantz Fanon, *Black Skin, White Masks* (New York: Grove, 1987).

12. Jacques Derrida, "Signature, Event, Context," in *Margins of Philosophy*, trans. Alan Bass (Chicago: University of Chicago Press, 1985); Judith Butler, "Afterword" to *The Scandal of the Speaking Body: Don Juan with J.L. Austin, or Seduction in Two Languages,* by Shoshana Felman (Stanford, Calif.: Stanford University Press, 2003), 122.

13. Jean Genet, *Journal du voleur* (Paris: Gallimard, 1949), 121 (emphasis in the original).

14. "Ficticious veut dire fictif, mais au sense ou j'ai deja articulé devant vous que toute verité á une structure de fiction." Lacan, *L'Éthique de la psychanalyse, 1959–1960* (Paris: Les Éditions du Seuil, 1986), 23.

15. Jean Genet, *The Declared Enemy,* trans. Jeff Fort (Stanford, Calif.: Stanford University Press, 2004).

16. "L'Enfant criminel," a radio address censored before broadcast, makes this point in stark and uncompromising terms. Jean Genet, *Oeuvres complètes,* vol. 5. (Paris: Gallimard, 1951).

17. Recent works that introduce alternate modernisms to Anglo-American modernist studies include Nicholas Brown, *Utopian Generations: The Political Horizon of Twentieth-Century Literature* (Princeton, NJ: Princeton University Press, 2005); Laura Doyle and Laura Winkiel, eds., *Geomodernisms: Race, Modernism, Modernity* (Bloomington: Indiana University Press, 2005); and Laura Winkiel, *Modernism, Race and Manifestos* (Cambridge: Cambridge University Press, 2008).

18. Richard Terdiman, *Discourse/Counter-Discourse: The Theory and Practice of Symbolic Resistance in Nineteenth-Century France* (Ithaca, NY: Cornell University Press, 1985).

19. The literary historical claim that decadence constitutes a repressed within literary modernism is suggested in the work of several literary critics. Peter Nicholls's *Modernisms* (Berkeley: University of California Press, 1995) surveys an array of American and European modernist literature to argue for the importance of aestheticist and decadent literature not as a "proto-modernism" but as the fecund source of the salient debates concerning the loss of what Nicholls calls a "classical ideal" that preoccupies later writers. Other critics working on the problem of fascism and literary modernism find the roots of a modern aesthetic appropriation of the political in the texts of the fin de siècle. For an example of the latter approach see Andrew Hewitt's *Political Inversions: Homosexuality, Fascism and the Modernist Imaginary* (Stanford. Calif.:

Stanford University Press, 1996), as well as his *Fascist Modernism: Aesthetics, Politics and the Avant-Garde* (Stanford, Calif.: Stanford University Press, 1993). Matei Calinescu's *Five Faces of Modernity: Modernism, Avant-Garde, Decadence, Kitsch and Postmodernism* (Durham, NC: Duke University Press, 1987), now a classic, covers this material from a literary historical perspective.

20. In the introduction to a recent issue of *Modernism/Modernities* (15, no. 3 [September 2008]), Cassandra Laity takes a critical distance from the Benjaminian version of Baudelaire that dominates some receptions of decadence in modernist studies. This is a Baudelaire transformed into a "father of modernism" with all the freight such a title will bear and credited with authorizing a critical indifference to the links between the decadence of the late nineteenth century and high modernism. This figuration is also associated with a caricature of decadence as effeminate and elitist. While Laity is right to indicate that such attitudes persist, it would be precipitous to attempt a "decentering" of a major modernist innovator, one whose global recognition has inspired modernist avant-garde writers in postcolonial and queer contexts and sometimes in the overlap of both. I would propose instead that we expose the homophobic, misogynist, and racist constructions of those who would reductively label a critical and social sensibility "elitist" when considering Baudelaire, Wilde, or Huysmans, three modernists whose decadent writings are seminal for the postcolonial avant-garde gesture of *Talismano*, for instance.

21. Foucault's early archaeologies began by signaling the importance of Freud's move away from physiological accounts of psychic dynamics. See the conclusion of Foucault's *Les Mots et les choses* (Paris: Gallimard, 1966). A decade later, in *History of Sexuality, Volume I,* he singles out psychoanalysis as the only science devoted to a resistant account of subjectivity; ethnography, to which psychoanalysis had been compared in the first book, is no longer a point of reference in 1976.

22. Terdiman, *Discourse/Counter-Discourse*.

23. Judith Butler, *Antigone's Claim: Kinship Between Life and Death* (New York: Columbia University Press, 2002), 8.

24. Foucault, *Fearless Speech*, 18.

25. Ibid., 21.

26. Stefania Pandolfo, "The Thin Line of Modernity: Some Moroccan Debates on Modernity," *Questions of Modernity*, ed. Tim Mitchell (Minneapolis: University of Minnesota Press, 2000). Hereafter cited as TLM.

27. Written in Beirut during the civil war, Huda Barakat's *hajr a-dhak*, an award-winning and widely translated novel, critiques the modernist legacy while it simultaneously references those modernists whose prose complexly thematizes minority identity. Self-consciously deploying allusions to Flaubert, Joyce, and Proust, the novel tracks the subjectivity of a male child who, rather than coming to consciousness during the war, grows into a hypermasculinized fighter. Critically revising a modernist metacritical discourse, the narrator reverses Flaubert's cross-gender identification in *Madame Bovary* by addressing her male protagonist directly to lament his transformation; such a critical reuse of a modernist tradition entangles that tradition in the modernity of its new site by knotting together formal and political insights. In this example,

Flaubert's invocation of gender in the midst of a major formal innovation ("Mme. Bovary c'est moi") finds a contemporary purchase in Arabic genre conventions, as the lamentation and songs of mourning foregrounded by Barakat function both as traditional genres of women's writing in Arabic and as the gendered labor of modern women's writing. Huda Barakat, *The Stone of Laughter* (London: Interlink, 1998).

28. Although Arabic free verse *(shi'r manthur)* had been practiced since Amin al-Rihani's Whitmanesque poems of 1905, free verse and prose poetry are most often associated with the three innovative Iraqi poets Badr Shakir al-Sayyab, Nazek al-Mala'ika, and al-Bayati, as well as others in Egypt. *Shi'r hurr* (literally, "free poetry") refers to mixed meter rather than strictly to what in English we call *free verse* and in French *vers libre*. Ahmad Zaki Abu Shadi is credited with coining the term in 1926, although the first free verse poem was likely penned by Niqula Fayyad in 1924. A second wave of innovation in *shi'r hurr* begins with al-Sayyab's practice of *vers irrégulier* in 1947. Baudelaire is an obvious reference here, and the transformative and sweeping influence of T. S. Eliot on Arabic poetry in the late 1940s is well known. See Shmuel Moreh, *Modern Arabic Poetry 1800–1970: The Development of Its Forms and Themes under the Influence of Western Literature* (Leiden: E. J. Brill, 1976). The Beirut avant-garde journal *Shi'r*, established in 1957 by Yusuf al-Khal and Adonis, became a center for intellectuals and writers in the post-1948 period; and while it is often argued that the eliotic influence is responsible for the resurgent interest in pre-Islamic, pre-Christian mythology in the Lebanese and Syrian poetry of the 1940s, this archaism was directly encouraged by the Syrian Social Nationalist Party as an ideological means to develop a regional nationalist identity that could produce national unity by overriding confessional difference. For an energetic and controversial discussion of these political origins, see Joseph Zeidan, "Myth and Symbol in the Poetry of Adūnīs and Yūsuf al-Khāl," *Journal of Arabic Literature* 10 (1979): 70–94. While the literary influence of the extraordinary number of translations of European and American modernism that flooded the Arabic literary scene in the early twentieth century is tremendously important, the political and ideological forces that motivate literary movements in nationalist or, following Robert Crawford's definition, provincializing directions are equally strong and bear the marks of another genealogy of influence. Like its counterparts in Europe and elsewhere, the Arab nationalism of the 1930s and 1940s "was clearly formulated with reference to Nietzsche, Spengler, Bergson and others," and this is true for nationalist and anticolonial movements whether they configured their notion of Arab unity through language, race, or continuous habitation of a region. Aziz Al-Azmeh, *Islams and Modernities* (London: Verso, 1993), 28; Robert Crawford, *Devolving English* (Edinburgh: Edinburgh University Press, 2001).

29. Bernard Aresu situates Kateb Yacine as a reader of Faulkner; Boudjedra names Faulkner along with the *nouveau roman* as sources for his own poetics; and Meddeb's *Talismano* includes fictional interviews with its precursors. Aresu, *Counterhegemonic Discourse from the Maghreb: The Poetics of Kateb's Fiction* (Tübingen: G. Narr, 1993).

30. *Nedjma* and *Le Passé simple* (two milestone novels of the 1950s from Algeria and Morocco), the new free verse poetry coming out of Lebanon in the 1950s, and the essays, fiction, and poetry of the Palestinian resistance after 1948 are instances of avant-garde modernist expression with deep political and aesthetic commitments. Thus the argument that modernism ends abruptly or that a figure like Beckett marks a transition between modernism and postmodernism may hold for Anglo-American literature but not for modernism's global reach.

31. Wilde's investment in the aesthetic techniques of sublimation and his failure to bring about such aesthetic triumph over tragic ruin signal the new limits that biopolitical subjection set to aesthetic self-invention even as those limits are materialized and revalued by the artwork.

32. Foucault, "Genealogy of Ethics: An Overview of a Work in Progress," in *Ethics: Subjectivity and Truth (Essential Works of Foucault, 1954–1982, Vol. I)* (New York: The New Press, 2006).

33. C. L. R. James, *Mariners, Renegades and Castaways: The Story of Herman Melville and the World We Live In*, intro by Donald Pease (Hanover, NH: The University Press of New England, 2001), xxvii. Hereafter cited as *MRC*. In addition to providing ample historical context, Pease's introduction and his subsequent essay in the *Arizona Quarterly* make a compelling case for *Mariners, Renegades, and Castaways* as a critique of imperialism and a commentary on American practices of indefinite detention at Guantanamo Bay. For a useful account of James's reception, see Grant Farred, ed., *Rethinking C. L. R. James: A Critical Reader* (London: Blackwell Publications, 1995), and his *What's My Name? Black Vernacular Intellectuals* (Minneapolis: University of Minnesota Press, 2003).

34. *MRC*, 125.

35. Ibid., 126.

36. Genet, *Declared Enemy*, 51.

37. *MRC*, 166.

38. Born of the McCarthy era, the McCarran-Walter Act of 1952 removed racial impediments to immigration but established national and ethnic quotas and new categories of undesirability in the national immigration policy. The act gave the INS wide latitude to discriminate on many bases, including national culture, sexual orientation, and political views, and through this license, the INS became a much-used tool of anti-communism. The ideological commitments authorized by the act remained well intact until 2003, when the INS became the ICE, which enjoys even wider powers of scrutiny, expulsion, and rendition.

39. Pease cites William E. Cain, Paul Buhle, and Timothy Brennan as scholars who agree that *Mariners* is a marginal text in the James oeuvre. Especially noteworthy in this critical history is Buhle's charge that James's appeal to the American people constitutes an apology for American capitalism. See the intro by Pease in *MRC*.

40. Felman, *Scandal of the Speaking Body*.

41. James's negotiation with class and race is itself a complex and nuanced one. Whereas the 1936 text *Black Jacobins* offers an argument against the

priority of race over class and situates the San Domingo slave rebellion of 1791 as a central event of European history, *Mariners* bluntly equates the consolidation of the nation-state with a racial doctrine that reaches its apotheosis in Nazi ideology. Unsteadily straddling the notions of race as ideological alibi or mask of class war and race as category of difference that congeals class differences, *Mariners* takes up the cause of the alien.

42. Walter Benjamin: "Some Motifs in Baudelaire," in *Charles Baudelaire: A Lyric Poet in the Era of High Capitalism,* trans. Harry Zohn (London: Verso, 1983).

43. Genet, *Declared Enemy,* 51–52.

44. Roberto Fernández Retamar, *Caliban and Other Essays,* trans. Edward Baker, foreword by Fredric Jameson (Minneapolis: University of Minnesota Press, 1989); Aimé Césaire *Une Tempête: Adaptation de "La Tempête" de Shakespeare pour un théâtre nègre* (Paris: Seuil, 1969); Edward Kamau Braithwaite, *The Arrivants: A New World Trilogy—Rights of Passage; Islands; Masks* (Oxford: Oxford University Press, 1973).

45. Georges Bataille, *Le Bleu du ciel* (Paris: Gallimard, 1979), 11. Bataille's use of *rage* is not to be confused with the "paranoid rage" that Julia Kristeva explores in her reading of Céline's phallic anti-Semitism. In French as in an archaic English usage, *rage* refers not only to anger and furor but to the fits of rabies as well. With typical ambivalence, Bataille hits upon a term that muddies the distinction between man and animal, reason and madness, and, crucially, body and affect. Bataille's rage is a moment of abjection, a sacrifice that opens the restricted economy of the given word to the general economy of the reprobate and excessive expenditure of language and self. In keeping with his critique of fascist brotherhoods, Bataille's inspiring rage exposes the self to the violence of its own breaching and never allows its ordeal to be displaced externally and projected or "embodied in the figure of a maleficent agent, both feminine and masculine, miserable and all-powerful" (Julia Kristeva, *Powers of Horror: An Essay on Abjection* [New York: Columbia University Press, 1982], 318). For his critique of fascism, see "The Psychological Structure of Fascism" and "Popular Front in the Streets," in Georges Bataille, *Visions of Excess: Selected Writings 1927–1939,* ed. Allan Stoekl (Minneapolis: University of Minnesota Press, 1985).

46. Bataille's late, unfinished trilogy reflects the progression of his thought from analysis of the perpetual and historical sublimation of sacrifice and sovereignty to the exploration of the same themes within subjectivity and the possibility of writing to address itself to communication.

47. In her fascinating study of the manifesto from the seventeenth-century populist pamphlets of the Diggers and Ranters to the SCUM manifesto of the 1960s, Janet Lyon relies upon the Habermasian model to explore the manifesto as the dominant modern genre of resistant speech. See Janet Lyon, *Manifestoes: Provocations of the Modern* (Ithaca, NY: Cornell University Press, 1999). Hereafter cited as *MPM*.

48. Retamar, *Caliban and Other Essays.*

49. Léopold Sédar Senghor and Jean-Paul Sartre, *Anthologie de la nou-*

velle poésie nègre et malgache de langue française; précedée de Orphée Noir par Jean-Paul Sartre (Paris: Presses Univérsitaire de France, 1948).

50. Cited in Fanon, *Black Skin, White Masks* (New York: Grove 1987), 29. Hereafter cited as *BSWM*.

51. See Robert Young, *White Mythologies* (London: Routledge, 1990), especially the chapter on Sartre and dialectics.

52. *BSWM*, 29.

53. Retamar mentions Fanon approvingly in "Caliban" but seems to retain only the Fanonian development of self-alienation manifest in the strategy of reinvesting the symbol of abjection. No mention is made of the Fanonian argument regarding the disalienation required to open revolutionary subjectivity to affirmation. By the time Sartre wrote in his introduction to *The Wretched of the Earth,* "in short, the Third World finds itself and speaks to itself through his voice," he had absorbed the new orientation of address heralded not only by Fanon's text but by the sea change in anticolonial struggles evident in 1961. Fanon's unstinting critique of his introduction to *Orphée Noir* notwithstanding, Sartre continues to address white Europeans in *Les Damnées de la terre.*

54. The two most sensitive readings of Fanon's poetics and politics can be found in Homi Bhabha, *The Location of Culture* (New York: Routledge, 1994), and Edward Said, *Culture and Imperialism* (New York: Vintage, 1994).

55. Martin Puchner takes speech act theory to task for shrinking from confrontation with the manifesto as performative, and even as a performative challenge to John Austin's taxonomy of illocutionary and perlocutionary statements. For Puchner the manifesto is exemplified by the "Communist Manifesto," a Marxist speech act negotiating its own double nature between a wished for performative force and a necessary theatricality or what one might call its fictional character. For Puchner, performativity is reduced to theatricality and the sovereign knowledge that one is putting on a performance. A more sophisticated notion of performativity that does not reduce the perlocutionary to success or failure, mimesis or rejection, has been alive and well in feminist gender and sexuality studies and theorized by Judith Butler as a negotiation between genre and intervention, gender norms and their iteration both perverse and conventional, in the social practice of becoming or remaining visible and legible in a world we do not make and which we enter always belatedly. It may be that the manifesto's desire for performative force cannot contend with, indeed, must blind itself to, the complexities of this belatedness so invested must it be in the fantasy of ex nihilo creative action in order to "prends langue" as Césaire puts it, or "capture speech," to quote de Certeau, but the capacity to issue demands and ultimatums in the voice of necessity and with the certainty that this must be or that must end is a very different animal from the event of ranting, which can be sure only of one thing: I am bound here and you are bound to hear. The conceit of sovereignty is itself open to breakdown and moments of unintelligibility; these can be moments of performative force as well, for performativity and sovereign agency are not identical.

56. "The manifesto's revolutionary speaking position constructs political certainty, in other words, not just by reinforcing polemical fields, but also by

assuming control of the language of history, the conditions of plot" (*MPM*, 60). This is an apt description of Retamar's rhetorical gambit and his use of history. In contemporary and modernist texts, even that certainty is undercut by textual ironies and the generalized insecurity that now attends the act of speaking in one's own name and in one's own voice.

57. Nancy Fraser, "Rethinking the Public Sphere: A Contribution to the Critique of Actually Existing Democracy," *Social Text* 25/26 (1990), cited in *MPM*, 55.

58. Jürgen Habermas, *Theory of Communicative Action*, vol. 2 (Boston: Beacon Press, 1985), 302.

59. *MPM*, 82.

60. Habermas's account of the decline of the public sphere and the rise of counterdiscourse does not so much diagnose an ill as it narrates a decline. Consistent trope of modernism, such a narrative of decline, in its refusal to attend to the marked particularity of the modern, fails to capture the alteration of subjection and subjectivity characteristic of modernity. Although his *Modernity* might give one pause, Habermas is no ranter and cannot include in his narrative of the public the violent history that founds the modern except as a tragic fall. Lewis and Adorno, on the other hand, diagnose a psychosexual component of public life, which inscribes a racial, bodily imagination at the heart of the public. Césaire's work offers a theater for the exploration of monstrous social relations, while Fanon's ability to read abjection and psychosexual projections of racial culture allow him to conceive of political possibilities beyond the impasses of modernity. Far from agreeing with Jameson's conclusion that globalization sounds the death knell for narratives of self, anti- and postcolonial understandings of political subjectivity illuminate the constitutive exclusions of prior metropolitan narratives. The anti- and postcolonial difference, when read back into narratives of the public sphere, allows us to understand the global as engendering practices of freedom in the spaces of apparent decline.

61. Butler, *Antigone's Claim*, 80.

62. Gayatri Spivak. *Critique of Postcolonial Reason: Toward a History of the Vanishing Present* (Boston: Harvard University Press, 1999), 111.

63. In a study of the ethics of travel and ethnographic writing, John Culbert approaches this history of enlightenment erasure and inscription and its modernist legacy in scientific and literary writing through the figure of the paralyzed traveler to argue that moments of breakdown and failures of mobility constitute an embedded discourse of ethical encounter within the enlightenment narrative of contact. John Culbert, *Paralyses: Literature, Travel and Ethnography in French Modernity* (Lincoln: University of Nebraska Press, 2010).

64. Michel Foucault, *Psychiatric Power: Lectures at the Collège de France, 1973–74* (New York: Palgrave Macmillan, 2006), 21.

65. Ibid., 55.

66. Butler, "Bodies and Power Revisited," in *Feminism and the Final Foucault*, ed. Dianna Taylor and Karen Vintges (Urbana: University of Illinois Press, 2004), 191.

67. Michel Foucault, *The Hermeneutics of the Subject: Lectures at the Collège de France, 1981–1982* (New York: Palgrave Macmillan, 2006).

68. Butler, "Bodies and Power Revisited," 191.

69. "Chargé de représenter ce point où la loi n'est pas comprise du sujet, mais jouée par lui." Jacques Lacan, *Le Séminaire, livre II: Le moi dans la théorie de Freud et dans la technique de la psychanalyse* (Paris: Seuil, 1978), 158.

70. Foucault, *Fearless Speech*, 18.

71. Canguilhem's analysis of the idealism of the human sciences influenced Foucault's thinking about normativity and the psychoanalytic difference. See George Canguilhem, *On the Normal and the Pathological* (Boston: D. Reidel, 1978).

72. Dina Al-Kassim, "Epilogue," in *Islamicate Sexualities,* ed. Afsaneh Najmabadi and Kathryn Babayan (Cambridge, Mass.: Harvard University Press, 2008).

73. See Butler, *Psychic Life of Power: Theories in Subjection* (Stanford, Calif.: Stanford University Press, 1997).

74. This critical anti-modernism is not a rare phenomenon, and certainly we could choose other figures to pursue this argument, including among the languages and national literatures considered here.

75. For Habermas, the development of the welfare state and increased commercialization transform the public sphere into a private forum for a particular class interest; thus a crisis of legitimacy in the public sphere results from a "re-feudalisation" or decline of the public sphere through a return to a media whose sole function is to reflect the interests of the bourgeois ruling class. Habermas, "The Public Sphere," *New German Critique* 1, no. 3 (1974): 49–55.

76. Bruce Robbins, ed., *The Phantom Public Sphere* (Minneapolis: University of Minnesota Press, 1993), viii.

77. Discourses of modern decline and alienation in the public sphere are not limited to political theory, of course, and in the period 1926 (Lewis) to 1963 (Adorno) literary sensibilities register anxiety and triumphalism with equal force. However, coupling modernist critiques of the public with postcolonial addresses to a public-yet-to-come reminds us that discussions of the public sphere, whether in its ideal form or as a haunting loss, must account for histories of colonial predation and the substantial qualification such histories offer to an abstract discourse on "publics." In line with the discourse of the decline of the public sphere and in a historical account of the role of *theatrum mundi* that accuses psychoanalysis of sanctioning a culture of narcissism, Sennett argues that changing attitudes toward theater and private life produced a shift in the importance of and place granted dissent in the public sphere. Richard Sennett, *The Fall of Public Man* (Cambridge: Cambridge University Press, 1976). Dana Villa compares Sennett and Habermas to Arendt on the subject of decline of the public sphere. See Villa, "Theatricality and the Public Realm," in *Politics, Philosophy, and Terror: Essays on the Thought of Hannah Arendt* (Princeton, NJ: Princeton University Press, 1999), 128–54.

78. In *Infancy and History: Essays on the Destruction of Experience* (London: Verso, 1993), Giorgio Agamben dwells on the loss of experience

and thus of a "common" sense in modernity and turns to infancy as a shared "experience" of the lack, being without language, which inheres in language.

79. Etienne Balibar, with Immanuel Wallerstein, *Race, Nation, Class: Ambiguous Identities* (London: Verso, 1991), 59.

80. Samir Amin, *Eurocentrism* (New York: Monthly Review Press, 1989), 75. Seshadri-Krooks, in a compelling psychoanalytic discussion of race and whiteness, relies upon this notion in Amin as well. "One historicist way of approaching whiteness is to regard it as the unconscious core of what Samir Amin has termed eurocentrism." Kalpana Seshadri-Crooks, *Desiring Whiteness: A Lacanian Analysis of Race* (New York: Routledge, 2000), 47.

81. Wyndham Lewis, *America and Cosmic Man* (Garden City, NY: Lewis-Doubleday and Co., 1948), and Marshall McLuhan, *The Gutenberg Galaxy* (Toronto: University of Toronto Press, 1962)

82. Wyndham Lewis, *The Art of Being Ruled* (Santa Rosa, Calif.: Black Sparrow Press), viii–ix. Hereafter cited as *ABR*.

83. Freud, "The Sexual Enlightenment of Children," in *The Sexual Enlightenment of Children* (New York: Collier Books, 1963), 19 (vol. 9: 131–39 in the Standard Edition).

84. Foucault, *History of Sexuality, Volume 1: An Introduction*, trans. Robert Hurley (New York: Vintage, 1990), 8.

85. Freud, *Three Essays on the Theory of Sexuality* (New York: Perseus Books, 2000), 39.

86. Gayle Rubin, "Thinking Sex: Notes for a Radical Theory of the Politics of Sexuality," in *The Lesbian and Gay Studies Reader,* ed. Henry Abelove, Michele Barale, and David Halperin (New York: Routledge, 1993).

87. Sigmund Freud, "Reflections on War and Death," in *Character and Culture* (New York: Collier Books, 1963), 112.

88. Theodor Adorno, "Sexual Taboos and Law Today," in *Critical Models: Interventions and Catchwords,* trans. Henry Pickford (New York: Columbia University Press, 1998), 77. Of particular interest are the texts of Adorno's last decade (1959–69), when he became a near-popular figure delivering radio addresses and consulted on controversial public issues such as the decriminalization of homosexuality.

89. Ibid., 80.

90. Ibid.

91. Ibid., 76.

92. Sigmund Freud, *Totem and Taboo: Some Points of Agreement between the Mental Lives of Savages and Neurotics,* trans. James Strachey (New York: W. W. Norton and Company, 1989). My treatment of Freud's myth of the primal father goes against the grain of a common understanding, as, for instance, found in Lacan's reading of the Hugo poem "Booz endormi" as the reproduction of Freud's myth before the fact. Jacques Lacan, *Ecrits: A Selection,* trans. Alan Sheridan (New York: W. W. Norton, 1977), 158. For my part, the paternal metaphor admits other potentialities, including the disappearance of the originary figure in the trace of its spectral instantiations as new forms of kinship.

93. Foucault, *Discipline and Punish: The Birth of the Prison,* trans. Alan Sheridan (New York: Vintage, 1979), and *History of Sexuality, Volume 1.*

94. Foucault, *Society Must Be Defended: Lectures at the Collège de France, 1975–1976* (New York: Palgrave Macmillan, 2003).

CHAPTER 1

1. Wilde's early career was built around publicity stunts that included posing as the inspiration for a fictional character. Richard D'Oyly Carte, sometime partner and producer for Gilbert and Sullivan, was also Wilde's agent and persuaded Wilde to portray in public the foppish poet, Bunthorne, from the operetta *Patience,* itself a send up of young aesthetes.

2. Note Basil's impassioned declaration of love for Dorian in Oscar Wilde, *The Picture of Dorian Gray* (London: Dent Everyman's Library, 1976), 16. Hereafter cited as *PDG.*

3. See Joseph Bristow, *Effeminate England: Homoerotic Writing after 1885* (New York: Columbia University Press, 1995).

4. Charles Bernheimer, *Decadent Subjects: The Idea of Decadence in Art, Literature, Philosophy, and Culture of the Fin de Siècle in Europe* (Baltimore, Md.: Johns Hopkins University Press, 2002), 6. Hereafter cited as *DS.*

5. Max Nordau's *Degeneration,* published in 1892, three years before Wilde's imprisonment, devotes a chapter to Wilde.

6. H. G. Wells's *The Island of Dr. Moreau* is one example of a political worry that science under capitalism will lead inexorably to degeneration of mind, body, and ethical substance.

7. Richard Gilman, *Decadence: The Strange Life of an Epithet,* cited in *DS,* 6.

8. Compare to Gautier's "Il n'y a de vraiment beau que ce qui ne peut servir à rien" and "La jouissance me paraît le but de la vie et la seule chose utile au monde."

9. Cited in Joseph Bristow, "Dorian Gray and Gross Indecency," in *Sexual Sameness: Textual Differences in Lesbian and Gay Writing* (London: Routledge, 1992). Youth provides the central affective pivot of the cross-examination at all three of Wilde's trials. Take, for instance, this sample from the testimony of April 26, 1895: "Why did you take up with these youths?—I am a lover of youth. (Laughter) So you would prefer puppies to dogs and kittens to cats?—I think so." Cited in Richard Ellmann, *Oscar Wilde* (New York: Random House, 1987), 464. That boys become puppies in the English arty press as in a courtroom is evidence, even if absurd, that the trial, like the scandal of the book four years before, was for some a prurient form of entertainment. The imagined danger to youth, however, had already become the signature narrative of the prosecution and criminalization of homosexuality in the Criminal Law Amendment Act of 1885. An examination of newspaper editorial responses to the trials as well as to letters written by citizens shows that the last two decades of the nineteenth century marked a shift in press politics and address as newspapers became beholden to advertising revenue,

which in turn demanded more attention to readership. The cultivation of the sex scandal as a major social diversion became an essential tool of newspaper sales and thus shaped the public culture of the time. Edward Cohen's *Talk on the Wilde Side* details precisely this aspect of the trials. See also Michael S. Foldy, *The Trials of Oscar Wilde: Deviance, Morality and Late-Victorian Society* (New Haven, Conn.: Yale University Press, 1997).

10. Oscar Wilde, "Soul of Man under Socialism," in *The Complete Works of Oscar Wilde,* with an introduction by George Bernard Shaw (New York: Barnes and Noble Books, 1994), 1100–1101 (hereafter cited as *CWOW*).

11. Wilde's criticism of rebellion in the arts or in the subcultural productions of his time is virtually the same as his misgivings about the socialist.

12. Eve Sedgwick, "Some Binarisms (II): Wilde, Nietzsche, and the Sentimental Relations of the Male Body," in *Epistemology of the Closet* (Berkeley: University of California Press, 1990).

13. Throughout Wilde's work, the aesthete exemplifies a failure to understand the iterative model of Individuality presented in *De Profundis,* which argues for the fecundity of the constraints of perpetual origination by imitation. In both the prison letter and the earlier lecture "The Soul of Man under Socialism," Wilde distinguishes the sterile repetition of the aesthete from the generative citationality of the Individual as he does the conformist from the singular and spectacular Artist. His practice of capitalization suggests that these terms are to be read and to circulate like proper names. The aesthete, then, misrecognizes the class character of his hoped-for individuality when he substitutes consumption for aesthetic invention. In failing to understand that the avant-gardism of his style robs him of the desired uniqueness of his "self"-invention, the aesthete is alienated from the social values that Wilde consistently relies upon to frame his political interventions, in "The Soul of Man under Socialism" as in his lectures of the 1880s on home decor and reform in women's dress.

14. Is not this critical intuition of self-relation as "homosexual" itself an artifact of homophobia, and therefore another species of what Sedgwick has dubbed a "paranoid reading practice"? Why does Allan Bloom's notion of modernism dominate Sedgwick's conception of *literary* modernism? "For Wilde, the progression from *homo* to same to self resulted at least briefly, as we shall see, in a newly articulated modernist 'self'-reflexiveness and anti-figurality, anti-representationism, iconophobia that struggles in the anti-sentimental entanglements of *Dorian Gray* and collapses in the sentimental mobilizations of *Reading Gaol* (Sedgwick, "Some Binarisms," 161). The charge of iconophobia is a difficult one to maintain with reference to *Salomé,* which moves narratively through the unfolding of tableaux and images. Indeed, the drama was inspired by, among other influences, the paintings of Moreau and the purple prose of Huysmans. Further, Wilde, the author of fairy tales and plays, who has said of his creative process, "I can only think in stories," deals in iconic symbols throughout his career; think only of "The Sphynx," *The House of Pomegranates,* or *The Portrait of W.H.* Sedgwick seems to appropriate Wilde to a particular interpretation of Mallarmesian poetics that emphasizes abstraction over ornament. For a discussion of the impossible demand consti-

tuted by the dream of pure language as a material conveyance of spiritual and sensible meaning in Mallarmé, see Maurice Blanchot, *The Book to Come*, trans. Charlotte Mandell (Stanford, Calif.: Stanford University Press, 2003). Wilde was courting Mallarmé in 1891, and, over Whistler's loud protest that Wilde was no more than a *farceur,* Mallarmé received Wilde as an esteemed guest in his *mardi* salon. Mallarmé responded warmly by letter upon receiving a deluxe copy of *Dorian Gray*. Still, Wilde seems to be more influenced by Huysmans and the symbolist movement, which Mallarmé substantially exceeds, and spends his honeymoon in Paris reading Huysmans's *A rebours (Against the Grain)*. Later he composes *Salomé* in French as a bid for membership in the French avant-garde and in direct competition with Mallarmé, whose poem "Hérodiade" was still unfinished when Wilde began his *Salomé*.

15. Ellmann, *Oscar Wilde*, 319.
16. Jean Laplanche, "To Situate Sublimation," *October* 28 (1984).
17. Oscar Wilde, "The Critic as Artist," in *CWOW*, 1045.
18. Jean Laplanche and J.-B. Pontalis, "Fantasy and the Origins of Sexuality," in *Formations of Fantasy,* ed. Victor Burgin, James Donald, and Cora Kaplan (London: Routledge, 1989). My use of the term "fantasy" relies upon the condensation of their theory (26) where fantasy derives from an enigmatic origin not unlike *influence*. Wilde presents us with a model of seduction as contagion and influence, and to the extent that Laplanche later develops seduction as an unconscious exchange of signs, both theories evoke a figure of implantation of desire as an enigma coming from the exterior. For Laplanche, the enigma of sexual nonknowledge incites the production of fantasy.
19. Sedgwick, "Some Binarisms," 148.
20. In *Shopping With Freud* (London: Routledge, 1993), Rachel Bowlby sets *Dorian Gray* within a highly charged atmosphere of burgeoning consumerism and amply cites from Wilde's essays to argue that he consciously constructs a portrait of the new consumerism split between the moral of renunciation and hedonistic appetite.
21. Oscar Wilde, "Pen, Pencil and Poison," in *Oscar Wilde: The Artist as Critic,* ed. Richard Ellmann (Chicago: University of Chicago Press, 1982). See also Ellmann's *Oscar Wilde* (300), where it looks as though he has in mind Nordau's comments on Wilde's "color mysticism."
22. Ellmann, *Oscar Wilde*, 365.
23. Cited in Sedgwick, "Some Binarisms," and explained in Ellmann, *Oscar Wilde*. The carnation had by the time of the trials already become a fad on the continent. So, the question of which nation Wilde might have been saluting becomes even more vexed: Ireland, France, or a queerness newly and parodically conceived on the model of national identity?
24. Laplanche, Jean, and J. B. Pontalis, *The Language of Psycho-Analysis,* trans. Donald Nicholson-Smith (New York: W. W. Norton, 1974), 317. Hereafter cited as *LP*.
25. Teresa Brennan, *The Transmission of Affect* (Ithaca, NY: Cornell University Press, 2004), 12.
26. "Writing, which allows one to recover, is equal to a resurrection. The writer, then, finds himself marked out for identification with Christ, if only in

order for him, too, to be rejected, ab-jected.... Contemporary literature ... propounds, as a matter of fact, a sublimation of abjection. Thus it becomes a substitute for the role formerly played by the sacred, at the limits of social and subjective identity. But we are dealing here with a sublimation without consecration. Forfeited." Julia Kristeva, *Powers of Horror: An Essay on Abjection* (New York: Columbia University Press, 1982), 26.

27. Neil Bartlett, *Who Was That Man: A Present for Mr. Oscar Wilde* (London: Serpent's Tail, 1988). See especially "Evidence," pp. 93–162.

28. On the green carnation Bartlett has this to say: "By wearing it Wilde ceased to be an individual homosexual with a flair for creating his own public image, and subscribed to a homosexual fashion. He declared himself to be one of an anonymous group of men for whom the wearing of the carnation *meant* homosexuality" (ibid., 50). Here, the signifier becomes a desiring sign equivalent to a speech act (declaring) with a definitive signified "homosexuality." While I share this reading and its investment in the sign and the signifying act, the label of "anonymous group" as a descriptor for the circle of friends in the theater audience that night indicates the problem with the class politics of Bartlett's approach. This group, far from anonymous to themselves and to scholars today, constitutes the kind of gay male kinship that Wilde did intend to cultivate.

29. "Elitism" does not capture the complexity of Wilde's class position, crossed as it was by his protestant Irish background, his identification with Catholic Ireland, and his promotion of Irish sovereignty; against the grain of his own politics, Bartlett's awareness of the class difference between Wilde and the soldiers and other young men whom Wilde paid for sex does little more than mark class miscegenation as another Wildean sin.

30. *PDG*, 16.
31. Ibid., 18.
32. Ibid.
33. Ibid., 17.
34. Ibid.
35. Ibid.

36. *New Foundations* proposes to rethink both the putative developmental model of subjectivity often thought to derive from psychoanalysis and the framework of interpellation that Althusser develops through the famous scene of a subject interrupted and thus called into being by the police or, less literally, by the name. Implantation allows for no such conscription of the subject into the being-subject to the officer's citation. Laplanche's organic model emphasizes the temporal lag between the seeding of an enigmatic signifier, the destiny of which cannot be known in advance, and the sequence of meanings that become attached to the site of this signifier. This temporal deferral we can recognize as the working of *nachträglichkeit;* it is the delayed fruition of the enigmatic signifier that reveals the properly traumatic character of implantation. Unlike the Althusserian fable of subjection, implantation offers no name by which to know oneself as other. The other is present from the outset as a producer of irritating nonsignifying secrets, which must be elaborated and imbued with meaning by the subject of becoming. The destiny of such an

enigmatic signifier is utterly singular and subject to typification only by virtue of the similarity of an originary setting. Implantation may fall, finally, into the trap of a phonologocentricism and thus repeat aspects of the model of interpellation; however, the enigmatic signifier offers no equivalent to the direct address of Althusserian interpellation, nor does it authorize an imagination of norming as a form of knowledge or rote learning of convention. Neither the fullness of inscription nor the immanence of human being, implantation offers us a model of decipherment without an origin.

37. Michel Foucault, *History of Sexuality, Volume I: An Introduction*, trans. Robert Hurley (New York: Vintage, 1990), 152.

38. Ibid., 154.

39. Sigmund Freud, "On Narcissism: An Introduction" (1914), in *General Psychological Theory* (New York: Macmillan, 1963), 70.

40. In a complex study of figures of homosexuality and the inversion model, Andrew Hewitt interprets the German context of the Narcissus myth and, important for any consideration of nineteenth-century theories of masculinity and homosexuality, discusses the very texts upon which Sedgwick's readings rely for their historical argument. Andrew Hewitt, *Political Inversions: Homosexuality, Fascism and the Modernist Imaginary* (Stanford, Calif.: Stanford University Press, 1996).

41. See Judith Butler, *Bodies That Matter* (London: Routledge, 1993).

42. Freud, "On Narcissism," 74.

43. "On the Mechanism of Paranoia" makes homosexual object-choice dependent upon the choice of "an outer object with similar genitals."

44. Laplanche and Pontalis, "Fantasy and the Origins of Sexuality," 27.

45. Ibid.

46. Foucault, *History of Sexuality*, 101.

47. *PDG*, 106.

48. Ibid.

49. Ibid., 108.

50. Michel Foucault, *Discipline and Punish* (New York: Vintage, 1979), 29.

51. Oscar Wilde, *The Soul of Man and Prison Writing*, introduction by Isobel Murray (Oxford: Oxford University Press, 1990), 55. Further references to *De Profundis* in the text will be cited as *DP*.

52. Isobel Murray notes that Wilfred Scawen Blunt had already published a volume of prison poems entitled "In Vinculis" and suggests this as an explanation for the change of title, chosen by Rob Ross, in Wilde, *The Soul of Man*.

53. See Caroline Walker Bynum, *Jesus as Mother: Studies in the Spirituality of the High Middle Ages* (Berkeley: University of California Press, 1984).

54. Foucault, *Discipline and Punish*, 191.

55. Foucault, *History of Sexuality*, 150.

56. Ibid.

57. Wilde was quite familiar with the literature on degenerescence and perversion. In his letter to the Home Secretary of July 2, 1896, he cites Lombroso and Nordau as evidence of a decriminalized, medical discourse on homosexuality, even going so far as to brag that the insidious Nordau had "devoted an entire chapter to me." There, he claims, "that such offenses are forms of sexual

madness and are recognised as such not merely by modern pathological science but by much modern legislation, notably in France, Austria and Italy, where the laws affecting these misdemeanors have been repealed, on the ground that they are diseases to be cured by a physician, rather than crimes to be punished by a judge." Later in the same letter and while arguing a connection between sexual madness and literary temperament, Wilde claims "that during the entire time he [Wilde] was suffering from the most horrible form of erotomania, which made him forget his wife and children, his high social position in London and Paris, his European distinction as an artist, the honour of his name and family." Wilde had much to gain by appearing to share this view of erotomania. Most particularly he had a library to gain, as this letter's purpose is to secure books with which to pass his time in Reading Gaol. What is striking, however, is the annexation of categories in the hyperbolic series of "forgettings" that swiftly move from erotomaniacal neglect of family to international status.

58. Oscar Wilde, "The Critic as Artist," in *CWOW*, 1058.

59. Philip E. Smith II and Michael S. Helfand, *Oscar Wilde's Oxford Notebooks: A Portrait of Mind in the Making* (New York: Oxford University Press, 1989), 34.

60. T.H. Huxley, *Evolution and Ethics: T.H. Huxley's Evolution and Ethics with New Essays on Its Victorian and Sociobiological Content*, ed. James Paradis and George C. Williams (Princeton, NJ: Princeton University Press, 1989), 82.

61. Cited in Smith and Helfand, *Oscar Wilde's Oxford Notebooks*, 76. See also the discussion of sexual selection and female bird spectatorship, with its odd echo of Rousseau, in the fourth chapter of *The Origin of Species by Means of Natural Selection*.

62. Foucault, *Discipline and Punish*, 30, and *The History of Sexuality*.

63. For Freud this kind of conglomeration is itself the structure of the symptom. See "Fragment of an Analysis of a Case of Hysteria (1905)," in *Dora: An Analysis of a Case of Hysteria*, by Sigmund Freud, with introduction by Philip Rieff (New York: Touchstone Edition, 1997).

64. Foucault, *History of Sexuality*, 120.

65. Ibid., 125.

66. Ibid., 149. Here Foucault discovers a totemism in the paranoid anxiety with blood purity; when the sovereignty of blood ties is grafted onto an "analytics of sexuality," totemism retroactively justifies the taboo on homosexuality as contributing to racial degenerescence. Purity of blood, like the primitive totem, must be protected, celebrated, and gloriously sacrificed in the scientific identification of deviance and in the late nineteenth-century practice of generating sex panics through tabloid journalism.

67. This can easily be corroborated from his letters. On May 31, 1898, he writes, "Yes: I think that, aided by some splendid personalities like Davitt and John Burns, I have been able to deal a heavy and fatal blow at the monstrous prison-system of English justice. There is to be no more starvation, nor sleeplessness, nor endless silence, nor eternal solitude, nor brutal floggings. The system is exposed, and so, doomed. But it is difficult to teach the English either pity or humility. They learn slowly. Next, the power of Judges

(an extremely ignorant set of men—ignorant, that is, of what they are doing, their power to inflict the most barbarous sentences on those who are brought before them) must be limited. A judge, at present, will send a man to two years' hard labour or to five years' penal servitude with utter callousness, not knowing that all such sentences are sentences of death. It is the lack of imagination in the Anglo-Saxon race that makes the race so stupidly, harshly cruel. Those who are bringing about Prison Reform in Parliament are Celtic to a man. For every Celt has inborn imagination." *The Letters of Oscar Wilde,* ed. Rupert Hart-Davis (New York: Harcourt, Brace and World, 1962).

68. Wilde, "The Soul of Man under Socialism" in *CWOW,* 1101.

69. Linda Dowling, in *Hellenism and Homosexuality in Victorian Oxford* (Ithaca, NY: Cornell University Press, 1994), traces the development of Oxford Platonism as a new discourse of empire. She persuasively argues that Wilde uses the terms of an imperial discourse of civic friendship to authorize and install a positively valued homosexual identity at the center of the imperial subject. However, her analysis ignores the register of biology and race that is fused to the self-conception of empire. Further, in her effort to correct the historical misconceptions of recent queer theory, or what she chooses to call "homosexual apologists," her analysis suffers from an uncritical identification with the indirect and idealized expressions of Oxonian homoerotic hellenism. In a paradigmatic instance, Dowling interprets Wilde's disdain for Lord Alfred Douglas's phrase "the love that dare not speak its name," which was cited in court as evidence of sexual misconduct and circulated throughout the trials and after as a name of homosexuality. "As Wilde realized, Douglas had indolently borrowed the notion of 'two loves' for his poem of the same title from the platonic doctrine of the Uranian and Pandemic eros—where its subtle axis is poised between a *telos* of intellectual aspiration and a *telos* of physical appetite. Douglas then transferred the notion of 'two loves' to a banal new polarity organized around sexual object choice. . . . Wilde, loyal to him even in this extremity, summons himself to defend Douglas's lame verse. Speaking his mighty peroration, Wilde briefly embodies the power of a mind saturated in Greek thought and Oxford Hellenism to stave off the invading horror, to overcome another man's intellectual indolence and imaginative vulgarity, and to transfigure even vapidity into something eloquent and fine" (142–43). Is it really so indolent, banal, lame, vulgar, vapid, and, finally, horrible to wrench a stylized sexuality into the modernity of object choice? Consistent with this tendency to deny the contemporaneity of contestatory discourses, she minimizes the influence and importance of the biological sciences at Oxford and in Wilde's notebook. For Dowling the importance of an aesthetic ontology is that it completely sublates phylogeny; for Wilde the sublation is never complete, the dialectic between body and spirit is always to be made anew. Otherwise, the creative energy of aesthetic invention would be completely dissipated; aesthetics would cease to be that sexual research he so plainly intends it to be.

70. Oscar Wilde, "The Critic as Artist." Gilbert's increasingly expansive speech rises to heights of hysterical truth telling only to lapse back upon itself in exhausted maxims, e.g., "There is no sin except stupidity" (1057). He seems to be the prototype of the Wildean ranter.

71. Ibid.

72. Ibid.

73. H. G. Wells's *The Time-Machine* (1895), published the year Wilde went to prison, offers a didactic narrative on this theme of social devolution.

74. Freud's discovery of unconscious fantasy marks the break with the biological determinism of his period. Though often represented as a "biologist of the mind," Freud, in his shift away from a literalist account of the seduction theory and toward a notion of primal fantasy, substantially departs from the dogma of inherited characteristics and organic cause of the period.

75. The sublimation of appetite into ego ideals and ideal forms in aesthetics is the place of overlap for understanding how an aestheticized ontology like Wilde's might demonstrate Freud's theory.

76. Sigmund Freud, "Mourning and Melancholia," in *General Psychological Theory* (New York: W. W. Norton, 1991), 176.

77. Sigmund Freud, "Reflections on War and Death," in *Character and Culture* (New York: Collier Books, 1963), 122.

78. Queensberry was an intimidating man whose disapproval could be so fierce that at least one of his gay sons preferred suicide to exposure by a blackmailer. Ellman speculates, "The conviction that one son had died in a homosexual scandal resolved Queensberry to make sure that a second did not die the same way" (*Oscar Wilde*, 427).

79. Sigmund Freud, *Totem and Taboo* (New York: Norton, 1989), 192.

80. Ibid., 193.

81. Ibid., 192.

82. The scene suggests that Wilde knew that pillory had been a punishment for sodomy in early modern England. See Louis Crompton, *Byron and Greek Love* (Berkeley: University of California Press, 1985).

83. These phrases are taken from the narration of Dorian's meditations before the portrait.

84. Huxley and Wells are examples of this tendency.

85. Freud, *Totem and Taboo*, 72.

86. Letter of May 31, 1898, in *Letters of Oscar Wilde*.

87. Sigmund Freud, *Ego and the Id* (New York: Norton, 1960), 27.

88. Jacques Lacan, "Aggressivity in Psychoanalysis," in *Ecrits: A Selection*, trans. Alan Sheridan (New York: W. W. Norton, 1977), 26.

89. Ibid.

90. Michael Banton, *Racial Theories* (Cambridge: Cambridge University Press, 1987). This field of study has exploded in the last decade, in part because of the availability of Foucault's lecture *Society Must be Defended*, first in its original version and then in 2003 in English translation.

91. Ibid., 76.

92. For a persuasive detailing of the national projections involved in consolidating a stereotyped Irishman as a national threat, see L. P. Curtis, *Anglo-Saxons and Celts: A Study of Anti-Irish Prejudice in Victorian England* (Bridgeport, Conn.: University of Bridgeport, 1968), as well as his *Apes and Angels: The Irishman in Victorian Caricature* (Washington, DC: Smithsonian

Institution Press, 1971), which includes the now famous cartoons illustrating Mr. MacSimius. For persistent attention to the sustained development of the "atavism" alleged to derive from Celtic culture, see David Lloyd, *Nationalism and Minor Literature: James Clarence Mangan and the Emergence of Irish Cultural Nationalism* (Berkeley: University of California Press, 1987), and *Anomalous States: Irish Writing and the Post-Colonial Moment* (Durham, NC: Duke University Press, 1993). For a history of the imbrication of state with race, see David Goldberg, *The Racial State* (London: Blackwell, 2001).

93. See George W. Stocking Jr., *Victorian Anthropology* (New York: The Free Press, 1987).

94. Cited in Vincent Cheng, *Joyce, Race and Empire* (Cambridge: Cambridge University Press, 1995), 7. Also in Banton, *Racial Theories*, 57. Neither of these critics explains how Knox's murderous racism toward the "Celts" can coexist with a relatively enlightened critique of empire, although Stocking understands this as an artifact of a very dark worldview (Stocking, *Victorian Anthropology*, 64). Banton cites this passage from *The Races of Man*: "[The Anglo-Saxons in South Africa] so debase the coloured races as to deprive them for ever of all chance of recovering that inestimable treasure beyond all price or value, freedom of speech, thought and action; in a word, the rights of man. How has this antagonism of race arisen? The truth is, it has always existed, but it never appeared in its terrible form until the Saxon race began to migrate over the earth, to establish free colonies as they are called—free to the white man and their own race—dens of horror and cruelty to the coloured" (59).

95. Banton, *Racial Theories*, 57, and Cheng, *Joyce, Race and Empire*, 30.

96. Banton, *Racial Theories*, 59.

97. Curtis, *Apes and Angels*, 2.

98. Stocking, *Victorian Anthropology*, 234.

CHAPTER 2

1. Jane Bowles, *Two Serious Ladies,* in *My Sister's Hand in Mine* (New York: Ecco Press, 1978), 194–201. References to this volume of Bowles's collected works will hereafter appear as *MS*.

2. The horizon of a modernist sacred, always hovering in the background, affords the perspective of judgment and failure, futility and incomprehension, by which character is judged in her fiction. My reading of these moments in Bowles differs from that offered by other critics who interpret this tendency of her prose either as an undoing of gender through the mobilization of queerness understood as indeterminacy or as an exploration of the alienation of existence. Cf. the essays by Carolyn Allen and Robert Loughy in Jennie Skerl, ed., *A Tawdry Place of Salvation: The Art of Jane Bowles* (Carbondale: Southern Illinois University Press, 1997).

3. Millicent Dillon, ed., *Out in the World: Selected Letters of Jane Bowles 1935–70* (Santa Rosa, Calif.: Black Sparrow Press, 1985), 41. Hereafter cited as *OW*.

4. Ibid., 71.

5. The superego is credited in *The Ego and the Id* with the power of reproachful speech that I am here identifying as directed toward that psychic agency.

6. Millicent Dillon, *A Little Original Sin: The Life and Work of Jane Bowles* (New York: Holt, Rinehart and Winston, 1981), 170 (hereafter cited as *AL*). The story of a writing block deriving from an inability to see appears also in Paul Bowles, *Paul Bowles Photographs: "How Could I Send a Picture into the Desert?"* ed. Simon Bischoff in collaboration with the Swiss Foundation for Photography (New York: Scalo Publishers, 1994). There Paul Bowles narrates the story in an interview that offers much evidence for the speculation that Jane Bowles was made to feel her difference from her husband and her writing peers as a difference of *gender*. Paul confidently ascribes her writing impediments, contrasted with his own ease, to her gender and to her overvaluation of her fictional characters.

> She was very different from me. Especially because she was a woman, she cared more about her characters, she felt close to them. And I only cared about how they behaved in my situation, about their words and their actions. About them, no, of course not! . . . One of her characters, some woman, said . . . she made her say: I've never dabbled in people. (Laughs) so wonderful: " . . . dabbled in people!" Just the opposite of the way Jane thought. She did dabble in people. People fascinated her. It was a different relationship with reality. She always wrote that she had to see in order to be able to write. . . . Not only did she have to see it, but she also had to know how it was made—which is often impossible. That only requires a little imagination, an image; but for her, the image wasn't enough!

The statement that an image is never enough for Jane seems consistent with the kind of work she does with gender. The image fails to gratify because so much is occluded in the forms granted to vision. The symbolic matrix of feminine abjection is not a fact given to sight but the making-see within a constrained angle of view, and for this reason the boundary of intelligibility, so rigorously policed, cuts across any vision Jane might have. Paul's unwillingness to "see" the work she does imagine authorizes his assumption that she lacks imagination; this imagined lack echoes the accusation of artless projection leveled at Jane by Toklas. In the same interview he claims that Jane was not capable of love, did not feel it for Cherifa, and substituted "obsession" for the romance of love. The evidence of her letters leads me to quite different conclusions. On this basis I tend to view him as an unreliable but telling interpreter of her motives, desires, and writerly aspirations.

7. For another consideration of the undecidability of the rhetorical "how?" see Paul de Man, "Semiology and Rhetoric," in *Allegories of Reading: Figural Language in Rousseau, Nietzsche, Rilke, and Proust* (New Haven, Conn.: Yale University Press, 1979). De Man uses the example of Yeats's "How can we know the dancer from the dance?" to demonstrate the indecision between literal and figural meaning produced by rhetorical uses of systematic grammatical forms. His argument stresses the difference between the effects of a rhetorization of grammar exemplified by the rhetorical question and a grammatization of rhetoric held to promise a demystificatory and critical reading of figures. "The former end[s] up in indetermination, in a suspended uncertainty

that was unable to choose between two modes of reading, whereas the latter seems to reach a truth, albeit by the negative road of exposing an error, a false pretense" (16). De Man's valorization of the latter promises for him a practice of critical truth "invisible to the reader caught in naive metaphorical mystification" (16), but this promised resting place for the critical subject undergoes a further twist as de Man points out that the voice of critical demystification is itself subject to the formal undoing it enacts elsewhere. Thus, he deduces an "anxiety of ignorance" that "becomes thematically clear . . . not as an emotive reaction to what language does, but as an emotive reaction to the impossibility of knowing what it might be up to" (19). Bowles responds to this anxiety of ignorance by believing in it so wholeheartedly that she brings it to a standstill, a strategy that in its aggressive demand to be told *how* would seem to condense the series of points of view and turns on the text—in short, the narrative of error and truth described by de Man—into a single scene or, even less, a single point, a particle of speech. The author, who writes obsessively in the margins of her unfinished novel, "It is impossible to live without a myth," cannot seem to find the zero point of blindness or insight to begin her fabulations, to sustain them, and certainly not to finish them.

8. Primitivist style had already been the subject of an issue of *View*, the New York surrealist journal produced by Charles Henry Ford and Parker Tyler. Paul Bowles contributed to the October 1943 issue and again to the October 1944 issue. He edited the "Tropical Americana" issue, *View* 5, no. 2 (May 1945), in which he wrote in praise of "primitive" art and advocated an aesthetic practice exploring so-called "naive," grotesque, or impoverished forms. Jane Bowles's style accords with the revaluation of "ordinary" forms of speech and the coupling of naive forms with fantasy. The reveries in *Two Serious Ladies,* as well as the unmotivated shifts in action, plot, and dialogue, suggest that she is working in modes advocated by the journal.

9. Sigmund Freud, *Totem and Taboo: Some Point of Agreement between the Mental Lives of Savages and Neurotics* (New York: W. W. Norton, 1989), 113.

10. See *AL*. Reviewed by the *New York Times* and the *Saturday Review,* Bowles's work did attract notice in major publications. What she did not receive is serious consideration by other writers sufficient to placate her violent internal critic. Carolyn Allen's "The Narrative Erotics of *Two Serious Ladies*" in *Tawdry Place* cites from the reviews, some of which are also cited in Dillon. Jennie Skerl's introduction to the volume *Tawdry Place* discusses the mixed reviews that greeted all of Bowles's publications.

11. Scenes of seduction and pursuit proliferate in the fiction, but the most explicit version of her signature narrative occurs in "Going to Massachusetts," a fragment of the unfinished novel. There we are introduced to Janet, a clumsy butch (reminiscent of Beryl in *Camp Cataract*) who is owner of a mechanic's garage, attempting to seduce the attractive, "bad" Sis Mcavoy. The latter, getting drunk on Janet's scotch, thinks to herself, "She was enjoying the compliments, although it was disturbing that they should be coming from a woman. She was very proud of never having been depraved or abnormal, and pleased to be merely mean and discontented to the extent of not having been able to stay with any man for longer than the three months she had spent with her hus-

band" (*MS,* 456). Bowles's butches are always awkward, dowdy, and slightly ridiculous; unlike her femmes, they are working-class, but no gender performance escapes the suggestion of failure in her fiction. Bowles consistently pursues the association between freedom from labor in her feminine characters and capability crossed with economic need in characters who perform a working-class masculinity that is sexually nonthreatening. For instance, prostitutes or other women willing to exchange sex for support are the only women represented as desirable. Note, for example, Pacifica in *Two Serious,* Harriet in *Camp Cataract,* and Sis Mcavoy. The precarious economy of a prostitute or homeless woman's life seems sufficient cause to extract her from the norms of kinship, while destitution makes her irresistible. Within this fantasyscape, a woman of no means attracts like no other whereas the butch-femme distinction seems less operative than destitution itself. Lillian Faderman, in "Butches, Femmes and Kiki's," in *Odd Girls and Twilight Lovers: A History of Lesbian Life in Twentieth-Century America* (New York: Penguin, 1991), describes the tensions in the postwar period between American middle- and working-class lesbians, for whom butch-femme roles provided a structured subculture. In the upper-middle-class lesbian circles that Jane Bowles frequented, butchness, according to Faderman, was an object of disdain. This claim is supported by John D'Emilio's work on American lesbian bar culture from the 1940s through the '60s, also cited in Faderman. Bowles seems at times to recapitulate this prejudice uncritically, while texts like "Emmy Moore's Journal" suggest the potency and necessity of female masculinity for the articulation of desire from the position of a destitute femme. Bowles's own desires are harder to gauge. Her long-term relationship with Helvetia Perkins was wrenching and came to a rancorous end; she seems to have turned toward very feminine women after that, until meeting Cherifa. I believe that Bowles's efforts to view Cherifa as primitive substitute that primitiveness for the masculinity she had desired in Helvetia. Other scholars working on the history and theory of butch women in America come to different conclusions than Faderman about class attitudes toward gender performance. See Sue-Ellen Case, "Toward a Butch-Femme Aesthetic," in *The Lesbian and Gay Studies Reader,* ed. Henry Abelove, Michele Aina Barale, and David M. Halperin (New York: Routledge, 1993); Esther Newton, "The Mythic Mannish Lesbian: Radclyffe Hall and the New Woman," in *Hidden From History: Reclaiming Gay and Lesbian Past,* ed. Martin Bauml Duberman, Martha Vicinus, and George Chancey Jr. (New York: NAL Books, 1989); Carroll Smith-Rosenberg, "The New Woman as Androgyne: Social Disorder and Gender Crisis, 1870–1936," in *Disorderly Conduct* (New York: Oxford University Press, 1985).

 12. Sigmund Freud, *Character and Culture* (New York: Macmillan, 1963), 45. Thanks to Celeste Langan for drawing my attention to this essay.

 13. Ibid., 47.

 14. *AL,* 27.

 15. Samuel M. Steward, ed., *Dear Sammy: Letters from Gertrude Stein and Alice B. Toklas* (Boston: Houghton Mifflin, 1977). The most damning entries are in Edward Burns, ed., *Staying on Alone: Letters of Alice B. Toklas* (New York: Liveright, 1973).

16. *AL*, 186.
17. Ibid., 191.
18. Ibid., 210. Letter of November 22, 1950, in Steward, *Dear Sammy*.
19. Given that it is perfectly ordinary for a playwright or director or leading man to become involved with the leading lady, the statement makes even less sense. Apparently, for Jane to behave with the same abandon and theatrical disregard for conventional morality as a man elicits only ire from the older woman. Toklas's responses to Jane's freedom set the standard for one consistent thread of censorious dismissal of her.
20. *AL*, 211. Letter of February 26, 1952, in Burns, *Staying on Alone*.
21. *AL*, 235. Letter of February 24, 1954, in Burns, *Staying on Alone*.
22. *AL*, 235.
23. Truman Capote, introduction to *My Sister's Hand in Mine*.
24. There can be no doubt that Jane was intimidated and insulted by Toklas. Unfortunately, Toklas represented a real entry into literary society, and this worked to Paul's advantage, as Toklas approved of his writing and let her opinions be known. She disapproved of Truman Capote, as borne out by a long, despairing letter of 1950 from Jane to Paul: "Alice T. was delighted that you didn't really care for him [Capote] very much. [I told her.] She said it was the one thing that really worried her. She could not understand how an intelligent person like you etc. She doesn't seem to worry in the least, however, about my liking him. So I'm insulted . . . again" (*OW,* 148).
25. Shari Benstock, "Paris Lesbianism and the Politics of Reaction, 1900–1940," in *Hidden from History*. See also Benstock's *Women of the Left Bank: Paris, 1900–1940* (Austin: University of Texas Press, 1986). The Parisian modernism of expatriate and French lesbian women would seem to challenge the model of butch-femme role-playing developed by scholars of American lesbian history in the period from the 1920s to the '50s. For the modernist lesbian, butch-femme identities were still legible and accessible as a glamorous feminine dandyism. That these women were either wealthy enough to feel themselves above the law or foreign enough to be excluded from the rigors of gender policing are significant facts. Benstock, *Women of the Left Bank*, covers this question. Recent work on queer and lesbian modernism complicates this picture of polymorphous dandyism abroad and gender parody at home. See Susan Raitt, "Lesbian Modernism," *GLQ* 10, no. 1 (2003).
26. Benstock, *Women of the Left Bank*, 341.
27. Ibid., 342.
28. Wyndham Lewis, *Time and Western Man*, ed. Paul Edwards (Santa Rosa, Calif.: Black Sparrow Press, 1993), 51.
29. Ibid., 35.
30. Ibid., 59.
31. Ibid., 61.
32. The overlap of queer unconscious preoccupation with primitivism and childhood and Lewis's censure is no accident. Lewis's constant harping on the alleged effeminacy of his contemporaries and glorying in the virility of still others would tend to suggest that his homosexual panic heightens his scrutiny of the very things that queer modernists are also reacting to—even as Lewis

may have been reinforcing a cultural preoccupation with the conflation of primitiveness and queerness. Many of his novels, most notably *Snooty Baronet,* model their heroes on Lewis's buddy Roy Campbell. That a thick strain of an unsteadily maintained homosociality circumscribed their relation cannot be doubted. They even exchanged thinly veiled erotic love poetry—larded through and through with images of phalli ascending the heavens—though the dedications read, respectably enough, "from Mr. and Mrs. Campbell to Mr. and Mrs. Lewis," and vice versa.

33. Freud, *Totem and Taboo,* 89.

34. Even as it crosses and is crossed by other discourses, the "context" of modernism extends to various other domains, yet we find the same kinds of judgments against Jane. In theatrical circles of New York, Jane's play *In the Summer House* mainly drew fire, though there were a few good reviews. Jane's letters of this period trace the ups and downs of this reception; not surprisingly, the negative reviews seem like echoes of Toklas's judgments. "Laurence Olivier's head reader saw my play and wrote that it was *morbid and depressing* and though not something to be dismissed, certainly *nothing they could think of doing*" (*OW,* 148). Sklar takes issue with Bowles's account of her reception and notes mainly good reviews.

35. Ibid., 147.

36. Ibid., 146.

37. From Gertrude Stein, "The Winner Loses: A Picture of Occupied France," cited in Benstock, *Women of the Left Bank,* 339.

38. Jane Bowles's attachment to food as a signifier of self is consistent throughout her best work. "A Quarreling Pair," "Camp Cataract," and "A Stick of Green Candy" all work out a poetics of food preparation, consumption, and taboo suggesting an entire cartography of desire and identification. In 1947 she had been reading Kierkegaard, Sartre, and de Beauvoir; during the protracted period of her convalescence and after her conversion to Catholicism she said to Sister Mercedes, at the Clinica de Los Angeles in Málaga, that she was very sorry for having been in a "field of existentialists." The comment reveals Bowles's own account of her "faith" during the years that concern us, while the complex link between faith, myth, and the gendering of food cannot be underestimated in Bowles's fiction. This seminal passage from *Being and Nothingness,* a text that there is reason to suspect she read in French well before the 1943 translation, may be an intertext for "A Stick of Green Candy."

> The synthetic intuition of food is in itself an assimilative destruction. *It reveals to me the being, which I am going to make my flesh. Henceforth, what I accept or what I reject with disgust is the very being of that existent, or if you prefer, the totality of the food proposes to me a certain mode of being of the being which I accept or refuse.* . . . It is not a matter of indifference whether we like oysters or clams, snails or shrimp, if only we know how to unravel the existential significance of these foods. . . . Every human reality is a passion in that it projects losing itself so as to found being. . . . Man is a useless passion.

On Sartre's vaginophobia in these passages from *Being and Nothingness,* see Marjorie Collins and Christine Pierce, "Holes and Slime: Sexism in Sartre's Psychoanalysis," in *Women and Philosophy: Toward a Theory of Liberation,* ed. C.

Gould and M. Wartofsky (New York: Putnam, 1976); and Michele Le Doeuff, "Operative Philosophy: Simone de Beauvoir and Existentialism," *Ideology and Consciousness* 6 (Autumn 1979): 47–57.

39. Freud, *Totem and Taboo*, 90.

40. Ibid., 21.

41. See Judith Butler, *Gender Trouble* (New York: Routledge, 1990), for the analysis of gender melancholia. There it is argued that a template of abandoned object choices, which come to model for subsequent identification, establishes the modality of gender as the gender lost and unrecoverable through mourning. "Gender identification is a kind of melancholia in which the sex of the prohibited object is internalized as a prohibition" (63). The force of such a taboo lies in the prohibition of non-normative desires and identifications.

42. Lacan, "Aggressivity in Psychoanalysis," in *Ecrits: A Selection* (New York: W. W. Norton, 1977), 26.

43. Freud, *Totem and Taboo*, 23

44. Ibid., 91.

45. Ibid., 81.

46. Ibid.

47. *AL*, 397.

48. Letter of August 1957, in *OW*, 32. All errors have been retained.

49. Nearly every biographical and critical discussion of Jane Bowles makes the claim that she spoke Arabic, the Moroccan dialect or "Moghrebi," a coinage found on the covers of Mohammed Mrabet's work as transcribed and "translated" by Paul Bowles. In an interview with Simon Bischoff in *Paul Bowles: Photographs,* Paul claims not to speak the Arabic dialect of Morocco; he and Mrabet converse in Spanish, a language that Paul knew well and from which he translated works of Latin American fiction into English. When pressed on this point, Paul Bowles replies, "I never had the desire. Then, I never had the time to devote to studying Arabic. I was busy working, writing, writing music. I wasn't interested in learning it because there wasn't anything I wanted to read in Arabic" (*Paul Bowles: Photographs,* 214). He adds that Jane studied Arabic dialect "everyday." This means that she studied the oral dialect of Tangier but never learned to read, because dialect is unwritten. Her notebooks, located at the Harry Ransom Humanities Research Center Collection, contain a few pages devoted to copying out Arabic letters and sentences in transliteration, but there is no archival evidence of an extensive or sustained effort to learn to read and write. We must conclude that although Jane was capable of communicating, her command of the language was nothing like what the critical references suggest. Her letters contain short transliterations of phrases, and the translations that accompany these mentions are often either incorrect or inexact. In a notebook entitled "History" and which contains the manuscript of "Camp Cataract," we find a single page on which someone has copied the first seven letters of the Arabic alphabet in a large, childish hand along with a French pronunciation guide (Jane Auer Bowles, Series 1.11, HRHC). Another notebook contains a lesson in oral dialect. On one side of the page is a story in French using *passé simple,* and on the other is the story transliterated in the oral dialect of Tangiers. Interspersed are pages of the Andrew section of "Out

in the World," her unfinished novel, and the Gertrude and Lionel play (Jane Auer Bowles, Series 2.3, HRHC). Thus the myth of Jane's prowess appears to be greatly exaggerated, while the specific erotic basis of her language study is often displaced by the critical reception into a fantasy of *prowess*. To my mind, her motivation to learn to talk to the people among whom she sought to live—and the women especially—sets her apart from the casual sexual tourist.

50. It is an oddity of their eventual domestic life that Cherifa went to the trouble to acquire from the Moroccan government a certificate of "permanent virginity," which she is reputed to have brandished whenever they quarreled.

51. Although the word *safi* could be translated as "okay," it might just as easily be the French *suffit*, "enough," which, in this multileveled context of knowledge and incomprehension, may mean much more than Jane is able to understand. Her statement "It does not mean always the same thing" indicates a degree of understanding about the limits of her own comprehension. Given the uncertainty and imprecision of their communication, it is striking that both of them seem to forestall the "bargaining moment." In their negotiations around the bargain Jane and Cherifa lay the ground for an erotic and a domestic relation. Their ways of declining—to act, to force the issue, to refuse—establish the paths to each other by constructing for them a form of civility.

52. Michael Lucey, *Gide's Bent: Sexuality, Politics, Writing* (New York: Oxford University Press, 1995), 61.

53. This commonplace racism is characteristic of at least some of the English-speaking queer expatriates in Tangier in the period following the war. Such hostilities and worse form the basis of the oft-cited Arno Schmitt and Jehoeda Sofers, eds., *Sexuality and Eroticism among Males in Moslem Societies* (New York: Harrington Park, 1992). For works touching on homosexuality in the Maghreb by Maghrebin scholars, see Abdelwahab Bouhdiba, *Sexuality in Islam* (London: Routledge, 1985); and Malek Chebel, *L'esprit de sérail* (Paris: Petite Bibliothèque Payot, 1995). For examples of the view of Moroccan sexuality described above, see Alfred Chester, "Glory Hole: Nickel Views of the Infidel in Tangiers," in *Head of a Sad Angel: Stories, 1953–1966* (Santa Rosa, Calif.: Black Sparrow, 1990), and the interview in *Paul Bowles: Photographs* in which Paul Bowles asserts that Moroccans have no concept of love, only sex, avarice, and obsession. Greg Mullins's *Colonial Affairs* engages the complexities of male-male relations between queer American expatriate writers and the Moroccan writers they dated.

54. Explicitly linked to lesbian desire, especially in scenes of lesbian childhood, belief is a key issue in Bowles's fiction. This narrative obsession with belief suggests that the construction of desire against the grain of heteronormativity is imagined by Bowles to be a negotiation with the symbolic as a matrix of fetishistic belief.

55. Octave Mannoni, *Clefs pour l'Imaginaire ou l'Autre Scène* (Paris: Éditions du Seuil, 1969), 11. For a study of the ways that commodification and fetishism attached to nineteenth-century constructions of the feminine, see Emily Apter, *Feminizing the Fetish: Psychoanalysis and Narrative Obsession in Turn-of-the-Century France* (Ithaca, NY: Cornell University Press, 1991); and also see Emily Apter and William Pietz, eds., *Fetishism as Cultural*

Discourse (Ithaca, NY: Cornell University Press, 1993), for a sampling of the diverse disciplinary uptake of notions of fetishism drawn from Marx and Freud.

56. Mannoni, *Clefs pour l'Imaginaire,* 18. Mannoni uses the term *repudiation* to translate *Verleugnung,* whereas in English *disavowal* is the more common translation. He makes the point of equating the two, but not in a way that necessarily implies an equation of disavowal with foreclosure.

57. Ibid., 32.

58. Dillon's biography of Jane, Paul's autobiography, and his letters and scores of interviews circulate the story that Cherifa may have poisoned Jane and caused her stroke. Sometimes Paul dismisses this as fantasy, claiming that the many charms—especially one buried in a potted plant—were, most likely, love potions designed to secure Jane's devotion. Others are not so scrupulous and continue to repeat the racist accusations and characterizations of Cherifa as a "witch." Stephen Bischoff goes so far as to describe her as "the black demon of death."

59. Edouard Roditi recalls frustrating discussions with Jane about her epilepsy, which she refused to treat.

60. Brain damage resulting from the stroke left her with a kind of aphasia that in its worst phases would not only blind her but made her substitute opposites for words she really meant to speak. For example, when Paul, seeing her blind for the first time, was greeted with the phrase "You smell good," he understood this to mean "I see bad," or "I am blind."

61. *AL,* 312.

62. Ibid. The errors and spacing appear as in Dillon's faithful reproduction of the original. This self-justification is written on a heavily creased piece of paper folded into quarters. From sources, Dillon corroborates what is evident upon physical examination of the document housed at the Harry Ransom Humanities Research Center. Jane Bowles carried it in her pocket for an extended period of time as if it were a final, most valuable testament to the diminished but interminable writing she lived (Jane Auer Bowles, Series I, Composition written during her illness—1.1, HRHC).

CHAPTER 3

1. Elisabeth Roudinesco, *Jacques Lacan and Co.: A History of Psychoanalysis in France, 1925–1985,* trans. Jeffrey Mehlman (Chicago: University of Chicago Press, 1990), 703. The Arabic text is a translation of the passage in *The Interpretation of Dreams* (chap. V, B) that relates Freud's childhood disappointment in his father's lack of heroism when an anti-Semite accosted Freud senior on a public byway, knocking his new fur hat into the mud and shouting, "Hey you, Jew, get off the sidewalk" (my translation from Arabic). This story is retold to the little boy Freud, who asks his father, "What did you do?" "I picked up my hat," is the reply that the son recounts in his own analytic text to support the theory that his subsequent childhood fantasies around the figure of Hannibal are related to this slight against his own father. The passage clearly links the development of the "martial ideal" to a national ideal

about which the adult analyst still feels great ambivalence, a fact noticeable in the first footnote to this section where Freud refers to the "strange" mistaking of Hasdrubal for Hannibal in the first imprint of his *The Interpretation of Dreams.*

2. Jacques Lacan, *The Four Fundamental Concepts of Psycho-analysis,* ed. Jacques-Alain Miller, trans. Alan Sheridan (London: Hogarth Press, 1977), 20.

3. Thrice *Jacques Lacan and Co.* refers to Lacan as Cato to Freud's Hannibal.

4. Louis Althusser and Etienne Balibar, *Reading Capital* (London: Verso, 1979), 28.

5. Abdelwahab Meddeb, *Talismano* (Paris: La Bibliothèque Arabe Sindbad, 1987), 50. Hereafter cited as in the text as *T.*

6. Jacques Lacan, *Ecrits: A Selection,* trans. Alan Sheridan (New York: W. W. Norton, 1977), 45. Hereafter cited as *Ecrits.*

7. "Shoot blood, splash tears, if only in these hours everywhere moribund; thought loiters, hesitating between banks: thought by turns imprisoning and paralysing the fingers; thought one casts out radiating, overflowing, atomized, refugied, morning dew drips sweetness on plants at the edges of so many towns. History, no more than words and corpses, tight coupling, moving in haste, edges reconciling the myths of a fugitive self."

8. More than once in its opening sections *Talismano* refers indirectly to Huysmans's *A Rebours*. In Huysmans's novel, for instance, Des Esseintes dwells on the pharaonic practice of inserting lotus petals into the vagina of the deceased. *Talismano* dwells on the more ancient Nubian practice of standing a palm frond in the corpse's vagina and calls this a stylus. The visual and conceptual pun here is multiple and deliberately transgressive, for not only does Meddeb stretch the reference backward in time, but he adds another layer. The Qur'an was originally written on the individual leaves of the palm frond (Meddeb, *Talismano,* 21).

9. Assia Djebar, *Le blanc de l'Algérie* (Paris: Éditions Albin Michel S.A., 1995). Of course, one could counter this assertion with the qualification that perhaps it is only the Arabic of the Maghreb that has never experienced a desacralization, for other dialects in other regions are much closer to the classical language. Further, particular domains of practice and theory—jurisprudence and legal philosophy, for example—maintain a close relationship with classical Arabic. Finally, when the entire Arabo-Islamic world manages its modernity in several registers (for instance, media news broadcasts are not rendered in dialect but in a lingua franca, modern standard Arabic, that, although not transparent to all, is certainly functional throughout a wide geographical area), it may be difficult to sustain any such grand thesis about the sacred or profane character of language practices. Her comments are far more valid for literary expression, but even this has been powerfully contested by the innovation of new styles, e.g., Salwa Bakr's "journalistic" style.

10. The argument is not that secularism has not and cannot be pursued in Arabic. The special status accorded the written language permits a conservative understanding of form and innovation which may be used as a politi-

cal tool against innovators of content and form, including seemingly simple innovations like Bakr's noted above. *Khbz al-hafi,* the first installment of Chukri's autobiography, was criticized on the grounds of its alleged inept use of language as much as for its portrayal of poverty and obscenity. See Christina Civantos, "Literacy, Sexuality, and the Literary in the Self-Inscription of Muammad Shukri," *Middle Eastern Literatures* 9, no. 1 (2006): 23–45.

11. Abdelkebir Khatibi, *Maghreb Pluriel* (Paris: Éditions Denoël, 1983).

12. Meddeb, *Talismano,* 15.

13. "Such a father taught in this profitable mosque: his masterful words, perfect knowledge of the hadith and the sources of law . . . erudite, honest father so modest in his manner of transmitting, without pretension, the exactitude of his knowledge . . . but how to impose the precision of numbers there where fable would best express that which cannot be measured? My first quarrel with the father erupted, mix of words, during the recitation of a text: rebel, I could not stand to repeat Qur'anic verses by heart; . . . such a father was not given to interpretation of the text; . . . through the lesson he hoped to facilitate a discipline. And I was less revolted by the meaning than by the submission to duty. I encountered the father through the practice of the text. It was painful for me to adapt to his coarse memorization" (Meddeb, *Talismano,* 104–7).

14. See Abdelkebir Khatibi, "Bilinguisme et littérature," in *Maghreb Pluriel,* and Ronnie Scharfman, "Thanatography: Writing and Death in Abdelwahab Meddeb's *Talismano,*" *Substance* 21, no. 3, issue 69 (1992), *Special Issue: Translations of the Orient: Writing the Maghreb.*

15. Judith Butler, *Bodies That Matter* (New York: Routledge, 1993), 189–90.

16. Ibid. See also the final chapter of Judith Butler, *Excitable Speech* (New York: Routledge, 1997), for a rethinking of censorship as a form of foreclosure.

17. There can be no doubt that for Lacan primordial law, symbolic law, and normativity are one and the same where culture supersedes nature with the effect that language becomes kinship. Consider, for instance, this definition of the symbolic law found in Lacan's "Function and Field," in *Ecrits*:

> The primordial Law is therefore that which in regulating marriage ties superimposes the kingdom of culture on that of a nature abandoned to the law of mating. The prohibition of incest is merely its subjective pivot, revealed by the modern tendency to reduce to the mother and the sister the objects forbidden to the subject's choice, although full license outside of these is not yet entirely open.
> This law, then, is revealed clearly enough as identical with the order of language. For without kinship nominations, no power is capable of instituting the order of preferences and taboos that bind and weave the yarn of lineage through succeeding generations. (66)

18. Jacques Lacan, *Le Séminaire, livre II: Le moi dans la théorie de Freud et dans la technique de la psychanalyse* (Paris: Seuil, 1978), 158–59.

> That is censorship in so far as there can never be any relation with the law in its entirety, since the law is never complete made one's own. Censorship and super-ego are to be located in the same register as that of the law. It is the concrete discourse, not only in so far as it dominates man and makes all kinds of fulgurations appear, it doesn't matter what, everything which happens, everything which constitutes discourse, but in so far as it gives man his own world, which we, more or less accu-

rately, call cultural. It is in this dimension that censorship is located, and you can see in what way it differs from resistance. Censorship is neither on the level of the subject, nor on that of the individual, but on the level of discourse, in so far as, as such, it [the discourse] constitutes, all by itself, a full universe, and at the same time there is something irreducibly discordant about it, in every one of its parts. It takes very little, very little at all, being locked up in the toilets, or having a father falsely accused of lord knows what crime, for the law all of a sudden to appear to you in a lacerating form. That is what censorship is.

Jacques Lacan, *The Seminar of Jacques Lacan: Book II. The Ego in Freud's Theory and in the Technique of Psychoanalysis 1954–55*, trans. Sylvana Tomaselli, ed. Jacques-Alain Miller, with notes by John Forrester (London: W. W. Norton & Company, 1991), 130.

19. This is not to say that the translation is a defective one, but rather that between the French and the English we have a circuit from *forming* to *constituting* and back again.

20. This passage is missing from the English translation.

That is censorship, inasmuch as in Freud, at the origin, it happens at the level of the dream. That is the superego, insofar as it effectively terrorizes the subject and constructs in him symptoms that are efficient, developed, lived and carried on (sued, prosecuted, pursued) and which undertake to represent that point where the law is not understood by the subject but performed by him. They have the responsibility of incarnating the law as such; they give the law its face/figure of mystery.

It is a completely different thing from the narcissistic relation to the image (mirror image, fellow, look-alike). It is the relation of the subject with the law as a whole inasmuch as there can never be a relation with the law as a whole since the law is never completely taken up (assumed, grasped). [My translation]

Lacan, *Le Séminaire, livre II*, 158.

21. Lacan will insist on the primacy of symbolic organization and orientation as that point of contact between the absolutely general and the utterly singular. Symptoms hinge the two registers, and as such they stand at the frontier of the imaginary, normally held to be a realm of egoic aspiration, hallucinatory fantasy, and perception. This early definition of the symptom tallies with the account given in *The Seminar of Jacques Lacan, Book VII: The Ethics of Psychoanalysis, 1959–1960* (London: W. W. Norton & Company, 1992), in which sublimation of the primordially foreclosed maternal body grants the subject his singularity in a sublimated activity of infinite variety. Sublimation and symptom formation resulting from foreclosure are not identical activities, yet both are the consequence of a surplus of prohibition that exceeds repression and are to be distinguished from it. When these two accounts of the productivity of foreclosure are juxtaposed, it is difficult to distinguish the symbolic from the imaginary. Complicating the taxonomy, resistance is held to be an instance of the "imaginary friction" between the analyst and the patient, whereas a genuine symptom would indicate the pressure point of the law. The example of the Muslim patient advanced in both seminars and discussed here below is instructive. Any protest that the "symbolic law" in effect in his symptom is not the religious law but something else could be dismissed as a mere resistance to the analysis/analyst. How would such a patient educate the analyst in such a scene? And would not a failure to correct the analyst be evidence of the per-

formance of another law? How are we to understand the distinction between the "mere" imaginary effect and a major symbolic cause? Or that between differing registers of kinship's inscription?

22. Butler, *Bodies That Matter,* 204.

23. Many thanks to Stefania Pandolfo, with whom I first encountered a postcolonial Lacan in her "Rapt de la voix," *Awal: Cahiers d'études Berbères* 15 (1997): 31–50.

24. Lacan, *Seminar of Jacques Lacan: Book II,* 129–30. In the first seminar, the Muslim patient also appears in relation to Lacan's evocation of the superego as a "discordant statement," which sounds like an even earlier attempt to characterize foreclosure. "Tradition and language diversify the reference to the subject. A discordant statement, unknown in law, a statement pushed into the foreground by a traumatic event, which reduces the law down to a point with an inadmissible, unintegrable character—this blind, repetitive agency is what we usually define in the term super-ego." Jacques Lacan, *Seminar I: Freud's Papers on Technique, 1953–1954* (London: W. W. Norton & Company, 1991), 198.

25. Roudinesco's history of psychoanalysis sheds no light on the identity of the "Muslim patient."

26. Lacan, *Seminar I,* 197.

27. Ibid.

28. Lacan's exoticism, though advanced as a kind of recognition of the fundamental cultural milieu of his patient, takes its cue from a long-standing orientalist tradition that seals off the Muslim in a space of fatalistic passivity with respect to scripture, with the difference that Lacan reads even resistance to religious law as evidence of the primordial, even fetishistic, importance of such a law. The peculiarity of Lacan's move is to take a writing and turn it into a nonwriting such that the law only functions as the letter of the law, as a literalization of punishment in words he cannot read. Consider the complexity of any Islamic prescription. First one must contend with the scriptural dogma asserting the Qur'an is the uncreated word of God. Writing is itself an abject activity—though not taboo, as are representations of the human form. Then, consider the laborious tradition of exegesis that renders even the *surah* "Al-Ma'idah," which details the various moral taboos and punishments for infractions and contains the single line condemning thieves, subject to rhetorical interpretation. The aspect of the sacred law of interest to Lacan is particularly infelicitous for his argument because the verb *qata'a,* meaning "to cut," is subject to a host of idiomatic uses and meanings. Presumably a child hearing that the hand of a thief shall be cut would be forced to negotiate the difficulties of rhetorical usage, but it is not clear which register, the literal or the idiomatic, would dominate his understanding. The Qur'an does not say that a thief shall have his hand cut off; it says that he shall have his hand cut, which can mean to have one's thievery cut short, as in the idiomatic use of the verb with *tongue,* meaning to have one's speech blocked. In English and French the same verb carries the same idiomatic meanings. Ahmed Ali, novelist and translator, remarks that as the next lines of the *surah* prescribing punishment for theft deal with repentance, forgiveness, and rehabilitation, the "literal" interpre-

tation is not the best one. He notes that during the Umayyad caliphate the punishment for theft was flogging. *Al-Quran,* trans. Ali Ahmed (Princeton, NJ: Princeton University Press, 1984), 113.

29. Lacan, *Seminar I,* 197.

30. Even when Algerians attempted to become citizens of France, their chances of becoming so were hardly encouraging. "In the decade between 1899 and 1909, 551 Algerians applied for citizenship, and 337 received it. Many of the 214 rejected were turned down on the vague grounds of 'unworthiness.'" John Ruedy, *Modern Algeria: The Origins and Development of a Nation* (Bloomington: Indiana University Press, 1992). On the judicial organization of colonial Morocco, see Alan Scham, *Lyautey in Morocco: Protectorate Administration, 1912—25* (Berkeley: University of California Press, 1970).

31. We can only marvel at this replacement of one orthodoxy by another where orientalist, folkloric "knowledge" about another culture is held to be a technological improvement over a lived knowledge of European child rearing practices.

32. Lacan, *Seminar I,* 197.

33. Ibid.

34. Lacan, *Seminar of Jacques Lacan: Book II,* 129.

35. Lacan, *Seminar I,* 197.

36. The third seminar presents psychotic foreclosure as

> the lack of the Name-of-the-Father in that place which, by the hole that it opens up in the signified, sets off the cascade of reshapings of the signifier from which the increasing disaster of the imaginary proceeds, to the point at which the level is reached at which signifier and signified are stabilized in the delusional metaphor.... But how can the name of the father be called by the subject to the only place in which it could have reached him and in which it has never been? Simply by a real father, not necessarily by the subject's own father, but by A-father.... Again this A-father must attain that place to which the subject was unable to call him before.

Foreclosure of the name of the father relegates the subject to psychosis and to the swarm of signifiers that stream out of the "place" of abjection or foreclosure that Lacan names the Real. Jacques Lacan, *The Seminar of Jacques Lacan, Book III: The Psychoses, 1955–1956,* trans. Russell Grigg (New York: W.W. Norton, 1993).

37. Lacan's first essay of the postwar period, "Aggressivity in Psychoanalysis" (1948), diagnoses this loss and its attendant subjective effects by situating the patient's aggressive projections onto the analyst in a context of global colonial predation, Paris in ruins, and the accumulation of capital in the metropole (Lacan, *Écrits*).

38. Lacan, *Seminar I,* 198. In this argument we see Lacan repeating the essentials of Freud's recourse to the analogy between primitive societies and modern neurosis from *Totem and Taboo.* The desire to find in Mediterranean cultures, especially Arabic and Islamic societies, the most "archaic" form of oedipal masculinity and heterosexual norms is not an isolated feature setting apart Lacan or Lacanianism from anthropology or political science. For an example of this analytic fantasy at work in a project that straddles anthropol-

ogy, sociology, and social theory and which claims to critique the "mythic overdetermination" of psychoanalysis, see Pierre Bourdieu, *Outline of a Theory of Practice,* trans. Richard Nice (Cambridge: Cambridge University Press, 1990), 92. For the critique of Bourdieu's orientalism that cogently points out his inability to perceive the hand of French colonial manipulation at work in Kabylian family structures, see Marnia Lazreg, *The Eloquence of Silence: Algerian Women in Question* (New York: Routledge, 1994).

39. Jacques Derrida's *Of Grammatology,* trans. Gayatri Chakravorty Spivak (Baltimore, Md.: Johns Hopkins University Press, 1976), makes the withering critique of this gesture in Levi-Strauss, in which the imputation of simple literalism to the writing of the primitive allows the anthropologist to claim writing "as such" for the West. Thus the word of the other is always already only the literal letter of the law severed from its spirit, and for this reason forever caught in a metaphysics that assigns to the absence of writing the status of foreclosed inscription.

40. Lacan, *Seminar II,* 127.

41. The failure to write in French might also be a way of warding off an evil, for the hand, in the symbolic register of the patient, is also a totem. Unfortunately Lacan, knowing no Arabic, cannot explore the possible significance of words pertaining to writer's cramp. A classical Arabic translation of "writer's cramp," and by no means the only one, *'uqqaal al-kaatib* leads to a semantic matrix including notions of consciousness, judgment, and intelligence but also to literal meanings, for instance, "to hobble a camel using a knot or cord," which has a pre-Islamic provenance. The root is, additionally, the source for the Arabic word for concentration camp. A host of meanings circling round judgment and trauma could be condensed into the symptom of writer's cramp—and this only from one of the patient's languages. Further, the words *la main,* or hand, sound like a redundant statement of "no, not" in Arabic. The possibilities are endless, but Lacan never justifies his interpretive choices by giving more details of the patient's history; rather, he is content to make the ethnocentric error of literalizing the word and the "law" of the other as merely the letter of the law.

42. Lacan, *Le Séminaire, livre II,* 158. "What I am telling you has the air of being a bit of an apologue/fable."

43. For a discussion of the Orient as spectacle imbued with Romantic exoticism, see Edward Said, *Orientalism* (New York: Vintage Books, 1979), 158.

44. Bataille will insist that primitive cave paintings attest to the drive for alteration or "self-mutilation" analogous to representations of the law as described by Lacan; the theory of art as an assault on "form" where the object seeks to stage its difference from what comes before—tradition—overturns the simple understanding of primitive art as unmediated ludic human expression. Whereas foreclosure can describe for Lacan a pathological form of resistance and rebellion, for Bataille alteration names the transgression that attests, in its negative form, to the existence of taboo and the important place or function of transgression of societal taboo, especially in ritualized and collective forms of transgression. The negotiation with Bataille's *La Part maudite* underway in Lacan's early seminars of the 1950s and again, obliquely and without mention-

ing Bataille, in the 1963 essay "Kant avec Sade," penned the year of Bataille's death, deserves its own investigation. For a discussion of Bataille, Lascaux, and the function of plastic arts, see Rosalind E. Kraus, *The Originality of the Avant-Garde and Other Modernist Myths* (Cambridge, Mass.: MIT Press, 1996).

45. See Said, *Orientalism*, especially chapter 4.

46. Abdallah Laroui, *La crise des intellectuels arabes: traditionalisme ou historicisme?* (Paris: Librairie François Maspero, 1974).

47. Under French rule the teaching of Arabic was systematically undermined in Algeria. In Tunisia and Morocco Islamic schools were allowed to operate, but French dominated as the language of colonial administration, becoming that of commerce and advanced education as well. Speaking French was clearly one medium of class advancement under colonial rule. In the postcolonial era national governments and the proponents of national culture have enforced policies of Arabization to redress the cultural harms of colonialism and have found themselves polemically opposed by an intellectual and political strain of Francophones advocating a neocultural synthesis that speaks only French. Significantly, neither camp took up as a serious cultural or national project the practical bi- and multilingualism of the international and national scenes in the 1960s, and this held true for Algeria and Tunisia. Instead, in Algeria a de facto divorce of the two languages came to represent a division between the language of technical modernity, French, and that of prayer and poetry, Arabic, a division legitimated by its repetition in the university. Complicating the picture even more is the history of French colonial manipulation of regional and ethnic differences into a fully blown modern racism, that of an imagined racial difference between Arab and Berber. For a detailed history of this colonial tool, see Patricia M. E. Lorcin, *Imperial Identities: Stereotyping, Prejudice and Race in Colonial Algeria* (London: I. B. Tauris & Co., 1995). Against a popular conceit of American Francophone studies that in many ways repeats the "Kabylian myth," it is interesting to note that in the important Algerian student demonstrations of the 1970s this linguistic hegemony was contested by the reiteration of three linked demands: freedom of speech; teaching of dialects, including Berber, at the university level; and generalization of Arabic, with the intention of opening the technical fields to the Arabophone citizens. In Algeria since at least 1976, Arabization has become entangled with efforts to affirm Islam as the state religion, efforts that have at times been in tension with the resurgent interest in the Berber patrimony of the entire Maghreb. In the American academy, but not only there, this fact is all too often exaggerated into a transhistorical and irreducible ethnic hostility between the repressive forces of the allegedly unredeemable Arabizing Islamist and the democratic impulses of the modern Berber. For a serious consideration of the role of the Algerian bureaucratic bourgeoisie in the manipulation of the state apparatus and the impetus toward fundamentalism, both Islamist and Berber, in the period before the Algerian civil war of the 1990s, see Rachid Tlemcani, *State and Revolution in Algeria* (London: Zed Books, 1986).

48. *Greffe*: notary, graft, transplant; sounds like *griffe*/claw.

49. *Tranchante frappe:* strike, stamp, typeface, impression. *Trancher:* judicial decision.

50. *Libération,* 1985, cited in Scharfman, "Thanatography."

51. "Return to wordless themes: body, ecstasy, death, desert; so many inexpressibles to transform [into] moments of speech passing through the language of metaphor, rendering them ancient to oneself, age-old."

52. Meddeb, *Talismano.*

53. Frantz Fanon, *The Wretched of the Earth* (New York: Grove Press, 2005). See especially chapter 4, "On National Culture."

54. *Calligraphesis* is my neologism for the practice of a figural rendering that contains within it both the specificity of meaning and the excess of its own staging. As *calligraphy* refers exclusively to the technique of ornamental writing, I distinguish the novel's transgraphing techniques with the term *calligraphesis.* This coinage takes its bearings from *Talismano's* long meditations on calligraphy, the use of calligraphy as a figure for the relation of egoic self-knowledge to the unconscious, and the formal technique of manipulating French grammatical and syntactic forms to the point of incomprehensibility. Calligraphesis is very close to what the novel names "allography," with the difference that allographic writing (allographesis) is bound within a network of textual tracks analogous to a vast transportation system that the novel calls the "networks of travel." One might think of the difference between calligraphesis and allography as that between a motion or operation and the genealogy of the many operations that constitute the distinctive path or identity of a particular passage. Essentially the difference between a practice of representing kinship and performatively materializing the attenuations of kinship as it changes through time and within the specific track of its own locale, calligraphesis and allography are both practices of transgraphing; the key difference lies in temporal orientation. In this sense, allography holds out the hope for a singular identity that might escape the fixity of the grid's standardized identity. If calligraphesis is akin to a resurgence of an older technology capable of critique and invention, allography is that hybrid partaking of both the grid and the spiral, a network of writing otherwise oriented toward a future. To recast these definitions within the aesthetic strategies of ranting, one might say that calligraphesis responds strategically to the dialectic of abjection by reusing the archaic against the instrumental reason of state narratives. In this sense, the ranting response to postcolonial enlightenment is limited to a well-known, though still viable, avant-garde strategy of resistance. But *Talismano* goes further than this into the temporal complexity of postcolonial resistance by insisting on allography, even as a dead and haunting form, as a means of reimagining alternative futures. Neither the transcendental critique of an outsider's indictment nor the immanent critique that might refuse history's monstrous inscriptions, ranting as performed by this novel becomes a poetics of continual address in a landscape saturated by the haunting absence of a public sphere.

55. Brinkley Messick, *The Calligraphic State: Textual Domination and History in a Muslim Society* (Berkeley: University of California Press, 1993). Hereafter cited as *CS.*

56. "The revealed whole, believe it or not, of the talisman, words and images surrendered to the Nubian who commissioned them, without myself knowing what they meant."

57. "I know you are not schooled in the magical arts, but I am sure that in this situation you have what it takes; without this intuition I would not have asked you for a thing. . . . I want this place restored to its former peace."

58. Rachid Boudjedra, Driss Chraibi, Tahar Djaout, and Assia Djebar are a few authors not treated here whose texts take up this theme.

59. Sigmund Freud, *Totem and Taboo: Some Points of Agreement between the Mental Lives of Savages and Neurotics,* trans. James Strachey (New York: W. W. Norton and Company, 1989).

60. Michel Foucault, *Discipline and Punish: The Birth of the Prison,* trans. Alan Sheridan (New York: Vintage, 1979).

61. *Pharmakon,* a term invoked by Messick, refers to the analysis of the metaphysics of writing found in Jacques Derrida's *Dissemination,* trans. Barbara Johnson (Chicago: University of Chicago Press, 1981), whereby writing is held to be both a cure for the loss of meaning and a poison that threatens the presence of truth or meaning through the unmasterable effects of interpretation and repetition.

62. Messick gives examples of spiral texts and other practices of signature linked to the older writing system, which date from the nineteenth century through the 1950s. He uses examples from the 1970s to demonstrate the abstraction of the grid form and the system of authorization to which it attests.

63. Abdelkebir Khatibi, *La blessure du nom propre* (Paris: Éditions Denoël, 1986); *L'art calligraphique arabe* (Paris: Chêne, 1976); and *Maghreb Pluriel.*

64. "I am not stretching things if I say my writing comes down [to storytelling], describing in another language the delirium of a city. . . . This tongue which lends me a body that I stamp with the seal of possession, this tongue to symbolize a metropolis."

65. Abdelkebir Khatibi, *La mémoire tatouée: Autobiographie d'un décolonisé* (Paris: Les Lettres nouvelles, 1971).

66. Tahar Djaout, "Quelques os, quelques ors," *Algérie-Actualité,* no. 1161, January 14–20, 1988; and Abdelwahab Meddeb, "Bistami est un aventurien de l'être," interview by Tahar Djaout, *Algérie-Actualité,* no. 1264, January 4–10, 1990.

67. Ronnie Scharfman, "Thanatography." Scharfman's essay and chapter 5 of Khatibi's *Maghreb Pluriel* are the significant critical approaches to Meddeb's novel to date. Both argue for the essentially transgressive and boldly subversive character of the text without considering the novel's explicit concern with nationalism and kinship.

68. "Our recent history, both personal and national, is inscribed between power and the letter. If this wound conveys an all-too blinding present, at the same time it masks the immense difficulty of thinking the concept of history." Khatibi, *La blessure,* 199.

69. "The calligraphic trace plays itself out in an interstitial space like a sacred festival of the sign. Far from being a simple graphic supplement added

to speech, the calligraphic trace is a composition interior to the text, a crystalline product of the linguistic body itself." Ibid., 20.

70. Though more appropriately indicating a spa-like treatment or therapy involving speech, "la cure du dire" plays on the phrase "talking cure," and by involving a more corporal reference again insists the body into the writing.

71. "In such an 'I,' unruly thoughts—in other words whose negativity allows for no betterment—must be weeded out; the talking cure calls upon you not to accept yourself as such but to acknowledge yourself an enigma irreducible to meaning, to the law, to proportion; the 'I' connects himself to history: these years that filled my birth, my origin, my childhood extend to the shaky foundations of a moribund class to be betrayed; 'I,' representative of an Arab generation that must contend with a cracked image, marked monstrous by Europe and France, must live the experience of exile, . . . must correct its social body through a backward approach."

72. Here and throughout the following discussion, I revert to the "self" as the name for that object/text drawn, entangled, illuminated, and obscured by the calligraphic conceit when it takes the *je* as its topic. The "self" in *Talismano* is an operation and ought not to be read as a retreat from psychoanalytic complexity or as the reassertion of a sovereign writing subject. In the vocabulary of subjection we might say that the self thus transcribed is a process of subjectivation without outcome; hence, the insistence of Meddeb's text on writing as a "reflection of bodily disorder rather than primordial law" (*T,* 50). Implicit in such a retranslation of "self" into the language of subjection is the aim, evident in the novel, to capitalize on the metaphoricity of kinship without falling back into a politics of the subject.

73. Meddeb uses the term *Hallajian motto,* where *Hallajian* refers to the first-century C.E. Sufi poet al-Hallaj, to describe a chanted phrase repeated until the participants achieve an exalted state of mind. Here, the Sufi calligraphers chant the motto without the name of god.

74. Khatibi, *Maghreb Pluriel,* chapter 5. Notice especially that "allah" reappears as "allo" in allographesis.

75. "Those who Islamicized themselves calligraph . . . or dissolve the meaning of writing in the calligrapher's ample and rapturous gesture. . . . And writing becomes monumental loss of meaning." (The term *s'islamisèrent* is a double pun in French and Arabic, for one hears both "to submit" and "la misère.")

76. Moustapha Safouan suggests that secularity ought to be thought not as the prohibition of religious tradition but as the fostering of culture in the "mode of creative transmission, [as] those movements of thought in which a whole people is implicated and divided into differing tendencies." "Two Modes of Transmission: Creative and Fixed," *Critical Quarterly* 36, no. 2 (1996): 2–12. Calligraphesis may be one instance of such a creative transmission; however, as Safouan's formulation indicates, secularity becomes such by being disseminated in a collective scene. The limit of *Talismano*'s powerful rescripting of the self and the social is kinship itself.

77. In the passages devoted to calligraphic writing and its challenge to

meaning—passages that invoke the name of god only to erase it—the postcolonial city grid is understood as a spatial enactment of foreclosure because the unlicensed mysticism that takes place happens within the confines of the casbah.

78. Scharfman, "Thanatography."

79. "The national warrant that legitimizes a political logic subservient to so-called universal norms of power!"

80. "To surrender ourselves in writing without giving you purchase, to tire your eyes with an arabesque of words, to offer you the networks of travel."

Bibliography

Adorno, Theodor. *Minima Moralia: Reflections on Damaged Life*. London: Verso, 1987.
———. "Sexual Taboos and Law Today." In *Critical Models: Interventions and Catchwords,* trans. Henry Pickford. New York: Columbia University Press, 1998.
Agamben, Giorgio. *Infancy and History: Essays on the Destruction of Experience*. London: Verso, 1993.
Al-Azmeh, Aziz. *Islams and Modernities*. London: Verso, 1993.
Al-Kassim, Dina. "Epilogue." In *Islamicate Sexualities,* ed. Afsaneh Najmabadi and Kathryn Babayan. Cambridge, Mass.: Harvard University Press, 2008.
Althusser, Louis. "Freud and Lacan." In *Lenin and Philosophy and Other Essays*. New York: Monthly Review Press, 1971.
———. "Ideology and Ideological State Apparatuses (Notes Towards an Investigation)." In *Lenin and Philosophy and Other Essays*. New York: Monthly Review Press, 1971.
Althusser, Louis, and Etienne Balibar. *Reading Capital*. London: Verso, 1979.
Amin, Samir. *Eurocentrism*. New York: Monthly Review Press, 1989.
Apter, Emily. *Feminizing the Fetish: Psychoanalysis and Narrative Obsession in Turn-of-the-Century France*. Ithaca, NY: Cornell University Press, 1991.
Apter, Emily, and William Pietz, eds. *Fetishism as Cultural Discourse*. Ithaca, NY: Cornell University Press, 1993.
Aresu, Bernard. *Counterhegemonic Discourse from the Maghreb: The Poetics of Kateb's Fiction*. Tübingen: G. Narr, 1993.
Balibar, Etienne, with Immanuel Wallerstein. *Race, Nation, Class: Ambiguous Identities*. London: Verso, 1991.
Banton, Michael. *Racial Theories*. Cambridge: Cambridge University Press, 1987.

Barakat, Huda. *The Stone of Laughter.* London: Interlink, 1998.
Bartlett, Neil. *Who Was That Man: A Present for Mr. Oscar Wilde.* London: Serpent's Tail, 1988.
Bataille, Georges. *The Accursed Share, Vols. 2 and 3: The History of Eroticism and Sovereignty.* New York: Zone Press, 1993.
———. *Le Bleu du ciel.* Paris: Gallimard, 1979.
———. *L'Expérience intérieure.* Paris: Gallimard, 1943, 1954.
———. *Inner Experience,* trans. Leslie A. Boldt. New York: SUNY Press, 1988.
———. *La Part maudite.* Paris: Les Éditions de Minuit, 1967.
———. *Visions of Excess: Selected Writings 1927–1939,* ed. Allan Stoekl. Minneapolis: University of Minnesota Press, 1985.
Benjamin, Walter. "Some Motifs in Baudelaire." In *Charles Baudelaire: A Lyric Poet in the Era of High Capitalism,* trans. Harry Zohn. London: Verso, 1983.
Benstock, Shari. *Women of the Left Bank: Paris, 1900–1940.* Austin: University of Texas Press, 1986.
Bernheimer, Charles. *Decadent Subjects: The Idea of Decadence in Art, Literature, Philosophy, and Culture of the Fin de Siècle in Europe.* Baltimore, Md.: Johns Hopkins University Press, 2002.
Bhabha, Homi. *The Location of Culture.* New York: Routledge, 1994.
Blanchot, Maurice. *The Book to Come,* trans. Charlotte Mandell. Stanford, Calif.: Stanford University Press, 2003.
Bouhdiba, Abdelwahab. *Sexuality in Islam.* London: Routledge, 1985.
Bourdieu, Pierre. *Outline of a Theory of Practice,* trans. Richard Nice. Cambridge: Cambridge University Press, 1990.
Bowlby, Rachel. *Shopping With Freud.* London: Routledge, 1993.
Bowles, Jane. *Two Serious Ladies,* in *My Sister's Hand in Mine.* New York: Ecco Press, 1978.
Bowles, Paul. *Paul Bowles Photographs: "How Could I Send a Picture into the Desert?"* ed. Simon Bischoff in collaboration with the Swiss Foundation for Photography. New York: Scalo Publishers, 1994.
Braithwaite, Edward Kamau. *The Arrivants: A New World Trilogy—Rights of Passage; Islands; Masks.* Oxford: Oxford University Press, 1973.
Brennan, Teresa. *The Transmission of Affect.* Ithaca, NY: Cornell University Press, 2004.
Bristow, Joseph. "Dorian Gray and Gross Indecency." In *Sexual Sameness: Textual Differences in Lesbian and Gay Writing.* London: Routledge, 1992.
———. *Effeminate England: Homoerotic Writing after 1885.* New York: Columbia University Press, 1995.
Brown, L. C., ed. *From Madina to Metropolis.* Princeton, NJ: Darwin Press, 1973.
Brown, Nicholas. *Utopian Generations: The Political Horizon of Twentieth-Century Literature.* Princeton, NJ: Princeton University Press, 2005.
Burgin, Victor, James Donald, and Cora Kaplan, eds. *Formations of Fantasy.* London: Routledge, 1989.

Burns, Edward, ed. *Staying on Alone: Letters of Alice B. Toklas.* New York: Liveright, 1973.
Butler, Judith. "Afterword" to *The Scandal of the Speaking Body: Don Juan with J.L. Austin, or Seduction in Two Languages,* by Shoshana Felman. Stanford, Calif.: Stanford University Press, 2003.
———. *Antigone's Claim: Kinship Between Life and Death.* New York: Columbia University Press, 2000.
———. "Bodies and Power Revisited." In *Feminism and the Final Foucault,* ed. Dianna Taylor and Karen Vintges. Urbana: University of Illinois Press, 2004.
———. *Bodies That Matter.* New York: Routledge, 1993.
———. *Excitable Speech.* New York: Routledge, 1997.
———. *Gender Trouble.* New York: Routledge, 1990.
———. *The Psychic Life of Power: Theories in Subjection.* Stanford, Calif.: Stanford University Press, 1997.
———. *Undoing Gender.* New York: Routledge, 2004.
Bynum, Caroline Walker. *Jesus as Mother: Studies in the Spirituality of the High Middle Ages.* Berkeley: University of California Press, 1984.
Calinescu, Matei. *Five Faces of Modernity: Modernism, Avant-Garde, Decadence, Kitsch and Postmodernism.* Durham, NC: Duke University Press, 1987.
Canguilhem, George. *On the Normal and the Pathological.* Boston: D. Reidel, 1978.
Case, Sue-Ellen. "Toward a Butch-Femme Aesthetic." In *The Lesbian and Gay Studies Reader,* ed. Henry Abelove, Michele Aina Barale, and David M. Halperin. New York: Routledge, 1993.
Césaire, Aimé. *Discourse on Colonialism,* trans. Joan Pinkham. New York: Monthly Review Press, 2000.
———. *Notebook of a Return to the Native Land,* trans. and ed. Clayton Eshleman and Annette Smith. Middletown, Conn.: Wesleyan University Press, 2001.
———. *Une Tempête: D'après "La Tempête" de Shakespeare: Adaptation pour un théâtre nègre.* Paris: Seuil, 1969.
Chebel, Malek. *L'esprit de sérail.* Paris: Petite Bibliothèque Payot, 1995.
Cheng, Vincent. *Joyce, Race and Empire.* Cambridge: Cambridge University Press, 1995.
Chester, Alfred. "Glory Hole: Nickel Views of the Infidel in Tangiers." In *Head of a Sad Angel: Stories, 1953–1966.* Santa Rosa, Calif.: Black Sparrow, 1990.
Civantos, Christina. "Literacy, Sexuality, and the Literary in the Self-Inscription of Muammad Shukri." *Middle Eastern Literatures* 9, no. 1 (2006): 23–45.
Cohen, Ed. *Talk on the Wilde Side: Towards a Genealogy of the Discourse on Male Homosexuality.* London: Routledge, 1992.
Collins, Marjorie, and Christine Pierce. "Holes and Slime: Sexism in Sartre's Psychoanalysis." In *Women and Philosophy: Toward a Theory of Liberation,* ed. C. Gould and M. Wartofsky. New York: Putnam, 1976.

Crawford, Robert. *Devolving English*. Edinburgh: Edinburgh University Press, 2001.
Crompton, Louis. *Byron and Greek Love*. Berkeley: University of California Press, 1985.
Culbert, John. Paralyses: *Literature, Travel, and Ethnography in French Modernity*. Lincoln: University of Nebraska Press, 2010.
Curran, J. "Rethinking the Media as a Public Sphere." In *Communication and Citizenship*, ed. P. Dahlgren and C. Sparks. London: Routledge, 1991.
Curtis, L. P. *Anglo-Saxons and Celts: A Study of Anti-Irish Prejudice in Victorian England*. Bridgeport, Conn.: University of Bridgeport, 1968.
———. *Apes and Angels: The Irishman in Victorian Caricature*. Washington, DC: Smithsonian Institution Press, 1971.
de Certeau, Michel. *The Capture of Speech and Other Political Writings*. Minneapolis: University of Minnesota Press, 1998.
———. "An Ethics of Speech." In *Heterologies: Discourse on the Other*. Minneapolis: University of Minnesota, 1986.
de Man, Paul. "Semiology and Rhetoric." In *Allegories of Reading: Figural Language in Rousseau, Nietzsche, Rilke, and Proust*. New Haven, Conn.: Yale University Press, 1979.
Dellamora, Richard. *Apocalyptic Overtures: Sexual Politics and the Sense of an Ending*. New Brunswick, NJ: Rutgers University Press, 1994.
Derrida, Jacques. *Dissemination*, trans. Barbara Johnson. Chicago: University of Chicago Press, 1981.
———. *Of Grammatology*, trans. Gayatri Chakravorty Spivak. Baltimore, Md.: Johns Hopkins University Press, 1976.
———. "Signature, Event, Context." In *Margins of Philosophy*, trans. Alan Bass. Chicago: University of Chicago Press, 1985.
Dillon, Millicent. *A Little Original Sin: The Life and Work of Jane Bowles*. New York: Holt, Rinehart and Winston, 1981.
———, ed. *Out in the World: Selected Letters of Jane Bowles 1935–70*. Santa Rosa, Calif.: Black Sparrow Press, 1985.
Djaout, Tahar. "Quelques os, quelques ors." *Algérie-Actualité*, no. 1161, January 14–20, 1988.
Djebar, Assia. *Le blanc de l'Algérie*. Paris: Éditions Albin Michel S.A., 1995.
———. *Fantasia: An Algerian Cavalcade*. Portsmouth, NH: Heinneman, 1993.
Dollimore, Jonathan. *Sexual Dissidence*. Oxford: Oxford University Press, 1991.
Dowling, Linda. *Hellenism and Homosexuality in Victorian Oxford*. Ithaca, NY: Cornell University Press, 1994.
Doyle, Laura, and Laura Winkiel, eds. *Geomodernisms: Race, Modernism, Modernity*. Bloomington: Indiana University Press, 2005.
Duberman, Martin Bauml, Martha Vicinus, and George Chauncey Jr., eds. *Hidden from History: Reclaiming the Gay and Lesbian Past*. New York: New American Library, 1989.
Ellmann, Richard. *Oscar Wilde*. New York: Random House, 1987.
Faderman, Lillian. "Butches, Femmes and Kiki's." In *Odd Girls and Twilight*

Lovers: A History of Lesbian Life in Twentieth-Century America. New York: Penguin, 1991.

Fanon, Frantz. *Black Skin, White Masks.* New York: Grove Press, 1967.

———. *The Wretched of the Earth.* New York: Grove Press, 2004.

Farred, Grant. *What's My Name? Black Vernacular Intellectuals.* Minneapolis: University of Minnesota Press, 2003.

———, ed. *Rethinking C.L.R. James: A Critical Reader.* London: Blackwell Publications, 1995.

Felman, Shoshana. *The Scandal of the Speaking Body: Don Juan with J. L. Austin, or Seduction in Two Languages.* Stanford, Calif.: Stanford University Press, 2003.

Foldy, Michael S. *The Trials of Oscar Wilde: Deviance, Morality and Late-Victorian Society.* New Haven, Conn.: Yale University Press, 1997.

Ford, Charles Henry, and Parker Tyler. *View: Parade of the Avant-garde: An Anthology of View Magazine (1940–1947).* New York: Thunder's Mouth Press, 1992.

Foucault, Michel. *Discipline and Punish: The Birth of the Prison,* trans. Alan Sheridan. New York: Vintage, 1979.

———. *Fearless Speech,* ed. Joseph Pearson. New York: Semiotext(e), 2001.

———. "Genealogy of Ethics: An Overview of a Work in Progress." In *Ethics: Subjectivity and Truth (Essential Works of Foucault, 1954–1982, Vol. I).* New York: New Press, 2006.

———. *The Hermeneutics of the Subject: Lectures at the Collège de France, 1981–1982,* ed. Frédéric Gros, trans. Graham Burchell. New York: Palgrave Macmillan, 2005.

———. *History of Sexuality, Volume 1: An Introduction,* trans. Robert Hurley. New York: Vintage, 1990.

———. *Les Mots et les choses.* Paris: Gallimard, 1966.

———. *Politics, Philosophy, Culture: Interviews and Other Writings, 1977–1984,* ed. and intro by Lawrence Kritzman. New York: Routledge, 1988.

———. "Preface to Transgression." In *Language, Counter-Memory, Practice.* Ithaca, NY: Cornell University Press, 1980.

———. *Psychiatric Power: Lectures at the Collège de France, 1973–74.* New York: Palgrave Macmillan, 2006.

———. *Society Must Be Defended: Lectures at the Collège de France, 1975–1976.* New York: Palgrave Macmillan, 2003.

———. "The Subject of Power." In *Power: Essential Works of Foucault, 1954–1984, Volume III,* ed. Robert Hurley, James D. Faubion, and Paul Rabinow. New York: New Press, 2001.

———. "What Is Critique?" In *The Politics of Truth,* ed. Sylvère Lotringer and Lysa Hochroth, trans. Lysa Hochroth, transcript by Monique Emery, revised by Suzanne Delorme et al. New York: Semiotext(e), 1997.

Fraser, Nancy. "Rethinking the Public Sphere: A Contribution to the Critique of Actually Existing Democracy." *Social Text* 25/26 (1990).

———. *Unruly Practices: Power, Discourse, and Gender in Contemporary Social Theory.* Minneapolis: University of Minnesota Press, 1989.

Freitag, George H. "Fine First Novel Probes Deep into the Human Mind"

Review of *Two Serious Ladies,* by Jane Bowles. *Book Week,* May 16, 1943: 3.
Freud, Sigmund. *Character and Culture.* New York: Macmillan, 1963.
——. *Civilization and Its Discontents.* New York: W.W. Norton, 1989.
——. *Ego and the Id.* New York: W.W. Norton, 1960.
——. *Group Psychology and the Analysis of the Ego.* New York: W.W. Norton, 1990.
——. *The Interpretation of Dreams.* London: Penguin Books, 1995.
——. *Jokes and Their Relation to the Unconscious.* London: Penguin Books, 1976.
——. "Mourning and Melancholia." In *General Psychological Theory.* New York: W.W. Norton, 1991.
——. "On Narcissism: An Introduction" (1914). In *General Psychological Theory.* New York: Macmillan, 1963.
——. "On the Mechanism of Paranoia" (1911). In *General Psychological Theory.* New York: Macmillan, 1963.
——. "Reflections on War and Death." In *Character and Culture.* New York: Collier Books, 1963.
——. "The Sexual Enlightenment of Children." In *The Sexual Enlightenment of Children.* New York: Collier Books, 1963.
——. *Three Essays on the Theory of Sexuality.* New York: Perseus Books, 2000.
——. *Totem and Taboo: Some Points of Agreement between the Mental Lives of Savages and Neurotics,* trans. James Strachey. New York: W.W. Norton, 1989.
Gautier, Théophile. *Mademoiselle de Maupin.* New York: Penguin Classics, 2006.
Genet, Jean. *The Declared Enemy,* trans. Jeff Fort. Stanford, Calif.: Stanford University Press, 2004.
——. *Journal du voleur.* Paris: Gallimard, 1949.
——. *Oeuvres complètes,* vol. 5. Paris: Gallimard, 1951.
Gilman, Richard. *Decadence: The Strange Life of an Epithet.* New York: Farrar, Straus & Giroux, 1980.
Goldberg, David Theo. *The Racial State.* London: Blackwell, 2001.
Habermas, Jürgen. *The Philosophical Discourse of Modernity: Twelve Lectures,* trans. Frederick G. Lawrence. Cambridge, Mass.: MIT Press, 1987.
——. "The Public Sphere: An Encyclopedia Article." *New German Critique* 1, no. 3 (1974): 49–55.
——. *Theory of Communicative Action,* vol. 2. Boston: Beacon Press, 1985.
Hewitt, Andrew. *Fascist Modernism: Aesthetics, Politics and the Avant-Garde.* Stanford, Calif.: Stanford University Press, 1993.
——. *Political Inversions: Homosexuality, Fascism and the Modernist Imaginary.* Stanford, Calif.: Stanford University Press, 1996.
Huxley, T.H. *Evolution and Ethics: T.H. Huxley's Evolution and Ethics with New Essays on Its Victorian and Sociobiological Content,* ed. James Paradis and George C. Williams. Princeton, NJ: Princeton University Press, 1989.

Huysmans, Joris-Karl. *A Rebours*. London: Penguin Classics, 2004.
James, C. L. R. *Mariners, Renegades and Castaways: The Story of Herman Melville and the World We Live In*. Intro by Donald Pease. Hanover, NH: University Press of New England, 2001.
Kelley, Robin D. G. "A Poetics of Anticolonialism." In *Discourse on Colonialism*, trans. Joan Pinkham. New York: Monthly Review Press, 2000.
Khatibi, Abdelkebir. *L'art calligraphique arabe*. Paris: Chêne, 1976.
———. *La blessure du nom propre*. Paris: Éditions Denoël, 1986.
———. *Maghreb Pluriel*. Paris: Éditions Denoël, 1983.
———. *La mémoire tatouée: Autobiographie d'un décolonisé*. Paris: Les Lettres nouvelles, 1971.
Kraus, Rosalind E. *The Originality of the Avant-Garde and Other Modernist Myths*. Cambridge, Mass.: MIT Press, 1996.
Kristeva, Julia. *Powers of Horror: An Essay on Abjection*. New York: Columbia University Press, 1982.
Lacan, Jacques. "Aggressivity in Psychoanalysis." In *Écrits: A Selection*, trans. Alan Sheridan. New York: W. W. Norton, 1977.
———. *L'Éthique de la psychanalyse, 1959–1960*. Paris: Les Éditions du Seuil, 1986.
———. *The Four Fundamental Concepts of Psycho-analysis*, ed. Jacques-Alain Miller, trans. Alan Sheridan. London: Hogarth Press, 1977.
———. *Le Séminaire, livre II: Le moi dans la théorie de Freud et dans la technique de la psychanalyse*. Paris: Seuil, 1978.
———. *Seminar I: Freud's Papers on Technique, 1953–1954*. New York: W. W. Norton, 1991.
———. *The Seminar of Jacques Lacan, Book II: The Ego in Freud's Theory and in the Technique of Psychoanalysis 1954–55*, trans. Sylvana Tomaselli, ed. Jacques-Alain Miller, with notes by John Forrester. New York: W. W. Norton, 1991.
———. *The Seminar of Jacques Lacan, Book III: The Psychoses, 1955–1956*, trans. Russell Grigg. New York: W. W. Norton, 1993.
———. *The Seminar of Jacques Lacan, Book VII: The Ethics of Psychoanalysis, 1959–1960*. New York: W. W. Norton, 1992.
Lacoue-Labarthe, Philippe. *The Subject of Philosophy*. Minneapolis: University of Minnesota Press, 1993.
Laity, Cassandra. "Editor's Introduction." *Modernism/Modernities* 15, no. 3 (September 2008): 427–30.
Laplanche, Jean. *Life and Death in Psychoanalysis*. Baltimore, Md.: Johns Hopkins University Press, 1970.
———. *New Foundations for Psychoanalysis*. London: Blackwell, 1989.
———. "To Situate Sublimation." *October* 28 (1984): 23–30.
Laplanche, Jean, and J. B. Pontalis. *The Language of Psycho-Analysis*, trans. Donald Nicholson-Smith. New York: W. W. Norton, 1974.
Laroui, Abdallah. *La crise des intellectuels arabes: traditionalisme ou historicisme?* Paris: Librairie François Maspero, 1974.
Lazreg, Marnia. *The Eloquence of Silence: Algerian Women in Question*. New York: Routledge, 1994.

Le Doeuff, Michele. "Operative Philosophy: Simone de Beauvoir and Existentialism." *Ideology and Consciousness* 6 (Autumn 1979): 47–57.
Lee, Jonathan Scott. *Jacques Lacan*. Amherst: University of Massachusetts Press, 1990.
Lerman, Leo. "Three Quite Different Spring Novels." Review of *Two Serious Ladies,* by Jane Bowles. *New York Herald Tribune Weekly Book Review,* April 15, 1943.
Lewis, Wyndham. *America and Cosmic Man*. Garden City, NY: Doubleday & Company, 1949.
———. *The Art of Being Ruled*. Santa Rosa, Calif.: Black Sparrow Press, 1989.
———. *Blast I*. Santa Rosa, Calif.: Black Sparrow Press, 1981.
———. *Hitler*. New York: Gordon Press, 1972.
———. *Time and Western Man,* ed. Paul Edwards. Santa Rosa, Calif.: Black Sparrow Press, 1993.
Lloyd, David. *Anomalous States: Irish Writing and the Post-Colonial Moment*. Durham, NC: Duke University Press, 1993.
———. *Nationalism and Minor Literature: James Clarence Mangan and the Emergence of Irish Cultural Nationalism*. Berkeley: University of California Press, 1987.
Lorcin, Patricia M. E. *Imperial Identities: Stereotyping, Prejudice and Race in Colonial Algeria*. London: I. B. Tauris & Co., 1995.
Lucey, Michael. *Gide's Bent: Sexuality, Politics, Writing*. New York: Oxford University Press, 1995.
Lyon, Janet. *Manifestoes: Provocations of the Modern*. Ithaca, NY: Cornell University Press, 1999.
Mannoni, Octave. *Clefs pour l'Imaginaire ou l'Autre Scène*. Paris: Éditions du Seuil, 1969.
McLuhan, Marshall. *The Gutenberg Galaxy*. Toronto: University of Toronto Press, 1962.
Meddeb, Abdelwahab. "Bistami est un aventurien de l'être." Interview by Tahar Djaout in *Algérie-Actualité,* no. 1264, January 4–10, 1990.
———. *Talismano*. Paris: La Bibliothèque Arabe Sindbad, 1987.
Messick, Brinkley. *The Calligraphic State: Textual Domination and History in a Muslim Society*. Berkeley: University of California Press, 1993.
Miller, Tyrus. *Late Modernism: Politics, Fiction and the Arts between the World Wars*. Berkeley: University of California Press, 1999.
Moreh, Shmuel. *Modern Arabic Poetry 1800–1970: The Development of Its Forms and Themes under the Influence of Western Literature*. Leiden: E. J. Brill, 1976.
Nicholls, Peter. *Modernisms*. Berkeley: University of California Press, 1995.
Newton, Esther. "The Mythic Mannish Lesbian: Radclyffe Hall and the New Woman." In *Hidden from History: Reclaiming Gay and Lesbian Past,* ed. Martin Bauml Duberman, Martha Vicinus, and George Chancey Jr. New York: NAL Books, 1989.
Pandolfo, Stefania. "Rapt de la voix." *Awal: Cahiers d'études Berbères* 15 (1997): 31–50.
———. "The Thin Line of Modernity: Some Moroccan Debates on Moder-

nity." In *Questions of Modernity,* ed. Tim Mitchell. Minneapolis: University of Minnesota Press, 2000.
Al-Quran. trans. Ahmed Ali. Princeton, NJ: Princeton University Press, 1984.
Raitt, Susan. "Lesbian Modernism." GLQ 10, no. 1 (2003).
Retamar, Roberto Fernández. *Caliban and Other Essays,* trans. Edward Baker, foreword by Fredric Jameson. Minneapolis: University of Minnesota Press, 1989.
Robbins, Bruce, ed. *The Phantom Public Sphere.* Minneapolis: University of Minnesota Press, 1993.
Roditi, Edouard. "The Fiction of Jane Bowles as a Form of Self-Exorcism." *The Review of Contemporary Fiction* 12, no. 2 (1992): 182–94.
Rothman, N.L. "The Dream of Freedom." Review of *Two Serious Ladies,* by Jane Bowles. *Saturday Review,* May 1, 1943: 20.
Roudinesco, Elisabeth. *Jacques Lacan and Co.: A History of Psychoanalysis in France, 1925–1985,* trans. Jeffrey Mehlman. Chicago: University of Chicago Press, 1990.
Rubin, Gayle. "Thinking Sex: Notes for a Radical Theory of the Politics of Sexuality." In *The Lesbian and Gay Studies Reader,* ed. Henry Abelove, Michele Barale, and David Halperin. New York: Routledge, 1993.
Ruedy, John. *Modern Algeria: The Origins and Development of a Nation.* Bloomington: Indiana University Press, 1992.
Safouan, Moustapha. "Two Modes of Transmission: Creative and Fixed." *Critical Quarterly* 36, no. 2 (1996): 2–12.
Said, Edward. *Culture and Imperialism.* New York: Vintage, 1994.
———. *Orientalism.* New York: Vintage Books, 1979.
Sartre, Jean-Paul. *Being and Nothingness: An Essay on Phenomenological Ontology.* London: Routledge Classics, 2003.
Sedgwick, Eve. "Some Binarisms (II): Wilde, Nietzsche, and the Sentimental Relations of the Male Body." In *Epistemology of the Closet.* Berkeley: University of California Press, 1990.
Senghor, Léopold Sédar, and Jean-Paul Sartre. *Anthologie de la nouvelle poésie nègre et malgache de langue française; précedée de Orphée Noir par Jean-Paul Sartre.* Paris: Presses Univérsitaire de France, 1948.
Scannell, P. "Public Service Broadcasting and the Modern Public Life." *Media, Culture & Society* 11, no. 2 (1989).
Scham, Alan. *Lyautey in Morocco: Protectorate Administration, 1912–25.* Berkeley: University of California Press, 1970.
Scharfman, Ronnie. "Nomadism and Transcultural Writing in the Work of Abdelwahab Meddeb." *L'Esprit Createur* 41 (2001): 105–13.
———. "Thanatography: Writing and Death in Abdelwahab Meddeb's *Talismano.*" *Substance* 21, no. 3, issue 69 (1992). Special Issue: *Translations of the Orient: Writing the Maghreb.*
Schmitt, Arno, and Jehoeda Sofers, eds. *Sexuality and Eroticism among Males in Moslem Societies.* New York: Harrington Park, 1992.
Sennett, Richard. *The Fall of Public Man.* Cambridge: Cambridge University Press, 1976.

Seshadri-Crooks, Kalpana. *Desiring Whiteness: A Lacanian Analysis of Race.* New York: Routledge, 2000.
Skerl, Jennie, ed. *A Tawdry Place of Salvation: The Art of Jane Bowles.* Carbondale: Southern Illinois University Press, 1997.
Smith II, Philip E., and Michael S. Helfand. *Oscar Wilde's Oxford Notebooks: A Portrait of Mind in the Making.* New York: Oxford University Press, 1989.
Smith-Rosenberg, Carroll. "The New Woman as Androgyne: Social Disorder and Gender Crisis, 1870–1936." In *Disorderly Conduct.* New York: Oxford University Press, 1985.
Solanas, Valerie. *The S.C.U.M. Manifesto.* London: Verso, 2005.
Spivak, Gayatri Chakravorty. *Critique of Postcolonial Reason: Toward a History of the Vanishing Present.* Boston: Harvard University Press, 1999.
———. *Outside in the Teaching Machine:* New York: Routledge, 1993.
Stein, Gertrude. "The Winner Loses: A Picture of Occupied France." In *Selected Writings of Gertrude Stein,* ed. Carl Van Vechten. New York: Random House, 1962.
Steward, Samuel M., ed. *Dear Sammy: Letters from Gertrude Stein and Alice B. Toklas.* Boston: Houghton Mifflin, 1977.
Stocking Jr., George W. *Victorian Anthropology.* New York: The Free Press, 1987.
Taussig, Michael. "Maleficium: State Fetishism." In *The Nervous System.* New York: Routledge, 1992.
Taylor, Charles. "Foucault on Freedom and Truth." In *Foucault: A Critical Reader,* ed. David Couzens Hoy. Oxford: Oxford University Press, 1986.
Terdiman, Richard. *Discourse/Counter-discourse: The Theory and Practice of Symbolic Resistance in Nineteenth-Century France.* Ithaca, NY: Cornell University Press, 1985.
Tlemcani, Rachid. *State and Revolution in Algeria.* London: Zed Book, 1986.
Villa, Dana. *Politics, Philosophy, and Terror: Essays on the Thought of Hannah Arendt.* Princeton, NJ: Princeton University Press, 1999.
Wells, H. G. *The Island of Dr. Moreau.* London: Penguin, 2005.
———. *The Time-Machine.* London: Penguin, 2005.
Wilde, Oscar. *The Complete Works of Oscar Wilde.* New York: Barnes and Noble Books, 1994.
———. *The Letters of Oscar Wilde,* ed. Rupert Hart-Davis. New York: Harcourt, Brace and World, 1962.
———. *Oscar Wilde: The Artist as Critic,* ed. Richard Ellmann. Chicago: University of Chicago Press, 1982.
———. *The Picture of Dorian Gray.* London: Dent Everyman's Library, 1976.
———. *The Soul of Man and Prison Writing,* ed. Isobel Murray. Oxford: Oxford University Press, 1990.
Winkiel, Laura. *Modernism, Race and Manifestos.* Cambridge: Cambridge University Press, 2008.
Young, Robert. *White Mythologies.* London: Routledge, 1990.
Zeidan, Joseph. "Myth and Symbol in the Poetry of Adānīs and Yūsuf al-Khāl." *Journal of Arabic Literature* 10 (1979): 70–94.
Žižek, Slavoj. *The Sublime Object of Ideology.* London: Verso, 1989.

Index

Page numbers in italics indicate an illustration

abject speech, and Jane Bowles, 119–20, 149–50
ABR (*The Art of Being Ruled;* Lewis), 51, 54, 57–58
actions, and influence of art in Wilde's writing, 81–82
Adorno, Theodor, 4–5, 27, 54–55, 56, 240n60, 242n88
aestheticism, 67–69, 99–103, 105, 244n13, 244–45n14, 248–49n67, 249n69, 250n75
Agamben, Giorgio, 241–42n78
allography, and Meddeb, 210, 211, 225, 226, 228–29, 232, 267n54, 269n74
alteration, 240n60, 265–66n44
Althusser, Louis, 179–80, 246–47n36
America and Cosmic Man (Lewis), 50–51
Amin, Samir, 50
Arabic cultures: Meddeb and, 204–7; sex and love in, 165–67, 258n51
Arabic language: Bowles, Jane, and skills in speaking, 157, 161, 257–58n49; Meddeb, and writing in, 184–85, 207, 260n9, 260–61n10, 266n47
Arabic literature: application of term modernity and, 21–22, 235–37nn27–30; Meddeb and, 184–85, 260n9, 260–61n10
Arabic script, as figure for the unconscious, 178–81

"Arguing with the Real" (Butler), 189–90
art, and Wilde, 65–66, 81–82, 244n11
The Art of Being Ruled [*ABR*] (Lewis), 51, 54, 57–58
art of wit, and social critique by Wilde, 66–67, 72, 245n20
Austin, J.L., 8
avant-garde, postcolonial, 14, 23, 41, 187–88, 223, 260n7

Balibar, Etienne, 50, 55
Banton, Michael, *Racial Theories*, 115–16, 117, 251n94
Bartlett, Neil, 75–76
Bataille, Georges, 1, 17, 24, 34–35, 238nn45–46, 265–66n44
Baudelaire, Charles, 12–13
Beddoe, John, 116, 117, 251n94
Benjamin, Walter, 4, 13, 32, 228
Benstock, Shari, 138–39
Bernheimer, Charles, 64–65
bilingualism, and social analysis of Meddeb's writing, 225–26. *See also under* Arabic language; French language
biography, in fiction, 124, 148–53, 186
"Black Orpheus" (Sartre), 37
Black Skin, White Masks [*BSWM*] (Fanon), 37–39
Bowles, Jane: abject speech and, 119–20, 149–50; antithetical sense of primitivism by, 131–32; Arabic language skills

281

Bowles, Jane *(continued)*
of, 157, 161, 257–58n49; on Arabs' concept of love and sex, 165–67, 258n51; biography in fiction of, 124, 148–53; Capote on, 137–38; character, and judgment from writing of, 121, 251n2; Cherifa, and relationship with, 142, 153, 156–57, 160–68, 171–72, 258nn50–51, 259n58; childishness and adult feminine character of, 126, 134–38, 140, 142, 172, 255–56n32; children in scenes of seduction and pursuit in writing of, 129–30; child's role of Cherifa, and relationship with, 168, 170–73, 259n56; colonial narratives and, 159–60, 162, 168; desire and, 25, 128–29, 157, 163, 167–70, 173, 252n6; "Emmy Moore's Journal," 148–51; epistolary writing, and career of, 14, 25–26, 123–24, 127, 153–54, 173–74, 177; eroticism, and erotic writing of, 127–28, 157; exclusion experience and, 158–59, 168; failure, and writing of, 15–16, 25–26, 125–26, 174–76; feminine gender markers for, 139, 141–42, 256–57n38; fetishism and, 14, 157–60, 169–73, 258n54; food gendering by, 141–42, 256–57n38; foreclosure and, 122, 123, 130–32, 139, 147, 172; French language, and writing of, 152–53; "The Iron Table," 148, 151–52; isolation and, 153–56; kinship, and family life with Cherifa and, 25, 157, 163, 167–70, 173; lesbian gender norms and, 15, 25, 134–35, 139, 140, 142–43, 256n34; literary reviews for writing by, 125, 127, 253n8, 253n10, 256n34; marriage between Paul and, 133, 157; melancholic speech and, 122, 155; money used in seduction of Cherifa by, 162–64, 167, 258n50; on "Oriental" women, 157; *Out in the World*, 148, 173, 174; picturing, and writing by, 126–27, 147–48, 252n6, 252–53n7; primitivism and, 130–32, 139, 167, 168, 172; primitivist style and, 125–26, 146–47, 152, 172, 253n8; projection and, 147; on prostitution turned into kinship and family life, 25, 157, 163, 167–70, 173; psychoanalytic argument of, 15, 24, 25; racial narratives and, 14, 157–60, 162, 168, 172–73; ranterism and, 4, 14, 25–26, 121, 122, 123, 252n5; regression and, 137–40, 142, 172–73; seduction adventures of, 157, 159–60; seduction and pursuit scenes, in writing of, 127–28, 129–30, 255–56n11; self-invention, in relationship between Cherifa and, 156–57; silence and, 120, 121; social foreclosure and, 15, 25, 134–35, 139, 140, 142–43, 256n34; "A Stick of Green Candy," 126, 129, 141, 154, 256–57n38; stroke, and effects suffered by, 174–75, 259nn58–60, 259n62; *In the Summer House*, 125, 253n8, 256n34; symbolic law, in writing of, 25–26, 121, 124, 153, 173–74; Toklas, and influence on, 132–34, 135–37, 140–41, 146–47, 172, 255n19; on "Turkish" type femininity and the world picture, 148–52; *Two Serious Ladies (MS)*, 119–20, 124, 127–28, 131–32, 253n10; unruly feminine character of, 4, 126, 134, 255n19; as woman modernist writer, 122–23; women in scenes of seduction and pursuit in writing of, 127–28, 255–56n11; writing block and, 14, 25–26, 124–27, 141–42, 147–48, 153–56, 172–74, 252n6, 252–53n7; writing process and, 153, 157

Bowles, Paul: on Arabs' concept of love and sex, 257n49; on Cherifa's alleged poisoning of Jane, 259n58; marriage between Jane Bowles and, 133, 157; Toklas-Stein household and, 132, 255n24; on writing block of Jane Bowles, 141, 142, 252n6

Brennan, Teresa, 74

brotherhood bond and father-son conflict, in Wilde's writing, 84, 90–91, 106–9

BSWM (*Black Skin, White Masks*; Fanon), 37–39

Bürger, Peter, 41, 68

Butler, Judith, 1, 2–3, 7, 9, 189–90, 239n55

Caliban character in Shakespeare, and Retamar on resistant speech, 35–38, 239n53, 239–40n56

calligraphesis, and Meddeb, 211–12, 225–26, 230–32, 267n54, 269n76

The Calligraphic State [CS] (Messick), 211, 218–19

calligraphy: desacralization in Meddeb's writing and, 227–30; the embodied character in Meddeb's writing and, 224–25; as instrument of power, 222–23; Khatibi, on the embodied character and, 223–25, 268n68, 268–69n69;

Index

national consciousness in Meddeb's writing and, 224-31; as reference point for the postcolonial avant-garde, 223; the self in Meddeb's writing and, 224-31; the talking cure in Meddeb's writing and forms in, 226, 269n70
Capote, Truman, 137-38, 255n24
Celtic racial imagination narrative, and Wilde, 112, 115
censorship: Lacan on, 190-93, 261-62n18, 262nn19-20; Wilde and, 61-65, 121-22
Césaire, Aimé, 5-8, 12, 233-34n9, 234n10, 239n55
childhood, infantalism and cult of, 26-27, 51-53, 139-40, 241-42n78
childishness and adult feminine character of Jane Bowles, 126, 134-38, 140, 142, 172, 255-56n32
children, in scenes of seduction and pursuit in writing of Jane Bowles, 129-30
Chraibi, Driss, 20, 21, 237n30
Christ, Wilde on the queer, 94-96, 100-101
class miscegenation, and Wilde, 76, 246n29
Clifford, W.K., 98, 106
colonialism: Bowles, Jane, and narratives on, 159-60, 162, 168; Césaire on, 233-34n9; decline of public space, and rant against, 60; Lacan on written law and, 197-99, 203, 265n41; Meddeb on postcolonial normativity and, 123, 215
common sense in modernity, loss of, 49, 241-42n78
communication in modernity, with simultaneous denial of rights of speech, 9-10
confession, and Wilde, 92, 96-97
conversion, and Wilde, 92-97
cosmopolitanism, Wilde on, 104
Criminal Law Amendment Act of 1885 and, 90, 101, 243-44n9
Critique of Postcolonial Reason (Spivak), 43
CS (*The Calligraphic State;* Messick), 211, 218-19
cult of childhood, and infantalism, 26-27, 51-53, 139-40, 241-42n78

Darwinism, 91, 98-99, 104-8, 250n74
DC (*Discourse on Colonialism;* Césaire), 6-7, 233-34n9
decadence, in modernity, 13, 15, 23, 183-84, 205-6, 234n19, 235n20

Decadent Subjects [DS] (Bernheimer), 64-65
de Man, Paul, 252-53n7
De Profundis [DP] (Wilde): the aesthete and, 244n13; art of wit and, 67; brotherhood bond and father-son conflict in, 84, 90-91, 106-9; collective indifference, and tragic comedy in, 111-12; confession, 92, 96-97; conversion in, 92-97; described, 14, 62, 63; heredity, and synthesis with idealism in, 97-99, 247-48n57; humiliation, projected outward in, 92-94, 96; humility and, 92-97; melancholic speech in, 121; nationalism, as cause for prejudice and, 104; oedipal strategy of resistance and, 98, 108-10, 112; the queer Christ in, 94-96, 100-101; queer kinship and, 24, 62-63, 75-76, 91, 107, 113, 115, 121-22; ranterism and, 15, 62, 63, 105-6, 115, 118, 121-22; rhetoric of race in, 90-91, 98, 104, 112-13; self-invention and, 15, 106, 115, 121-22; subjectivity, and function of the primitive in, 118; on title of, 92, 247n52; writing, and role of sublimation in, 75-77, 245-46n26
Derrida, Jacques, 8, 265n39
desacralization, and calligraphic forms in writing of Meddeb, 227-30, 269nn73-76, 269-70n77
desire, and Jane Bowles, 25, 128-29, 157, 163, 167-70, 173, 252n6
Dictionnaire des idées reçues (Flaubert), 12-13
Discipline and Punish (Foucault), 24, 48, 92, 216
Discourse on Colonialism [DC] (Césaire), 6-7, 233-34n9
Douglas, Lord Alfred, and affair with Wilde, 71, 73, 90, 92, 106-9, 249n69, 250n78
Dowling, Linda, 249n69
DP (*De Profundis;* Wilde). See *De Profundis [DP]* (Wilde)
DS (*Decadent Subjects;* Bernheimer), 64-65

Ecrits (Lacan), 180, 182, 261n17
elitism, and Wilde, 76, 246n29
the embodied character, Khatibi on calligraphic writing and, 223-25, 268n68, 268-69n69. See also subjectivity
"Emmy Moore's Journal" (Bowles), 148-51

epistolary writing, and career of Jane Bowles, 14, 25–26, 123–24, 127, 153–54, 173–74, 177
eroticism, and erotic writing of Bowles, Jane, 127–28, 157
Eurocentrism, 50, 242n80
Eurocentrism (Amin), 50
exclusion experience, and Jane Bowles, 158–59, 168

failure, and writing of Jane Bowles, 15–16, 25–26, 125–26, 174–76
family life: Bowles, Jane and Cherifa, and prostitution turned into kinship and, 25, 157, 163, 167–70, 173; Wilde on tragedy of English, 109–10, 115. *See also* kinship
Fanon, Franz: on alteration of subjection and subjectivity, 240n60; *Black Skin, White Masks (BSWM)*, 37–39; on national consciousness, 209–10; ranterism and, 8, 38; resistant speech and, 37–38, 239n53; subjection and, 38–39, 240n60; *The Wretched of the Earth*, 209; on writing and subjection, 38–39
fantasy: Arabic script, as figure for, 178–81; Brennan on psychoanalysis and, 74; Freud on, 109, 216, 250n74; of social and psychic cohesion under authority figure, 216–18; Wilde on homosexual desire and, 62–63, 70–72, 75–76, 84, 87–89, 113, 245n18, 247n40; Wilde on psychoanalysis and, 73–75; Wilde on subjectivity, and function of, 103–4, 118
Fearless Speech (Foucault), 1, 17–18
Felman, Shoshana, 8–9, 15
fetishism, and Jane Bowles, 14, 157–60, 169–73, 258n54
Flaubert, Gustave, 12–13
food, Jane Bowles's gendering of, 141–42, 256–57n38
foreclosure: boundaries of lesbian gender norms for Jane Bowles, and social, 15, 25, 134–35, 139, 140, 142–43, 256n34; Bowles, Jane and, 122, 123, 130–32, 139, 147, 172; Lacan on, 189, 190–91, 261–62n18; Lacan on psychotic, 201, 264n36; in language, and Lacan, 193–95, 262n20, 262–63n21; the law and, 10–12, 43–44, 189–90; manifestos and, 43; Meddeb and, 15, 181, 183, 188–89, 189–90, 261n13; orientalism, and Lacan on, 178–80; politics of address and, 43; primitivism, and Lacan on, 201–3, 265n39;

ranterism and, 10–12, 43–44; reproduction of, 240n63; status of symptoms, and Lacan on, 193–95, 262n20, 262–63n21; *Verwerfung* and, 10, 43; Wilde and, 61–65, 84, 121–22
Foucault, Michel: *Discipline and Punish*, 24, 48, 92, 216; on fantasy of social and psychic cohesion under authority figure, 216–17; *Fearless Speech*, 1, 17–18; *The Hermeneutics of the Subject*, 17–18; *History of Sexuality*, 47, 48, 49, 82, 235n21; homosexuality as hereditary disease and, 101–2; oedipal guilt as regulatory mechanism, 49, 57; on *parrhesia*, 16–18; on power and subjection, 24, 44, 45, 59; *Psychiatric Power*, 44–45; on psychoanalysis as form of modernism, 15, 47–48, 235n21, 241n71; on race and forms of social management, 102, 248n66; "Society Must Be Defended," 1, 116; on speech and subjection, 1–2, 3, 5, 23, 46, 233n3; on subjection, 1–2, 3, 5, 23, 24, 44, 45, 46, 59, 233n3; on sublimation, 47–48, 82–83
French language: Bowles, Jane, and writing in, 152–53; Meddeb's writing, and use of, 185–86, 187–88, 208–9, 215, 267n51
Freud, Sigmund: on antithetical sense of primitivism, 131; on authority figure, 216; on fantasy, 109, 216, 250n74; on gendered identity, 84; on homosexual desire, 87, 247n40; on homosexuality defined, 87; on idealization theory, 85–86; on incest and metaphoric relation, 143–45, 257n41; on infantalism, 52–54; *The Interpretation of Dreams*, 178–79, 259–60n1; *Jokes and Their Relation to the Unconscious*, 67; on kinship and metaphoric relation, 56–57, 109, 143–45, 257n41; on narcissism, 83–85; oedipal structure, 52, 56–57; "On Narcissism," 83; on parricide, 56–57, 109; on primal father myth, 56–57, 108, 242n92; on primitivism and modernity, 114–15, 126–27, 131, 144–47, 250n74; on prohibition and repression of impulse, 146; on psychology and primitivism, 146–47; on race, use of term, 114; on racial fantasy, 109; on racial industry of modernity, and psychoanalysis, 48–49; on subjection and oppression in modern culture, 52–54; on taboo as social institution, 140, 142, 144, 146; *Totem and Taboo*, 91, 109, 114, 115, 216; on

Index

universality, 57; *Verwerfung* and, 10, 43
"The Function and Field of Speech and Language in Psychoanalysis" (Lacan), 181–82, 261n17

Gautier, Théophile, 65–66, 243n8
gay men. *See* homosexual desire; homosexuality
gendered identity: Bowles, Jane and feminine, 139, 141–42, 256–57n38; Freud on, 84; Sedgwick on, 81; speech in Meddeb's writing and, 187; Wilde and, 15, 80–81, 83–85
Genet, Jean, 9–10, 32–33, 34
Gilman, Richard, 65
the global village, and Lewis, 50–51
Greek friendship, and Wilde, 109, 112–13
green color, and Wilde, 72–73, 246n28
grid city plan, and shift from spiral old city plan, and Meddeb, 222
"grid" system, and shift from spiral handwritten document, 211, 219–22, 220, 221, 229, 268n62

Habermas, Jürgen, 35, 39–40, 41, 240n60, 241n75
Helfand, Michael S., 98
heredity, and synthesis with idealism by Wilde, 97–99, 247–48n57
The Hermeneutics of the Subject (Foucault), 17–18
Hill, Christopher, 4
History of Sexuality (Foucault), 47, 48, 49, 235n21
homosexual desire: Freud on, 87, 247n40; Sedgwick on, 84, 247n40; Wilde on fantasy and, 62–63, 70–72, 75–76, 84, 87–89, 113, 245n18, 247n40
homosexuality: Foucault on hereditary disease, and classification of, 101–2; Freud, and definition of, 87; as hereditary disease, 101–2; open secrecy and, 64, 69, 72; Sedgwick on self-reflection and, 64, 68–70, 244n14; sex panics and, 53, 66, 243–44n9, 255–56n32; Wilde on homosexual culture and, 69, 74–76, 246nn28–29; Wilde on subjectivity and, 68–69, 103–4, 118. *See also* lesbian gender norms; *specific main entries for queer*
humiliation, suffered by Wilde, 92–94, 96, 110–12, 250n82
humility, and Wilde, 92–97
Huxley, T. H., 98, 99

Huysmans, Joris-Karl, 89, 183–84, 260n8

idealization theory, and Freud, 85–86
the Imaginary, Lacan on, 182
incest and metaphoric relation, Freud on, 143–45, 257n41
infantalism, and cult of childhood, 26–27, 51–54, 139–40, 241–42n78
initiation, and Wilde, 77–79, 84–85
The Interpretation of Dreams (Freud), 178–79, 259–60n1
In the Summer House (Bowles), 125, 253n8, 256n34
Islamic cultures. *See* Arabic cultures
isolation, and Jane Bowles, 153–55, 155–56

Jacques Lacan and Co. (Roudinesco), 178–80, 259–60n1
James, C. L. R.: *Mariners, Renegades and Castaways* (MRC), 27–35, 37–38; *parrhesia* caught up in apologia and, 18, 27; prison narratives and, 33–34; on subjection and writing, 27–35, 38–39, 237n33, 237nn38–39, 237–38n41
Jameson, Fredric, 36, 240n60
Jokes and Their Relation to the Unconscious (Freud), 67
Journal de voleur (Genet), 9–10

Khatibi, Abdelkebir: on calligraphic writing and the embodied character, 223–25, 268n68, 268–69n69; on labor of decolonization, 38; *La mémoire tatoué*, 223–24
kinship: Adorno on oedipal family, 54–56; Bowles, Jane on prostitution turned into family life and, 25, 157, 163, 167–70, 173; Freud on familial fantasy and, 109; Freud on metaphoric relation and, 56–57, 143–45, 257n41; Lacan on metaphoric extension and, 178; Lewis on oedipal family and, 52; Meddeb, and meditation on, 212, 214; Wilde, and queer, 24, 62–63, 75–76, 91, 107, 115, 121–22
knowledge and nonknowledge, and politics of address, 18
Knox, Robert, 116–17, 251n94

Lacan, Jacques: on Arabic culture and modernity, 207; on Arabic script as figure for the unconscious, 180; on censorship, 190–93, 261–62n18, 262nn19–20; *Ecrits*, 180, 182, 261n17;

Lacan, Jacques *(continued)*
  on foreclosure, 189, 190–91, 261–62n18; on foreclosure and orientalism, 178–80; on foreclosure and primitivism, 201–3, 265n39; on foreclosure in language, and status of symptoms, 193–95, 262n20, 262–63n21; "The Function and Field of Speech and Language in Psychoanalysis," 181–82, 261n17; on the Imaginary, the Symbolic, and the Real, 182; on kinship and metaphoric extension, 178; on the law, 46, 189, 190–92, 205, 261n17, 261–62n18; Meddeb, and reworking of psychoanalytic theories of, 14, 181–83; on modernity, 113; on the Muslim patient with writer's cramp tale, 196–204, 207–8, 263n24, 263–64n28, 264nn30–31, 265n41; Oedipus complex and, 194, 202, 264–65n38; the performative speech act and, 8; on primitivism and modernity, 114, 144–45, 202–3, 264–65n38, 265n39; on psychoanalysis, 19, 181–82; on psychotic foreclosure, 201, 264n36; on social alienation, 201, 264n37; on speech in psychoanalysis, 181–82; on subjection, 46; on the superego, 193–96, 262n20, 263n24; the talking cure in modern psychoanalysis and, 19; on translation, 192, 262n19; on written colonial law, 197–99, 203, 265n, 265n41
language: Lacan on foreclosure in, 193–95, 262n20, 262–63n21; Meddeb on image and literary, 182. *See also* Arabic language; French language
The Language of Psychoanalysis [LP] (Laplanche and Pontalis), 74, 75
Laplanche, Jean, 71, 88, 245n18, 246–47n36
Laroui, Abdallah, 20, 205–7
law(s): Bowles, Jane and symbolic, 25–26, 121, 124, 153, 173–74; Criminal Law Amendment Act of 1885, 90, 101, 243–44n9; foreclosure and the, 10–12, 43–44, 189–90; Lacan on colonialism, and written, 197–99, 203, 265n41; Lacan on sacred, 199–201, 203, 264n31; Meddeb, and symbolic, 15, 181, 188–89, 194–95, 261n13; ranterism, and symbolic, 13; Wilde, and rant against the, 14, 62, 63
lesbian gender norms: Bowles, Jane, and boundaries of, 15, 25, 134–35, 139, 140, 142–43, 256n34; Toklas and, 132, 138–39, 255nn24–25
Lewis, Wyndham: *America and Cosmic Man*, 50–51; *The Art of Being Ruled (ABR)*, 51, 54, 57–58; on cult of childhood, 26–27, 51–53, 139–40; on the global village, 50–51; homosexual panic of, 255–56n32; oedipal family and, 52; on public space, 240n60; on sociopolitical theory and body of subject, 57–59; on speech, 41; *Time and Western Man*, 47, 51, 139–40
L'Expérience intérieure (Bataille), 1
love and sex, and Arab cultures, 165–67, 258n51
Lyon, Janet, 4, 39–42, 238n47, 239–40n56

the male figure, constructed by Wilde, 65–77
Manifestoes [MPM] (Lyon), 39–42, 239–40n56
manifestos: Césaire on, 22–23, 239n55; foreclosure and, 43; as modernist genre, 39–40, 43, 239–40nn55–56; as the performative speech act, 239n55; as resistance speech, 4, 39–42, 238n47, 239–40n56
Mannoni, Octave, 169–71, 173, 259n56
Mariners, Renegades and Castaways [MRC] (James), 27–35, 37–38
Marxism, 3, 4, 20, 205–7, 239n55
McCarran-Walter Act 1952, 30, 31, 44, 237n38
melancholic speech, 121–22, 155
La mémoire tatoué (Khatibi), 223–24
Messick, Brinkley: *The Calligraphic State (CS)*, 211, 218–19, 229; on *pharmakon* of writing, 218, 268n61; on power of legal documents, 211, 219–22, 220, 221, 268n62; on shift from spiral handwritten document to "grid" system, 211, 219–22, 220, 221, 229, 268n62; on the social space of writing, 229; on Yemen template for document writing, 218–19
Minima Moralia (Adorno), 4–5
modernism: defined, 22–23; Arabic literature, and application of term, 21–22, 235–37nn27–30; Francophone literature, and application of term, 21–23, 235n27, 237n30; queer, 21–24, 135, 140
MPM (*Manifestoes*; Lyon), 39–42, 239–40n56
MRC (*Mariners, Renegades and Castaways*; James), 27–35, 37–38
MS (*My Sister's Hand in Mine*; Bowles), 128–30, 148–51, 251n1, 253–54n11. *See also Two Serious Ladies* (Bowles)

Index 287

the Muslim patient with writer's cramp tale, Lacan on, 196–204, 207–8, 263n24, 263–64n28, 264nn30–31, 265n41
My Sister's Hand in Mine [MS] (Bowles), 128–30, 148–51, 251n1, 253–54n11. See also *Two Serious Ladies* (Bowles)

narcissism: Freud on, 83–85; Wilde and, 67–69, 72–73, 84, 85–86, 244n13, 244–45n14, 247n40
national consciousness: calligraphy in Meddeb's writing and, 224–31; as cause for prejudice in Wilde's writing, 104; Fanon on, 209–10; Meddeb and, 183, 207, 209–12, 224–31, 266n47, 267n54
North African. See *specific main entries for Arabic*

Oedipus complex: Adorno on oedipal family and, 54–56; Foucault on oedipal guilt as regulatory mechanism and, 49, 57; Freud on oedipal structure and, 52, 56–57; Lacan and, 194, 202, 264–65n38; Lewis on oedipal family and, 52; Wilde on oedipal strategy of resistance and, 63, 66, 67, 73, 81, 85, 98, 108–10, 112
"On Narcissism" (Freud), 83
open secrecy, 64, 69, 72
orientalism: Arabic script, as figure for, 178–81; foreclosure and, 178–80; Lacan on foreclosure and, 178–80
Out in the World (Bowles), 148, 173, 174

Pandolfo, Stefania, 19–21
parrhesia (fearless speech), 5, 16–18, 27, 45–46, 52
parricide, 56–57, 108–10. See also Oedipus complex
Le Passé Simple (Chraibi), 20, 21, 237n30
PDG (*The Picture of Dorian Gray*; Wilde). See *The Picture of Dorian Gray [PDG]* (Wilde)
Pease, Donald, 28–30, 237n33, 237n39
the performative speech act: Austin on, 8; Butler and, 1, 2–3, 7, 9, 239n55; Derrida and, 8; Lacan and, 8; manifestos as, 239n55; Puchner on, 239n55; Wilde and, 8, 72–73, 76, 246n28. See also speech
pharmakon, of writing, 218, 268n61
The Picture of Dorian Gray [PDG] (Wilde): actions, and influence of art in, 81–82; the aesthete in, 67–69, 244n13, 244–45n14; art of wit in, 67, 72, 245n20; confession and, 90; fantasy, 62–63, 70–76, 84, 87–89, 103–4, 118, 245n18, 247n40; foreclosure and, 84; gendered identity in, 80–81, 83–85; green color and, 72–73; homosexual desire in, 62–63, 70–72, 75–76, 84, 87–89, 245n18, 247n40; initiation and, 77–79, 84–85; narcissism in, 67–69, 72–73, 84, 85–86, 244n13, 244–45n14, 247n40; oedipal strategy of resistance and, 63, 66, 67, 81, 85; open secrecy in, 72; the primitive in subjectivity and, 103–4, 118; psychoanalysis, and fantasy in, 73–75; rhetoric of race in, 103; seduction and, 79–80, 87; self-invention and, 71; sex panic in, 66, 243–44n9; sexual normativity challenged in, 67–68; subjectivity and, 79–80, 103–4, 118; sublimation in, 82–83, 85–86, 89–90
picturing, and writing by Jane Bowles, 126–27, 147–48, 252n6, 252–53n7
politics of address, 1–5
Pontalis, J.-B., 71, 88, 245n18
postcolonial avant-garde, 14, 23, 41, 187–88, 223, 260n7
power: calligraphy in Meddeb's writing as instrument of, 222–23; disciplinary, 44–45; Foucault on subjugation and, 24, 44, 45, 59; of legal documents, and shift from spiral handwritten document to "grid" system, 211, 219–22, 220, 221, 268n62; in queer modernism and, 24; seizing upon, participating in its reach, and rerouting potential, 23–24; writing and, 24, 26–27
primal father myth, Freud on, 56–57, 108, 242n92
primitivism: of the body in literature, 46–47; Bowles, Jane and, 130–32, 139, 167, 168, 172; foreclosure and, 201–3, 265n39; Freud on modernity and, 114–15, 126–27, 144–47, 250n74; Freud on psychology and, 146–47; Lacan on foreclosure and, 201–3, 265n39; Lacan on modernity and, 114, 144–45, 202–3, 264–65n38, 265n39; Meddeb and, 14, 26, 123, 196, 202, 265n39; Wilde on modernity and, 114–15
primitivist style, and Jane Bowles, 125–26, 146–47, 152, 172, 253n8
prison narratives, 32–33. See also *De Profundis [DP]* (Wilde)

prohibition, and Freud on repression of impulse, 146
prostitution, turned into kinship and family life by Jane Bowles, 25, 157, 163, 167–70, 173
Psychiatric Power (Foucault), 44–45
psychoanalysis: Bowles, Jane on psychoanalytic argument and, 15, 24, 25; as form of modernity, and Foucault, 15, 47–48, 235n21, 241n71; Freud on primitivism and, 146–47; Freud on racial industry of modernity and, 48–49; psychoanalytic approach of Wilde and, 14–15, 24–25, 63–64, 69, 237n31; the talking cure and, 19, 226, 269n70
psychotic foreclosure, Lacan on, 201, 264n36
public space: Adorno on, 240n60; counterdiscourse increase in modernity during decline of, 41, 49, 60, 240n60, 241nn74–75, 241n77; Habermas on, 35, 39–40, 41, 240n60, 241n75; Lewis on, 240n60; Meddeb on postcolonial era and, 181, 183, 205–6, 212; Meddeb on shift from old city spiral plan to new city grid plan and, 222, 222, 229–30, 269–70n77; politics of address and, 38–41, 43; Wilde, and humiliation in, 110–12, 250n82
Puchner, Martin, 239n55

Queensberry, Marquess of, and Wilde's affair with Douglas, 72, 90, 106, 107, 108, 250n78
the queer Christ, and Wilde, 94–96, 100–101
queer kinship, and Wilde, 24, 62–63, 75–76, 91, 107, 113, 115, 121–22
queer modernism, 21–24, 135, 140

race: Celtophobia and, 116–18, 251n94; as coding for social issues and culture, 5–6, 116–17, 251n94; Foucault on forms of social management and, 102, 248n66; Freud on, 48–49, 109, 114; as ideological alibi, 31, 237–38n41. *See also* rhetoric of race
The Races of Man (Beddoe), 116, 251n94
Racial Theories (Banton), 115–16, 117, 251n94
rant: defined, 3–4; Bataille on rage of experience and, 17, 34–35, 238n45; Baudelaire and, 12–13; Bowles, Jane and, 4, 14, 25–26, 121, 122, 123, 252n5; Césaire and, 5–8, 12, 234n10; decline of public space and anticolonial, 60; Fanon and, 8, 38; Flaubert and, 12–13; foreclosure and, 10–12, 43–44; as genre, 4, 15–16, 18; historical, 3–4; James and, 30–35; the law and, 10–12, 43–44, 46; literary texts, and sites of, 15; Meddeb, and rant as poetics, 4, 14, 15, 21, 123, 182–83; in modernity, 13, 15, 18, 234n19, 235n20; power and, 13, 26, 27; primitivism and, 13–14, 26, 59; speech rights denied in modernity and, 9–10, 46; subjectivity and, 13–14, 26, 59; symbolic law and, 13; Wilde and, 3–4, 15, 45, 62, 63, 105–6, 115, 118, 121–22
the Real, Lacan on, 182
À Rebours (Huysmans), 89, 260n8
Redonnet, Marie, 11
regression, and Jane Bowles, 137–40, 142, 172–73
resistant speech: Caliban character in Shakespeare, and Retamar on, 35–38, 239n53, 239–40n56; Fanon and, 37–38, 239n53; manifestos and, 4, 39–42, 238n47, 239–40n56; Sartre and, 37. *See also* speech
rhetoric of race: Bowles, Jane and, 14, 157–60, 162, 168, 172–73; Meddeb and, 14, 15; racial decline and, 50–51; Wilde and, 90–91, 98, 102–4, 112–15, 248–49n67, 249n70. *See also* race
Roudinesco, Elisabeth, *Jacques Lacan and Co.*, 178–80, 259–60n1
Rubin, Gayle, 53

the sacred, Meddeb on desacralization in calligraphy, 227–30, 269nn73–76, 269–70n77
sacred law, Lacan on, 199–201, 203, 264n31
Safouan, Moustapha, 269n76
Sartre, Jean-Paul, 37, 239n53
Scharfman, Ronnie, 224, 268n67
Sedgwick, Eve, 64, 244n14, 247n40; on abstraction, 86–87; on gendered identity, 81; on homosexual desire, 84, 247n40; on open secrecy, 69; on self-reflection and homosexuality, 64, 68–70, 244n14
seduction: Bowles, Jane, and adventures in, 157, 159–60, 162–64, 167, 258n50; Bowles, Jane, and writing with scenes of pursuit and, 127–28, 129–30, 255–56n11; Wilde's writing and, 79–80, 87

the self, and calligraphic forms in Meddeb's writing, 224–31, 269n72
self-invention: Foucault on, 17–18; of Jane Bowles, 156–57; postcolonial avant-garde and, 23; Wilde and, 15, 70–71, 98, 106, 115, 121–22, 244n13
sex and love, and Arab cultures, 165–67, 258n51
sex panics, and homosexuality, 53, 66, 243–44n9, 255–56n32
sexuality, in modernity, 15, 47, 58, 59, 67–68, 88. *See also* lesbian gender norms
sexual taboos, 54–57, 242n88
Shakespeare, William, *The Tempest*, 35–38, 239n53, 239–40n56
silence, and Jane Bowles, 120, 121
Smith, Philip E., II, 98
social Darwinism, 91, 98–99, 104–8, 250n74
social foreclosure, and Jane Bowles, 15, 25, 134–35, 139, 140, 142–43, 256n34
"Society Must Be Defended" (Foucault), 1, 116
Solanas, Valerie, 121
"Some Binarisms (II)" (Sedgwick), 64
"Some Motifs in Baudelaire" (Benjamin), 32
the soul, and Foucault, 92
"The Soul of Man Under Socialism" (Wilde), 102–3, 115, 244n13
"speaking truth to power," 2, 5, 28
speech: Adorno on oppositional, 4–5; Bataille on sovereignty and, 1, 17, 24, 238nn45–46; Bowles, Jane, and abject, 119–20, 149–50; Butler on intersubjective event of, 1, 2–3, 7, 9; communication in modernity, with simultaneous denial of rights of, 9–10; denial of rights of, 9–10; Foucault on subjection and free, 1–2, 3, 5, 23, 46, 233n3; Lewis on, 41; *parrhesia* and, 5, 16–18, 27, 52. *See also* the performative speech act; resistant speech
speech act theory. *See* the performative speech act
spiral handwritten document, and shift to "grid" system, 211, 219–22, 220, 221, 229, 268n62
spiral old city plan shift to new city grid plan in public space, and Meddeb, 222, 222, 229–30, 269–70n77
Spivak, Gayatri, 43
Spleen de Paris (Baudelaire), 12
Stein, Gertrude, 132, 138–40, 141, 255n24

"A Stick of Green Candy" (Bowles), 126, 129, 141, 154, 256–57n38
subjection: Fanon and, 38–39, 240n60; Foucault on, 1–2, 3, 5, 23, 24, 44–46, 59, 233n3; Freud on oppression and, 52–54; James on, 27–35, 38–39, 237n33, 237nn38–39, 237–38n41; Lacan on, 46; Meddeb and, 15; Wilde on modern, 45
subjectivity: Althusser on model of, 246–47n36; Bataille on politics of address and, 1, 17, 24, 238nn45–46; contradiction confronting modern, 19–21; Laplanche, and model of, 246–47n36; Lewis on sociopolitical theory and, 57–59; Wilde and, 68–69, 79–80, 103–4, 118
sublimation: Foucault on, 47–48, 82–83; Wilde's writing, and role of, 75–77, 245–46n26; Wilde's writing and, 75, 76–77, 82–83, 85–86, 89–90, 245–46n26
subversive literature, and Meddeb, 224–25, 268n67
the superego, Lacan on, 193–96, 262n20, 263n24
the Symbolic, Lacan on, 182
symbolic law: Bowles, Jane and, 25–26, 121, 124, 153, 173–74; Meddeb and, 15, 181, 188–89, 194–95, 261n13
symptoms, Lacan on foreclosure and status, 193–95, 262n20, 262–63n21

taboos, 54–57, 140, 142, 144, 146, 242n88
Talismano (Meddeb): about opening images in, 186–87; allography and, 210, 211, 225, 226, 228–29, 232, 267n54, 269n74; Arabic cultures and, 204–7; Arabic language and, 184–85, 207, 260n9, 260–61n10, 266n47; Arabic literature and, 184–85, 260n9, 260–61n10; Arabic script and, 178–81; avant-garde in postcolonial era and, 14, 187–88, 223, 260n7; bilingualism, and social analysis of, 225–26; biography in fiction of, 186; calligraphesis and, 211–12, 225–26, 230–32, 267n54, 269n76; calligraphy, and national consciousness in, 224–31; colonialism, and postcolonial normativity in, 123, 215; as critique of postcolonial era, 123; decadence in modernity and, 183–84, 205–6; desacralization, and calligraphic forms in, 227–30, 269nn73–76, 269–70n77;

Talismano (Meddeb) *(continued)*
the embodied character, and calligraphy in, 224–25; fantasy of social and psychic cohesion under authority figure in, 216–18; foreclosure and, 15, 181, 183, 188–89, 189–90, 261n13; French language, and use in, 185–86, 187–88, 208–9, 215, 267n51; gendered identity, and speech in, 187; gendered speech in, 187; Huysmans's writing, and association with, 183–84, 260n8; kinship meditation in, 212, 214; Lacanian psychoanalytic theories, and reworking in, 14, 181–83; the law and foreclosure in, 189–90; literary language, and image in, 182, 183; Marxist critiques and, 205–7; the Muslim patient with writer's cramp tale and, 196–204, 207–8, 263n24, 263–64n28, 264nn30–31, 265n41; national consciousness and, 183, 207, 209–12, 224–31, 266n47, 267n54; orientalism and, 178–81; power, and calligraphy in, 222–23; primitivism and, 14, 26, 123, 196, 202, 265n39; psychoanalytic theory and, 14; public space, and shift from old city spiral plan to new city grid plan in, 222, 222, 229–30, 269–70n77; public space in postcolonial era and, 181, 183, 205–6, 212; rant as poetics in, 4, 14, 15, 21, 123, 182–83; rhetoric of race and, 14, 15; the self, and calligraphic forms in, 224–31, 269n72; the social space of writing and, 229–30, 269n71, 269–70n77; speech, and foreclosure in, 181, 183, 188–89, 261n13; subjection and, 15; subjectivity in postcolonial state and, 14, 181, 212, 224–25; subversive literature and, 224–25, 268n67; the symbol and its law, and opposing understandings in, 15, 181, 188–89, 194–95, 261n13; the talisman in, 212–15, 213, 268nn56–57; the talking cure, and calligraphic forms in, 226, 269n70; the tongue as writing's body and, 223, 268n64; transgraphing techniques in, 211, 215, 228, 267n54; writing and, 207–9, 212, 226–27, 231–32, 266n48, 270n80; writing theory and, 210. *See also* Messick, Brinkley
the talking cure, 19, 226, 269n70
The Tempest (Shakespeare), 35–38, 239n53, 239–40n56
"The Iron Table" (Bowles), 148, 151–52
The Wretched of the Earth (Fanon), 209

"Thinking Sex" (Rubin), 53
"The Thin Line of Modernity" *[TLM]* (Pandolfo), 20
Time and Western Man (Lewis), 47, 51, 139–40
Toklas, Alice: Bowles, Jane, and influence of, 132–34, 135–37, 140–41, 146–47, 172, 255n19; lesbian gender norms of, 132, 138–39, 255nn24–25
the tongue as writing's body, and Meddeb, 223, 268n64
Totem and Taboo (Freud), 91, 109, 114, 115
transgraphing techniques, and Meddeb, 211, 215, 228, 267n54
"Turkish" type femininity, and the world picture by Jane Bowles, 148–52
Two Serious Ladies (Bowles), 119–20, 124, 127–28, 131–32, 253n10

Undoing Gender (Butler), 1
universal humanism and universality, 50, 56–57

Verwerfung, and Freud, 10, 43
vision, and writing by Jane Bowles, 126–27, 147–48, 252n6, 252–53n7

Wilde, Oscar: aesthetic selection theory, 99–103, 105, 248–49n67, 249n69, 250n75; on art, 65–66, 81–82, 244n11; art of wit and, 66–67; celebrity of, 61, 243n1; Celtic racial imagination narrative, 112, 115; censorship, and career of, 61–65, 121–22; on cosmopolitanism, 104; Criminal Law Amendment Act of 1885 and, 90, 101, 243–44n9; Douglas, and affair with, 71, 73, 90, 92, 106–9, 249n69, 250n78; elitism and, 76, 246n29; on family life in England, 109–10, 115; foreclosure and, 61–65, 84, 121–22; gendered identity and, 15, 80–81, 83–85; Greek friendship and, 109, 112–13; green color and, 72–73, 246n28; homosexual culture and, 69, 74–76, 246nn28–29; homosexuality as hereditary disease and, 101–2; humiliation suffered by, 92–94, 96, 110–12, 250n82; imprisonment of, 90, 91–92; initiation and, 77–79, 84–85; the male figure constructed by, 65–77; oedipal strategy of resistance and, 63, 66, 67, 73, 81, 85, 98, 108–10, 112; open secrecy and, 64, 69; the performative speech act and, 8, 72–73, 76, 246n28; on primitivism and modernity, 114–15; psychoanalytic approach and, 14–15, 24–25, 63–64, 69, 237n31; Queensberry, and Douglas's affair with, 72, 90, 106, 107, 108, 250n78; ranterism and, 3–4, 15, 45, 62, 63, 105–6, 115, 118, 121–22; rhetoric of race and, 90–91, 98, 102–3, 104, 112–15, 248–49n67, 249n70; self-invention of, 70–71, 98, 244n13; on sexual normativity, 15, 67–68; as social critic and theorist, 68–69; social Darwinism and, 91, 98–99, 104–8; "The Soul of Man Under Socialism," 102–3, 115, 244n13; subjectivity and, 68–69, 79–80, 103–4, 118; on subjegation and writing, 45. See also *De Profundis [DP]* (Wilde); *The Picture of Dorian Gray [PDG]* (Wilde)

wit, Wilde and art of, 66–67, 72, 245n20

the world picture, and "Turkish" type femininity by Jane Bowles, 148–52

writing: Bataille on, 24, 35, 238n46; Bowles, Jane, and epistolary, 14, 25–26, 123–24, 127, 153–54, 173–74, 177; Bowles, Jane as modernist woman writer and, 122–23; Fanon on subjection and, 38–39; handwritten spiral document, and shift to Western-style "grid" system and, 211, 219–22, 220, 221, 229, 268n62; James on subjection, and technology of, 27–35, 38–39, 237nn33, 237nn38–39, 237–38n41; Meddeb and, 207–9, 212, 226–27, 229–30, 231–32, 266n48, 269n71, 269–70n77, 270n80; Messick on, 218, 229, 268n61; power and, 24, 26–27; the social space of, 229–30, 269n71, 269–70n77; the West, and claim on, 265n39; Wilde, and role of sublimation in, 75–77, 245–46n26; Wilde, on modern subjegation and, 45; the word of the other, and claim for absence of, 265n39. *See also* calligraphesis; calligraphy

writing block, and Jane Bowles, 14, 25–26, 124–27, 141–42, 147–48, 153–56, 172–74, 252n6, 252–53n7

writing theory, and Meddeb, 210

Yemen template for document writing, and Messick, 218–19

Text:	10/13 Sabon
Display:	Sabon
Compositor:	BookMatters, Berkeley
Indexer:	Naomi Linzer
Printer & binder:	Odyssey Publications

www.ingramcontent.com/pod-product-compliance
Lightning Source LLC
Chambersburg PA
CBHW032052220426
43664CB00008B/965